# St Petersburg

**Steve Kokker**
**Nick Selby**

LONELY PLANET PUBLICATIONS
Melbourne • Oakland • London • Paris

**St Petersburg**
**3rd edition** – January 2002
**First published** – February 1996

**Published by**
**Lonely Planet Publications Pty Ltd**  ABN 36 005 607 983
90 Maribyrnong St, Footscray, Victoria 3011, Australia

**Lonely Planet offices**
**Australia** Locked Bag 1, Footscray, Victoria 3011
**USA** 150 Linden St, Oakland, CA 94607
**UK** 10a Spring Place, London NW5 3BH
**France** 1 rue du Dahomey, 75011 Paris

**Photographs**
Many of the images in this guide are available for licensing from
Lonely Planet Images.
email: lpi@lonelyplanet.com.au
Web site: www.lonelyplanetimages.com

**Front cover photograph**
So much to see. The Hermitage. (John King)

ISBN 1 86450 325 4

text & maps © Lonely Planet Publications Pty Ltd 2002
photos © photographers as indicated 2002

Printed by SNP SPrint (M) Sdn Bhd
Printed in Malaysia

# Contents – Text

## PLACES TO STAY                                                     137

## PLACES TO EAT                                                      142

## ENTERTAINMENT                                                      154

## SHOPPING                                                           161

## EXCURSIONS                                                         165

## LANGUAGE                                                           175

## GLOSSARY                                                           183

## THANKS                                                             185

## INDEX                                                              189

## MAP LEGEND                                                   back page

## METRIC CONVERSION                                    inside back cover

# Contents – Maps

# The Authors

## Steve Kokker

When he first visited St Petersburg in 1992, Steve was dumb-founded, perplexed – hooked. The place was beautiful, lots of fun. But why did it feel like slipping through the rabbit hole when arriving? He kept returning every summer, eventually moving there for a year in 1997, determined to try and figure out the puzzling society and the contradictions in its inhabitants. Had he read Tyuchev before ('You can't understand Russia with reason...you can only believe in her'), he might have saved himself a lot of trouble. Despite having travelled widely, Steve, whose hometown is Montreal, Canada, has been changed most by the city on the Neva. It gave him the best and worst times of his life and taught him more than he thought possible about humanity and fate. A graduate in psychology and an ex-film critic, Steve also directs video documentaries. He's currently based in Tallinn, Estonia, close enough to Russia to keep stimulated and far enough to keep sane.

## Nick Selby

Nick was born and raised in New York City. In 1990 he moved to Europe and then Russia in 1991, where he wrote *The Visitor's Guide to the New St Petersburg*. Since then, Nick has been travelling and writing guides for Lonely Planet including *Brazil*, *Germany*, *Russia*, *Texas* and *St Petersburg*.

## FROM THE AUTHOR

**Steve Kokker** The depth of my thanks to the city and its eccentric residents is boundless. Much gratitude to those directly helpful to this project: Peter Kozyrev, my perambulatory partner in the discovery of haunting decay and tasty bliny; Oxana Yakimenko and Volodya Egorov for culinary suggestions and philological stimulation; Misha Shpinyov for being such an eager, earnest, effective assistant; Irina Yakimenko for her palace tours and her palatial goodness; to Tatyana, Boris, Galya and Nastya for unforgettable days and nights in magical Staraya Ladoga; Andrei Udalov who taught me so much about Russian mentality; Igor Tokarenko and Dima for some 'inside' info; and to all the nameless museum babushkas who were so forthcoming in the secrets of their charges. I am even more indebted to these same people (babushkas excluded!) for their friendship, because, in the end, that's what it's all about, really. Thanks also to Oxana's students for my lessons in clubland, and to the nameless dozens of friends, acquaintances and passersby whose words and gestures have shaped, little by little, my experiences there, all of which are reflected in this book. A final thanks to Nick Selby, who had done such a great job on the first edition of this book. May fate finally smile kindly upon this special city and its lovely inhabitants.

# This Book

The 1st and 2nd editions of *St Petersburg* were written by Nick Selby. This 3rd edition has been written and updated by Steve Kokker.

## From the Publisher

This book was produced at Lonely Planet's Melbourne office. Celia Wood drew the maps and laid out the book, assisted by Csanad Csutoros. The book was edited by Darren O'Connell with help from Helen Yeates and Melanie Dankel. Margaret Jung designed the cover. Matt King coordinated the illustrations which were drawn by Kelli Hamblett (KH), Clint Curé (CC), Melissa Kirby (MK), Martin Harris (MH), Kate Nolan (KN) and Trudi Canavan (TC). Thanks to Emma Koch and Inna Zaitseva for their work on the language section, Mark Germanchis for assistance with layout, Barabara Dombrowski in LPI for assistance with colour and to Brigitte Ellemor, Mark Griffiths and Kieran Grogan for checking the artwork.

THANKS
Many thanks to the travellers who used the last edition and wrote to us with helpful hints, advice and interesting anecdotes. Your names appear in the back of this book.

# Foreword

## ABOUT LONELY PLANET GUIDEBOOKS

The story begins with a classic travel adventure: Tony and Maureen Wheeler's 1972 journey across Europe and Asia to Australia. Useful information about the overland trail did not exist at that time, so Tony and Maureen published the first Lonely Planet guidebook to meet a growing need.

From a kitchen table, then from a tiny office in Melbourne (Australia), Lonely Planet has become the largest independent travel publisher in the world, an international company with offices in Melbourne, Oakland (USA), London (UK) and Paris (France).

Today Lonely Planet guidebooks cover the globe. There is an ever-growing list of books and there's information in a variety of forms and media. Some things haven't changed. The main aim is still to help make it possible for adventurous travellers to get out there – to explore and better understand the world.

At Lonely Planet we believe travellers can make a positive contribution to the countries they visit – if they respect their host communities and spend their money wisely. Since 1986 a percentage of the income from each book has been donated to aid projects and human rights campaigns.

**Updates** Lonely Planet thoroughly updates each guidebook as often as possible. This usually means there are around two years between editions, although for more unusual or more stable destinations the gap can be longer. Check the imprint page (following the colour map at the beginning of the book) for publication dates.

Between editions up-to-date information is available in two free newsletters – the paper *Planet Talk* and email *Comet* (to subscribe, contact any Lonely Planet office) – and on our Web site at www.lonelyplanet.com. The *Upgrades* section of the Web site covers a number of important and volatile destinations and is regularly updated by Lonely Planet authors. *Scoop* covers news and current affairs relevant to travellers. And, lastly, the *Thorn Tree* bulletin board and *Postcards* section of the site carry unverified, but fascinating, reports from travellers.

**Correspondence** The process of creating new editions begins with the letters, postcards and emails received from travellers. This correspondence often includes suggestions, criticisms and comments about the current editions. Interesting excerpts are immediately passed on via newsletters and the Web site, and everything goes to our authors to be verified when they're researching on the road. We're keen to get more feedback from organisations or individuals who represent communities visited by travellers.

Lonely Planet gathers information for everyone who's curious about the planet – and especially for those who explore it first-hand. Through guidebooks, phrasebooks, activity guides, maps, literature, newsletters, image library, TV series and Web site we act as an information exchange for a worldwide community of travellers.

**Research** Authors aim to gather sufficient practical information to enable travellers to make informed choices and to make the mechanics of a journey run smoothly. They also research historical and cultural background to help enrich the travel experience and allow travellers to understand and respond appropriately to cultural and environmental issues.

Authors don't stay in every hotel because that would mean spending a couple of months in each medium-sized city and, no, they don't eat at every restaurant because that would mean stretching belts beyond capacity. They do visit hotels and restaurants to check standards and prices, but feedback based on readers' direct experiences can be very helpful

Many of our authors work undercover, others aren't so secretive. None of them accept freebies in exchange for positive write-ups. And none of our guidebooks contain any advertising.

**Production** Authors submit their raw manuscripts and maps to offices in Australia, USA, UK or France. Editors and cartographers – all experienced travellers themselves – then begin the process of assembling the pieces. When the book finally hits the shops, some things are already out of date, we start getting feedback from readers and the process begins again ...

## WARNING & REQUEST

Things change – prices go up, schedules change, good places go bad and bad places go bankrupt – nothing stays the same. So, if you find things better or worse, recently opened or long since closed, please tell us and help make the next edition even more accurate and useful. We genuinely value all the feedback we receive. A well-travelled team reads and acknowledges every letter, postcard and email and ensures that every morsel of information finds its way to the appropriate authors, editors and cartographers for verification.

Everyone who writes to us will find their name listed in the next edition of the appropriate guidebook. They will also receive the latest issue of *Planet Talk*, our quarterly printed newsletter, or *Comet*, our monthly email newsletter. Subscriptions to both newsletters are free. The very best contributions will be rewarded with a free guidebook.

We may edit, reproduce and incorporate your comments in all Lonely Planet products, such as guidebooks, Web sites and digital products, so let us know if you don't want your comments reproduced or your name acknowledged.

Send all correspondence to the Lonely Planet office closest to you:

**Australia:** Locked Bag 1, Footscray, Victoria 3011
**USA:** 150 Linden St, Oakland, CA 94607
**UK:** 10a Spring Place, London NW5 3BH
**France:** 1 rue du Dahomey, 75011 Paris

Or email us at: talk2us@lonelyplanet.com.au

**For news, views and updates see our Web site: www.lonelyplanet.com**

## HOW TO USE A LONELY PLANET GUIDEBOOK

The best way to use a Lonely Planet guidebook is any way you choose. At Lonely Planet we believe the most memorable travel experiences are often those that are unexpected, and the finest discoveries are those you make yourself. Guidebooks are not intended to be used as if they provide a detailed set of infallible instructions!

**Contents** All Lonely Planet guidebooks follow roughly the same format. The Facts about the Destination chapters or sections give background information ranging from history to weather. Facts for the Visitor gives practical information on issues like visas and health. Getting There & Away gives a brief starting point for re-searching travel to and from the destination. Getting Around gives an overview of the transport options when you arrive.

The peculiar demands of each destination determine how sub-sequent chapters are broken up, but some things remain constant. We always start with background, then proceed to sights, places to stay, places to eat, entertainment, getting there and away, and getting around information – in that order.

**Heading Hierarchy** Lonely Planet headings are used in a strict hierarchical structure that can be visualised as a set of Russian dolls. Each heading (and its following text) is encompassed by any preceding heading that is higher on the hierarchical ladder.

**Entry Points** We do not assume guidebooks will be read from beginning to end, but that people will dip into them. The tradi-tional entry points are the list of contents and the index. In addition, however, some books have a complete list of maps and an index map illustrating map coverage.

There may also be a colour map that shows highlights. These highlights are dealt with in greater detail in the Facts for the Visitor chapter, along with planning questions and suggested itin-eraries. Each chapter covering a geographical region usually begins with a locator map and another list of highlights. Once you find something of interest in a list of highlights, turn to the index.

**Maps** Maps play a crucial role in Lonely Planet guidebooks and include a huge amount of information. A legend is printed on the back page. We seek to have complete consistency between maps and text, and to have every important place in the text captured on a map. Map key numbers usually start in the top left corner.

Although inclusion in a guidebook usually implies a recommen-dation we cannot list every good place. Exclusion does not necessarily imply criticism. In fact there are a number of reasons why we might exclude a place – sometimes it is simply inappropriate to encourage an influx of travellers.

# Introduction

St Petersburg weaves a strange magic around those who open themselves to it, taking visitors by surprise, often compelling them to return. It's a city unlike any other in Europe and certainly in Russia, without question one of the planet's most exciting cities at the moment. That's not only due to the grand beauty of its architectural splendour and charming waterways, not only because of the wealth of its cultural treasures and the intrigue of its rich history, which one senses at every step.

St Petersburg is a dust-devil of influences and styles, a bewitching vortex of life's extremes. It's breathtakingly gorgeous, it's ruefully falling apart; it's viscerally sensual, it's crude and vulgar; its very essence gets under your skin, but remains forever outside your grasp. It's precisely this fine interplay of beauty and decay, of frivolity and gravity that forms upon the traveller such an indelible impression.

On bright and airy summer nights, when people sing on the street and play guitar by the riverbanks after midnight, the city's spirit seems so light and wispy that it might lift off at any moment. And at other times, the dour history witnessed by its colossal monuments and fantastic buildings seems to transcend reality and weigh heavily upon all who walk its streets.

'There are few more grim, harsh, and strange influences on a man's soul than in Petersburg!' says one character in Dostoevsky's *Crime and Punishment*.

There's been an other-worldliness to St Petersburg since its very inception. Forced into being on inhospitable lands by a driven, fierce ruler, and built upon the blood and bones of hapless labourers, it rose from low-lying wetlands to become the capital of the world's largest country – a shining jewel whose glitter caught the eye and imagination of the world.

This apparent victory over nature inspired a population, already prone to superstition, to spin legends and tales of a mystical and esoteric nature about the city and its 'spirit'. This is easily felt even today – try counting all the books about the legends, secrets and mysteries of St Petersburg (whereas there isn't one about the hidden mysteries of Moscow!). Rare is the city whose residents so deeply feel and so eagerly share its history, and who talk so earnestly about its spirit and soul as if about an enigmatic personage. Eccentric, friendly Petersburgers revel in the intrigues of tsars and princesses, boast about its world-famous arts scene, and shudder at the memory of purges and war-torn strife. All that goodness and badness is wrapped up into one insoluble conundrum called 'Piter'.

At the dawn of the new millennium, St Petersburg is in the process of reinventing itself, dressed up in its Sunday best for the first time in decades, looking better than it has in a century, and more than ever before open to receiving guests and hosting parties. And while so much emphasis is given to the city's glorious, even notorious history, it can escape the danger of identifying itself only with a past long gone, for its present is itself so varied and stimulating.

Alongside the treasures of the Mariinsky Theatre's ballet and the red-faced opulence of the Hermitage are some of Europe's most exciting dance, theatre and avant-garde art movements. In healthy contrast to the lush imperial balls of yesterday is the club scene of today – more hedonistic, experimental and sexy than in many other European cities. The city is rejuvenating itself, still finding its balance on the foundations of a rich and troubled history in order to take on and shape its future boldly, confidently and with rarefied spirit.

# Facts about St Petersburg

## HISTORY

Alexandr of Novgorod defeated the Swedes near the mouth of the Neva River in 1240, earning him the title Nevsky (literally, 'of the Neva'). Sweden took control of the region in the 17th century and it was the desire of Peter I (the Great) to crush this rival and make Russia a European power that led to the founding of the city. At the start of the Great Northern War (1700–21) he captured the Swedish outposts on the Neva, and in May 1703 he founded the Peter & Paul Fortress on the river a few kilometres in from the sea and named his city after his patron saint, Sankt Pieter Burkh, in Dutch style.

## Peter the Great

Those Swedes were no pushovers; Peter's victory was the result of ruthlessness and determination. The rapid growth of St Petersburg from a swamp to the lavish capital of a world empire was not accomplished through the good will of the peasants who built it.

They and Swedish prisoners of war became forced labourers, thousands dropping like flies from disease, exhaustion and starvation. To raise money for the city's construction, Peter taxed everything he could think of, including beards, coffins and even death itself via the infamous 'Soul Tax' (essentially a death duty, imposed on all lower-class adult males).

Architects and artisans were brought from all over Europe; canals were dug to drain the marshy south bank, and in 1712 Peter made the place his capital, forcing grumbling administrators, nobles and merchants to move here from Moscow and build new homes. What's more, anyone entering the city had to bring building supplies with them – wagons were checked at the city line.

The upper classes were also thrown into a tizzy by Peter's edicts on their performance: aristocrats had to serve in either the army or the civil service, or lose their titles and land. Birth status counted for little, as state servants were subject to Peter's new Table of Ranks, a performance-based ladder of promotion with only the upper grades conferring hereditary nobility. Some aristocrats lost all they had, while capable state employees of humble origin and even foreigners became Russian nobles.

Peter mobilised Russian resources to compete on equal terms with the West, eclipsing all but the most powerful nations of the day – a startling achievement. His territorial gains were small, but the strategic Baltic Sea territories added a new class of German traders and administrators that formed the backbone of Russia's commercial and military expansion.

By the time of his death in 1725, Peter's city on the Neva had a population of 40,000 (one eighth of the country's urban population), and 90% of Russia's foreign trade passed through it. The south bank around the Admiralty had become the centre of the now-bustling town.

Peter died without naming a successor. Had it not been for a government structure built on the Table of Ranks as well as a

Peter the Great

LPP

professional bureaucracy with a vested interest in its preservation, Peter's reforms might well have died with him.

## Catherine II (the Great)

Peter's immediate successors moved the capital back to Moscow but Empress Anna Ioannovna (r. 1730–40) returned it to St Petersburg. Between 1741 and 1825 under Empress Elizabeth, Catherine the Great and Alexander I, it became a cosmopolitan city with a royal court of famous splendour These monarchs commissioned great series of palaces, government buildings and churches, which turned the city into one of Europe's grandest capitals.

Of Russia's female leaders, none is more (in)famous than Catherine II. Born Sophie Friederike Auguste in what is now Szczecin, Poland, on 2 May 1729, Catherine was the daughter of the German prince of Anhalt-Zerbst. At 15, young Sophie went to Russia to marry Peter, Empress Elizabeth's nephew and heir to the Russian throne (later, Catherine said of Peter: 'I believe the Crown of Russia attracted me more than his person'). On Elizabeth's death, Christmas Day 1761, Peter became Peter III.

Peter III was not only widely disliked, he was despised by powerful members of his own military who saw in his wife a better leader (she was in full agreement). This was accomplished in June 1762 when a party of officers (led by the brother of one of Catherine's lovers) arrested and subsequently assassinated Peter. Catherine became ruler of Russia.

While legends persist about Catherine's rapacious sexual appetite (rumours of her fondness for horses have been greatly exaggerated), it would seem that she was the target of some deft propaganda by jealous male members of the court. Her diaries are said to list fewer than 10 lovers, and even if some of them were engaged concurrently, by modern standards she would have appeared quite conservative, if not extraordinarily generous: many of her favourites were given palaces and large estates.

Catherine's legacy stems from her constant self-education and love of culture. She

Catherine II (the Great)

was a great exponent of the Enlightenment and westernised Russia in leaps and bounds, all the while ensuring that any public spirit of liberalism didn't grow unchecked; the French Revolution appalled her and she went to lengths to avoid any similar occurrence on her territory.

Catherine's most visible bequest was to bring Russia on to the world stage of arts and her letters (her most famous correspondent was Voltaire). She freed regulations and restrictions on publishing. Her vast collection of paintings turned the Hermitage into a world-class museum. And Catherine went on an architectural commissioning spree, inviting dozens of Western European architects to bring neo-classicism to St Petersburg.

## Alexander I

When Catherine died in 1796 the throne passed to her son, Paul I. An old-school autocrat, he antagonised the gentry with attempts to reimpose compulsory state service and in 1801 his own courtiers murdered him in the palace he only got to occupy for 40 days (today's Engineers' Castle, part of the Russian Museum).

Paul's son, Alexander I (who had been Catherine's favourite grandson), kicked off his reign with several reforms, including expanding the school system to bring it within reach of the lower-middle classes. The early days of his reign were relative halcyon days for the populace, and Russia's wars against Napoleon galvanised disparate elements of society.

After several defeats by Napoleon's troops, Alexander negotiated the Treaty of Tilsit (1807) which (in theory) united them against England. This alliance lasted only until 1810, when Russia resumed trade with England. A hopping-mad Napoleon decided to crush the tsar with a Grand Army of 600,000, the largest force the world had ever seen for a single military operation.

Rather than meet the Grand Army in Prussia or Poland, Alexander shrewdly drew it into the vast Russian countryside in the summer of 1812. A bloody but inconclusive battle was fought at Borodino, 130km west of Moscow.

In September, Napoleon entered a largely deserted Moscow; a few days later the city was burnt down around him. With winter coming, Napoleon ordered a retreat. His troops, harassed by Russian partisans, froze and starved. Only one in 20 made it as far as Poland, and the Russians pursued them all the way to Paris. Alexander rode triumphantly into the city on a white horse.

## The Decembrists

Alexander's unexpected death without a clear heir in 1825 sparked the usual crisis. His reform-minded brother Constantine, married to a Pole and living happily in Warsaw thank you very much, had no interest in the throne. Officers who had brought back liberal ideas from Paris in 1815 preferred Constantine to Alexander's youngest brother, the militaristic Nicholas, who was due to be crowned on 26 December 1825. Their rally in St Petersburg was quashed by troops loyal to Nicholas, who threw those who weren't killed into the Peter & Paul Fortress. Nicholas looked each so-called Decembrist in the eyes before pronouncing sentence, psychologically terrorising many (executing some, while subjecting others to mock executions only to tell them at the last moment that their sentences had been 'commuted' to exile).

The remainder of Nicholas I's reign was as inauspicious as the beginning; though he granted title to peasants on state land (effectively freeing them), his foreign policy accomplished little else than to annoy everyone in the Balkans, most of the rest of Europe, and to start the Crimean War in which England and France sided against Russia. Inept

**Retreat of Napoleon's Grand Army from Russia**

LPP

command on both sides resulted in a bloody, stalemated war. At home, his obsession with military order stifled the capital from expressing any independent thought.

## Alexander II – the 'Great Reformer'

When Nicholas died in 1855, St Petersburg was the fourth largest city in Europe. His son, Alexander II (r. 1855–81), put an end to the Crimean War, which had revealed the backwardness behind the post-1812 imperial glory. The time for reform had come, and he engaged it on all levels of society.

The serfs were freed in 1861. Of the land they had worked, roughly a third was kept by established landholders. The rest went to village communes which assigned it to individuals in return for 'redemption payments' to compensate former landholders – a system that pleased no-one.

But the abolition of serfdom opened the way for a market economy, capitalism and an industrial revolution. Railroads and factories were built and cities expanded as peasants left the land. Nothing, though, was done to modernise farming methods and the peasants found their lot had not improved in half a century.

During the reign of Alexander II and his son, Alexander III (r. 1881–94), Central Asia came under Russian control. In the east, Russia acquired a long strip of Pacific coast from China and built the port of Vladivostok, but sold the 'worthless' Alaskan territories to the US in 1867 for just $7.2 million.

The loosening of restrictions and rapid change in the make-up of Russian society took its toll, however. Industrialisation and the emancipation of the serfs brought a flood of poor workers into St Petersburg, leading to overcrowding, poor sanitation, epidemics and festering discontent. Revolutionary sentiment was rife and radicals were plotting the overthrow of the tsarist government as early as the second half of the 19th century. After seven attempts on his life, Alexander II was assassinated in 1881 in St Petersburg by a terrorist bomb.

Suspected reactionary members of society were rounded up and either executed or exiled, and the reign of Alexander III was marked by repression of revolutionaries and liberals alike.

## The Russo-Japanese War

Port Arthur, home of the Russian Fleet during China's Boxer Uprising, was attacked by Japanese forces on 8 February 1904, after Russia refused to withdraw its troops from the region. The Russo-Japanese war that followed was quick, humiliating and devastating – nearly all of Russia's navy was obliterated.

Tsar Nicholas II (crowned in 1894) used a traditional Russian strategy for engaging in military offences: throw as many men (in many cases forcibly-drafted and ill-prepared peasants) as he could at the Japanese. The subsequent butchering of young Russians caused a huge political backlash and the series of defeats took their toll in the form of ever increasing civil unrest in St Petersburg. Under the terms of the peace treaty signed on 5 September 1905, Russia not only gave up Port Arthur, the larger half of Sakhalin Island and other properties, but also recognised Japanese predominance in Korea.

## The 1905 Revolution & WWI

St Petersburg became a hotbed of strikes and political violence as well as the hub of the 1905 revolution, sparked by 'Bloody Sunday', 9 January 1905 when a strikers' march to petition the tsar in the Winter Palace was fired on by troops. The group, led by Father Georgy Gapon, was made up of about 150,000 workers who were imploring for better living conditions. The protesters were fired upon throughout the city; estimates of the number of dead reach into the thousands. Despite the thorough witch hunt for revolutionaries that followed, the incident galvanised and united opposition factions against the common enemy.

In the months to follow, peasant uprisings, mutinies (most famously that aboard the Battleship Potyomkin) and other protests across the nation abounded. Soviets, or 'workers' councils', were formed by social democrat activists in St Petersburg and Moscow. The St Petersburg Soviet, led by

Mensheviks (Minority People, who in fact outnumbered the Bolshevik, or Majority People's, party) under Leon Trotsky, called for a massive general strike in October, which brought the country to a standstill.

These protests resulted in Tsar Nicholas II's grudgingly issued 'October Manifesto' which, along with granting hitherto unheard of civil rights, created the (largely powerless) State Duma, Russia's elected legislature. By 1914, when in a brief wave of patriotism (or at least anti-German sentiment) at the start of WWI, the city's name was changed to the Russian-style Petrograd, it had a population of 2.1 million people. A few years later, after countless defeats on the battlefield and literally millions of lives lost in the unpopular war, Petrograd would again be the cradle of revolution.

## The 1917 Revolution

Actually, there were two. With the deprivations caused by the war, along with a breakdown in the chain of command, morale was very low. People were also incensed at the strong influence the randy Siberian spiritualist Grigory Rasputin had on the throne, via the empress Alexandra. Nicholas was blamed for failures of the Russian armies. Political fragmentation had resulted in a reincarnation of the Petrograd Soviet of Workers & Soldiers Deputies, based on the 1905 model. Workers' protests turned into a general strike and troops mutinied, forcing the end of the monarchy.

On 1 March Nicholas abdicated after he was 'asked to' by the Duma. The Romanov dynasty of over 300 years officially came to an end. A short time later, Nicholas and his entire family were exiled to Yekaterinberg, east of the Ural Mountains, where they were later murdered and buried in a mass grave. Some of the bodies have been exhumed and re-buried at the Peter & Paul Fortress (see the boxed text 'Reburying the Past' in the Things to See & Do chapter).

A provisional government announced that general elections would be held in November. The Petrograd Soviet started meeting in the city's Tauride Palace alongside the country's reformist Provisional Government. It was to Petrograd's Finland Station that Vladimir Lenin travelled in April to organise the Bolshevik Party. The Smolny Institute, a former girls' college in the city, became the locus of power as the Bolsheviks took control of the Petrograd Soviet which had installed itself there.

During the summer, tensions were raised considerably by the co-existence of two power bases: the Provisional Government and the Petrograd Soviet. The Bolsheviks' propaganda campaign was winning over a substantial number of people who, understandably, thought that the slogan 'Peace, Land and Bread' was a good maxim by which to live. Tensions were high; Lenin thought that it was now the time for a Soviet coup. But a series of violent mass demonstrations in July, inspired by the Bolsheviks but in the end not fully backed by them, was quelled. Lenin fled to Finland, and Alexandr Kerensky, a moderate Social Revolutionary, became prime minister.

In September, the Russian military Chief-of-Staff, General Kornilov, sent cavalry to Petrograd to crush the Soviets. Kerensky's government turned to the left for support against this insubordination, even courting

Vladimir Lenin

the Bolsheviks, and the counter-revolution was defeated. After this, public opinion massively favoured the Bolsheviks, who quickly took control of the Petrograd Soviet (chaired by Trotsky, who had joined them) and, by extension, all the Soviets in the land. Lenin (who had cowered in Finland through all this) again decided it was time to seize power and returned from Finland in October.

The actual 'Great October Soviet etc etc' revolution wasn't nearly as dramatic as all those red-tinted, massive Soviet canvases dedicated to the event would have you believe. Bolsheviks occupied key positions in Petrograd on 24 October. Next day, the All-Russian Congress of Soviets appointed a Bolshevik government. That night, after some exchanges of gunfire and a blank shot fired from the cruiser *Aurora* on the Neva (a symbol of the navy's allegiance to the uprising), the Provisional Government in the Winter Palace surrendered to the Bolsheviks.

Armistice was signed with the approaching Germans in December 1917, followed by the Treaty of Brest-Litovsk in March 1918 that surrendered Poland, the Baltic provinces, Ukraine, Finland and Transcaucasia to the Germans. This negotiation for a separate peace with Germany enraged the Allied forces, who would later back anti-Bolshevik fighters in a nose-thumbing effort to punish the revolutionaries for taking their ball and going home.

## The Civil War

There was wide dissent after the revolution, and a number of political parties sprang up almost immediately to challenge the Bolsheviks' power. The power struggle began peacefully in the November elections for the Constituent Assembly; the Socialist Revolutionaries won a sweeping victory, only to have the assembly shut down by a very mad Vlad. A multi-sided civil war erupted. Trotsky founded the Red Army in February 1918 and the Cheka, Russia's secret police force designed to fight opposition, was established.

The new government operated from the Smolny until March 1918, when it moved to Moscow, fearing attacks on Petrograd

from outside and from within. The loss in status was a crushing blow to the city, already suffocating from food shortages and unrest. By August 1920, the population of the city had fallen to 722,000, only one third of the pre-revolutionary figure. Civil war ravaged the country until 1921, by which time the Communist Party had firmly established one-party rule thanks to the Red Army and the Cheka, which continued to eliminate opponents. Those who escaped joined an estimated 1.5 million citizens in exile.

The Bolsheviks instituted a number of reforms, including modernising orthography and introducing the use of the Gregorian calendar in 1918. But the 1921 strikes in the city and a (bloodily crushed) revolt by the sailors of nearby Kronshtadt helped bring about Lenin's more liberal New Economic Policy (NEP).

Petrograd was renamed Leningrad after Lenin's death in 1924. It was a hub of Stalin's 1930s industrialisation program and by 1939 had a population of 3.1 million people, producing 11% of Soviet industrial output. But Stalin feared the city as a rival power base and the (likely Stalin-ordered) assassination of the local communist chief Sergey Kirov at Smolny in 1934 was the perfect excuse to start his purges.

## WWII

When the Germans attacked the USSR in June 1941, officially beginning what the Russians refer to as the Great Patriotic War, it took them only 2½ months to reach Leningrad. Hitler hated the place as the birthplace of Bolshevism, and he swore to wipe it from the face of the earth, but not before his expected New Year's victory ball at the Hotel Astoria. Nazi troops surrounded and besieged Leningrad from 8 September 1941 until 27 January 1944. Over two million people (and three-quarters of the industrial plant) had been evacuated. Nevertheless, between 500,000 and a million people died from shelling, starvation and disease in what's called the '900-day siege' (actually 872; see the boxed text 'The Blockade of Leningrad' in the Things to See & Do chapter). By comparison, the US and

## What's in a Name?

No wonder this city has suffered from identity crises. It's not enough that architecturally, it looks like its parents couldn't decide which clothes to dress it up in and so draped it in every style imaginable. It's also been forced to change its name three times and still its residents call it by yet another!

Established in honour of Peter the Great's patron saint, Sankt Pieter Burkh was soon-after changed to Sankt Peterburg. But in a wave of anti-German sentiment on the eve of WWI, Nicholas II ordered the German-sounding city to be renamed Petrograd in August 1914 (in the process making it the city of Peter the man, not the saint). To this day, the name Petrograd conjures unpleasant notions of tanks, wars and revolutions.

After Lenin died in 1924, it was Petrograd Communist Party leader Grigory Zinoviev's idea to re-name the city Leningrad (he figured he'd be in the game for a long while, and that the new name would increase the city's status – and thus his own). No matter that Lenin himself hadn't spent much time in the place and that he reportedly didn't like it. The renaming was good communist PR: cra-dle of the revolution and all that.

To some Russians, superstitious as always, the move was ominous. To betray the city – and city's founder – in such a way, and to remove it from the 'protection' of the saint after whom it was named, could only lead to no good. Look what happened in the 10 years of 'Petrograd'! The major flood of September 1924 seemed to prove all the Cassandras right. And, we can say now, so did the next 63 years.

Despite its different monikers, however, the city has always been affectionately known by resi-dents and admirers alike as simply 'Piter'. So it was little surprise that a public referendum in June 1991 led to the re-establishment of 'St Petersburg'. And it's been uphill ever since. Maybe fate shouldn't be messed with after all.

the UK together suffered about 700,000 deaths in all of WWII.

## The Postwar Period

After the war, Leningrad, now buffered from future attacks by territories won from Finland in the Winter War of 1939–40, was reconstructed and reborn, though it took until 1960 for the population to exceed pre-war levels. The centre and most of the inner surrounding areas were slowly repaired, and eventually the outlying areas were lined with concrete apartment blocks. Through-out the Khrushchev and Brezhnev years, the state stifled Leningrad's artistic voice, yet despite the stagnation, it was indisputably the Soviet Union's cultural and artistic cen-tre. Many of the period's more innovative artistic contributions, such as rock music, came to the Soviet world via Leningrad.

## The 1980s & Gorbachev

After Brezhnev's death in 1982 (it was only noticed in 1984), he was replaced by former KGB director Yuri Andropov, who shortly thereafter also died. His successor, Kon-stantin Chernenko, followed suit just 13 months later.

Seeing the need for some new, or at least circulating, blood, Mikhail Gorbachev was installed in 1985. He launched an immedi-ate turnover in the politburo, the bureau-cracy and the military, replacing many of the Brezhnevite 'old guard' with his own, younger supporters. He tried to clamp down on alcohol sales in an unsuccessful attempt to address alcoholism (of all his reforms, this was his most unpopular). He announced a policy of *glasnost* (openness), hoping to spur the economy by encouraging manage-ment initiative and rewarding efficiency.

Gorbachev stunned the world by adopting a conciliatory attitude towards the West, and in his first summit meeting with US Presi-dent Ronald Reagan in 1985, Gorbachev uni-laterally suggested a 50% cut in long-range nuclear weapons. This was followed by sig-nificant cuts in arms and troop numbers.

## Chernobyl & Perestroika

The shock of the Chernobyl nuclear disaster in April 1986 fuelled the drive towards political restructure. It had taken a very un-glastnost-like 18 days to admit the (underplayed) extent of the disaster to the West, even longer to the neighbouring Warsaw Pact countries. It is worth noting that a now unclassified KGB document, commissioned and signed by Yuri Andropov on 21 February 1979, predicted the disaster over seven years before it occurred.

It was becoming clear that no leader who relied on the Party could survive as a reformer. *Perestroika* (restructuring) became the new cry. This meant limited private enterprise and private property, not unlike Lenin's New Economic Policy, and further efforts to push towards decentralisation.

The forces unleashed by Gorbachev's laudable but awkwardly instituted reforms precipitated the fall of the Soviet Union. The reduced threat of repression spurred a growing clamour for independence: first in the Soviet satellite states of Eastern Europe, followed by the Baltic republics, Moldova, and the Transcaucasian republics. The floodgates, once opened, were impossible to close, despite occasional shows of force.

Residents of the city of Leningrad voted to rename the city St Petersburg in a June 1991 referendum (the surrounding region, a separate governmental body, refused to join in the fun and to this day is called the Leningradskaya oblast). Mayor Anatoly Sobchak cheered the results. In presidential elections, also held in June 1991, Boris Yeltsin won the title of President of the Russian Republic by a good majority.

## 1991 Coup

On 19 August 1991, a group of hardline communists staged what was perhaps the most inept coup of the 20th century. While Gorbachev was on holiday at his Crimean dacha, it was announced in Moscow that a 'state of emergency' was in effect; a self-appointed Committee of the State Emergency announced that it was in power.

Tanks and armed soldiers appeared on the streets of Moscow and Yeltsin joined a group of protesters at the Russian Parliament's headquarters, the White House. When tanks approached, Yeltsin, in full view of CNN, leapt aboard one and implored its crew to use their heads and hold their fire. As hordes of protesters grew, the disorganised plot crumbled.

As hundreds of thousands of St Petersburg protesters filled Dvortsovaya pl, Sobchak, who had earlier talked a group of soldiers out of obeying their Moscow-issued orders to arrest him, appeared on local television denouncing the coup and asking local residents to do the same. Fearful but determined residents spent a jittery evening awaiting tanks that never appeared.

When Yeltsin proclaimed the Communist Party an illegal organisation, what fragile threads remained of the Soviet Union were ripped apart. On 25 December 1991, Gorbachev resigned and the Soviet Union was officially pronounced dead. Next day, the Russian Federation's flag of red, white and blue flew over the Kremlin.

## The New St Petersburg

St Petersburg and Moscow immediately set about attracting foreign business. Unfortunately, the 74 years of Soviet rule had created a deeply entrenched bureaucracy that believed that the way to attract foreigners was to intimidate and humiliate them, change regulations without warning, to swindle money as often as possible and to send taxes through the roof. The foreigners, blinded by the lust for quick profits, and not shy to engage in some swindling themselves, proved them right and came in droves. Even the economic crisis of August 1998, when the rouble was devalued, did not scare off foreign investment.

The 1990s were particularly hard times for most citizens of St Petersburg, as for the country as a whole, whose politicians and oligarchs siphoned tens of billions of dollars out of the country and into foreign bank accounts. As many citizens would say, yes, the shops were full and they could travel anywhere they wanted, but no one had the money to take advantage of this 'freedom'. St Petersburg also gained the nickname of

Russia's crime capital, thanks to a series of high-profile political and Mafia killings.

Yet in many ways the city itself has been burgeoning from an attention it hadn't received since before the revolution. True, most of the foreign and domestic capital that somehow stayed in Russia has been channelled into polishing Moscow, but central St Petersburg has been largely cleaned up and restored. Russians love to dazzle foreign guests, so it's no surprise that in the months preceding the 1994 Goodwill Games and the 2000 World Hockey Championships, the

city was suddenly allocated millions of roubles to patch potholed streets (the roads are still reputed to be among Russian's worst), re-paint, clean and restore decaying palaces, build stadiums, manicure parks and estates, and rejuvenate the city's main thoroughfare, Nevsky prospekt.

Vladimir Putin's election to the presidency in March 2000 signalled a further boost to the city on the Neva: Putin, having spent most of his life there – when he wasn't busy gathering intelligence in East Germany – is reputedly very fond of the city; his first meeting with a foreign head of state, Tony Blair, took place there, not in Moscow; he has continued to meet heads of states in St Petersburg palaces en lieu of the Kremlin; there is talk of moving the Ministry of Culture to St Petersburg; and he has announced that his St Petersburg residence is to be the crumbling Konstantinovsky Palace, designed by Ratrelli, located just outside the city on the way to Petrodvorets.

The city is also in the throes of preparation for its 300th anniversary, which will turn into a year-long series of celebrations and festivals in 2003 (see the boxed text 'Happy Birthday!'). After spectacular federal disregard of the city's infrastructure during the Soviet era, much of what was crumbling and decaying has or is being preserved and rebuilt. St Petersburg is in the process of re-inventing itself.

## GEOGRAPHY

St Petersburg, whose latitude is 59°57' N and longitude 30°19' E, straddles the Neva River delta and is made up of 42 islands, connected by some 340 bridges. Branches of the Neva River divide the city's busiest areas. Since the 18th century, 67 smaller rivers, canals, islands and ponds within the city limits have been filled in or changed (for example, present-day Ligovsky pr used to be a canal, dug in 1718–21, and filled in in stages from 1891–1969). The entire area surrounding St Petersburg is flat, the highest peaks reaching only some 200m in far-away Karelia. The historical centre of the city itself is nowhere higher than 4m above sea level; parts are actually below it.

---

### Happy Birthday!

On the newly pedestrianised Mal Sadovaya ul, there's a spacey-looking metal-and-LED contraption that shows how many days, minutes and seconds are left before what is sure to be St Petersburg's most enthusiastically celebrated birthday ever. The date 27 May 1703 is considered to be the official birth of St Petersburg, with the laying of the first stone for the Peter & Paul Fortress. With its tri-centennial just around the corner, the already party-happy city is busy preparing for a bash to end all bashes.

Though June 2003 will be a month-long bacchanalia of festivals, concerts, sports events, exhibits and merry-making on a grand scale, special events are being organised for the entire year. Even more importantly for the city, some $1.3 billion has been allocated to St Petersburg for the celebrations, much of which will be poured into repairing roadways, restoring architectural treasures in the city and environs and ensuring the participation of all sectors of society in the fun and games. It hasn't hurt that the head of the State Committee overlooking the 300th anniversary has been none other than ex-St Petersburger Vladimir Putin.

The city hopes to attract even more than the 2.5 million tourists who already visit the city each year. The city even opened its first tourist office abroad in early 2001, in Paris, to attract even more *joie de vivre* that's sure to embrace it.

## CLIMATE

St Petersburg's climate is maritime and much milder than its northern latitude would suggest. January temperatures average -8°C; a really cold day will get down to -15°C. It's a windy city though and in some areas exposed to the Gulf of Finland the wind chill is quite fierce, so bring a good warm hat and scarf.

Summer is cool and takes a while to get going: snow in late April is not uncommon as temperatures suddenly drop when the melting ice blocks from Lake Ladoga come floating through the city's main waterways. Warm weather doesn't really start until the period between June and August, when temperatures usually surpass 20°C. On the rare hot days of highs up to 30°C, the city becomes unbearable and residents flee to the beaches on the north bank of the Gulf of Finland or to their dachas in cool but mosquito-infested forests.

The city's northern latitude means long days in summer and long nights in winter. During the summer White Nights festival, around the time of the summer solstice, night is reduced to a brief dimming of the lights at around 1am, only to turn to dawn a couple of hours later. And in winter the city seems to be in constant dusk.

## ECOLOGY & ENVIRONMENT
### Pollution

**Air** Thanks to St Petersburg's wide streets and prevalent winds, the place is relatively smog-free, but that's not for lack of trying. Cars roam free without the encumbrance of catalytic converters or pollution control devices and trucks and buses emit unbelievable clouds of soot-filled exhaust – and that's only part of the story. St Petersburg's industrial plants are major air and water polluters. But at the end of the day, the air quality here is about on a par with that of other developing cities; your Kleenex after a stroll around London will be blacker than after a day in St Petersburg.

**Radiation** St Petersburg's disaster-in-waiting, the Sosnovy Bor nuclear power plant, 60km west of the city, threatened to blow its stack in 1992 (it didn't). It's an

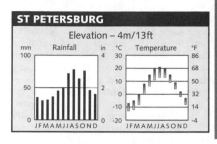

ST PETERSBURG
Elevation – 4m/13ft

RBMK-style reactor, the same model as the doomed Chernobyl reactor, except this one's older. Its waste dumps have been threatening to overflow for several years already, but the closest thing to a solution that has been approved is the opening, in May 2001, of EKOMET-S, a factory on the nuclear station's grounds that plans to produce anywhere from 5000 to 150,000 tonnes of cleaned metal products a year. That is, it plans on utilising raw, reactive waste metal, clean and refine it to produce everything from kitchen utensils to cars. The plant insists its products will only emit twice the accepted level of radiation. Radiation levels in St Petersburg are said to be consistent with the international norms. Incidentally, the most radioactive statue in the city is said to be the one of General Suvorov, standing in between the Mars Field and the Troitsky most.

## GOVERNMENT & POLITICS

The city is managed by Governor Vladimir Yakovlev, whose first act after defeating Mayor Anatoly Sobchak in June 1996 was to change the title from mayor to governor. Though he has presided over St Petersburg in its time of increasing prosperity, his reign has been marred by serious allegations of wrongdoings. In 1999, he narrowly escaped being charged by the Interior Ministry for using city money to fund his All Russia Congress (this after spending the better part of his first two years in office trying to publicise the supposed corruption of Sobchak). And, a year later, the city's police chief was quickly fired after publicly announcing that an investigation would follow from documented proof that a number of city government officials were also part of local Mafia bands.

A string of high-level political assassinations have also occurred since Yakovlev came to office, and his name has been linked to within a few degrees of separation with these (most notably of Duma Deputy Galina Starovoitova in 1998, shot down in her apartment building). A deputy in the Legislative Assembly, Yury Shutov, elected with Yakovlev's support, was eventually charged with ordering seven contract killings in the city.

Since Putin's election to the presidency, Yakovlev's future has been uncertain. Both worked together under Sobchak in the early 1990s and Putin's dislike of Yakovlev was no secret. Still, the two have made several chummy public appearances, and Yakovlev has made loud announcements of his wish to move Russia's Parliament back to St Petersburg. In early 2001, rumours were flying that Putin is not about to let Yakovlev survive as governor to reap the glory of the city's 300th anniversary in 2003. Instead, newspapers were writing, Putin would place him at the head of the commission for the union between Belarus and Russia, together with another well-known defender of freedom and democracy, Belarus president Alexander Lukashenko – which would show that Putin has a nice sense of irony.

## ECONOMY

The Russian economy has enjoyed an upswing since the economic crash of August 1998 when the rouble fell from six to the dollar to 23 to the dollar. This has in part been due to a rise in global oil prices and to tighter fiscal policies. In 2000, the economy grew 7% while household incomes grew 5%. In the first quarter of 2001 alone, GDP grew by 4%, an increase matched by industrial output.

Muscovites, of course, enjoy the benefits of any economic upswing more than anyone else in the land, but St Petersburg and its surrounding areas are in a healthy second place. The country's middle class is estimated to comprise about 7% of the population, but growing all the time (in contrast, 64% of Americans are considered middle-class). These are people earning from $500 to $1500 a month. The national average monthly wage is about $40.

While the gap between rich and poor has narrowed a smidgen, the top 10% of the population earned 14.3 times more than the poorest 10% in 2000. The forecasted inflation rate for 2001 is between 12% and 14%.

St Petersburg is a high-tech centre – one in 10 Russian scientists work here – and is the country's largest commercial seaport. The region's natural resources include timber and bauxite, an element used in aluminium production.

Almost every major multinational corporation has a presence in town (see Doing Business in the Facts for the Visitor chapter).

## POPULATION & PEOPLE

The number of residents in the city in 2000 was estimated to be 4.2 million, though the figure of 4.7 million (which includes the outlying areas) is more frequently used. The city has the lowest birth rate in all of Russia's 89 administrative regions and, on average, its population is among Russia's oldest. As in much of the Russian Federation, the make-up of St Petersburg's population is mostly composed of ethnic Russians. Minorities include Jews (still considered to be a nationality in Russia), Ukrainians, Belarusians and other nationalities from within the former Soviet Union. The expatriate community of Western businesspeople and students is continually growing; in 2000 there were an estimated 20,000 such residents, among them about 5000 Americans and a greater number of Germans.

## EDUCATION

St Petersburg has a high concentration of some of the country's best schools and colleges. Their sheer numbers are mind-boggling: 22 military colleges, some 70 sports schools, several dozen universities (see Universities in the Facts for the Visitor chapter), some 200 technical, medical, economic and trade colleges, over 400 primary and secondary schools, 250 kindergartens and dozens of specialised schools. The Soviet primary and secondary education system was excellent, outstripping most Western countries in scope, and its continuing legacy happily remains. However, in the city's top universities, competition is very tough and students complain that another legacy of old times, bribery and need for personal contacts, is necessary to ensure a place. Another factor marring the quality of education is the astoundingly meagre teachers' salaries (a professor could earn as little as $30 a month).

## SCIENCE & PHILOSOPHY

The history of science in Russia and the Soviet Union has been a confusing blend of sheer brilliance and confounding stagnation. The Russian Academy of Sciences was established in 1726 and has since produced great results. Students the world-over learn about the conditional reflex experiments on Pavlov's puppies, and about Dmitri Mendeleev's 1869 discovery of the Periodic Table of Elements (Russians often say, with a sigh, 'Russia's lands have everything in Mendeleev's Table and yet we live so poorly!'). Yet visitors may be surprised to hear from locals about Russia's invention of the telephone and the radio (didn't you know?). The country's history of scientific achievements has very much been that of brilliant, capable individuals limited by the whims of the state and by prevailing, ever-shifting ideologies.

In the USSR, science, hampered by secrecy, bureaucracy and lack of technology, was dependent on the ruling Party. Funding would come sporadically, and then in great bursts for projects which served propaganda or militaristic concerns. Thus the space race received lots of money, and even though very little of scientific consequence was achieved during the first missions, the PR was priceless. In other fields, however, the USSR lagged behind the West: genetics, cybernetics and the theory of relativity all at one point were deemed anathema to communism. Physics – especially theoretical and nuclear – was supported and Russia has produced some of the world's brightest scientists in the field. Andrei Sakharov, (1921–89) 'father of the H-bomb', was exiled to Gorky in 1980, five years after receiving the Nobel Peace Prize, for his vocal denunciations of the Soviet nuclear program and the military crackdown in Afghanistan. He became one of the most vocal and influential dissidents of his time.

Russian science also gets distracted by the enthusiastic pursuit of less than realistic, even mystical goals. Sure, great discoveries start as fanciful dreams. Yet flights of fancy can also waste resources. After wrapping the Periodic Table, Mendeleev, a fan of science fiction, devoted much of the remaining 38 years of his life to searching for universal ethers and rarefied gases which allegedly rule interactions between all bodies. In Russia, hard science can blend with supernatural mysticism without a burp of contradiction.

Russia is not wanting in great ideas, though, and let's hope some of them work: in late 2000, St Petersburg's Institute of Bioregulation and Gerontology announced that they had come up with a recipe of bioregulators called cytamines and cytamedines guaranteed to slow the human ageing process.

See what else is cooking in the St Petersburg scientific pot at Ⓦ http://spb.ru/000/science/scientific/index.en.

## ARTS

St Petersburg has been at the forefront of all avenues of Russian art, not only as the nation's capital for the 200 years when artistic life flourished, but also as a natural magnet for creativity. Russian tendencies towards eccentricity and theatricality collide in this city, itself built as a work of art, and the innovative, experimental and occasionally brilliant results have in some cases gone on to be achievements of a world-class level.

### Literature

St Petersburg's status as artistic and cultural centre of Russia has much to do with the writers and poets associated with the city. The list is a veritable *Who's Who* of literary figures: Pushkin, Dostoevsky, Lermontov (whose *Death of a Poet* accused the government of plotting Pushkin's death), Nabokov, Blok, Akhmatova…

Alexandr Pushkin, Russia's best-loved poet, was born in 1799. He was the great-grandson of Abram Hannibal, an Ethiopian

## Dostoevsky

No other figure in world literature is more closely connected with Russia – and St Petersburg – than Fyodor Dostoevsky. He was among the first writers to navigate the murky, uninvestigated waters of the human subconscious, blending powerful prose with psychology, philosophy and spirituality.

He, like most intellectuals, had deep but mixed feelings about his home country, calling it a 'sublime, universal, ordered chaos' and Russians themselves 'half-saint, half-savage'. Increasingly religious as he grew older, he quoted two inspirations for his life views: the New Testament, and the Russian people. He felt Russians have an unrealised Christ-like harmony that could redeem humanity if acknowledged. Yet he all too clearly saw, and depicted, the squalid reality around him, framed by a society that stifled individuality.

His first novel, *Poor Folk*, written when he was 24 years old, was immediately seen as the work of a genius, though his next offerings, *The Double* and *White Nights*, disappointed the other literary figures of the time, namely Nekrasov and Belinsky, who had championed him as the best writer in Russia since Gogol.

His career was halted – but ultimately shaped – by his casual involvement with a group of young free-thinkers who would meet weekly at the home of an eccentric socialist, Mikhail Petrashevsky, and free-associate liberal ideas. Nicholas I decided to make an example of the harmless group to any burgeoning revolutionaries and had 34 of their members arrested and sentenced to death, including Dostoevsky. After spending a few months in the Peter & Paul Fortress prison, he, along with 20 others, were marched out to Semyonovskaya pl (today's Pionerskaya pl) on 22 December 1949 for the execution which, as the guns were aimed and ready to fire, was suddenly called off, commuted to a sentence of hard labour. The mock execution was Nicholas I's idea of a good, sick joke.

In a labour camp in Omsk, Siberia, Dostoevsky witnessed incredible suffering at the hands of wicked brutality, yet also limitless courage and acts of unforgettable kindness. After he was pardoned by Alexander II and allowed to return to St Petersburg, he wrote *Notes from the House of the Dead* (1861), a vivid recounting of his prison sojourn. His life was marred by personal tragedy in the following years, with the death of his wife and beloved brother in 1864 plunging him into grief. Addicted to gambling, he was also always in debt.

The ultimate St Petersburg novel, and a classic of literature, is his *Crime and Punishment* (1866), which depicts in great detail the squalor of anti-hero Raskolnikov's surroundings. As well as it being a tale of frustrated individuality and redemption, it also acknowledged the 'other side' of the regal, pretty capital that was now becoming industrialised, gritty and spawning shifty, unsavoury characters.

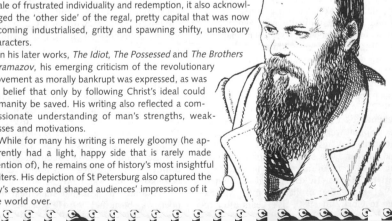

In his later works, *The Idiot*, *The Possessed* and *The Brothers Karamazov*, his emerging criticism of the revolutionary movement as morally bankrupt was expressed, as was his belief that only by following Christ's ideal could humanity be saved. His writing also reflected a compassionate understanding of man's strengths, weaknesses and motivations.

While for many his writing is merely gloomy (he apparently had a light, happy side that is rarely made mention of), he remains one of history's most insightful writers. His depiction of St Petersburg also captured the city's essence and shaped audiences' impressions of it the world over.

slave who went on to become a general under Peter the Great. There is probably not a soul in all of Russia who could not recite at least a few lines of his poetry by heart. After his graduation in 1817, Pushkin enjoyed the high life in St Petersburg and committed many of his liberal ideas to paper. These papers eventually made their way to the police, who were not amused; Pushkin was exiled from St Petersburg in 1820, which probably is the only reason he wasn't standing with the Decembrists in 1825 (he said so himself, later, to Nicholas I who appreciated the poet's forthrightness).

In the 1830s Pushkin had lost popularity with the general Russian reading public and had married Natalya Goncharova with whom, some say, he was obsessed. On 27 January 1837, Pushkin challenged Baron Georges D'Anthés, a French nobleman who had been openly courting Natalya, to a duel. Pushkin was shot and died two days later His last place of residence is now a museum (see the Things to See & Do chapter).

Pushkin's most famous work, published posthumously in 1841, is *The Bronze Horseman*, depicting the great flood of 1824. In it, the hopes and wishes of the people – represented here by the lowly clerk Yevgeni, who has lost his beloved in the flood – take on the conquering, empire-building spirit of Peter the Great, represented by the animation of the bronze statue of him installed by Catherine the Great. His other famous works include *Eugene Onegin* and *Queen of Spades*.

Fyodor Dostoevsky's (1821–81) descriptions of St Petersburg's slums are legendary, and he was the first major writer to show fully the seedy, dangerous and filthy side of life in the grand Russian capital.

Alexandr Blok (1880–1921) took over where Dostoevsky left off, writing of prostitutes, drunks, Gypsies and other assorted 'rabble'. Blok's sympathies with the revolutions of 1905 and 1917 were held up by the Bolsheviks – as was the work of Mayakovsky – as an example of an established writer who had seen the light; Blok's *The Twelve*, published in 1918, is pretty much a love-letter to Lenin. However, he soon grew deeply disenchanted with the revolution, consequently fell out of favour, and died a sad, lonely poet. In one of his last letters, he wrote, 'She did devour me, lousy, snuffling dear Mother Russia, like a sow devouring her piglet'. The flat where he spent the last, sad eight years of his life is now a museum (see the section on Teatralnaya pl in the Things to See & Do chapter).

No literary figure, though, is as inextricably linked to the fate of St Petersburg-Petrograd-Leningrad as Anna Akhmatova (1889–1966), the long-suffering poet whose work contains bittersweet depictions of the city she so loved. Akhmatova's life was filled with sorrow and loss – her family was imprisoned and killed, her friends exiled, tortured and arrested, her colleagues were constantly hounded – but she refused to leave her beloved city, and died there in 1966 (see Akhmatova Memorial Museum in the Things to See & Do chapter). Her work depicts the city with realism and monumentalism, painted with Russian as well as personal history. Her major work is *Poem Without a Hero*. While the Communist Party's condemnation of her work (in a denunciation in August 1946) as 'the poetry of a crazed lady, chasing back and forth between boudoir and chapel' may not have been fair, her love for her city was unconditional but unblinking: 'The capital on the Neva; Having forgotten its greatness; Like a drunken whore; Did not know who was taking her'.

## Dance

First brought to Russia under Tsar Alexis Mikhailovich in the 17th century, Russian ballet evolved as an offshoot of French dance combined with Russian folk and peasant dance techniques. It stunned Western Europeans when it was first taken on tour in the 19th century.

The 'official' beginnings of Russian ballet date to 1738 and the establishment by French dance master Jean Baptiste Lande of a school of dance in the Winter Palace, the precursor to the famed Vaganova School of Choreography (see the Things to See & Do chapter). Catherine the Great created the Bolshoi Theatre to develop opera and ballet in 1765 and imported foreign composers and teachers.

Marius Petipa (1819–1910) is considered to be the father of Russian ballet. The French dancer and choreographer acted first as principal dancer, then Premier Ballet Master of the Imperial Theatre. All told he produced more than 60 full ballets (including Tchaikovsky's *Sleeping Beauty* and *Swan Lake*).

At the turn of the 20th century, the heyday of Russian ballet, St Petersburg's Imperial School of Ballet rose to world prominence, producing superstar after superstar. Names such as Vaslaw Nijinsky, Anna Pavlova, Mathilda Kshesinskaya, Georges Balanchine, Mikhail Fokine and Olga Spessivtzeva turned the Mariinsky Theatre into the world's most dynamic display of the art of dance. Sergei Diaghilev's *Ballets Russes* took Europe by storm. The stage decor was unlike anything seen before. Painted by artists (like Alexandr Benois) and not stagehands, it suspended disbelief and shattered the audience's sense of illusion.

Under the Soviets, ballet was treated as a natural resource. It enjoyed highly privileged status, which allowed schools like the Vaganova and companies like the Kirov to maintain a level of lavish production and no-expense-spared star-searches. Still, the story of 20th-century Russian ballet is connected with the West, to where so many of its brightest stars emigrated or defected. Pavlova, Nijinsky, Nureyev, Mikhail Baryshnikov, Balanchine, Kshessinskaya, Natalia Makarova, to name a few, all found fame in the Europe or America.

The Kirov, whose home is the Mariinsky Theatre (the company is sometimes referred to as the Mariinsky Opera and Ballet), has been rejuvenated under the fervent directorship of Valery Gergiev, a charismatic Ossetian who has made the Mariinsky once again one of the top companies in the world. Not afraid to take chances, he has revived with great success some lesser-known operas by his personal favourite Prokofiev, such as *War and Peace* (the premiere of which was attended by Putin and guest Tony Blair). In 1998 he also opened the Academy of Young Singers at the Mariinsky, now one of the only major theatres in the world to cast young, fresh talent in some of opera's juiciest roles. In late 2000, the theatre was given a boost via a $14 million donation by billionaire Alberto Vilar for the production of two operas or ballets for the next three years.

Valery Mikhailovsky's fantastic St Petersburg All-Male Ballet company (W www.maleballet.spb.ru), formed in 1992, has also made an international name for itself, dressing world-class male dancers in tutus and staging innovative, emotional productions of classical and modern ballets.

## Music

**Classical** The roots of Russian music lie in folk song and dance and Orthodox Church chants. Epic folk songs of Russia's peasantry, *byliny*, preserved folk culture and lore through celebration of particular events such as great battles or harvests. More formal music slowly reached acceptance in Russian society; first as a religious aid, then for military and other ceremonial use, and eventually for entertainment.

The defining period of Russian music was from the 1860s to 1900. As Russian composers (and painters and writers) struggled to find a national identity, several influential schools formed, from which some of Russia's most famous composers and finest music emerged. The Group of Five – Mussorgsky, Rimsky-Korsakov, Borodin, Kui and Balakirev – believed that a radical departure was necessary, and they looked to byliny and folk music for themes. Their main opponent was Anton Rubinshteyn's conservatively-rooted Russian Musical Society, which became the St Petersburg Conservatory in 1861, the first in Russia.

The middle ground was, it seems, discovered by Pyotr Tchaikovsky (1840–93), a student of the conservatory, who embraced Russian folklore and music as well as the disciplines of the Western European composers. Tchaikovsky is widely regarded as the father of Russian national composers.

Far from the middle ground was composer Dmitri Shostakovich (1906–75), who

## The Monarchs of the Ballet World

In the West, most people associate Russian ballet with the male stars whose notoriety and well-documented flights from the Soviet Union made them household names: Nureyev, Nijinsky, Baryshnikov. But to St Petersburgers, the true magic of their rich ballet lore is tied to two women – Anna Pavlova and Mathilda Kshesinskaya.

Pavlova, born just outside St Petersburg in 1881, first danced at the Mariinsky in 1899. Within a decade she and Nijinsky were dancing together in some of the most excitingly choreographed productions the world had seen, mainly by Michel Fokine. In 1909, when Diaghilev's Ballets Russes in Paris produced Fokine's *Les Sylphides* (*Chopiana* in Russia), audiences were rapturous. Pavlova's light-as-air grace was an instant sensation.

In 1912 she emigrated to form her own ballet company in the West. Her ambassadorial skills (representing ballet, that is) remain unmatched – in an age without seat sales and air-mile points, she travelled some 500,000km across the globe in 15 years. A dessert was even named after her in Australia! She is largely credited for bringing ballet to the US. Her most remembered role is in Fokine's *The Dying Swan*, written especially for her.

She died in a hotel room in The Hague in 1931, and was cremated close to her London home. Over the years there have been many attempts to bring her ashes back to Russia for a proper burial, but these were always marred by beaurocracy and indecisiveness on the Russian side, which at one point called the proposition 'of highly dubious legality'. Problems were settled, and Pavlova's ashes were finally sent to Moscow for a September 2001 burial.

Mathilda Kshesinskaya, born in 1872 near Petrodvorets, graduated from the Imperial Ballet School and instantly became its star, she was the first Russian dancer to master 32 consecutive *fouettés en tournant* (spins done in place on one leg), considered then the ultimate achievement in ballet. She was also the subject of curiosity and admiration for her private life – she was the lover of Nicholas II in his pre-tsar days, and later married his cousin, the Grand Duke André. She hosted glamorous balls in her mansion that were attended by the elite of St Petersburg society.

She emigrated to France in 1920, where she lived and taught ballet until she died in 1971. She is revered as a heroine of her times – for her outspokenness, her professional mastery, and for the debonair way she controlled her own affairs (only men were supposed to do all that!).

Her old mansion now houses the Museum of Political History, but there's a wonderful exhibit on the ballerina inside (see the Things to See & Do chapter), and the ladies working inside will be happy to fill you in on details of Kshesinskaya's life.

**Anna Pavlova**                    MK

wrote alternately brooding, bizarrely dissonant works, as well as accessible traditional classical works. His belief that music and ideology went hand in hand meant that his career would be alternately praised and condemned by the Soviet government; after official condemnation by Stalin, Shostakovich's 7th Symphony – the Leningrad – brought him honour and international standing when it was performed by the Leningrad Philharmonic during the Siege of Leningrad. The authorities changed their mind again and banned his anti-Soviet music in 1948, then 'rehabilitated' him after Stalin's death.

Igor Stravinsky spent some 30 years in America but in his memoirs credits his childhood in St Petersburg as having had major effects on his music, such as *Petrouchka*. The official Soviet line was that he was a 'political and ideological renegade', but after visiting the USSR in 1962 and being received by Khrushchev himself, he was rehabilitated.

**Opera** When Peter the Great began throwing Western culture at his fledgling capital, the music of Western European composers was one of the chief weapons in his arsenal. He held weekly concerts of music by composers from the West – Vivaldi was a favourite. Catherine the Great further encouraged Western music and it gained popularity. St Petersburg was the birthplace of Russian opera when Mikhail Glinka's *A Life For The Tsar*, which merged traditional and Western influence, was performed on 9 December 1836. It told the story of peasant Ivan Susanin who sacrifices himself to save Mikhail Romanov. Another pivotal moment was the 5 December 1890 premiere of Tchaikovsky's *Queen of Spades* at the Mariinsky. His adaptation of the famous Pushkin tale surprised and invigorated the artistic community at the time as Tchaikovsky's deviations from the original text – infusing it with more cynicism, a brooding sense of doom – tied the piece to contemporary St Petersburg itself, and to its future. Tchaikovsky had successfully merged opera with topical social comment.

Classical opera was performed regularly in the Soviet period, though audiences went mad for the occasional foreign tour, to see something new and different, like a series of Benjamin Britten operas in 1964 performed at the Mariinsky. Valery Gergiev (see Ballet) has revitalised the Mariinsky, and operas are as popular as ever.

**Rock** Russian rock was born in the 1960s when the 'bourgeois' Beatles filtered through, despite official disapproval (Joseph Brodsky's translation of *Yellow Submarine* was widely circulated!). Rock developed underground, starved of decent equipment and the chance to record or perform to big audiences, but it gathered a huge following among the disaffected, distrustful youth of the 1970s (the Soviet hippy era) and 1980s. Vladimir Rekshan, leader of the band Sankt Petersburg, became one of the first rock stars in Russia.

Bands in the 1970s started by imitating Western counterparts but eventually homegrown music emerged. In the early 1980s, many influential bands sprung up in Leningrad. Mitki was a band of artists, poets and musicians who self-styled a Russian variation of hippiedom, donning sailor gear, drinking fantastic amounts of alcohol and putting a Russian accent on the term bohemian. Boris Grebenshikov and his band Akvarium (Aquarium), caused sensations wherever they performed; his folk rock and introspective lyrics became the emotional cry of a generation. Yury Shevchuk and his band DDT, also from Leningrad and penning very strong lyrics, emerged as the country's main rock band. At first, all of their music was circulated by illegal tapes known as *magizdat*, passed from listener to listener; concerts were held, if at all, in remote halls in city suburbs, and even to attend them could be risky. All three bands continue to record to this day.

The god of Russian rock, though, was Viktor Tsoy, originally from Kazakhstan. His group Kino was the stuff of legends. A few appearances in kung fu-type flicks helped make Tsoy the King of Cool, and his early death in a 1990 car crash ensured the legend a long life. To this day, fans gather on the anniversary of his death (August 15) and play his music. His grave, at the Bogoslovskogo Cemetery in St Petersburg has been turned into a shrine.

There are few forms of pop culture on earth more gosh-awful than Russian pop music. A few minutes of Russian MTV will leave you clambering for Roxette, Celine Dion and others you *thought* were bad. But standing just outside the mainstream are interesting St Petersburg rock bands like Mumii Troll, led by the literate, androgynous Ilya Lagushenko; Alicia, a more heavy-rock group that puts on kick-ass concerts; Splin; and the talented pop-folk singer Pavel Kashin. Russian music fans are more sensitive to the lyrical content of the music they like than your average fan in the West.

## Painting & Sculpture

St Petersburg was the birthplace of many Russian avant-garde art movements, as well as futurism and neo-primitivism. More recently, neo-academism, the most important Russian artistic movement of the late 20th century, found its birthplace there.

**Peredvizhniki** In the 18th century, when Peter the Great encouraged Western trends in Russian art, Dmitry Levitsky's portraits were outstanding. The major artistic force of the 19th century was the Peredvizhniki (Wanderers) movement, a group formed by 14 artists who broke away from the conventions of the powerful but conservative Academy of Arts, and who saw art as a force for national awareness and social change. Their name refers to their idea of travelling around the country with yearly exhibits, so that not only Petersburgers would have access to art. They became very famous in their time, and counted Alexander III as one of their main patrons.

Its members included Vasily Surikov, who painted vivid Russian historical scenes, Nikolay Ge (biblical and historical scenes), Arkhip Kuindzhi (moonlit Crimean landscapes) and Ilya Repin, perhaps the best loved of all Russian artists, whose works ranged from social criticism *(Barge Haulers on the Volga)* through history *(Zaporozhie Cossacks Writing a Letter to the Turkish Sultan)* to portraits of the famous.

Isaak Levitan, who revealed the beauty of the Russian landscape, was one of many others associated with the Peredvizhniki. The end-of-century genius Mikhail Vrubel, inspired by sparkling Byzantine and Venetian mosaics, showed early traces of Western influence.

**Futurism** Around the turn of the 20th century the Mir Iskusstva (World of Art) movement (and art magazine) in St Petersburg, led by Alexandr Benois and Sergey Diaghilev under the motto 'art pure and unfettered', opened Russia up to Western innovations like Impressionism, Art Nouveau and symbolism. They also wished their movement to be the linchpin for broad cultural change. From about 1905 Russian art became a maelstrom of groups and -isms as it absorbed decades of European change in a few years before giving birth to its own avant-garde futurist movements, which in turn helped Western art go head over heels.

Natalya Goncharova and Mikhail Larionov were at the centre of the Jack of Diamonds group (a Cézanne-influenced group with which Vasily Kandinsky was associated) before developing neo-primitivism, based on popular arts and primitive icons.

In 1915 Kazimir Malevich announced the arrival of suprematism, declaring that his utterly abstract geometrical shapes, with the black square representing the ultimate 'zero form', finally freed art from having to depict the material world and made it a doorway to higher realities. Another famed futurist, who managed to escape subordinate -isms, was acclaimed poet Vladimir Mayakovsky.

**The Soviet Era** It was the Futurists who with mixed enthusiasm supplied the revolution with posters, banners and education. They now had a chance to act on their theories of how art shapes society. Even by the early 1920s, formalist art fell sharply out of official favour. Workers felt dispassionate and vaguely confused at the sight of abstract, cubist shapes and coloured panels draping bridges, buildings and posters. The Party wanted socialist realism. Striving workers, heroic soldiers and inspiring leaders took over; Malevich ended up painting penetrating portraits of workers and doing designs for Red Square parades; Mayakovsky committed suicide.

After Stalin, an avant-garde 'conceptualist' underground was allowed to surface. Ilya Kabakov painted, or sometimes just arranged, the debris of everyday life to show the gap between the promises and realities of Soviet existence. Erik Bulatov's 'Sotsart' pointed to the devaluation of language by ironically reproducing Soviet slogans or depicting words disappearing over the horizon. In 1962 the authorities set up a show of such 'unofficial' art at the Moscow Manezh; Khrushchev called it 'dog shit' and sent it back underground.

Eventually a thaw set in and the avant-garde became international big business.

**Neo-Academism** The main wave in Russian art in the post-Soviet period is undoubtedly neo-academism, founded by St Petersburg artist Timur Novikov in the early 1990s as an antidote to 'the barbarism of modernism'. The neo-academism movement sprung from a short-lived wave of so-called Necro-Realists, who focused on decay as a symbol of a dying social system.

Novikov has been a leader of the St Petersburg and Russian arts scenes for over a decade. He continues to be the movement's guru, and despite suffering from meningitis – he is now practically blind – continues to produce and exhibit, as well as inspire other artists. In 1982 his theory of 'Zero Object' acted as one of the foundations of Russian conceptual art, and his work with some of Russia's best artists and musicians in the 1980s and 1990s culminated in his Museum of the New Academy of Fine Arts, otherwise known as its address, Pushkinskaya 10, established in 1993. Neo-academic artists, including co-founder Bella Matveeva, digital artist Olga Tobreluts and Oleg Maslov and Viktor Kuznetsov, once prided themselves on – and even advertised – their propensity

towards drugs and alcohol while turning out works that pay homage to classicism (some even dress ominously in Victorian clothes) though infusing it with a street-level, almost junk-shop feel. One common thread which binds them is a hatred for modernism, which they feel killed contemporary art. Their works – not only paintings, but photographs, sculptures, collages, videos, set and graphic designs, music – have been shown throughout the world.

## Architecture
St Petersburg is an architect student's dream city, where examples of nearly every style imaginable, from rococo to Soviet Realist, via neo-Byzantine, Art Nouveau and Russian eclecticism, are represented in one city; a cornucopia of world styles on a larger-than-life scale display. Throughout the centre, you'll get the feeling that every building has its own face, if not facade: the caryatids, telamons, and ornamental figures that adorn so many buildings all have stories to tell. On an architectural level, this is easily one of the most impressive cities in the world.

Unrestricted by winding old streets or buildings from the past, the early European and European-trained designers of St Petersburg created a unique waterside city of straight avenues, wide plazas and grand edifices in the baroque, rococo and classical styles of the 18th and early 19th centuries.

Few major buildings had reached their final form by the time of Peter the Great's death in 1725, though his version of Petergof Palace was complete and the SS Peter & Paul Cathedral and the Twelve Colleges were well under way. Empress Elizabeth (r. 1741–61) commissioned the first grand wave of buildings from Bartolomeo Rastrelli, an Italian who engraved her lighthearted, fanciful spirit on the city's profile. His inspired creations, like the Winter Palace, Smolny Cathedral and the Great Palace at Pushkin, were playful in their rococo detail yet majestic in form.

Catherine the Great and Alexander I launched hosts of projects to make St Petersburg Europe's most imposing capital, employing an international array of designers to beat the West at its own architectural games. Both monarchs rode the new wave of classical taste, whose increasing severity can be traced through some of their chief buildings. The Academy of Arts by JBM Vallin de la Mothe (France), Pavlovsk Palace by Charles Cameron (England) and the Hermitage Theatre by Giacomo Quarenghi (Italy) display the simpler, earlier classicism of Catherine's reign. Quarenghi's Smolny Institute for Alexander was halfway towards the later, heavier works of another Italian, Carlo Rossi, who created the Mikhailovsky Palace (now the Russian Museum), the General Staff building and ploshchad Ostrovskogo.

The more grandiose branch of later classicism known as Russian Empire style is typified by the Kazan Cathedral and the Admiralty, both built by Russian designers for Alexander I. The huge-domed St Isaac's Cathedral by Frenchman Ricard de Montfer rand, mostly built under the reign of Nicholas I, was the city's last major classical building.

Most of the extended city centre was thankfully spared the aesthetic wasteland that was Soviet architecture, even though dozens of churches in the city were torn down to build ugly, grey or beige concrete buildings (the present-day Oktyabrsky Concert Hall and the Nevskie Bani both stand on ground once occupied by handsome churches).

## Theatre

Theatre in Russia has its roots in religious battles between Western Christian and Russian Orthodox churches, which were vying for members as early as the 16th century. As Jesuits used dramatic scenes to propagandise and spread their message, the Russian Orthodox Church found it had to do likewise to stop an exodus to Catholicism. Over the next few centuries, drama was almost exclusively used in a similar fashion by schools and the Church, until tsars and nobility began importing tragedy and comedy from the West.

Vaudeville – biting, satirical one-act comedies that had been created on the streets of Paris and poked fun at the rich and powerful – found its way into Russia in the 19th century and the practice of using theatre to put forth the Party or church line on social issues came under attack by playwrights like Pushkin and Lermontov. Other writers, such as Gogol, Griboedov and Ostrovsky, wrote plays that attacked not just the aristocracy but the bourgeoisie as well.

Anton Chekhov wrote for St Petersburg newspapers before writing one-act, vaudevillean works. Yet it is his full-length plays, especially *Uncle Vanya* and *The Seagull*, which are his legacy. Towards the end of the 19th century, Maxim Gorky's *The Stormy Petrel*, which raised workers to a level superior to that of the intellectual, earned him reverence by the Soviets as the initiator of Socialist Realism.

The Futurists had their day on the stage, mainly in the productions of the energetic and tirelessly inventive director Vsevolod Meyerhold, one of the most influential figures of modern theatre. His productions of Blok's *The Fair Show Booth* (1906) and Mayakovsky's *Mystery-Bouffe* (1918) caused sensations at the time, and his 1935 production of Tchaikovsky's *Queen of Spades* was cited as strongly influential by Akhmatova and Dmitri Shostakovich.

The Soviet period saw drama used primarily as a propaganda tool and when foreign plays were performed it was usually for a reason – hence the popularity in Russia of *Death of a Salesman*, which showed just what Western (US) greed and decadence will lead to. However, just after the revolution, theatre artists were given great, if short-lived, freedom to experiment – anything to make theatre accessible to the masses. Avant-garde productions flourished for a while, notably under the mastery of poet and director Igor Terentyev. Artists such as Pavel Filonov and Malevich participated in production and stage design.

Even socialist theatre was strikingly experimental: the Theatre of Worker Youth, under the guidance of Mikhail Sokolovsky, used only non-professional actors, encouraged improvisation, sudden plot alterations and interaction with audience members, and strove to redefine the theatre-going experience. Free theatre tickets were given out at factories, and halls which once echoed with the jangle of their upper-class audience's jewellery were now filled with sailors and workers. The tradition of sending army regiments and schoolchildren to the theatre continues to this day.

## Cinema

The Russian and Soviet directors whose films Western film scholars analyse to the last frame – Eisenstein, Vertov, Shub, Pudovkin, Kuleshov – draw blanks from most Russians. The battle between ideology and box-office success, between art and the need to provide inexpensive entertainment for the masses, resulted in a system that alternately produced touching human drama, blatant propaganda and sensationalist crap. The stereotype of Soviet films being about happy workers harvesting wheat is much exaggerated.

Genre, as understood in the West, was a limited phenomenon in Russia. Yet this often gave rise to curious hybrids. For example, while the USSR produced only a handful of musicals, every major film had characters who burst into song once or twice (kind of like Russians do in real life); these songs remain some of the most popular and recognised in pop culture. Eldar Ryazanov made a string of popular comedy-dramas including the all-time favourite *Ironia Sudby* (The Irony of Fate), which shows on TV every New Year's Eve, and *Zhestoky Romans* (A Cruel Romance).

Film production in Russia has always mainly been centred in Moscow, but Lenfilm, a world-famous studio formed in 1918 that still produces films and television series in St Petersburg, has played a crucial role in Soviet film history. Lenfilm became known for its artistic and intellectually-inclined films and for its daring stylistic experimentations merged with expert storytelling. The mix captivated audiences, and, toeing the Party line in terms of content, became Stalin's darling. After the war, however, as part of the overall repression of Leningrad, Stalin had the studio all but shut down. Several renowned Shakespeare adaptations by Kozintsev (with translations by Boris Pasternak) pulled the studio out of the doldrums again.

In 1996, the studio, once again falling on hard times, had only one film in production. Things have picked up for Lenfilm slightly since then, mainly from several successful TV crime series and from the international reputation of one of its star directors, St Petersburger Alexander Sokurov, whose *Mother and Son* (1997), *Moloch* (1999) and *Taurus* (2001) are visually challenging and lyrical explorations of human emotion. An excellent Web site on his films is at **W** www.sokurov.spb.ru.

With the fall of the Soviet Union the Russian film-making infrastructure was sent into a tailspin. Many talented Russians have headed to more artistically promising countries. Andrei Konchalovsky made several Soviet classics before emigrating to the USA in 1980 (where his output has been rather dismal). Vitaly Kanievsky's *Freeze, Die, Come to Life* (1991), a hit in international festivals, was produced in France. Russian production bottomed out in the mid-1990s (20 features were made in 1996, versus over 200 in 1990), but has since seen a mild upswing, thanks in part to foreign investment and an increase in overall cinema attendance.

Many of the big-budget films in Russia today are co-productions, made with foreign money. *East-West* (1999, dir Régis Wargnier) was an epic Euro melodrama starring two of Russia's hottest actors, Oleg Menshikov and Sergei Bodrov – and Catherine Deneuve! – telling the story of Russian emigrants who returned to the Soviet Union to help build socialism but found themselves arrested or shot.

The current king of Russian cinema is Nikita Mikhailkov, whose *Burnt by the Sun* won the 1994 Academy Award for Best Foreign Film, but who now makes thin, weepy epics like *The Barber of Siberia* (1999), which tried to pander to foreign and domestic audiences alike. More interesting figures include Sokurov, Kira Muratova, whose *Three Stories* was a delightful gust of stylistic fresh air when released in 1997, and Alexander Balabanov (also from St Petersburg). He proved his mastery with *Of Freaks and Men*, and had huge domestic hits with *Brother* and its enormously popular sequel *Brother 2* (which upset a few US critics as it dared portray Americans as materialistic fools who get their comeuppance).

US movies are unquestionably the most popular form of cinema for movie-goers in Russia, even if they only get the schlockiest of US-made films. Aside from *Brother 2*, the only other Russian film of the past 10 years to enter public consciousness in a big way is Sergei Rogozhkin's alcohol-soaked *Peculiarities of the National Hunt*.

## SOCIETY & CONDUCT

The key to harmonious interaction with Russians depends not just on you behaving inoffensively, but also in your reaction to what you may consider highly offensive behaviour. Blowing your top in reaction to a surly waiter, irascible ticket clerk or cheeky coat-check babushka is (a) unlikely to remedy the situation, (b) asking for further trouble and (c) offensive to those around you, who will look upon you as being 'uncultured'. However, being mousy and apologetic will just get you more of the same. Patience, here more than anywhere, is a virtue. A smile, along with a stern but friendly rebuttal, go further than everything up to and perhaps including a revolver.

Russians tend to personalise official relationships, so don't be taken aback if you walk into an office to ask for some factual information and you're asked your nationality and marital status before you get your answer. More often you'll simply be asked, 'And who are you?'. This is done out of curiosity, not impoliteness. And if you answer their questions, you're likely to hear about their salary in return.

Inside Russian Orthodox churches and cathedrals, men must never wear hats and women should cover their heads, though women often get away with not doing so. Women in miniskirts and men in shorts are big no-nos. Standing around with your hands in your pockets will also get you glares. Photography at services is generally not welcome. Always feel out the situation first, and ask if in doubt.

In everyday life, the role of men and women is still rather old-worldly by Western standards; men are expected to be gentlemanly by holding open doors, lighting cigarettes, pulling out chairs etc for women. Women, likewise, are often seen playing the sweet, silent, feminine role at mixed social gatherings.

At theatres and cinemas, when advancing along a row to your seat, walk facing the people already seated, not with your backside to them, no matter how shapely it might be.

On public transport, you're expected to give your seat to the elderly – stand up, point to your seat and say '*pazhalsta*'. People manoeuvre their way out by confronting anyone in the way with '*Vy vykhodite?*' ('*vih vih-kho-dee-tye?*', meaning 'Are you getting off?'). If you're asked this and you're not getting off, step aside – quickly.

When visiting someone's house, always remove your shoes before entering – you'll be given slippers *(tapochki)* to wear inside. Coats and jackets should also not be brought too far into the apartment (they're dirty!). If invited to someone's house, a small gift is expected, but if you bring flowers, make sure there are an odd number of them (even-numbered bouquets are for funerals). Also, may as well prepare a toast before you arrive, because you'll be expected to make one during one of the many rounds of drinks considered impolite to decline.

Avoid nationalistic sentiment ('Boy, you Russians sure got whupped in the Cold War!') in your conversation. Swearing is frowned upon and considered vulgar, though nothing will make you 'one of the guys' quicker than a well-chosen swear word or phrase (especially in Russian) in all-male company only.

Superstition plays a large part in many customs, sometimes overtly (like never shaking hands across the threshold of a doorway) and sometimes covertly (like never shaking hands with gloves on). Big no-nos are (a) returning home to get something you forgot (that's what Pushkin did on his way to the duel and look where it got him!), (b) leaving empty bottles on the table during dinner parties and (c) stepping on someone's foot (remedies: (a) look in the mirror before leaving again, (b) put them under the table immediately and (c) offer your foot back to be stepped on). If you've unwittingly breached some other superstition known only to the person you're with, don't be surprised to see them make three spitting motions over their left shoulder or knock on wood.

It's also partly superstition that makes Russians who are asked, 'How are you?' answer with '*Normalno*' (somewhere between 'so-so' and 'OK'). Answering with a Yank-style, confidently vigorous 'Great! Amazing! Couldn't be better!', no matter the truth, is only asking for the opposite to happen. Plus, as most people's lives in Russia have been traditionally difficult, it is considered extremely distasteful to appear boastful of one's good fortunes, however small.

## RELIGION

The Russian Federation officially recognises four faiths: Orthodoxy, Judaism, Buddhism and Islam. All other churches must apply to be officially registered in order to operate missions in Russia. This attempt to limit the number of sects in the country has not prevented the appearance of numerous minority religious groups. In 2001, the Salvation Army was denied official registration in Moscow (despite the fact that they were already registered and operate in five other Russian cities); courts judged that they 'pose a national security threat'.

## Russian Orthodox Church

During the Soviet regime, hundreds of churches were torn down, gutted, and turned into swimming pools, skating rinks, factories, warehouses or used for military target practice. Believers faced victimisation, deportation and execution. But belief was never stamped out. Since the 1990s, the Russian Orthodox Church (Russkaya

Pravoslavnaya Tserkov) has enjoyed a big revival. The Church is an intimate part of many Russians' notions of Russia and 'Russianness', despite recriminations over its infiltration by the KGB during the Soviet era – three metropolitans (senior bishops) were accused in 1992 of having been KGB agents. Putin has shown himself to be a believer, has held public meetings with the Moscow Patriarch Alexy II and has even mentioned God in speeches.

Many people nonetheless decry a hypocrisy among a number of churchgoers, accusing them of merely following a trend (check out an Easter church service and try to spot all the 'repentant' Mafia bosses and bandits). The Orthodox Church now comprises over 17,000 full-time priests and bishops, and has 462 operational monasteries throughout Russia.

**History & Hierarchy** Prince Vladimir of Kyiv effectively founded the Russian Orthodox Church in 988 by adopting Christianity from Constantinople. The church's headquarters stayed in Kiev until 1300, when it moved north to Vladimir and then in the 1320s to Moscow.

Patriarch Alexy II of Moscow & All Russia is head of the Church; Metropolitan (Senior Bishop) Vladimir is St Petersburg's and Ladoga's spiritual leader and has a residence in the Alexandr Nevsky Lavra (a lavra is a monastery of the highest rank). The Russian Orthodox Church is one of the main fellowship of 15 autocephalous (self-headed) orthodox churches, in which Constantinople is a kind of first among equals.

**Beliefs & Practice** Russian Orthodoxy is highly traditional and the atmosphere inside a church is formal and solemn. Priests dress imposingly, the smell of candles and incense permeates the air, old women bustle about sweeping and polishing. However, to Catholics and Protestants, used to standing, kneeling and praying on command, things look a tad chaotic during a service: there are no seats so visitors move freely about the church, seemingly engaged in their own affairs, kissing or kneeling before

Great move, Vladimir.

St Petersburger in national costume

Clowning around at the Peter & Paul Fortress

Enjoying a bike ride around St Petersburg

Ice cream is a favourite for Russians of all ages.

St Isaac's Cathedral dominates the skyline of St Petersburg.

SS Peter & Paul Cathedral and its needle-thin spire sits in the middle of the Peter & Paul Fortress.

The frozen Fontanka River passes through the heart of St Petersburg.

icons and such, and priests engage in complex, mysterious motions no-one fully seems to follow. As a rule, working churches are open to one and all but, as a visitor, take care not to disturb any devotions or offend sensibilities (see Society & Conduct earlier in this chapter).

The Virgin Mary (*Bogomater;* Mother of God) is greatly honoured. The language of the liturgy is 'Church Slavonic', the old Bulgarian dialect into which the Bible was first translated for Slavs. Easter *(Paskha)* is the focus of the Church year, with festive midnight services to launch Easter Day. Christmas *(Rozhdestvo)* falls on 7 January because the Church still uses the Julian calendar that the Soviet state abandoned in 1918.

In most churches, Divine Liturgy *(Bozhestvennaya Liturgia)*, lasting about two hours, is at 8am, 9am or 10am Monday to Saturday, and usually at 7am and 10am on Sunday and festival days. Most churches also hold services at 5pm or 6pm daily. Some of these include an akathistos *(akafist)*, a series of chants to the Virgin or saints.

**Church Names** In Russian, *sobor* means cathedral; *tserkov* and *khram* mean church. Common church names include:

| | |
|---|---|
| Blagoveshchenskaya | Annunciation |
| Nikolskaya | St Nicholas |
| Petropavlovskaya | SS Peter & Paul |
| Pokrovskaya | Intercession of the Virgin |
| Preobrazhenskaya | Transfiguration |
| Rozhdestvenskaya | Nativity |
| Troitskaya | Trinity |
| Uspenskaya | Assumption or Dormition |
| Vladimirskaya | St Vladimir |
| Voskresenskaya | Resurrection |
| Voznesenskaya | Ascension |
| Znamenskaya | Holy Sign |

**Old Believers** The Russian Church was split in 1666 by the reforms of Patriarch Nikon, who thought it had departed from its roots. He insisted, among other things, that the translation of the Bible be altered to conform with the Greek original, and that the sign of the cross be made with three fingers, not two. Those who wouldn't accept these changes became known as Old Believers *(Starovery)*, some of Russia's earliest social dissidents. Escaping official persecution, they fled west to the border of Estonia or east to the Siberian forests and remote parts of Central Asia. Only in 1771–1827, 1905–18 and again recently have Old Believers had real freedom of worship. They probably number over a million but in 1917 there were as many as 20 million. Old Believers have two churches in St Petersburg, returned to them in 1988 (see Religious Services at the end of this section).

## Other Christian Churches

Russia has small numbers of Roman Catholics and Lutheran and Baptist Protestants, mostly among the German and other non-Russian ethnic groups. Other groups such as the Mormons, Jehovah's Witnesses, Seventh Day Adventists and the Salvation Army are sending missionaries into the fertile ground of a country where God officially didn't exist for 70 years.

### Islam

Islam has, like Christianity, enjoyed growth since the mid-1980s. Though it has been some Muslim peoples – notably the Chechens and Tatars among Russian minorities – who have most resisted being brought within the Russian national fold since the fall of the Soviet Union in 1991, nationalism has played at least as big a part as religion in this. Militant Islam has so far barely raised its head in Russia.

Islam in Russia is fairly secularised, eg, women are not veiled, the Friday Sabbath is not a commercial holiday. St Petersburg's working Sunni-Muslim mosque (see the Things to See & Do chapter) is closed to women and often to non-Muslim men, though men may occasionally be invited in.

### Judaism

Many of Russia's 700,000 or so Jews have been assimilated into Russian culture and do not seriously practise Judaism. However, there were approximately 30 synagogues in Russia by 1991. Jews have long been the target of prejudice and even pogroms – ethnic cleansing – in Russia. Since glasnost, hundreds of thousands of Jews have emigrated to Israel and other countries to escape the state-sponsored anti-Semitism that existed under the former government and which is subtly felt today. St Petersburg has two working synagogues and a Jewish cemetery.

## Buddhism

The members of St Petersburg's Buddhist Datsan (Map 4; ☎ 430 03 41, Ⓦ www .datsan.spb.ru; Primorsky pr 91) belong to the Gelugpa or 'Yellow-Hat' sect of Tibetan Buddhism, whose spiritual leader is the Dalai Lama. However, a battle for ownership of the datsan (monastery) between two rival Buddhist groups still occasionally flares up. See the datsan's 'renegade' Web site at Ⓦ http://snark.ptc.spbu.ru/~uwe/ datsan for more details. Buddhism was tolerated by the Soviet state until Stalin nearly wiped it out in the 1930s.

## Religious Services

There are a number of English and other Western-language services in town; check the *St Petersburg Times* for current information during your stay. Places of worship, and information on some services in English (E), German (G), Hebrew (H), Russian (R) and Latin (L), follow:

**Anglican/Episcopalian Open Christianity Centre** (Map 8; ☎ 542 37 94, nab reki Fontanki 24, apt 22) Services 11am Sunday (E).

**Armenian Church of St Catherine** (Map 8; ☎ 219 41 08, Nevsky pr 40/42) Services 6pm Saturday.

**Buddhist Datsan** (Map 4; ☎ 239 03 41, 430 03 41, Primorsky pr 91) Services 9am and 5pm daily (R).

**Choral Synagogue** (Map 6; ☎ 114 11 53, Lermontovsky pr 2) Shabbas services sundown Friday, services 9.30am daily (H).

**Church of Jesus Christ of Latter Day Saints** (Map 8; ☎ 346 75 67, nab reki Fontanki 56) Services 2pm Sunday (E).

**Evangelical Lutheran Church** (Map 8; ☎ 311 07 98, Nevsky pr 22/24) Services 6pm Wednesday (G); and **St Michael's Lutheran Church** (Map 4; ☎ 218 04 77, Sredny pr 18) Services 9.30am Sunday (E).

**Mosque of the Congregation of Muslims** (Map 5; ☎ 233 98 19, Kronverksky pr 7) Services from 10am to 7pm daily (R, E).

**Old Believers** (☎ 107 55 22, Karavaevskaya ul 16) and (☎ 262 25 87, Aleksandrovskoy Fermy pr 20) (R).

**St Catherine Roman Catholic Church** (Map 8; ☎ 311 71 70, Nevsky pr 32/34) Mass 9.30 am Sunday (E), 8am and 6.30pm weekdays (R).

Russian Orthodox services are available at several locations throughout the city. Check the *St Petersburg Times* or *Luchshee V Sankt Peterburge* for listings.

## LANGUAGE

Russian is the national language of Russia. See the Language chapter at the back of this book for a short guide to Russian pronunciation and a list of useful words and phrases.

# Facts for the Visitor

## WHEN TO GO

St Petersburg is a year-round destination. Although some call wintertime bleak and depressing, others see a romance in the twinkling magic of watching a heavy snowfall from, say, the Anichkov most. Another plus about winter is finding the museums and hotels less crowded. A minus is not seeing Petrodvorets and other surrounding areas in their full glory. Most tourists prefer visiting during White Nights, at the end of June. The only really ugly time of the year is March, when snow and ice turn to rivers of black slush and falling icicles are forever menacing. If you do go in winter, remember to bring along good waterproof boots.

## ORIENTATION

St Petersburg sprawls across and around the delta of the Neva River, at the end of the easternmost arm of the Baltic Sea, the Gulf of Finland. Flowing eastward from Lake Ladoga and entering St Petersburg at its south-eastern corner, the Neva divides in the city's middle into several branches, forming the islands which make up the delta. The two biggest branches, which diverge where the Winter Palace stands on the south bank, are the Bolshaya (Big) and Malaya (Small) Neva; they flow into the sea either side of Vasilevsky Island.

The heart of St Petersburg is the area spreading back from the Winter Palace and the Admiralty on the south bank. Nevsky pr, stretching east-south-east from the Admiralty, is the main drag, with many of the city's sights, shops and restaurants.

The northern side of the city has three main areas. The westernmost is Vasilevsky Island, at whose east end – the Strelka – many of the city's fine early buildings still stand. The middle area is Petrograd Side, a cluster of delta islands whose south end is marked by the tall gold spire of the SS Peter & Paul Cathedral. This is where the city began. The third, eastern, area is Vyborg Side, stretching east along the north bank of the Neva.

## MAPS

There are dozens of maps of St Petersburg available at hotels and bookshops across the city. Check out Lonely Planet's handy *St Petersburg City Map*, a durable, full-colour, laminated fold-out map with a full index of streets and sights. It also features maps of Petrograd, Pushkin and Petrodvorets.

A recommended one is *Marshruty gorodskogo transporta Sankt Peterburg*, published by Karta, which lists all the city's transport routes. It also publishes a smaller 1:13,000 map of the centre that's easy to read (though it's in Cyrillic). Evrokarta publishes an excellent series of beautifully designed and detailed maps of the surrounding suburbs such as Peterhof, Pushkin and Pavolvsk. There are also numerous maps in English or German. Dom Knigi (second floor) and the Lensprav Information Kiosk outside the Moscow Station has a large selection. The best selection of maps, including old, out-of-print maps and maps of other Russian regions, can be found at the bookshop at Bolshoy pr 57, Petrograd Side.

## Street Names

In the early to mid-1990s, St Petersburg went on a rampage, changing the Soviet-era names of dozens of its streets, bridges and parks back to their pre-revolutionary names. Ten years on, only their 'new' names are used, though Griboedova Canal has not, and likely never will, replace its tsarist-era name, Yekaterinsky (Aleksander Griboedov was a 19th-century playwright who lived in a house on this canal). Only two fairly recent changes may cause confusion to tourists: Kirochnaya ul and Kazanskaya ul may occasionally be referred to by their Soviet names ul Saltykova-Shchedrina and ul Plekhanova respectively.

St Petersburg has two streets called Bolshoy pr: one on Petrograd Side, one on Vasilevsky Island. The two sides of some Vasilevsky Island streets are known as lines *(linii)* and opposite sides of these streets have different names – thus 4-ya linia (4th line) and 5-ya linia (5th line) are the east and west sides of the same street – which collectively is called 4-ya i 5-ya linii (4th and 5th lines).

## RESPONSIBLE TOURISM

This is one country where trying to 'cheat the system' or get free rides may not be so cool. Though the idea of a 'foreigner's price' (see the boxed text 'Dual-Pricing System') may have you up in arms, remember that many of the smaller museums which follow this policy may be in a severe state of under-funding, staffed by people who may earn less in a month than you spend for one night in your hotel. Try not to get angry at the ticket-sellers; they didn't institute the policies.

Striking a balance between doing the right thing and not being taken advantage of takes some getting used to here, but is an essential part of travel in Russia.

While snapping touristy shots shouldn't be a problem, you may encounter a high sensitivity about photographing and videotaping people on the street, public events, marketplaces, and even some statues and buildings. Doing so intrusively or obviously may lead to altercations ('Do you have permission to photograph this building?') or at least being looked at with great suspicion (spy paranoia is rampant and seeing one around every corner a favourite pastime of many Russians).

Try not to photograph beggars, drunks or people selling their wares on the streets – people are hypersensitive to the fact that foreigners tend to train their cameras at the 'shock' side of Russia, and it is humiliating to those photographed, who may even fear that you will report them to the authorities.

If you're taking professional photographs, you should ask permission to shoot before you do. Incredibly, even photographing the exteriors of famous buildings like the Hermitage and the Russian Museum technically require official permission to do so. Unofficially, few bother to go through the labyrinthine procedures to get permission (which is often denied anyway) and snap away. If reproached for photographing a, say, pretty dwelling house which turns out to

be a vital object of national security, make polite excuses and walk away. See Society & Conduct in the Facts about St Petersburg chapter for more tips on local customs.

## INFORMATION

The word 'information' is still among the dirtiest in the Russian language thanks in part to a long tradition of secrecy that has dictated that the less anyone knows, the better. When requesting information from official sources, you'll get a better response if you use the word *'pomosh'* (help) instead. Though getting information from any official source can raise blood pressure, things are getting easier for tourists all the time. When you ask for locations and opening times, people now won't *always* look at you suspiciously and answer, 'And what do you want this information for?'.

### City Reference Books

The Russian-language (and English-indexed) *Luchshee V Sankt Peterburge* and its shorter, English-language version, *The Traveller's Yellow Pages*, are fairly comprehensive and accurate pocketbook-sized yellow pages. They have good city centre maps as well as seating plans to major theatres. They are available at most bookshops, and well worth it if you're planning an extended stay. Published by Telinfo, it can be accessed on the info-packed Web site at W www.infoservices.com.

### Telephone Directory Inquiries

☎ 09 and ☎ 009 are, respectively, free and paid directory inquiry services. ☎ 063 will give you opening and showtimes for museums, concerts, cinemas and theatres.

## TOURIST OFFICES

In 2000, the city finally opened its first Tourist Information Office (Map 8; ☎ 311 29 43, 311 28 43, fax 315 97 96, e tourism@ gov.spb.ru, W www.tourism.spb.ru, Nevsky pr 41). Opening hours are 10am-7pm daily and it is situated on the 1st floor of the Beloselsky-Belozersky Palace in the city centre, it can suggest accommodation and city excursions, provide maps, booklets

## Dual-Pricing System

Call it what you like – insulting, outrageous, unfair (even the Russian courts have called it unconstitutional) – but at museums, large concert halls and hotels, you'll still be treated as 'not one of us' and charged many times more than Russians.

Ask Russians why this is so and they'll give you a variety of justifications. 'It is not so much for you, I think', 'You have more money than us', 'How much would you pay for this back home?' and 'This museum is here for Russians, not for foreigners' top the list of frequently heard responses. For others, it's a source of embarrassment, like when Russians go to the Hermitage with foreign friends and have to hear, 'That'll be 15 roubles for *you*', as the cashier's eyes narrow fixedly on their guest, 'and 300 roubles for *her*'.

To be fair, the situation is getting better each year. There is no longer a dual pricing system for train and airplane travel within Russia, and many hotels now treat all guests as equals. Also, at some smaller museums, staffed by people making $30 a month, and where the need for money is so painfully evident, it doesn't seem so bad to pay a reasonable $2 instead of $0.30 entrance fee. Other times, it is damn maddening, like at the Hermitage (nearly $11 vs $0.55) or the Mariinsky Theatre, where performances cost about 10 times more for foreigners (and where they'll run after you and holler until you pay the difference if you manage to sneak in with a Russian ticket).

At hotels you have no choice but to pay the rate they command. At museums you can either convince them that you study or work in Russia (if this is the case, you are charged the local rate), or speak Russian as best you can and try this: as gruffly as possible say '*ah-deen bil-let pa-zhal-stuh*', which means 'one ticket please', and glower at the ticket-seller. Say 'Da' to whatever he or she says next, proffer the Russian ticket price (learn to scan the price list quickly) and get the hell away as fast as possible.

At many places, however – usually those which need the money most – you'll find sympathetic cashiers willing to help you out (they know a thing or two about needing to save money). If they ask you, 'Do you work or study here?' while nodding conspiratorially, say 'Da!'. Of course, knowledge of Russian helps a great deal here.

Use student and senior citizen discount cards as often as possible and fight for the discount, although some places will honour ISIC and not ITSC cards, or only give discounts to *their* students, not *yours*. Showing your student or business visa usually works. If all else fails, just bite the bullet and tell yourself that your cash is going to a good cause!

and information free of charge and try to help with any of your queries. Its computer data bank is far from complete, but the multilingual staff will try their best to answer any of your questions. By winter 2001–02, it plans to open information kiosks at the Peter and Paul Fortress, on Dvortsovaya pl, at Pulkovo-2 airport and in Petrodvorets.

There is also a Tourism Information Help Line (☎ 327 78 78) that can give out museum opening times and the like. No English is spoken.

## TRAVEL AGENCIES

There are a number of travel agencies offering tours to St Petersburg and further afield in Russia:

**Sindbad Travel** (Map 8; ☎ 327 83 84, fax 329 80 19, e sindbad@sindbad.ru, w www.sindbad.ru, 3-ya Sovetskaya ul 28) Owned by the HI St Petersburg Hostel, it has two offices in town. The first is inside the hostel itself; the second (☎ 324 08 80) is inside the green St Petersburg Philological Faculty building on Vasilevsky Island, Universitetskaya nab 11 (Map 6). Both are genuine Western-style air ticket offices. Staffed by friendly, knowledgeable people, Sindbad operates as a full-service ticketing centre for STA and Kilroy Travel, sells and issues train tickets, can service any student-issued tickets and can book youth hostel accommodation through the IBN system. It also sells ISIC/ITIC cards.

**Ost-West Kontaktservice** (Map 8; ☎ 327 34 16, 279 70 45, fax 327 34 17, e info@ostwest.com, w www.ostwest.com, ul Mayakovskogo 7) Here's another winner. Staff can arrange tourist and business visas for you, find you an apartment to rent, organise tours and tickets – heck, they'll even sell you a Lomo (they're the city's official distributor of the nifty little Russian camera). The multilingual staff at Ost-West are down-to-earth and willing – and able – to help.

**Wild Russia** (Map 7; ☎ 273 65 14, e yegor@wild russia.spb.ru, w www.wildrussia.spb.ru, ul Mokhovaya 28–10) If you like Russia so much that you feel inspired to go on a wilderness expedition in the far reaches of the country, contact Wild Russia. Based in St Petersburg, it has loads of experience of placing fearless trekkers on the mountaintops of Altai and Kamchatka, and into the wilds of Karelia.

**American Express** (Map 8; ☎ 329 60 60, fax 329 60 61, w www.americanexpress.com) It is in the Grand Hotel Europe.

## VISAS

All foreigners visiting Russia need visas. A Russian visa is a passport-sized paper document. The visa lists entry/exit dates, your passport number, any children travelling with you, visa type, and the cities you intend on visiting (even though you can legally travel anywhere you like in Russia with a visa, except military sites and other closed towns). It's an exit permit too, so if you lose it (or overstay), leaving the country can be harder than getting in. It is highly recommended that you photocopy your passport and visa (preferably after it has been registered). You may wish to carry these with you to avoid loss or pickpocketing of the originals which could be left in a hotel safe or other safe place. Alternatively, keep the originals with you and the copies in a safe place – replacing lost documents is much easier if you can provide copies of them.

## Types of Visas

Six types of visas are available to foreign visitors and are listed here.

For all visas you'll need:

- a passport valid for at least a month beyond your return date – usually only a photocopy of the data page is required, but some consulates may require to see the original;
- three passport-size (4x4.5cm), recent full-face photos;
- a completed application form, available at the consulate;
- a handling fee (see Processing Fees).

**Tourist Visa** These are the most straightforward and inflexible visas available. In theory you're supposed to have booked accommodation for every night you'll be in the country, but in practice you can often get away with only booking a few, even just one. Then, once you've had your visa registered, you can freely move to another hotel or apartment as you like.

Getting an extension of a tourist visa can be an expensive hassle – they are best for trips when you know exactly what you're doing, when and where and for how long you'll be doing it. To obtain one, you will need, in addition to the items mentioned previously, a letter confirming your hotel or hostel reservations (see also Russian Visa Support Services under Getting a Visa).

**Business Visa** Far more flexible and desirable for the independent traveller is a business visa supported by a Russian company. The invitation eliminates the need for pre-arranged hotel confirmations because the company inviting you ostensibly puts you up for the duration of your stay.

To obtain a business visa you must have an invitation from a registered Russian company, which it usually must clear with the Ministry of Foreign Affairs. Bring the original (not a fax or copy) of the invitation to your local consulate. The fastest and most reliable way to get a business invitation is through hostels or travel agencies (see Russian Visa Support Services under Getting a Visa).

**Student Visa** Student visas are flexible and extendable. You'll need proof of enrolment at an accredited Russian school or university, which usually requires prepayment.

**Private Visa** Also referred to as an 'ordinary' visa, you get this when a Russian citizen sends you a personal invitation, approved at their local OVIR *(Otdel Viz i Registratsii)* office, the Department of Visas & Registration. This can take several weeks. Your friend then sends you the approval *(izveshchenie)* which you take to your local consulate. This process can be a headache for your host and lead to delays at your consulate; with easier ways of getting a visa (see Getting A Visa), there doesn't seem much point in pursuing this one.

**'On-the-Spot' Visa** These are fast-track business visas, freed from the requirement for advance invitations. Individuals arriving at Moscow's Sheremetevo-2 or St Petersburg's Pulkovo-2 airports can get short-term visas at a special consular office before going through passport control. To get one of these visas, you'll have to have a copy of an MID (Ministry of Foreign Affairs) invitation and have a representative of your inviting company meet you at the airport. This kind of visa is good for up to a month and costs $150.

**Transit Visa** Transit visas are given at Pulkovo-2 airport to passengers with proof that they are continuing to another country – air or train tickets will suffice, in addition to a visa for the destination country if one is required. A transit visa for up to 12 hours costs $50, and for a maximum of two days cost $90. These are not given out at land border crossings.

## Getting a Visa

A general rule of thumb is: apply as early as possible. Any number of unforeseen circumstances can arise to delay the processing of your visa. A second must: patience. Many travellers have been so put off by gruff service at consulates, or by having any query as to why their visa cannot get processed on time or at all answered with a series of very final-sounding *Nyet!*, that they've been tempted to cancel their trip and visit Spain instead. In Russia (and with Russians) everything is possible, it just sometimes takes a while to figure out exactly how.

**On Your Own** Don't believe travel agencies in North America or Europe who tell you that you must book hotels through them in order to get a visa. It's likely they deal only with the pricier hotels. If you want to save money, the cheapest way of getting your visa is to take a letter of hotel/hostel confirmation (both the HI St Petersburg Hostel and the Holiday Hostel can send these) or approved business or personal invitation (all of which you can arrange yourself), head to your local Russian consulate, fill out the application form and try to puzzle out the bewildering line-up system. Oh, then wait. The longer you're able to wait for your visa, the cheaper it will be (see Processing Fees).

**Russian Visa Support Services** There are many organisations in St Petersburg that will fax or mail you the documents you need to get a tourist or business visa from your local Russian consulate. Dealing with one of these can save endless headaches down the road. If you're booking with a major hotel, they'll send you what you need as par for the course. Otherwise, here are a few options:

**HI St Petersburg Hostel** (Map 8; ☎ 329 80 18, fax 329 80 19, e ryh@ryh.ru, w www.ryh.ru, 3-ya Sovetskaya ul 28) Organised through the hostel, a tourist visa costs $25 including registration, plus $10 for the fax, payable by credit card. Check with its partner firms in many European countries which can also get you a visa.
**Ost-West Kontaktservice** (Map 8; ☎ 327 34 16, fax 327 34 17, e sales@ostwest.com, ul Mayakovskogo 7) If you don't want hotel/hostel accommodation and just need a visa, this is one of the most reliable places in the city to get it. It charges $35 for an invitation for a two-week tourist visa, $50 for a month, and can also get

you the invitation for a three to 12-month business visa with at least six weeks advance notice (the cost is about $200 for a multi-entry business visa valid for a year). It can arrange for visa registration and accommodation as well, if needed.

**Hotel Oktyabrskaya** It has few partnerships with travel agencies abroad, so tourists making bookings from home are rarely suggested this hotel, though it is the most affordable decent hotel (see Place to Stay under Budget and Mid-Range accommodation) in the centre city – and it can arrange visa support. Just send your passport details and dates of travel to its Sputnik travel agency (☎ 277 61 21, fax 277 61 27, e hotel@ spb.cityline.ru) and it'll fax your tourist visa support, with hotel reservations for $50 a person.

## Visa Support Services in Neighbouring Countries

If you're travelling to St Petersburg overland from Finland or Estonia, you'll likely find getting a Russian visa there much easier than from further abroad. There are dozens of travel agencies in Helsinki and Tallinn that specialise in getting these critters by the carload every day. A few recommended options:

**RTT Matkapalvelut Travel Agency** (☎ 09-659 052, Laivasillankatu 14, Helsinki) This agency charges Americans $86 for an invitation and all visa processing at the Helsinki consulate for five-day service, and $190 for same-day service. Other nationalities pay less. Note that its prices include the Russian consulate's visa fees in addition to RTT's invitation fees.

**Neiris** (☎ 372-627 0627, W www.neiris.ee, Vana-Posti tänav 2, Tallinn) A US citizen can get a two-week tourist visa for $95; costs are slightly cheaper for other nationalities.

## Visa Agencies

The Internet is full of companies offering to set you up with a Russian visa by mail. Russia Link (W www.russialink.org.uk/embassy/visa_support), out of the UK, seems one of the most reliable. A single-entry tourist visa good for a month costs $46; a single-entry business visa $55.

## By Mail

It's possible to communicate with Russian consulates by mail, with stamped, self-addressed envelopes or, if you have them, FedEx, Airborne, DHL or TNT airbills,

complete with your account number for all requested forms and completed documents. When you receive the visa, check it carefully – especially the expiry, entry and exit dates and any restrictions on entry or exit points.

**Internet Resources** Those crazy, hacking diplomats in the American-Russian diplomatic corps have come up with a couple of Web resources; for the embassy, try the superb W www.russianembassy.org, with good up-to-date information, and W www.russia.net/travel/visas.html, an informative visa regulations section produced by the Russian consulate in Seattle, and you can download a copy of the application form from it.

## Processing Fees

Each Russian consulate charges as much as it can, so rates fluctuate depending on where and when you apply, and on your nationality. US citizens pay more than anyone else for their visas – a retaliatory measure imposed by Russians who have been shamefully treated when applying for US visas. As a ballpark figure, count on around $20 for a single-entry tourist visa, double or triple that for express service (depending on the consulate this can mean two days or one week, however, with gentle prodding and some extra cash, many consulates will offer to make your visa on the spot).

## Registration

*All* Russian visas must be registered with OVIR within three business days of your arrival in Russia. No ifs or buts about it. Leaving the country with an unregistered visa could be a pricey venture – fines up to several hundred dollars have been reported, depending on the border crossing. Then again, the border guard may just yawn and wave you through, or let you go after a stern lecture. In any case, it's not worth the risk.

Though your visa should ideally be registered by the hotel or hostel you are staying in (a small handling fee of a few dollars might be charged), or through the company that invited you, you may be in the hapless situation of having to go to a local OVIR office to register it yourself. A complete list of these offices, with opening hours, is available in *Luchshee V Sankt Peterburge*, and for general inquiries, try your luck at its main office (☎ 278 24 81, Kirochnaya ul 4). Opening hours are 9am to 5pm, Monday to Friday. Headache pills can be economised by getting your visa registered at any hotel or hostel that can do so, even if you are not staying there, usually for a fee equivalent to the price of one night in their cheapest room. Ost-West Contact Service can also help you with visa registration.

## Visa Extensions & Replacement

Try to avoid this by thinking ahead, before you leave home, and by going for the maximum possible period of validation on your visa. If you think you'll only be in town for a week, take a two-week visa just in case – you can always leave earlier, but trying to leave later will waste time and money. Many trains out of St Petersburg to Eastern Europe cross the border after midnight; make sure your visa is valid up to and including this day. Don't give border guards any excuses to give you trouble.

If you lose your visa, the office of the Ministry of Foreign Affairs at Puloko-2 airport (☎ 104 34 15) can replace it for $150. You will have trouble if you don't at least have a photocopy. This office can also extend your tourist visa (a 24-hour extension costs $70; a four- to 10-day extension $250). Travellers report that they have extended their visas there on the spot, which makes it easier than trying the main OVIR office, which requires 10 days' advance notice and a good explanation. However, the Ministry states that it needs official proof via a travel agency that you are staying on for a special tour or to show additional hotel bookings before granting an extension. Sindbad and Ost-West can help you sort these things out.

## DOCUMENTS

It is wise to travel to Russia with some, if not full, medical coverage. Always carry your agent's contact numbers with you. An International Driving Permit may come in handy if you decide to navigate the potholes.

## HIV/AIDS Testing

HIV/AIDS testing is officially required for foreigners staying in the Russian Federation longer than three months. The medical certificate must be in English and in Russian. By definition, this does *not* affect tourist visas, which are only issued for shorter stays, and in practice, even holders of business visas valid for a year are rarely asked for proof at the border. As the AIDS crisis in Russia worsens, though, they may eventually start enforcing this law.

## Student, Youth & Senior Cards

Full-time students and people aged under 26 or over 59 tend to get a substantial discount on admissions, transport and in some restaurants. The Hermitage is free for ISIC-holders, most other museums also recognise the card, and the list of establishments offering ISIC/ITIC discounts in St Petersburg has grown steadily over the years. The admission prices listed in the Things to See & Do chapter quote student prices where applicable; these usually mean presenting your ISIC card. Sometimes you may get away with another form of identification, but – good luck.

Full-time students 34 years old or younger can get an International Student Identification Card (ISIC), and teachers are eligible for an ITIC card from student agencies worldwide and at Sindbad Travel (in the HI St Petersburg Hostel). If you're not a student but you are under 26, try for an ISIC Youth Card. Check out Ⓦ www.istc.org for places that honour these cards in Russia.

Brit Rail and the American Association for Retired People both issue identification cards for senior travellers, and similar organisations exist in other Western countries.

## Copies

All important documents (passport data page and visa page, credit cards, travel insurance policy, air/bus/train tickets, driving licence etc) should be photocopied before you leave home. Leave one copy with someone at home and keep another with you, separate from the originals.

## EMBASSIES & CONSULATES

Check **W** www.russianembassy.net for changes in the following list.

### Russian Embassies Abroad

**Australia**
*Embassy*: (☎ 02-6295 9033, 6295 9474, fax 6295 1847) 78 Canberra Ave, Griffith, ACT 2603
*Consulate*: (☎ 02-9326 1866) 7 Fullerton St, Woollahra, NSW 2025

**Canada**
*Embassy*: (☎ 613-235 4341, fax 236 6342) 285 Charlotte St, Ottawa
*Visa Department*: (☎ 613-236 7220, fax 238 6158)
*Consulate*: (☎ 514-843 5901, fax 842 2012) 3655 Ave Du Musee, Montreal, Quebec, H3G 2EI

**Estonia**
*Embassy*: (☎ 646 4169) Pikk tänav 19, Tallinn
*Consulate*: (☎ 641 4166, fax 646 4130) Lai tänav 18, Tallinn

**Finland**
*Embassy*: (☎ 09-66 14 49, fax 66 10 06) Tehtaankatu 1B, FIN-00140 Helsinki

**France**
*Embassy*: (☎ 01 45 04 05 50, fax 01 45 04 17 65) 40–50 Boulevard Lannes, F-75116 Paris
*Consulate*: (☎ 91-77 15 25, fax 77 34 54) 8 Rue Ambrois Pare, F-13008 Marseille

**Germany**
*Embassy*: (☎ 0228-312 08 5/6/7, fax 311 56 3) Waldstrasse 42, 53177 Bonn;
*Consular affairs*: (☎ 0228-312 08 3, fax 384 56 1)
*Consulate*: (☎ 030-229 14 20, fax 2299 397) Unter den Linden 63–65, 10117 Berlin
*Consulate*: (☎ 040-229 52 01, fax 229 77 27) Am Feenteich 20, 22085 Hamburg

**Ireland**
*Embassy*: (☎ 01-494 3525, fax 492 3525) 186 Orwell Rd, Rathgar, Dublin 6

**Latvia**
*Embassy*: (☎ 733 21 51, fax 783 02 09) Antonijas iela 2, Riga

**Lithuania**
*Embassy*: (☎ 721 763) Latviu gatve 53/54, Vilnius

**Netherlands**
*Embassy*: (☎ 070-345 13 00/01, fax 361 7960) Andries Bickerweg 2, NL-2517 JP The Hague

**New Zealand**
*Embassy*: (☎ 04-476 6113) 57 Messines Rd, Karori, Wellington

**Poland**
*Embassy*: (☎ 022-621 55 75) ulica Belwederska 49, PL-00-761 Warsaw
*Consulate*: (☎ 012-22 26 47, 22 92 33, 22 83 88) ulica Westerplatte 11, PL-31-033 Kraków

**Ukraine**
*Embassy*: (☎ 044-294 79 36, fax 292 66 31) ulitsya Kutuzova 8, UKR-252000 Kyiv

**UK**
*Embassy*: (☎ 0171-229 3628/29, fax 727 8624/25) 13 Kensington Palace Gardens, London W8 4QX
*Consular Section*: (☎ 0171-229 8027, visa information message ☎ 0891-171 271, fax 0171-229 3215) 5 Kensington Palace Gardens, London W8 4QS
*Consulate*: (☎ 0131-225 7098, fax 225 9587) 9 Coates Crescent, Edinburgh E13 7RL

**USA**
*Embassy*: (☎ 202-298 5700, fax 298 5749) 2650 Wisconsin Ave, NW, Washington DC 20007
*Visa Department*: (☎ 202-939 8907, fax 939 8909) 1825 Phelps Place NW, Washington DC 20008
*Consulate*: (☎ 212-348 0926, fax 831 9162) 9 East 91 St, New York, NY 10128
*Consulate*: (☎ 415-928 6878, fax 929 0306) 2790 Green St, San Francisco, CA 94123

### Foreign Consulates in St Petersburg

**Canada** (☎ 325 84 48) Malodetskoselsky pr 32
**China** (☎ 114 76 05) nab Kanala Griboedova 134
**Estonia** (☎ 238 18 04) Bol Monetnaya ul 14
**Finland** (☎ 273 73 21) ul Chaikovskogo 71
**France** (☎ 312 11 30) nab reki Moyki 15
**Germany** (☎ 327 31 11) Furshtadtskaya ul 39
**Latvia** (☎ 327 60 53) 10-ya Linia 11 (Vasilevsky Island)
**Sweden** (☎ 329 14 30) Mal Konyushennaya ul 1/3
**UK** (☎ 325 60 36, 325 61 66) pl Proletarskoy Diktatury 5
**USA** (☎ 275 17 01) Furshtadtskaya ul 15

Australian and New Zealand citizens must contact their embassies in Moscow, though in emergencies you can seek help at the British, Canadian and US consulates.

### Your Own Embassy

It's important to realise what your own embassy can and can't do to help you if you get into trouble. Generally speaking, it won't be much help in emergencies if the trouble you're in is remotely your own fault. Remember that you are bound by the laws of the country you are in. Your embassy will not be sympathetic if you end up in jail after committing a crime locally, even if such actions are legal in your own country.

In genuine emergencies you might get some assistance, but only if other channels have been exhausted. For example, if you need to get home urgently, a free ticket home is exceedingly unlikely – the embassy would expect you to have insurance. If you have all your money and documents stolen, it might assist with getting a new passport, but a loan for onward travel is out of the question.

## CUSTOMS

Russian customs laws and regulations are in a state of flux and are not consistently enforced across all border points (starting to sound familiar?). You may be asked to fill out a declaration form when you enter the country; you are obliged to fill this in if the currency and goods you are bringing in exceed $1500. This is to ensure that you will not be bringing out more money than you arrived with. This *deklaratsia* will be stamped and handed back to you. You are to keep it and show it to the border guard on your way out, where they may ask you to account for the difference in money brought in and taken out. Most travellers find it simpler to just tell them that you have nothing to declare (нечего декларировать, *nyechego deklarirovat*); the less paperwork the better. One minor consequence of this is a new system in which changing money in the city without a declaration form can leave you stuck with a worse exchange rate (see Exchanging Money later in this chapter).

### What You Can Bring In

You may bring in modest amounts of anything for personal use except, obviously, illegal drugs and weapons. Cameras, notebook computers, video cameras and Walkmans are OK. If you're bringing in hypodermic needles or what looks like a suspicious amount of medicine, make sure you bring in a prescription for them and declare them under the line 'Narcotics and appliances for use thereof'.

Five litres of alcohol and 1000 cigarettes are allowed, though these don't concern customs agents as much as any object brought in a quantity that looks saleable.

You can get a receipt *(kvitantsia)* for any confiscated item and you might succeed in reclaiming the item when you leave.

### What You Can Take Out

Anything bought from a legitimate shop or department store can go out, but saving receipts isn't a bad idea. Leaving with Russian roubles is no longer the problem it used to be.

Anything vaguely 'arty' or old-looking, such as manuscripts, instruments, coins, jewellery, antiques or antiquarian books (meaning those published before 1975), must be assessed by the Ministry of Culture in St Petersburg (Map 8; ☎ 311 51 96, Mal Morskaya ul 17). It's open 11am to 5pm Monday to Friday. There the bureaucrats will issue a receipt for tax paid (up to 100% of the purchase price   bring along your sales receipt, on which you can ask the store to mark a lower price). A photograph will suffice if it's a large object.

A painting bought at tourist art markets, in a department store or from a commercial gallery should be declared and receipts should be kept. Don't expect customs agents to be able to tell that yours is 'obviously' just a souvenir – in short, don't give them any reason to make trouble for you. Show them as many documents as possible (preferably ones that have been stamped with official-looking seals). Customs in airports tend to be more strict than at any other border crossing.

## MONEY

Most prices in this book are presented in US dollars, except some local prices, such as bus tickets, which are given in roubles (R).

### Currency

The Russian unit of currency is the rouble *(roo-bl)*, whose name is its most consistent property. After fluctuating wildly throughout the 1990s, with several periods of stability, the big crash came in August 1998 when the rouble was devalued (from six to the dollar to 23 to the dollar in one fell swoop) and the populace once again lost huge chunks of their life savings. Since then, the exchange rate has been relatively stable.

The rouble is the only legal tender in Russia, even if many prices may be listed in more expensive restaurants and shops in mysterious 'conditional units' (conditional on the exchange rate of the dollar).

This is to ensure that if the rouble goes frenetic again, their goods will not be undersold. Still, in Russia, the word 'dollar' is bandied about as much as in the US, and some of your personal financial transactions (renting an apartment, buying something from an acquaintance etc) are likely to be in dollars.

## Exchange Rates

These exchange rates were valid at time of printing and are likely to change:

| country | unit | | rouble |
| --- | --- | --- | --- |
| Australia | A$1 | = | R14.7 |
| Canada | C$1 | = | R19.1 |
| euro | €1 | = | R24.9 |
| Finland | FIM1 | = | R4.19 |
| Japan | ¥100 | = | R0.22 |
| UK | UK£1 | = | R41.1 |
| USA | US$1 | = | R29.2 |

## Exchanging Money

Aside from the almighty greenback and Finnish markka are the most common foreign currencies in town, though you'll have no problem changing almost any other world currency. Bring new and undamaged notes with you.

To change money, you will usually be asked for your passport. An official receipt will be filled out showing your transaction; in the olden days (say, mid-1990s) you had to show these at the border to prove that you'd exchanged money legally. Now, these are for your records only (ie, you can trash them).

Since 2000, a semi-legal practice has begun giving holders of foreign passports a lower rate of exchange (usually about 1% less) – unless you provide your declarations slip, which you may or may not have been given at the border (see Customs earlier in

this chapter). This can be avoided by having a Russian you know change your money, or by smiling at the cashier, who will sometimes engage in the semi-legal practice of putting the transaction through on his or her own passport (I know, I'm scratching my head too). This goes for exchange bureaus; banks, which offer a lower rate of exchange to begin with don't require a declarations form.

A complete list of banks, exchange offices and locations of ATMs in St Petersburg can be found in *Lutshche V Sankt Peterburge*.

**Banks & Exchange Offices** There are legal exchange offices – many open around the clock – practically everywhere within St Petersburg – in hotels, restaurants, boutiques, back alleys etc. One place with consistently good rates for a large variety of currencies, including East European, is Ligovsky, at Ligovsky per 2 (Map 8; ☎ 325 10 93), near the Moscow Station, open 9am to 9pm daily. Promstroy Bank (Map 8) is one of the more prominent of the dozens of banks across the city. Its head office is at Nevsky pr 38 (enter across from the Grand Hotel Europe).

**Travellers Cheques & Credit Cards** Though they don't have the same status as in Europe or North America, credit cards will come in very handy, as they are widely accepted in restaurants and shops. Cash advances on all major credit cards is also no problem at banks and many exchange bureaus, if you don't mind paying at least a 3% commission fee (see ATMs).

American Express's full service (including emergency cashing and card replacement) office (Map 8; ☎ 329 60 60, at the Grand Hotel Europe) is open 9am to 5pm Monday to Saturday. American Express or Optima cardholders can use personal cheques to buy travellers cheques there. Though travellers cheques can be exchanged at the main banks (like Promstroy), using them in all but the largest shops and major hotels is still almost unheard of – they are not particularly handy in Russia. If you want to use travellers cheques, US dollar American Express is your best bet.

**Black Market** Though black market exchanging has all but died, it can revive within hours of some economic turmoil (the morning after the rouble devaluation in 1998, young entrepreneurs – some shifty-eyed folk, but honest students and regular joes are also trying their hand at speculation trading – appeared standing outside exchange bureaus). If someone approaches you as you are about to enter an exchange bureau or bank and offers you a marginally better rate, keep walking. These are likely to be thieves whose polished methods of chicanery are able to trick even the most street-wise.

**ATMs** There are reliable and safe-to-use ATMs throughout the city. Inside every metro station, all train stations, major post offices, banks, hotels, even some clubs, you'll find ATMs accepting Visa, MasterCard, American Express, Eurocard and/or Diners Club. Many of them have a limit of 1000 roubles (about $35) per transaction. For information about the location and opening times of Promstroy's ATMs, call ☎ 329 83 29.
ATM cash advances in US dollars are hard to come by, but Alpha Bank (Map 8; ☎ 329 80 50) ATMs can do this – and with no commission fee! The one at its headquarters, kanal Griboedova 6/2, gives a maximum of $100 per transaction (it can be accessed 8.30am to 8.30pm daily), while its other ATMs (eg, inside the Sheraton Nevskij Palace Hotel) give out $50 max per transaction.

**Wire Transfers** Western Union is still the fastest, most reliable – and most expensive – way of wire-transferring money to Russia. It has branches in dozens of banks (including the previously mentioned branch of Alpha Bank) and at the Grand Hotel Europe.
Direct bank-to-bank wire transfer is also possible. You'll need to open an account at a local bank and pay fees and a percentage of the money wired into that account. Depending on the bank, transferring money can take anything from one to five days.

## Costs
Depending on how you spend your holiday in St Petersburg, it can be more expensive than other European cities, or way cheaper. It's no trouble to go from your $250-a-night hotel to a $100-a-head restaurant, and then to a nightclub where the cover charge is $30 and inside a mixed drink will set you back $6.
Generally speaking, however, costs here will be significantly lower than in the rest of Europe (even Eastern Europe, and even Moscow). Finding good and cheap places to eat is a piece of cake. Your major cost will be accommodation; even hostels here aren't cheap, and unless you're willing to stay far from the centre, or share a triple or quad room at one of the cheaper hotels, you're likely to spend a minimum of $15 a day. For longer stays, renting an apartment makes sense (see the Places to Stay chapter for more details).
If you stay at the cheapest hotels or hostels, stick to self-catering or eat in inexpensive bistros and cafes, visit the sights at discounted rates and use public transportation, you may be able to squeeze by on $25 a day.

## Tipping
Tipping is far less common in Russia than in the West, where barbers, waiters and taxi drivers look ready to throttle you if you don't fork out at least 15% tip, even for lousy service. Here, it's standard in the better restaurants to leave about 10% tip; elsewhere 5% to 10% of the total is fine. However, unlike in the West, tipping for personal services is accepted, sometimes expected practice. Tipping a private tour guide with money or a gift, for example, is usually welcomed. Even in situations where an acquaintance drives you somewhere, a small contribution 'for the gas' is, shall we say, not unwelcome.

## Taxes & Refunds
There is no system in place for tax refunding upon departure.

## POST & COMMUNICATIONS
### Post
St Petersburg's Main Post Office (Map 6; *glavpochtamt;* ☎ 312 83 02, Pochtamtskaya ul 9) is located two blocks south-west of St

Isaac's Cathedral and is open 9am to 8pm Monday to Saturday and 10am to 6pm Sunday. All non-book parcels, or anything weighing over 5kg, leaving the country must be sent from here, from Window 24 (this keeps changing though – just walk to the far left side of the main hall and look for the sign).

Most hotels will sell stamps, postcards and envelopes. There are also over 400 smaller post offices scattered throughout the city, varying in services usually in proportion to their size. A convenient one is at Nevsky pr 65, near the Sheraton Nevskij Palace Hotel. A particularly friendly one is at Stremyannaya ul 14, on the other side of the same hotel. It's not usually busy, open 10am to 8pm Monday to Friday and until 5pm on weekends. The sweet, almost motherly staff will help you wrap your book or souvenir parcels (up to 5kg) and help you fill out those ubiquitous forms.

To send a letter weighing up to 20g/ 20g to 100g abroad air mail costs $0.50/ $1.25. To send a 20g letter within Russia costs $0.07. The dismal quality of Russian postal service has been grossly exaggerated.

**Express Services** Inside the Main Post Office, you can organise a special overnight service to Moscow and Minsk at Window 16. Euroletter at Window 26 will send letters and parcels up to 2kg, charging $6 for up to 250g, $10 for 2kg. It uses express until Sweden, then Swedish Post, and swears it only takes five days to the US and Australia.

Express Mail Service (EMS) is provided by EMS Garantpost (Map 6; ☎ 311 11 20, 325 75 25, e ems@comset.net). It has several outlets in the centre, but head office is at Konnogvardeysky bul 4, near the Main Post Office. Documents up to 2kg (500g to America costs $21; to Australia, $30) and packages up to 31kg (5kg to America costs $56; to Australia $78) take five days to reach their destination, three to European capitals. Small packages only can be sent from Window 15 inside the Main Post Office.

US-managed Westpost (Map 8; ☎ 275 07 84, 327 30 92, e westpost@westpost.ru, w www.westpost.ru; Nevsky pr 86) is a reliable, international mail service for monthly and one-time clients. Mail is transported daily from St Petersburg to Lappeenranta, Finland, and mailed from there. To the US, a 20g letter costs $1.15, and a 2kg parcel sent express costs $53. It has a full range of delivery and courier services.

The main global express mail services in town offer two-day delivery to Europe and the USA/Canada, and three-day delivery to Australia/New Zealand, all with services starting at $38 for letters. They are DHL (☎ 326 64 00, Izmailovsky pr 4), Federal Express (☎ 311 98 31, kanal Griboedova 16), and UPS (☎ 327 85 40, Shpalernaya ul 51). They all have pick-up service.

**Sending Mail** Address outgoing international mail as you would from any country, in your own language, though it might help to *precede* it with the country name in Cyrillic. Some Cyrillic country names are:

America (USA) – Америка (США)
Australia – Австралия
Canada – Канада
France – Франция
Germany – Германия
Great Britain – Великобритания
New Zealand – Новая Зеландия

**Receiving Mail** The most reliable option for those not staying in luxury hotels or the HI St Petersburg Hostel (which provide mail service via Finland) is limited to American Express and Optima cardholders. American Express (☎ 329 60 60) will hold mail (letters only) for cardholders and holders of travellers cheques for up to 30 days; the mailing address is American Express, PO Box 87, SF-53501 Lappeenranta, Finland – mail is brought from Lappeenranta to the American Express office daily, at no charge if you have an AmEx card or travellers cheques.

Westpost (see Express Services earlier) offers post boxes in Lappeenranta, with daily pick up or delivery to the Westpost office, or, for corporate clients, to an address in St Petersburg.

When sending mail from abroad to Russia, it's best to put Latin characters on top to get it to Russia, and Cyrillic on the bottom to get it to its ultimate destination.

Embassies and consulates won't hold mail for transient visitors.

## Telephone

Russia's country code is ☎ 7. St Petersburg's city code is ☎ 812.

You will be able to make long-distance calls from all hotels and hostels but their prices (yes, even at the hostels) will be more expensive than the following options.

**Private Telephones** Dialling abroad from a private phone is the simplest, though no longer necessarily the cheapest option. To call internationally, dial ☎ 8, wait for the second tone, then dial ☎ 10 plus the country and city codes, then the number.

Omit any noughts (zeros) from the city code you need to use (eg, to call Sydney the code would be 8 (tone) 10 61 2 and then the phone number).

When calling abroad, some useful country codes are:

| | |
|---|---|
| Australia | ☎ 61 |
| Canada | ☎ 1 |
| Denmark | ☎ 45 |
| Estonia | ☎ 372 |
| Finland | ☎ 358 |
| France | ☎ 33 |
| Germany | ☎ 49 |
| Latvia | ☎ 371 |
| Lithuania | ☎ 370 |
| New Zealand | ☎ 64 |
| Norway | ☎ 47 |
| UK | ☎ 44 |
| USA | ☎ 1 |

**Payphones** Payphones – таксофон *(taksofon)* – are located throughout the city. The green ones are the most common (not the cheapest), and accept prepaid telephone cards (with the letters SNM – CHM – on them) readily available from metro token booths or, at slightly higher prices, from telephone offices. Occasionally you'll need to press the star button as soon as you hear your party answer (you know you'll need to if they scream 'Allo? Allo?' after you start speaking).

Newly installed coin-operated phones are now quite popular; you can find one inside every metro station. On these, the rate is ostensibly R1/min or $0.04/min, though coins seem to disappear quicker than that. They accept 50 kopeck, and 1, 2 and 5 rouble coins.

There are several types of card payphones (Peterstar, ☎ 329 90 90, has better prices but so far fewer phones; BCL charge the highest prices), and cards are not interchangeable.

There has been a recent proliferation of prepaid, pin code-operated long-distance phone cards. Scan the *St Petersburg Times* for ads. Their pricing systems are mind-boggling, but still end up cheaper to use than dialling direct or using the SNM cards. These cards can be used from any private or public phone and are very handy. Peterstar has good deals, as does Fon-Mezhsvyaz (☎ 233 65 87). Only thing, these cards are (at least for the time being) not available anywhere but directly from them. However, representatives of these companies will meet you anywhere in the city and bring them to you for no extra charge.

**State/Central Telephone Office** There are several telephone offices in the centre, the most convenient being the main branch at Bol Morskaya ul 3/5 (Map 8; ☎ 312 20 85), and a smaller, user-friendly one at Nevsky pr 88. At either place you can direct dial calls anywhere, or order them through the operator. Prices are identical to those of private phones, but without cheap rate discounts.

**Cellular Service** Though pagers still outnumber cellphones in St Petersburg, 'mobiles' are fast gaining ground. You no longer need special permission to bring your mobile phone into Russia. European cellphones work here (double-check with your service provider before leaving home), yet the costs will be sky-high. You can rent a cellphone at ATS Telecome, which has many branches throughout town, most conveniently at Bol Morskaya ul 19 (☎ 326 86 40). A $150 deposit is needed, but then rental is about $3 a day, plus all your calls.

## Fax & Telegram

Faxes are able to be sent and received at the Central Telephone Office; the incoming fax number is ☎ 314 33 60 (at Nevsky pr 88 the number is ☎ 314 14 80), and the cost to retrieve them is $0.40 per page. Faxes can also be sent and received at the business centres in all major hotels and in the Moscow Station, as well as at the two youth hostels, at much higher prices.

International telegrams can be sent from many of the larger post offices, as well as from Window 38 at the main post office.

If you can speak Russian, you can also send telegrams from a private telephone via ☎ 066 (charged to the resident's line).

## Email & Internet Access

There are many options to surf the net around the clock. So what if you have to compete with pubescent video-game enthusiasts at most of them!

Nordic (Map 8; ☎ 269 42 22, W www .nordicclub.spb.ru, Sadovaya ul 8/7), open 24 hours, is the most comfortable place of its kind in town – friendly staff, trendy, mirrored interior, great espresso and low prices ($1.40 per hour). Kro Magnon (Map 8; ☎ 279 57 26, Nevsky pr 81) is your cheapest option. Also open 24 hours (but the guys running it like to close shop to have a smoke outside every so often), Internet access is just $1.10 an hour. Enter via the courtyard, and walk up the steep, rickety metal staircase to the 2nd floor (1st floor is for those ubiquitous hordes of pubescent video gamers).

The Central Telephone Office (Bol Morskaya ul 3/5) has comfy, though stuffy, individual booths with computers and printers in each one. Available 9am to 9pm daily, they cost from $1.40 to $2.80 an hour. There are also Internet booths at the telephone offices at Nevsky pr 88 and on 3-ya linia 8 on Vasilevsky Island.

There are more expensive options with no special benefits: at Westpost, Internet access is $7.20 an hour, at the HI St Petersburg Hostel $6 an hour; the hotel business centres charge even more.

Check the *St Petersburg Times* for providers' ads. Cityline (Map 8; ☎ 329 55 49, 279 11 22, W www.cityline.spb.ru), next to the telephone office at Nevsky pr 88, is one of the more reliable. It also has some terminals for surfing.

## DIGITAL RESOURCES

There's no better place to start your Web explorations than the Lonely Planet Web site (W www.lonelyplanet.com). Here you'll find succinct summaries on travelling to most places on earth, postcards from other travellers and the Thorn Tree bulletin board, where you can ask questions before you go or dispense advice when you get back. You are also able to find travel news and updates to many of our most popular guidebooks, and the sub-WWWay section links you to the most useful travel resources elsewhere on the Internet.

There is no shortage of useful and quirky information about St Petersburg on the Web. Listed here are some of the best, but see individual sections for more suggestions.

W **www.cityvision2000.com** – One of the best places to start. There's info on sights, current events and listings, a city virtual tour, online hotel booking, and a great, up-to-date traveller's message board.

W **www.spb.ru** – A good general starting point for St Petersburg information, including links to the *St Petersburg Times*.

W **www.online.ru/sp/fresh** – The Fresh Guide's cheeky irreverence overflows with perceptive, amusing and informative information.

W **www.russia.net/country/stpetersburg_sights** – Good general overview of the main sites and museums of St Petersburg.

W **www.museum.ru** – More detailed information about the city's museums.

W **www.exile.ru** – The homepage of Russia's cheekiest English-language paper, out of Moscow. Something to offend everybody! There are dozens of links and stain-your-pants funny articles about all things Russian. Best are its dissections of the ignorant pedantry that poses for journalism in articles about Russia by Moscow-based foreign correspondents.

W **www.online.ru** –Links to Russian Web cams, Internet radio stations, news and services.

W **http://dove.net.au/~punky/Stpetbg** – Some live Web cam views of St Pete.

## BOOKS
### Lonely Planet
If you're travelling outside St Petersburg, Lonely Planet's *Russia, Ukraine & Belarus* is *the* most comprehensive practical guide available on those countries. Lonely Planet also has guides to many neighbouring countries including *Scandinavian Europe, Estonia, Latvia & Lithuania* and *Eastern Europe*. See the Lonely Planet Web site for more details.

### Travel
Colin Thubron's forays into Eternal Russia have produced books considered to be among the best in their field. *Where the Nights are Longest* details his exploits driving through late-Soviet western European Russia. His latest, *In Siberia*, recounts his meeting with an alleged descendant of Rasputin, and his existential wanderings around ruined Gulag sites in Siberia. His style is often arch and humourless, and all his time among the Russians has sharpened his sense of the overdramatic, but his writing is filled with perspicacious accounts of the ordinary people he meets.

Though written after his journey through western Russia in 1839, the Marquis de Custine's *Empire of the Tsar* (also known by several other titles, including *A Journey Through Eternal Russia*) is still a blast today. He rivals Oscar Wilde in short, witty quips. One of the bitchiest travel writers ever, he has nary a kind word to say about anything and his facts are often jumbled, but his mordant observations are frequently bang-on: 'Russia is like a vigorous person suffocating for want of external air'; 'I am not surprised that the Russians neglect their ancient architectural monuments; these are witnesses of their history, which, for the most part, they are glad to forget'.

### History, Politics & Culture
Since the late 1990s, many books have attempted to explain the seeming failure of democracy and capitalism to take root in Russia in the ways the West expected it to. Dominic Lieven's *Empire* (2001) is an astute, scholarly book but written with great

love for Russia. Lieven believes the Soviet Union was to be the last one the planet will ever know and provides much material to understand contemporary Russia by. Edmund Wilson's *To the Finland Station* (1940) remains the authoritative account of the development of socialism and communism.

*Night of Stone: Death and Memory in Russia* by Catherine Merridale (2001) is a fascinating mix of history, psychology and philosophy, and reveals much about the way history – particularly of war and death – is remembered and rationalised by the Russian psyche. *A People's Tragedy* by Orlando Figes is an enthralling opus detailing little-known incidents surrounding Russia's revolutionary movements. Wright Miller's *Russians as people* (1960) remains one of the most astute descriptions of the Russian psyche ever published.

*The Sexual Revolution in Russia* by Igor S Kon is a comprehensive history of the sexual mores and habits among Russians throughout history. It's particularly good on the changing face of sexual life in the late and post-Soviet era.

Robert K Massie's *Peter the Great: His Life and World* is an excellent read on the history of St Petersburg's founder, while *Pushkin's Button* by Serena Vitale absorbingly recounts the writer/poet's fatal duel. W Bruce Lincoln's eminently readable *Romanovs: Autocrats of All the Russias*, is a complete history of the Romanov dynasty.

The most comprehensive book available on St Petersburg's contribution to the world of art is Solomon Volkov's *St Petersburg: A Cultural History*. This is essential reading for anyone with more than a passing interest in the city. Volkov, a musician who emigrated to the US in the 1970s, is passionate about his home city, and insightfully pries into its depths to reveal its influence on some of the world's greatest artists, themselves shaped by the city's unique character.

### Literature
The city of St Petersburg figures prominently in numerous works of fiction which mainly underscore its dark, mysterious side. Andrei Bely's 1913 symbolist masterpiece,

*Petersburg* stands on top of the heap. A Moscovite who loathed St Petersburg, his fantastical tale – loosely following the exploits of revolutionaries who hunt down a local official – has the city fulfill its dark destiny by disappearing into a hole.

An incomplete list of works greatly influenced by St Petersburg includes the prose of Fyodor Dostoevsky *(Crime and Punishment, Poor Folk, White Nights)*, Nikolai Gogol *(The Overcoat, The Nose, Nevsky Prospekt, Diary of a Madman)* and Andrei Bitov *(Pushkin House)*; the poems of Alexander Pushkin *(The Bronze Horseman)*, Daniil Kharms *(Incidents, Comedy of the City of St Petersburg)* and Nikolai Zabolotsky; the memoirs of Vladimir Nabokov *(Speak, Memory!)*, Dmitri Shostakovich *(Testimony)* and Georgy Ivanov *(Petersburg Winters)*; and both the poetry and prose of Anna Akhmatova, Mikhail Zoshchenko and Joseph Brodsky.

More recently, there's JM Coetzee's *The Master of Petersburg*, a powerfully-written tale of grief and an homage to Dostoevsky, as well as Duncan Farrell's *One Hot Night in St Petersburg* which contains a few brilliant descriptions of the city before getting bogged down in the author's melodramatic attachment to a handsome soldier.

## NEWSPAPERS & MAGAZINES

The Russian print media is still a bit of a grey area on the objectivity front. The freeing of the press in Russia throughout the 1990s paved the way for top-notch and brave journalistic feats in the investigation of scandals, high-level corruptions, government coverups and gross mismanagement. Many of these journalists paid for their daring with their lives, others with forced silence.

Though a far cry from the one-note news days of the Soviet era, most all of Russia's biggest papers are to some degree mouthpieces for the various powerful bodies that own them, be they political parties or rich businessmen. The public, already used to reading between the lines in the Soviet days, have once again learned to take a bit from here, a bit from there, and imagine a truth that's somewhere in between. Especially

amid cries of a Putin-enforced crackdown on dissenting voices in the media, the notion of a truly independent newspaper (if one exists anywhere at all) is getting further away with each passing month.

The most popular Russian dailies are *Izvestya, Kommersant* and *Komsomolskaya Pravda*. The government's official newspaper (which doesn't mean it doesn't control any others) is the *Rossiskaya Gazeta*. The tabloids category is covered by *Moskovsky Komsomolets*, and by rags like *Slukhi I Fakty*. For a gander at fringe party papers (by anarchists, fascists and the like), pass by Gostiny Dvor on Saturday afternoons, where representatives of such groups sell their wares. The weekly *Argumenty I Fakty* is one of the most popular papers in the country, selling over 30 million copies a week. Reputed to be relatively free from outside influences, it covers politics, economics and the social scene.

Two worthwhile local affairs magazines out of St Petersburg are the monthly *Na Nevskom* and *Prospekt*, published every two months, both available free of charge around town. They mix city history with contemporary happenings and interviews with city movers and shakers.

There are three *Details* and *The Face* clones on the national market: *Ptyouch, Om* and *Medved*. Their graphic design is as slick and inventive as you'd expect, though their glam and sex-obsessed content is as thin as bliny. Everyone was expecting more from *Aktivist*, an alternative monthly magazine with Finnish backing that appeared in 2000. Its Web site, however, is well-worth checking out for listings, features, the weather and the occasional obscure titbit about St Petersburg: W www.aktivist.ru.

### English-Language Print Media

The lifeline for English speakers in the city is the *St Petersburg Times*, a high quality, free English newspaper, published every Tuesday and Friday. It is available throughout town in hotels, cafes and travel agencies. Though it can be dry, sensationalist and alarmist, it's an excellent source of local and national news, and its well-researched features are always interesting. Its Friday listings are the most complete you'll find in English. They're online at W www.sptimes.ru.

*Pulse* is a slick, free monthly, also widely available, that used to actually boast an edgy opinion but which has now turned itself blatantly commercial. Published in English and Russian versions, it still does have the odd good feature and review, and its listings are a good complement to those in the *St Petersburg Times*.

The city's other English-language offering, the touchingly hyper-patriotic *Neva News*, has somehow managed to cling to life. It's mostly of interest as a source of amusing grammatical errors and to see how many interviews with dull expats who wax lyrical about St Petersburg can fit into one thin paper. Still, it often prints useful historical facts about the city.

## RADIO & TV

Most of St Petersburg's popular radio stations play a mix of trashy Euro pop and its even more over-the-top Russian variant. Still, their playlists are often unexpectedly eclectic. Some of the more popular FM stations include Eldoradio (101.4 MHz), Radio Modern (104 MHz), the grating Europa Plus (100.5 MHz) and the more diversified Radio Nostalgie (105.3 MHz) which broadcasts live from a windowed booth on Nevsky pr, 100m west of Sadovaya ul. More Russian content can be heard on Kanal Melodia (91.1 MHz), Russky Shanson (100.9 MHz) and Russkoe Radio (104.4 MHz). Two stations focus almost exclusively on St Petersburg-related news, music and features: Echo Peterburga (91.5 MHz) and Severnaya Stolitsa (105.9 MHz).

Television has had even less luck with freedom of expression than the beleaguered print media in Russia (see the boxed text 'Putin vs the Dolls').

One very popular series across Russia and filmed in St Petersburg is *Street of Broken Streetlamps*, nicknamed *Menty*, the slang for 'cops'. It's a gritty crime show with tongue-in-cheek humour, and plots often based on real happenings. It is only one of the many crime shows to hit the air

since the mid-1990s, most of which are filmed and based in St Petersburg. This has helped give the city the somewhat unjust nickname 'Bandit Petersburg'.

You can catch satellite TV broadcasts in all major hotels. The British Council has a TV perennially tuned to BBC World, whose reporters' peculiar intonation patterns can be heard free of charge (see Cultural Centres later in this chapter). The main state channels are ORT and RTR and St Petersburg has several local channels, including Peterburg and Kanal 6.

## English-Language Radio

The clearest BBC World Service shortwave (SW) frequencies in the morning, late evening and at night are near 9410, 12,095 (the most reliable) and 15,070 MHz. You can tune in to the BBC from:

| | |
|---|---|
| 2am to 5am & 3pm to 9pm | GMT/UTC |
| | 9410 MHz |
| 2am to 5am & 6pm to 8pm | 6195 MHz |
| 5am to 9pm | 12,095 MHz |
| 6am to 3pm | 15,565 MHz |
| 7am to 3pm | 17,640 MHz |
| 8pm to midnight | 5930, 6180 and 7325 MHz |

## VIDEO SYSTEMS

Hi8 and SVHS cassettes are easy to find in St Petersburg (at any of the electronic shops along Nevsky pr, or at the previously-mentioned Photo Master). If your camera records in NTSC (ie, bought in North America), these cassettes will be fine, even if they say PAL on them. You only might have a hard time connecting your camera to a TV or transferring onto a VHS, depending on whether or not the TV reads or the VCR records NTSC.

## PHOTOGRAPHY & VIDEO

One-hour drop off places for Kodak, Agfa and Konica are found everywhere throughout the centre, including inside many metro stations.

The most visible chain of photo labs in the city is Yarky Mir, but these are not recommended for anything other than purchasing supplies (constant complaints of

## Putin Vs The Dolls

The country's only major, non government-backed station, NTV (which translates as Independent TV), frequently upset the populace with its insolent and vituperative critique of the government. But everyone watched it. Many people would gripe endlessly about it yet watch it daily. After its spicy editorials and relatively daring programming, state-sponsored TV seemed so dull.

Throughout the Yeltsin years, the station screened *Kukli* (The Dolls), Russia's favourite TV show for a long while. Inspired by the British *Spitting Image* it is a social satire masterminded by Viktor Shenderovich which features politicians as grotesque dolls in absurd situations. The Kremlin was often not amused, but the show managed to sidestep attempts at censure. Until Vladimir – Putin, that is – came along.

Almost from his first day in office, Putin began putting pressure on the errant NTV, deciding at last to hound another Vladimir – Gusinsky, this time, multimillionaire owner of the station – for tax evasion and other charges of corruption. This led Vladimir to flee to Spain (that's Gusinsky), where he was placed under arrest but not extradited to face criminal prosecution in Russia.

No-one figured Gusinsky to be any less corrupt than any other oligarch (or high-level politician for that matter), but why he was being singled out seemed a clear signal that Putin's new government wished to control, if not silence, voices of dissent and encourage pro-government reporting. (Anyone doubting this should be reminded of a $6.25 million, government-sponsored program to begin in 2002 designed to bolster waning patriotism in the populace in part by increasing patriotic TV programming, ie, more WWII movies.)

A surprise buy-out of a controlling portion of NTV shares by the state gas giant Gazprom in April 2001 brought tens of thousands of protesters out in the streets of Moscow, demanding that NTV be left alone. Dozens of reporters quit the station, and its programming and acerbic tune were changed overnight.

The story of NTV is an important one in the annals of post-Soviet Russia if only for the issues of freedom of speech, rights and patriotism it brought to the forefront of a populace scarcely used to having public discussions about them.

**Vladimir Putin**

---

scratched negatives, ruined photos and unprofessional service haunt them).

There's an excellent Fuji lab in the centre (Map 8; reki Fontanki 23) open 10am to 6pm Monday to Friday and 11am to 5pm Saturday and Sunday. A major Fuji lab should be open at Bolshoy pr 35, Petrograd Side by the time this book is published. Another place with careful service (including slide developing) is Photo Master (Map 7; ☎ 314 46 51, Mal Morskaya ul 23) open 10am to 7pm daily. It also has a large selection of pro and amateur film and photo paper.

You can find good deals on truly cool Soviet photographic equipment at Bik Photo (Map 5; ☎ 272 09 35, Kirochnaya ul 36), and in the basement photo kiosk at Nevsky pr 54 (Map 8). At the latter location, you can also get passport photos done: B&W ($1 for six the next day; $2 in two hours) in the basement, and colour ones on the 4th floor.

### TIME

Russia uses a 24-hour clock; midnight is 0000, 7am is 0700, 9pm is 2100.

From the early hours of the last Sunday in September to the early hours of the last

Sunday in March, St Petersburg time is GMT/UTC plus three hours. From the last Sunday in March to the last Sunday in September, 'summer time' is in force and it's GMT/UTC plus four hours.

## ELECTRICITY

Electricity is 220 volts, 50Hz AC, and very reliable in St Petersburg. Sockets require a Continental or European plug adaptor with two round pins. American and Japanese appliances need a 220V to 110V/100V converter.

## WEIGHTS & MEASURES

The metric system is in use. Drinks are served in measures of 50g or 100g, about 1.75 or 3.5 ounces (whoo). Russian restaurant menus list food and drink servings by weight; a cup of tea is about 200g. Individual items, such as eggs, are usually sold by the 'piece': штука (shtuka) or шт. (sht.).

Numbers are written with the comma and decimal point reversed relative to US, Canadian, Australian and English standards (so, for example, $1,000.00 would appear written as $1.000,00 in Russia).

## LAUNDRY

Most hotels offer a laundry service. Otherwise, there is only one Western-style 'beautiful laundrette' in the city, Laundromat (Map 4; ☎ 323 74 98) at 11-ya linia 46, near metro Vasileostrovskaya. It'll cost about $4 to wash and dry 5kg while you wait, slightly more if you drop off your dirty stuff and pick it up later. It's open 8am until 10pm daily. All other places in town offer next-day service at best, usually longer.

## TOILETS

Free or inexpensive toilets are scattered around town, marked with the Latin characters 'WC' or the Russian Платный туалет (platny tualet; pay toilet). There are also free or inexpensive toilets at bus and train stations. Some may even be clean. In any toilet, Ж stands for zhenskiy (women's), and M for muzhkoy (men's). Your best bet is to use McDonald's, the toilet inside the Idealnaya Chashka coffee shop at Nevsky pr 15,

or the facilities on the main floor of the Grand Hotel Europe.

## LEFT LUGGAGE

There is a left luggage room at the Moscow Station, best accessed through the archway to the right of the main entrance on pl Vosstania. Look for the suitcase symbol on your right. Hotels usually only let guests leave bags with them.

## HEALTH
### Predeparture Planning

Most visitors to St Petersburg don't experience any serious health problems providing they adhere to the golden rule regarding drinking the city's water, but comprehensive travel insurance (covering theft, loss and medical problems, as well as medical evacuation if necessary) is recommended.

Make sure childhood vaccinations, including polio, diphtheria and tetanus, are up to date. In wintertime, it would be wise to get a flu shot; there are nasty strains every year that keep you sick for a month. There is no problem getting round-the-clock supplies at the many pharmacies in town, but take along your favourite brands just in case. Homeopathic and herbal remedies are available (see Pharmacies), but the selection of herbals is much smaller here, so bring your own.

### Medical Services

If all the advice of your Russian friends proves insufficient to curing whatever ails you (what, that mustard powder in your socks didn't reduce your fever?), you may need medical treatment. Though services in St Petersburg may not be as polished as back home, there is good routine, and some emergency, treatment. Serious medical emergencies are best treated outside Russia; Finland is the best option.

*Luchshee V Sankt Peterburge* has a long list of medical clinics in the city, including pediatricians, gynaecologists, homeopathic clinics, and clinics offering treatment services abroad.

The best bet for Western-quality treatment in St Petersburg is the American Medical Center (Map 7; AMC; ☎ 326 17 30,

## Medical Kit Check List

Following is a list of items you should consider including in your medical kit – consult your pharmacist for brands available in your country.

- [ ] **Aspirin or paracetamol (acetaminophen in the USA)** – for pain or fever
- [ ] **Antihistamine** – for allergies, eg, hay fever; to ease the itch from insect bites or stings; and to prevent motion sickness
- [ ] **Cold and flu tablets, throat lozenges and nasal decongestant**
- [ ] **Multivitamins** – consider for long trips, when dietary vitamin intake may be inadequate
- [ ] **Antibiotics** – consider including these if you're travelling well off the beaten track; see your doctor, as they must be prescribed, and carry the prescription with you
- [ ] **Loperamide or diphenoxylate** – 'blockers' for diarrhoea
- [ ] **Prochlorperazine or metaclopramide** – for nausea and vomiting
- [ ] **Rehydration mixture** – to prevent dehydration, which may occur, for example, during bouts of diarrhoea; particularly important when travelling with children
- [ ] **Insect repellent, sunscreen, lip balm and eye drops**
- [ ] **Calamine lotion, sting relief spray or aloe vera** – to ease irritation from sunburn and insect bites or stings
- [ ] **Antifungal cream or powder** – for fungal skin infections and thrush
- [ ] **Antiseptic (such as povidone-iodine)** – for cuts and grazes
- [ ] **Bandages, Band-Aids (plasters) and other wound dressings**
- [ ] **Water purification tablets or iodine**
- [ ] **Scissors, tweezers and a thermometer** – note that mercury thermometers are prohibited by airlines

Serpukhovskaya ul 10). This US-run facility offers a full range of medical services including gynaecological and paediatric care, dentistry, 24-hour emergency care, an emergency room, ambulance services, house calls and medical evacuations. Prices are stellar, with a basic (often required)

consultation costing $215; a check-up won't be less than $100, and an HIV test will cost $75. Prices are marginally cheaper for members, but they're already paying $55 a month for the privilege.

For routine matters, a Russian *poliklinika* provides perfectly adequate care. One of the best is Poliklinika No 2 (Map 7; ☎ 316 62 72, Moskovsky pr 22), the former clinic of choice for diplomatic staff. It charges $70 for house calls, $26 for in-house visit with doctors, and $31 for an HIV test. Free, anonymous HIV tests and Hepatitis B tests for under $1 are available at the City Centre for Fighting AIDS (Map 6; ☎ 259 94 05, nab Obvodnogo Kanala 179, near metro Baltiskaya).

### Pharmacies

Pharmacies (singular *apteka*), are located all over the city and most are well stocked with Western medications and toiletries. Apteka Petrofarm (Map 8; Nevsky pr 22) is open 24 hours. After hours, use the side entrance on Bol Konyushennaya ul (under the archway of house No 14 and to the right). The particularly well-stocked Apteka Baltik, (Map 8; Nevsky pr 66) is open 9am to 9pm Monday to Saturday and noon to 8pm Sunday. There's a great homeopathic pharmacy at Nevsky pr 50, 2nd floor.

To find out which drug is available where, call ☎ 325 09 00, 9am to 7pm Monday to Friday. Medicines can also be delivered for a fee via ☎ 554 34 74 (Russian-speaking).

### Sexually Transmitted Diseases

If your night of passion resulted in anything superfluous, visit one of the many so-called Skin and Venereal Dispensers *(kozhno-venericheskie dispanser)* for a quick and anonymous diagnosis (with sometimes medieval treatments thrown in for fun!). A central one is at Stremyannaya ul 4 (Map 8; ☎ 113 12 94).

Russia is experiencing the fastest rise of reported HIV and AIDS cases in the world. Until now, nearly all cases were drug use-related; the second wave of infection, from sexual transmission, has now begun. In 2000, there were over 50,000 registered

## Don't Drink That Stuff!

No matter how thirsty you are, never drink unboiled tap water in St Petersburg. In addition to heavy metal pollutants and harmful bacteria, it contains *Giardia lamblia*, a nasty parasite that causes unpleasant stomach cramps, nausea, bloated stomach, diarrhoea and frequent gas. There is no preventative drug. Metronidazole (brand name Flagyl) or Tinidazole (known as Fasigyn), are the recommended treatments. Antibiotics are of no use. Symptoms may not appear for up to several weeks after infection, and may recur for years.

To be absolutely safe, only drink water that has been boiled for 10 minutes or filtered through an antimicrobial water filter (PUR brand makes a good portable one). Treat ice with suspicion and avoid fruits and vegetables that may have been washed in the water – vegetables that peel are safest. While accepting tea or coffee at someone's house should be safe, it's best to always stick to bottled water, even for brushing your teeth. Bathing, showering and shaving, though, should cause no problems at all. Just in case, though, pick up some Imodium, a most effective treatment for diarrhoea; it may become your most trusted friend in St Petersburg!

cases of AIDS; in 1999 the figure was 13,500. Some reports even say that up to one million Russians could die of AIDS by the year 2010. All the necessary precautions of safe sex need to be exercised here.

## WOMEN TRAVELLERS

You are unlikely to experience sexual harassment on the streets, but sexual stereotyping remains strong. If you're with a man, finer restaurants may hand you a 'ladies' menu' without prices. Russian men have heard that 'American feminists' get upset when a man opens a door for a woman, or helps her with her coat – as is customary for Russian men to do – and cannot comprehend this. On a date, expect the Russian man to act like a 'traditional' gentleman; he may be expecting you to act like a 'traditional' lady.

However, Russian and International Women's Rights organisations highlight a severe problem of domestic violence in Russia. Some estimates have it that as many as 12,000 to 16,000 women a year die at the hands of their partners. (Alcoholism, unemployment and feelings of passivity and impotence in men are related problems.) Activists ridicule as hypocritical 8 March Women's Day celebrations in Russia – it is one of the year's major celebrations, a national holiday where businesses shut down for as many as three days, and when women are traditionally presented with flowers.

Any young or youngish woman alone in or near flashy foreigner-haunt bars risks being mistaken for a prostitute. With lawlessness and crime on the rise, you need to be wary; a woman alone should certainly avoid private taxis at night.

Russian women dress up and wear lots of make-up on nights out. If you wear casual gear, you might feel uncomfortable at dinner in a restaurant, or at a theatre or the ballet.

## GAY & LESBIAN TRAVELLERS

While women walking hand in hand and drunk men being affectionate are common sights throughout Russia, open displays of same-sex love are not condoned (you rarely even see blatant displays of opposite-sex love). In general, the idea of homosexual acts is well tolerated, while overtly gay behaviour is greatly frowned upon.

In St Petersburg, there are a number of gay discos (see the Entertainment chapter) and male cruising areas, such as the park surrounding the statue of Catherine the Great on Nevsky pr, and the colonnades of Gostiny Dvor at night. Be warned that these are also frequented by convincing hustlers and military cadets who expect you to pay for their time or who work in gangs that might

FACTS FOR THE VISITOR

## St Pete for Kids

There's heaps to do with kids in St Petersburg! Please see the appropriate chapters for addresses and opening times. If your kids usually nod off at the mention of the word 'museum', that'll change here. The Kunstkammer inside the Museum of Anthropology and Ethnography is an all-time favourite for its display of jarred and pickled mutants. The Artillery Museum with its rugged ammunition is another winner for more aggressive runts, while the Museum of Zoology has some of the best stuffed animal and dinosaur displays anywhere. The Kirov Museum has an exhibit of how children lived in the Soviet era. Both the Hermitage and Russian Museum can provide tours specially geared to children (even in English!) if contacted in advance.

The Botanical Gardens offers year-round, unexpected treats, and the Flowers Exhibition Hall near Smolny also has great tropical plants to gawk at. Then, of course, there's the zoo, circus and the Planetarium, all of which hold special kids' programs. The D-2 Submarine will wow them too.

The city's parks are first rate; there's a full-scale amusement park in the Alexandrovsky Park behind the Peter & Paul Fortress, and a much more humble one in the Tauride Gardens with a small children's park. There's a great children's playground on the east side of Bol Pushkarskaya ul, Petrograd Side. And there are rowing and pedal-boat rental outlets behind the Peter & Paul Fortress, and on Yelagin Island.

A few theatres in town cater to kids, and these can be a real treat, even if they don't understand the language (see Theatre in the Entertainment chapter).

For restaurants, try Arlekino (Map 8; ☎ 279 83 86, ul Belinskogo 6) which is open 9am to midnight daily. Situated near the circus, its colourful interior has a fun clown thematic. It can organise special birthday parties with entertainment, and no-one could resist the chocolate fondue ($11/22 for 2/4 people). DaVinci has a children's menu, but you may want to leave before its spicy evening show starts. And all kids will love Bliny Domik.

For teens, contact the Palace of Youth Creativity; located inside the Anichkov Palace (☎ 325 96 57), it regroups over 10,000 teens

**Kids at play on an icy slide**

STEVE KOKKER

---

attempt to rob or beat you up. Make sure you are not followed out of these areas. These guys often work the bars too, targeting rich, foreign (aren't the two words synonymous?) men. Many have been robbed by their pickups; trust your instincts – is it really your winning charm and dimples, or the size of your wallet that make his eyes sparkle so?

Krilija (Wings; ☎ 312 31 80, 🄴 krilija@ilga.org, Ⓦ www.geocities.com/TheTropics/Cove/6377) is Russia's oldest officially registered gay and lesbian community organisation that also runs the Neva Banks Gay Travel Agency and is happy to assist tourists with information (in English), accommodation, and tours. On the women's side, things are less organised, but the Labrys

Women Public Foundation (🄴 labrys@mail.admiral.ru) should be able to provide information. Caprice, a lesbian bar outside the centre occasionally operates Sunday evenings – try ☎ 584 0953.

On the Web, Ⓦ www.gay.ru has some (dated) information on bars and clubs in St Petersburg and a list of links to gay Russian sites. If you read Russian, K Rotikov's 1998 book *Drugoy Peterburg* (Another Petersburg) is a fascinating history of homosexual life in the city over the ages.

## DISABLED TRAVELLERS

Inaccessible transport, lack of ramps and lifts and no centralised policy for people with physical limitations make St Peters-

## St Pete for Kids

in some 500 after-school clubs. There's always lots going on there – call to find out about special events, or to see about just hanging out with young Russians who are learning to speak your native tongue! It could be a great place to make friends.

### Ramses Playground

The most unique site in town for kids is the Ramses Playground (Map 3; ☎ 254 53 57), outside the centre in the middle of a concrete jungle suburb, on ul Ziny Portnovoi between houses No 6 and 8 (from metro Leninsky Prospekt, walk west along Leninsky pr one block to ul Ziny Portnovoy and turn right).

When circus clown Arkady Kontsepolsky read Brezhnev's declaration at the 26th Party Congress, 'Comrades! We must beautify our courtyards!', he took it to heart and started hand-building a playground in his own courtyard, putting together found objects and scrap material to make a fantasy village of fairy tale-inspired shacks. Though he first started building it in 1979, he only received official permission to do so in the mid-1990s; he was forced to go through a Kafkaesque series of 11 commissions, navigate bureaucracy and fight spiteful neighbours who viewed personal initiative with suspicion and worried about the noise.

STEVE KOKKER

Named after his beloved dog Ramses, who died in 1980 (he is survived by a friendly, pony-sized grandson who takes kids on 'rides' on weekends), the little village has a garden, a Puss 'n Boots castle, a lit fountain, a tree house on chicken legs, several sculptures, makeshift windmills, even a miniature cinema. A tiny bed is there too, in case toddlers get sleepy. Some evenings the disco ball is turned on and melodia-era tunes are played.

Don't expect Disneyland – this is one man's gift to neighbourhood children, not an official or commercial enterprise. A donations box is there to help with upkeep; a clown's pension is a pittance, and he receives no other funding. Kontsepolsky himself lives in an adjacent building (look for the window adorned with the miniature version of the Summer Garden fence).

**Arkady Kontsepolsky**

burg a challenging destination for wheelchair-bound visitors. Still, each passing year sees more ramps, and several pedestrian walkways have made downtown marginally more navigable. However, even renovated sidewalks have drainage canals built into them which could prove awkward. More mobile travellers will have a relatively easier time, but keep in mind that there are obstacles along the way. Toilets are frequently accessed from stairs in restaurants and museums, for example. While disabled people are treated with respect and people do go out of their way to be helpful, many are still unaccustomed to dealing with the disabled, and the experience may be frustrating.

There are exceptions. The Grand Hotel Europe, Hotel Astoria and the Sheraton Hotel are wheelchair accessible, as are their restaurants. While the HI St Petersburg Hostel has no lift, it has a good amount of experience with wheelchair-bound visitors. Other major hotels will all provide assistance. The Hermitage and, to a greater degree, the Russian Museum are wheelchair accessible, even if that sometimes means being carried up their grand staircases. Patience and forward planning are required, however.

## Organisations

There are a number of organisations and tour providers around the world that specialise in the needs of disabled travellers.

FACTS FOR THE VISITOR

**Australia** Independent Travellers (☎ 08-232 2555, toll-free ☎ 008-811 355, fax 232 6877, 167 Gilles St, Adelaide SA 5000) A travel agent that provides specialised advice for disabled travellers to a number of destinations.

**Russia** The All-Union Association for the Rehabilitation of the Disabled (☎ 095-298 87 37, fax 230 24 07, 1 Kuibyakhera pl, Moscow)

**UK** RADAR (☎ 0171-250 3222, 250 City Rd, London) A good resource centre for travellers with disabilities.

**USA** Mobility International USA (☎ 503-343 1284, fax 343 6812, e miusa@igc.apc.org, PO Box 3551, Eugene, OR 97403) Advises disabled travellers on mobility issues. It also runs an exchange program and has run several programs in Russia.

### Digital Resources

Disabled Peoples' International has a home page at w www.dpi.org. It has loads of listings and great links. The disability-friendly w www.everybody.co.uk has an airline directory that provides information on the facilities offered by various airlines.

### SENIOR TRAVELLERS

Travellers over age 60 can expect senior citizen discounts and a good degree of respect from Russian ticket agents. Respect for the elderly is far more ingrained in the Russian mentality than in some countries, such as America. *Babushka* and *dedushka* (grandmother and grandfather) are monikers of esteem, applied to any senior, even if not a relative. Seniors are more a part of everyday life here, and so there's less of a need for special 'seniors cruises' or 'seniors clubs'; they go on cruises and join clubs along with everyone else. Organisations, like the American Association of Retired Persons (w www.aarp.org), can assist with information before you leave.

### USEFUL ORGANISATIONS

If you're staying in town for business, you may want to attend a monthly meeting of the St Petersburg International Business Association, a group of Western businesspeople that addresses problems and concerns of expatriate residents. For more information contact SPIBA (☎ 325 90 91,

e spiba@ online.ru). See also Doing Business later in this chapter.

### LIBRARIES

Don't expect to just waltz in and start browsing. This is Russia, so have your passport and visa with you, and expect to fill out a few forms before being let inside.

The National Library of Russia (Map 8; ☎ 310 71 37, Sadovaya ul 18, entrance via pl Ostroskogo) is St Petersburg's biggest and has some 31 million books, nearly a sixth of which are in foreign languages.

The enormous Mayakovskogo City Central Public Library (Map 8; ☎ 310 36 58, nab reki Fontanki 44) has 1.5 million books in over 20 languages, including English. It boasts a mediateque, and there's an enchanting wood-panelled reading room with international newspapers. Before using the facilities, register in room 102.

There are other English libraries at the British Council and the American Center (see Cultural Centres). The Prince George Vladimirovich Golitsyna Memorial Library (☎ 311 13 33, nab reki Fontanki 46) is a reading room containing books in English and Russian pertaining to Russian culture and British-Russian links.

To check out a Virtual Russian Library (in Russian), see w www.rvb.ru.

### UNIVERSITIES

St Petersburg has long been an academic centre and its numerous universities and trade schools have, since tsarist days, produced some of the country's leading scholars, engineers, scientists and professionals.

For a complete list of the city's two dozen universities, check *Luchshee V Sankt Peterburge* or *The Traveller's Yellow Pages*.

St Petersburg State University (☎ 218 20 00), with its main campus on the Strelka, has over 20 schools including languages, philosophy and geology. It is held to be the finest in the country after the State University in Moscow. Students from its programs won the International Collegiate Computer Programming Contest World Finals in 2000 and 2001.

St Petersburg Technical University (☎ 552 78 82) produces some of the best engineers in Eastern Europe and some of Russia's best computer technicians. Its schools range from electronics and engineering to computers and network security to satellite communications.

## CULTURAL CENTRES

The best organised – and busiest – cultural centre in the city is the British Council (Map 8; ☎ 325 60 74, nab reki Fontanki 46) which organises concerts, lectures, theatre and other cultural events and arranges for exchanges between Russia and the UK of students and professionals. It has a great resource centre for foreign teachers of English. There's a membership fee to use its library ($3 for teachers; $12 for non-teachers), but its selection of books is wide and up-to-date.

The Goethe Institute St Petersburg (Map 8; ☎ 311 21 00) is in the same building and also has a well-stocked library.

The Institut Francais (Map 8; ☎ 311 0995, W www.fr.spb.ru, nab reki Moyki 20) is abuzz with activity, teeming with French-language books (over 12,000 of them), magazines, videos and CDs. It also organises numerous cultural events and it's open 10am to 7pm Monday to Friday.

The American Center (Map 5; ☎ 311 89 05) at the Marble Palace disseminates American culture (snigger) and has a resource centre focused on (surprise!) helping Americans do business in Russia. It's open 9am to 5.30pm at Millionnaya ul 5.

## DANGERS & ANNOYANCES
### Street Crime

St Petersburg's streets are as safe or dangerous as any large European city – most say safer. However, caution must be exercised.

Pickpocketing is an especially common problem, particularly on crowded buses and trolleys that run along Nevsky pr and in metros during rush hour. *Karmaniki* (pickpockets) work in small gangs, usually three: one to divert your attention, a second to steal your wallet, and a third to whom it is passed.

Here are some anti-crime tips (see also the boxed text 'Fitting In'):

- Bum bags are out; they're easily cut with a razor and announce that you have something worth stealing. Better use the under-the-clothes model so your money is next to your skin.
- An exciting way to meet Russian photo enthusiasts is to walk down Nevsky pr with your Nikon slung carelessly over your shoulder. Bag it.
- Keep your wallet in your front pants pocket, or better, in a zippered or inside jacket pocket – never in a back or outside pocket.
- Be alert in crowds. Assume any displays of anger or altercations to be diversionary tactics and act accordingly.

### The 'Mafia'

The Western media has had a field day exaggerating the dangers of the Russian Mafia, portraying a country where Al Capone types race through the streets firing Kalashnikov rifles at tourists. In fact, the Mafia, whose fingers are indeed in the pies of most businesses and industries, couldn't be less interested in piddling tourists. Though they can be spotted in the city's more expensive restaurants, entertaining their equally expensive dates, the Mafia poses less trouble to tourists than do the mosquitoes.

St Petersburg's Mafia and gang-related violence occurs among themselves and in the form of high-profile contract killings and political assassinations.

### Theft & Burglary

Break-ins to flats and cars are epidemic so don't leave anything of value in a car. Leaving valuables lying around hotel rooms is tempting providence. If you'll be living in a flat, it's imperative that you invest in a steel door.

Some debonair male tourists at upscale bars and clubs have been picked up by young, enterprising ladies who have later drugged and robbed them in their hotel room or apartment, sometimes working alone or in gangs (and he thought she loved him for who he was!). Be suspicious of excessive interest in you or of money and job-related questions (the average Russian is rarely interested in the details of your job).

## Reporting Theft & Loss

If you're here in a group, your tour guide or service bureau should be your first resort if you want to report a theft or loss. If not, calling your consulate for advice is your best bet (the British Council is used to advising foreigners about these matters). If you are a foreigner and the victim of a crime, you can report this to the police at a special number set up for that purpose, ☎ 164 97 87. It supposedly has a multilingual staff. Just in case, *vorovstvo* and *krazha* both mean theft in Russian.

## Racism

Overt aggression against minorities is quite rare in St Petersburg, but there is a high level of entrenched racist attitudes across Russian society. Ask a Russian if Russians are prejudiced or bigoted and you'll be lectured about how tolerant and accepting they are, but scratch the surface and the racism seeps out: 'There are good and bad people of every nationality! I wouldn't mind having anyone as a neighbour if they're a good person – even a Jew or Chechen!'.

The word for 'nigger' *(negr)* is not regarded here as anything other than racially descriptive, and the word is liberally used when speaking about anyone with dark skin, including people from the Caucasus region, like Georgians and Chechens. Black Americans are widely considered to be 'cool', but people from the Caucasus are deeply disliked and considered criminals (occasionally, bands of young skinheads harass dark-skinned peoples at the marketplaces where they often work).

Jews in Russia have experienced centuries of discrimination and were the targets of state-sponsored anti-Semitism during the communist reign. However, they tend to be more distrusted and resented than openly hated. The Roma, or Gypsies, however, are openly reviled.

## Mosquitoes & Fleas

Mosquitoes are an absolute nightmare. Though the swarms that'll feed off of you in the Karelian forests can be compared to dive-bombers, the city-dwelling variants found in St Petersburg are among the fiercest, most obnoxious, determined and just plain *evil* creatures on the planet. They will even pierce through sheets and blankets. A strong repellent should keep them at bay, and the plug-in gizmos that heat pieces of repellent-coated cardboard (sold in kiosks and practically any store) are remarkably effective. If you don't want to douse yourself with DEET, taking large doses of Vitamin B complex allegedly keeps mosquitoes away. Passing out in an alcoholic stupor has also been known to make the problem disappear – for a while.

The problem is not only the city's swamp-front location, but also the fact that nearly every basement in town is uninhabited, damp and festering; in such conditions mosquitoes thrive, and that's why you'll sometimes still see the buggers inside 4th-floor apartments in January!

The perennially damp basements also produce fleas which every autumn, after the weather turns cool but before central heating has been switched on, come up through the floorboards and infest 1st-floor apartments only in the city centre. Don't snicker – fleas are quite happy to gnaw into human flesh when their usual sup (rats) isn't around. If you notice black specs on your sheets that hop when you touch them, or angry red welts around your ankles (which won't disappear for months), get out of where you're staying fast. Fleas can carry some of humanity's most horrendous diseases (including the bubonic plague!).

## Icicles

If the word 'icicle' conjures up sweet childhood memories of frozen lips on Popsicle-sized chunks of ice, forget them if you plan on visiting St Petersburg in springtime. The ones here are deadly. Every year in early spring and during winter thaws, several people die when child-sized, sword-shaped icicles plummet from St Petersburg's rooftops and balconies. Walking at this time can be exhausting: while avoiding slipping on sheer ice, negotiating pot holes and avoiding pedestrians, you must also crane your neck skywards to make sure one of these monsters is not dangling above your head.

## Fitting In

If you're trying to ward off excess attention to dissuade souvenir peddlers, thieves and beggars from pestering you on the street, there's more you can do than just not waving wads of cash around or holding back from screeching out, 'Oh my *gawd* Henry! Look at that *gorgeous* building!'.

Foreigners in St Petersburg for any length of time quickly learn to shelve (if not burn) that golf hat, to use as rags any article of clothing with a daring splash of colour, or to resist aching temptation to wear shorts even in the most sweltering summer heat – all the better to pass for a local. St Petersburg street fashion dictates: the darker the better. For men, a nice, cheap black leather coat (no matter the weather) should do the trick, and for women, a ruddy dark brown jacket (OK, OK, maybe deep crimson) will ensure you slip unseen into the masses. Here, even if people dare to don red, yellow or pink, these must assuredly be of the very darkest, dullest possible shade.

Other sure-fire tips to pass as a local: Try to match your new fashion sense with a comely scowl, frown or a look of vague dissatisfaction. Never smile for no discernible reason. Attention men! A nice accessory to your angry-looking physiognomy would be swaggering shoulders while you walk to indicate that you'd know what to do if messed with. Women! Keep those lips pursed and eyes narrowed!

Don't get the wrong idea – most St Petersburgers are extremely friendly people who'll go out of their way to, say, help you reach your destination if you're lost, often suggesting a staggering array of possibilities on how to get there or even taking you there themselves. It's just that life in this big city is tough for most people, and, as no-one trusts each other, many tend to wear a mask that says 'Don't mess with me – *ponyal* (get it)?'.

## General Annoyances

Some of your most hated Russian words are sure to be обед (*obed*, lunch), ремонт (*remont*, repairs), санитарный день (*sanitarny deng*, sanitarny day) and закрыто (*zakryto*, closed), which is often followed by по техническим причинам (*po technicheskim prichinam*, for technical reasons). All these, when printed on a sign and posted on a locked door tell you that your intended destination is closed for a host of seemingly arbitrary reasons.

Though many major shops, museums and cafes no longer close for lunch, you'll still find a number of places shut for an hour between noon and 4pm. No use getting flustered – ask a shopkeeper about this practice and you'll have the following conversation: 'Why do you close for an hour every day?'; 'Don't people in your country eat lunch?'; 'Yes, but they do so in shifts.'; 'Ah, who wants to eat by themselves? That's boring!'.

Russian driving habits are sure to cause exasperation as well – if not near heart failures. Those dirty little Ladas see pedestrians as the enemy, and like Stephen King's *Christine* will appear to be heading straight for you with intent to kill. Cars make U-turns on main, busy roads (legally), shoot around corners unexpectedly, barrel across pedestrian walkways (which drivers consider merely nice decorative touches) and will always try to thunder across an intersection as yellow turns to green (hint: cross the street a few seconds after the light has turned green, just in case).

Isn't there policing of such heinous behaviour, you ask? Why yes, traffic police are ever-present, you'll see them stopping cars all the same. No, not because they aren't wearing their seat belt (in the city they don't have to, go figure). No, not because they almost killed that lady at the last intersection (her fault for getting in the way). That officer randomly selected that car to do a document check – his licence just might be expired!

Other things you might find annoying are people hanging up on you when you phone for information; men clearing their nostrils on the sidewalks in wintertime; men spitting on the sidewalks all other times; late-night door banging in hotel corridors; over-sensitive car-alarms; the redolent

## Keepers of the Piece

One thing foreigners always notice when first visiting St Petersburg: the men in uniform. With soldiers and cadets from 22 military academies marching throughout the city, members of every branch of local and federal police and special services, not to mention the ubiquitous and much-hated traffic police (called the DPS, but still known by their old acronym, GAI, *gai-ee*), you just might get the impression that you were in a militaristic state!

Although policemen in any country tend not to win popularity contests, at least in many countries they don't behave like the robbers and thieves they're supposed to catch (or if they do, ordinary citizens aren't usually troubled by it). Here, sadly, along with pickpockets and swindlers, we have to list the police *(militsia)* as people to watch out for. In St Petersburg, people are often warier of the police than of bandits and thieves.

There are constant reports from travellers about being searched on the street and having money disappear out of their pockets, or, more rarely, drugs planted on them (all the better to levy an on-the-spot-fine, my dear).

This most often happens to young to middle-aged males walking alone or in small groups, often late at night along Nevsky pr. A group of two or three police will stop you and politely ask to see your documents. No matter what you might hear, *you actually are not obliged by law to carry your passport with you at all times*; however, to avoid problems, it's best to carry a photocopy of your visa and/or passport with you. Often, some minor or invented problem will be found with your documents and a fine might be levied, which they'd want you to pay right away. If you are drunk, loose bills might be lifted from your wallet or pockets.

Here's what one traveller reported to us:

If you're stopped at night, make sure you don't have any loose notes on you. If searched, those notes might mysteriously disappear after the search. It happened more than once to friends. Most famously, one friend, who had already experienced the militsia's light-fingeredness, caused two other officers a deal of embarrassment one night on Dvortsovy most. When they approached, he leapt up into the air clutching a fistful of rouble notes and shouting (in English) 'The money's here! The money's here!' Moral dilemma aside, this seemed to put them off, and both made a hasty retreat.

**Niall Munro, Oxfordshire**

While we can't recommend the same behaviour in every case, it might be good to follow a few cautionary steps, particularly if walking late at night: Either do not carry your money alongside your ID; purposefully keep a small amount of cash that you're willing to part with near your ID and hide the rest; or hide all your money (in your socks, for example).

You should also ask to see the policeman's hands before they slip into your coat to search you (*pokazhitye ruki, pozhalusta*, please show me your hands) to ensure they don't have any little unexpected packages in them. You can also avoid Nevsky pr late at night (cops love to wait at the corner of Griboedova Canal for drunk foreigners coming out of the expensive clubs and restaurants on that street).

If you speak some Russian, you might try politely but firmly stating your case – that you are not required to have your passport, or that you insist on being brought to a station and get a receipt if you pay a fine. They are counting on you being nervous and unsure of your rights – prove them wrong.

clouds of cigarette smoke that billow from most gatherings of Russians; and prostitutes who will sometimes call your room offering sex.

## EMERGENCIES

Emergency telephone numbers (Russian-speaking operators) are ☎ 01 for fire, ☎ 02 for police. The state-run ambulance service is still free, at ☎ 03. If you're trying to find out if someone's been in an accident and been picked up by ambulance, dial ☎ 278 00 55.

## LEGAL MATTERS

If you are arrested, the Russian authorities are obliged to inform your embassy or consulate immediately and allow you to communicate with it without delay. You can insist on seeing an official from your embassy or consulate straight away. Be polite and respectful and things will go far more smoothly for you. *'Pazhalsta, ya khatelbi pozvanit v posoltstvo moyay strani'* means 'I'd like to call my embassy'.

## BUSINESS HOURS

Government offices are open 9am or 10am to 5pm or 6pm Monday to Friday. Most shops are open Monday to Saturday, often until 7pm or 8pm. Food shops tend to open 8am to 8pm except for an hour break *(pereryv)* sometime in the afternoon; many are open Sunday until 5pm. Food and alcohol shops open 24 hours abound throughout the city.

Most museums shut entrance doors 30 minutes or an hour before closing time and may have shorter hours on the day before their day off. Beware the *sanitarny den* (sanitary day). Once a month, usually near the end of the month (the last Tuesday, for example), nearly all establishments – shops, museums, restaurants, hotel dining rooms – shut down for cleaning, each on its own day and not always with much publicity.

## PUBLIC HOLIDAYS & SPECIAL EVENTS

After more than seven decades of official atheism, religious holidays are once again kosher in Russia. During the last 10 days of June, when night barely falls, many St Petersburgers stay out all night celebrating White Nights (particularly on the weekends). There's a tourist-oriented White Nights Dance Festival with events ranging from folk to ballet, but the main Kirov Ballet company doesn't always take part – more often its students do. The Russian Winter and Goodbye Russian Winter festivities centre outside the city, with *troyka* (horse-drawn sleigh) rides, folk shows and performing bears.

Less tourist-oriented are the Christmas Musical Meetings in Northern Palmyra, a classical music festival held the week before Christmas. The locations change; check the *St Petersburg Times* for details. The St Petersburg Music Spring is an international classical music festival held in April or May, and the mid-November International Jazz Festival, *Osenie Ritmy* (Autumn Rhythms), is centred around St Petersburg's jazz clubs.

### January

**New Year's Day** 1 January.
**Russian Orthodox Christmas (Rozhdestvo)** 7 January. Begins with midnight church services.

### February & March

**Mariinsky Ballet Festival** 10–18 February.
**Defenders of the Motherland Day** 23 February. A new holiday from 1996 to celebrate the anniversary of the founding of the Red Army. Commonly referred to as 'Men's Day'.
**Goodbye Russian Winter** Late February–early March. Festivities centre outside the city, with troyka rides, folk shows etc.
**Monocle International Theatre Festival of One-Man Shows** Early March.
**International Festival of Jazz Dance and Music** Early March.
**International Women's Day** 8 March. The city shuts down and all women walk around with flowers.

### April & May

**Kuryokhin Music Festival** Late April. A three-day fest bringing together a stunning array of international figures of alternative modern music and performance.
**International Labour Day/Spring Festival** 1–2 May.
**Easter *(Paskha)*** The main festival of the Orthodox Church year.
**Victory (1945) Day** 9 May.
**St Petersburg Music Spring International classical music festival** Mid-May.
**City Day** 27 May. Mass celebrations and merry-making, throughout the city centre.

### June–August

**Russian Independence Day** 12 June.
**Beer Festival** Mid-June. This has fast become one of the city's best-attended festivals.
**Message to Man** Mid-June. A well-respected documentary, short and animated film festival.

**Festival of Festivals** Late June. International film festival.
**St Petersburg White Nights** Last 10 days of June. General merrymaking and staying out late, plus dance festival and marathon.
**Sailing Week** August.

### November
**Day of Reconciliation & Accord** 7 November. The former Great October Socialist Revolution Anniversary is a good time to see demonstrations and parades of communist old-timers.
**Autumn Rhythms** *(Osenie Ritmy)* Mid-November Jazz festival.

### December
**Russian Constitution Day** 12 December.
**Christmas Musical Meetings in Northern Palmyra** Late December–early January. A classical music festival that runs for three weeks.
**Russian Winter Festival** 25 December–5 January. Tourist-oriented troyka rides, folklore shows, games.
**Sylvestr & New Year** 31 December–1 January. The main winter and gift-giving festival. Gifts are put under the traditional fir tree *(yolka)*. See out the old year with vodka and welcome the new one with champagne while listening to the Kremlin chimes on radio and TV.

## DOING BUSINESS
All major hotels have full-service business centres. There is also one inside the Moscow Station. Westpost (see Post & Communications earlier in this chapter) is another option. For all professional printing and photocopying needs, head to one of Ipris' two locations (Map 8; ☎ 315 48 18, Shvedsky per 2; Map 4; ☎ 325 28 74, ul Lenina 16, Petrograd Side).

## WORK
Most foreigners working in St Petersburg will have already lined up their jobs through contacts before they move to Russia; the days are gone when you could count on getting a decent position on the basis of your CV and foreign passport alone.

Teaching foreign languages is still a favourite for younger transients who don't mind trading 'normal' wages for the chance to get a deeper knowledge of the country. Even here, however, your qualifications should be up to snuff; a TESL or equivalent is often required. The city is teeming with language schools for Russians; if you think you've got what it takes, try contacting Lingua Consult (☎ 325 22 41, W www.lidenz .ru) or the British Council (☎ 325 22 77, W www.britishcouncil.ru). Also see *Luchshee V Sankt Peterburge* for more foreign language schools.

To work for a foreign company in St Petersburg, you'll almost always need a headhunter; there are several agencies, like Kelly Services (☎ 325 73 00, fax 325 73 01, W www.kellyservices.ru, Nevsky pr 11, office 6), that specialise in long and short-term placement of foreigners and Russians. The *St Petersburg Times*' classified section is often filled with advertised positions.

While regulations on foreigners working in Russia are arcane and visa procedures Byzantine, getting permission to work here is, practically speaking, more a question of lining up a job than fumbling with paperwork. Once you have an employer, all the red tape seems to magically disappear and a multiple-entry business visa will be yours once your company's facilitators are on the job.

An excellent contact source for any issue related to working or doing business in St Petersburg is the St Petersburg International Business Association (SPIBA; ☎ 325 90 91, 279 18 15, W www.spiba.spb.ru, Shpalernaya ul 36).

## The Expat Community
Foreign business associations are well established in St Petersburg. The network of expatriates looks after its own and, once you're accepted as a serious resident, it's as chummy as any old-boy network the West has to offer. The St Petersburg International Business Association (see Useful Organisations earlier) is a good place to start. To just hang out with other expats, there are bars that attract a foreign crowd, as well as organised outings to banyas, Frisbee games and pub crawls (see the Things to See & Do and Entertainment chapters). The British and American consulates will have more details on other such clubs.

Narva Triumphal Arch is a tribute to the defeat of Napoleon.

Piskaryovskoe Cemetery

The Russian Revival Church on Spilled Blood has been lovingly restored.

Watch out for the icicles.

Statues at Beloselsky-Belozersky Palace

Church on Spilled Blood from Mikhailovsky Gardens

Rush hour at the Atrium Business Complex

Moskovsky prospekt pays tribute to the past.

Faces of history decorate a bridge over the Moyka.

Lomonsov most over the Fontanka

Lenin addresses the faithful at Finland Station.

# Getting There & Away

We list a number of ways to purchase your air, train and bus tickets, but remember that a handy place to get any and all of these tickets is the Central Airline Ticket Office (Map 8; ☎ 311 80 93) at the corner of Nevsky pr and Mal Morskaya ul. It's open 9am to 8pm Monday to Friday and 9am to 6pm Saturday and Sunday.

## AIR
Pulkovo-1 (☎ 104 38 22) and Pulkovo-2 (☎ 104 34 44), respectively the domestic and international airports that serve St Petersburg, are 17km south of the city centre (Map 3), about a half-hour taxi ride and about an hour by public transport. Plans are under way to build a third terminal.

There are regular direct services to St Petersburg from many European cities such as Amsterdam, Berlin, Budapest, Vienna, Hamburg, Hanover, Copenhagen, Munich, Prague, Stockholm and Helsinki.

There is a currency exchange office inside the arrivals hall at Pulkovo-2 airport which has poorer rates than in the city, but it's still worth changing a small sum before you get out into the big world.

There's a Russian-language online booking service at Ⓦ www.fly.ru.

See the Getting Around chapter for information on transport to and from the airport.

### Departure Tax
There is an air departure tax of $11, payable when you buy your ticket.

### Bargain Tickets & Flights
Airlines are not the place to buy cheap tickets, but their best deals, usually advance-purchase tickets, will give you a reference point. Cheaper and more convenient are agencies that specialise in finding low fares, like STA Travel (worldwide), Trailfinders and Usit Campus in the UK, Kilroy Travel in Finland, Travel Overland in Germany, Council Travel in the USA and Travel Cuts in Canada.

See the following sections for more country-specific information. Transaero has partnership programs with Virgin Atlantic and Continental and can book overseas flights via London or Frankfurt from the US (☎ 800-957 2658).

**Apex (Advance-Purchase Excursion) Fares** You get sizable discounts from some carriers by booking well ahead (eg, a 28-day advance booking knocks 25% off the London–St Petersburg return fare). But Apex fares come with big penalties for changes or cancellations.

**Charter Flights** Group-tour charters can be as much as a third cheaper than scheduled flights in the low season. You may be able to arrange one of these in advance but normally it's a last-minute affair.

**Discount Flights** Some airlines drop prices as they get closer to the departure

## Air Travel Glossary

**Alliances** Many of the world's leading airlines are now intimately involved with each other, sharing everything from reservations systems and check-in to aircraft and frequent-flyer schemes. Opponents say that alliances restrict competition. Whatever the arguments, there is no doubt that big alliances are the way of the future.

**Courier Fares** Businesses often need to send urgent documents or freight securely and quickly. Courier companies hire people to accompany the package through customs and, in return, offer a discount ticket which is sometimes a bargain. However, you may have to surrender all your baggage allowance and take only carry-on luggage.

**Fares** Airlines traditionally offer 1st class (coded F), business class (coded J) and economy class (coded Y) tickets. These days there are so many promotional and discounted fares available that few passengers pay full fare.

**Lost Tickets** If you lose your airline ticket, an airline will usually treat it like a travellers cheque and, after inquiries, issue you with another one. Legally, however, an airline is entitled to treat it like cash and if you lose it then it's gone forever. Take very good care of your tickets.

**Onward Tickets** An entry requirement for many countries is that you have a ticket out of the country. If you're unsure of your next move, the easiest solution is to buy the cheapest onward ticket to a neighbouring country or a ticket from a reliable airline which can later be refunded if you do not use it.

**Open-Jaw Tickets** These are return tickets where you fly out to one place but return from another. If available, this can save you backtracking to your arrival point.

**Overbooking** Since every flight has some passengers who fail to show up, airlines often book more passengers than they have seats. Usually excess passengers make up for the no-shows, but occasionally somebody gets 'bumped' onto the next available flight. Guess who it is most likely to be? The passengers who check in late. If you do get 'bumped', you are normally offered some form of compensation.

**Reconfirmation** Some airlines require you to reconfirm your flight at least 72 hours prior to departure. Check your travel documents to see if this is the case

**Restrictions** Discounted tickets often have various restrictions on them – such as needing to be paid for in advance and incurring a penalty to be altered or cancelled. Others are restrictions on the minimum and maximum period you must be away.

**Round-the-World Tickets** RTW tickets give you a limited period (usually a year) in which to circumnavigate the globe. You can go anywhere the carrying airlines go, as long as you don't backtrack. The number of stopovers or total number of separate flights is decided before you set off and they usually cost a bit more than a basic return flight.

**Ticketless Travel** Airlines are gradually waking up to the realisation that paper tickets are unnecessary encumbrances. On simple one-way or return trips, reservations details can be held on computer and the passenger merely shows ID to claim their seat.

**Transferred Tickets** Airline tickets cannot be transferred from one person to another. Travellers sometimes try to sell the return half of their ticket, but officials can ask you to prove that you are the person named on the ticket. On an international flight, tickets are compared with passports.

date. In many large cities, 'bucket shops' – discount clearing houses – offer some of the best bargains, but some are just crooks in disguise. Check that they're licensed by the International Air Transport Association (IATA) or an equivalent national body and get the tickets before you pay.

Bucket shops usually advertise in Sunday-paper travel sections. In London, see also *Time Out*. The *Village Voice* (New York) is another good place to check.

The following sections include travel agencies specialising in Russian or discount travel from abroad.

## Other Parts of Russia

Transaero, a high-quality Russian airline offering Western-standard service aboard mostly Western-made aircraft (mainly Boeing 737s and 757s), and Pulkovo Airlines, the 'baby-flot' that previously had the route monopoly, fly between St Petersburg and Moscow.

Both also offer flights to dozens of other Russian cities and international destinations. On many routes, they are in competition with each other, with Transaero coming out a bit cheaper most times.

Tickets for both Pulkovo and Transaero can be purchased from travel agencies such as Sindbad Travel (☎ 327 83 84) at the HI St Petersburg Hostel, and from the Central Airline Ticket Office.

Within Russia, the Moscow–St Petersburg route is the most frequently travelled. There are several daily flights by Pulkovo (single/return for $110/190) and Aeroflot ($130/183).

## The UK

London is arguably the world headquarters for bucket shops, which are well advertised and usually beat published airline fares.

Intourist UK (☎ 0171-538 8600, fax 538 5967, 🅦 www.intourist.com, 219 Marsh Wall, Isle of Dogs, London E14 9FJ) may be the best of its ilk. Its office is in the Docklands and offers a huge range of tours throughout Russia, especially Moscow and St Petersburg with prices in the UK£500 to UK£700 range.

For students or travellers under 26 years, popular travel agencies in the UK include STA Travel (☎ 020-7361 6262, 🅦 www.sta travel.co.uk, 86 Old Brompton Rd, London SW7) and Usit Campus (☎ 0870-240 1010, 🅦 www.usitcampus.co.uk, 52 Grosvenor Gardens, London SW1), which both have branches throughout the UK. Both of these agencies sell tickets to all travellers but cater especially to young people and students.

There are also a growing number of discount airlines, and if you don't mind taking a roundabout way of getting to St Petersburg, these may well save you money. Most require online booking and do not issue actual tickets. Out of Ireland, Ryanair (🅦 www.ryanair.com) has incredible deals out of London and Dublin. The closest it flies to Russia is Stockholm, usually for about UK£120 return. But it sometimes has unbelievable seat sales, like London-Stockholm for UK£10 return, plus taxes. Buzz Air (🅦 www.buzzaway.com), a KLM subsidiary, has London-Helsinki returns for about UK£100, and from there, St Petersburg is just a bus or train ride away. One-way flights are possible and are usually half the price of returns.

## Continental Europe

In Germany, an awesome travel discounter for students and non-students alike is Travel Overland, with offices in several cities; for the nearest one, contact its Munich office (☎ 089-27 27 63 00, 🅦 www.travel-over land.de, Barerstrasse 73, 80799 München) or see the Web site. In Berlin, try Die Neue Reisewelle (☎ 030-323 10 78). Usit Campus (call centre ☎ 01805-788336, Cologne ☎ 0221-923990, 🅦 www.usitcampus.de) has several offices in Germany (you'll find details on the Web site), including one at 2a Zuelpicher Strasse, 50674 Cologne.

From Warsaw, the terrific folk at LOT Polish Airlines and other carriers offer round trips to St Petersburg for about $250. Expect similar fares from Prague and Budapest.

## North America

A heavily restricted discount flight from New York to St Petersburg was about $600 at the time of writing (slightly more from Los Angeles). LOT Polish Airlines often has great deals through travel agents or bucket-shop agents, sometimes as low as $399 return from New Jersey off-season.

A reliable, small travel agency with mysterious ways of finding the cheapest prices out of New York (and that can courier your ticket anywhere) is ABS Travel (☎ 212-447 1717, 800-335 1717, e abs trav@aol.com). STA Travel (☎ 800-777 0112, W www.sta travel.com) has offices in Boston, Chicago, Miami, New York, Philadelphia, San Francisco and other major cities. Call the toll-free 800 number for office locations or visit its Web site.

Ticket Planet (W www.ticketplanet.com) is a leading ticket consolidator in the USA. Travel Cuts (☎ 800-667 2887, W www.travel cuts.com) is Canada's national student travel agency and has offices in all major cities. An inexpensive online booking service is at W www.tiss.com.

## Australasia

Two well-known agents for cheap fares are STA Travel and Flight Centre. STA Travel (☎ 03-9349 2411, W www.statravel.com.au) Its main Melbourne office is at 224 Faraday St, Carlton, Victoria with offices in all major cities and on many university campuses. Call ☎ 131 776 Australiawide for the location of your nearest branch. Flight Centre (☎ 131 600 Australiawide) has a central office at 82 Elizabeth St, Sydney, and there are dozens of offices throughout Australia. Its Web address is W www.flightcentre.com.au.

In New Zealand, STA Travel (☎ 09-309 0458) has its main office at 10 High St, Auckland, and has other offices throughout the country.

## Airline Offices

All airlines accept credit cards and almost all offer same-day ticketing. Most are open from 9am to 5pm.

**Aeroflot** (☎ 327 38 72) Kazanskaya ul 5
**Air France** (☎ 325 82 52) Bol Morskaya ul 35
**Austrian Airlines** (☎ 325 32 60) Sheraton Nevskij Palace Hotel, Nevsky pr 57

**British Airways** (☎ 329 25 65) Mal Konyushennaya ul 1/3
**CSA Czech Airlines** (☎ 315 52 59) Bol Morskaya ul 36
**Delta Airlines (USA)** (☎ 311 58 19) Bol Morskaya ul 36
**Finnair** (☎ 326 18 70) Kazanskaya ul 44
**KLM** (☎ 325 89 89) Zagorodny pr 5
**LOT Polish Airlines** (☎ 273 57 21) Karavannaya ul 1
**Lufthansa** (☎ 314 49 79) Voznesensky pr 7
**Malev Hungarian Airlines** (☎ 315 54 55) Voznesensky pr 7
**Pulkovo Airline** (☎ 303 92 68) ul 1 Krasnoarmeyskaya 4
**Scandinavian Airlines System (SAS)** (☎ 325 32 55) Sheraton Nevskij Palace Hotel, Nevsky pr 57
**Swissair** (☎ 325 32 50) Sheraton Nevskij Palace Hotel, Nevsky pr 57
**Transaero** (☎ 279 64 63) Liteyny pr 48

## BUS

St Petersburg's only bus station (*avtovokzal*) is an inconvenient kilometre from Ligovsky Prospekt metro, at nab Obvodnogo kanala 36 (Map 7; ☎ 166 57 77) which serves Tampere, Vyborg, Pskov, Novgorod, Moscow, Novaya Ladoga, Petrozavodsk and many smaller destinations. Many short- and long-distance buses, however, leave from outside the Baltic Station, including all Eurolines buses.

## Finland

There's a daily bus to Tampere from the bus station, leaving at 9.30am, for $34. Finnord (Map 8; ☎ 314 89 51) runs buses to Helsinki via Vyborg and Lahti from its office at Italyanskaya ul 37. A one-way ticket costs $35. Buses leave at 3.40pm and 11pm and arrive in Helsinki at 10.30pm and 6am. From Helsinki, buses leave at 9am and 11pm, arriving at 5.35pm and 6.40am.

Sovavto (☎ 123 51 25) has two daily coaches to Helsinki and Turku via Lappeenranta, as well as two daily Vyborg-Lappeenranta-Jyväskylä buses. Its buses to Helsinki cost $40 and leave from the Grand Hotel Europe at 8.40am and 12.15pm, arriving at 3.45pm and 7.15pm respectively. From Helsinki, its buses leave at 6.45am and 11.35am, arriving at 4.30pm and 9pm.

It has several other stops in St Petersburg – call to see which is most convenient. For complete details and prices, see W www .pohjolanliikenne.fi.

## Other Countries

Eurolines (☎ 168 27 48) operates four or five daily buses to Tallinn ($11 to $14, seven to 8½ hours), and daily buses to Tartu ($10, eight hours) and Riga ($18, 11 hours). It also has two or three buses a week to Stuttgart (DM150). Eurolines' head office (Map 6) is at Shkapina ul 10 (50m west of the Baltic Station), but you can also buy tickets at its kiosk inside the Central Airline Ticket Office from 11am to 6pm Monday to Friday. Stat Express (☎ 168 20 03, fax 316 24 31), inside the Warsaw Station, has twice weekly buses to Germany, stopping in 20 cities and towns.

## TRAIN

The main international rail gateways to St Petersburg are Helsinki, Tallinn, Warsaw and Berlin. Trains leave daily from St Petersburg to these and, by connections, to many European capitals. You can also use Moscow as a gateway, opening up the possibility of more connections. Rail passes are not valid in Russia. Prices quoted here are for one-way travel; buying a return ticket is about 25% cheaper for all routes except Moscow and Helsinki. For travellers going to Hungary, the Czech Republic or Poland, make sure citizens of your country do not require a visa.

St Petersburg has four chief main-line stations. Finland Station (Finlyandsky Vokzal; Map 5; ☎ 168 76 87, pl Lenina, Vyborg Side) serves trains on the Helsinki line. South of the river, Moscow Station (Moskovsky Vokzal; Map 8; ☎ 168 43 74, pl Vosstania on Nevsky pr) handles trains to/from Moscow, the far north, Crimea, the Caucasus, Georgia and Central Asia; Vitebsk Station (Vitebsky Vokzal; Map 7; ☎ 055, Zagorodny pr 52) deals with Smolensk, Belarus, Prague, Kyiv, Odesa and Moldova; and Warsaw Station (Varshavsky Vokzal; Map 6; ☎ 168 26 90, nab Obvodnogo kanala 118) covers Estonia, Latvia, Lithuania, Pskov, Lviv (Lvov) and Eastern Europe.

Baltic Station (Baltiysky Vokzal; Map 6; ☎ 168 28 59), just along the road from Warsaw Station, is mainly for suburban trains.

## Moscow

Most of the 12 or more daily trains to Moscow take about eight hours to complete the journey, including five overnight trains. There are two express trains, the *Aurora*, leaving from St Petersburg at 4pm daily, arriving in Moscow at 9.45pm, and the *ER-200*, leaving St Petersburg at 12.05pm every Thursday and arriving in Moscow at 5.12pm. The *Aurora* leaves Moscow at 5.20pm daily; the *ER-200* leaves Moscow at 12.11pm every Friday.

Now that foreigners pay the same as Russians for their tickets, they have a dizzying range of price options, each train having its own pricing system and range of options from a place in a sitting compartment, to luxury 1st-class cabins. You can make the journey in a *kupe* (compartment) for as little as $6! The express trains will cost you about $20 to $30.

**Security** St Petersburg–Moscow trains are among the safest in Russia – well supervised and often crowded. Reports of robberies on over-night trains have decreased substantially. Nevertheless, try to get a bottom bunk and place your belongings in the bin beneath your bed when you go to sleep. Make sure that the lock on your door is operational, and flip up the steel latch – about two-thirds of the way up on the left hand side of the door – to prevent entry by thieves who may have a skeleton key to carriages. Jam a piece of paper or cork underneath the latch to prevent it being flipped down again by the keener thieves who use bent coat-hangers for that purpose.

## Finland

On the heavily travelled Helsinki-Vyborg-St Petersburg corridor the rail crossing is at Vainikkala (Luzhayka on the Russian side). There are two daily trains between St Petersburg and Helsinki. The *Repin*, a Russian-run train that's cleaner than most, departs from St Petersburg's Finland Station (Finlyandsky Vokzal) at 7.42am and arrives in Helsinki at 12.30pm. Tickets cost $54/83 sitting/kupe each way. From Helsinki, it leaves at 3.34pm and arrives at 10.37pm.

The *Sibelius*, a pleasant, Finnish-run train costs the same, and leaves St Petersburg at 5.12pm, arriving in Helsinki at 9.28pm. This train leaves Helsinki at 6.30am, getting to St Petersburg at 1.07pm.

You can save yourself about $12 by spending a lot of time: From St Pete's Finland Station, take any *elektrichka* (suburban train) to Vyborg Station, where you can meet the Helsinki-bound *Repin* at 10.44am, or the *Sibelius* at 6.52pm. The trip to Vyborg takes approximately 2½ hours and costs about $1. Double-check arrival and departure times before doing this. In St Petersburg's Finland Station, buy tickets in the separate ticket sale hall alongside platform 1.

### Czech Republic & Hungary

Prague to St Petersburg trains ($97 one way) connect through Warsaw's Central Station (Warszawa Centralna); the 10.38pm train from Prague on Friday and Sunday arrives in Warsaw at 6.50am and connects with the 9am Warsaw-Moscow train (24 hours).

Alternatively, you can stick around for the day (check out Warsaw's Old Town) and catch the night train at 12.31am from Warsaw's Gdansk Station to St Petersburg's Vitebsky Station at 8.35am (27 hours). From St Petersburg, trains leave at 2.53pm on Wednesday and Friday and arrive almost 41 hours later (at 5.41am). The Wednesday train continues on to Budapest, arriving at 7.42am.

On Friday, a St Petersburg-bound train leaves Budapest at 8.55pm, stops in Prague and leaves there at 8.38pm, and arrives in St Petersburg at 2.41pm.

### Poland

There's a service six times a week from St Petersburg to Warsaw costing $57 for *kupe* class. On Tuesday, Thursday and Sunday, trains leave at 11.45am and on Tuesday, Friday and Sunday at 11.16pm (27 to 31 hours). These trains cross at Kuznica which is near Hrodna (Grodno) in Belarus. You'll

change wheels (this takes about three hours) just east of Bialystok Station.

You are required to hold a transit visa for Belarus if your train passes through it – your Russian visa will not suffice. See Ⓦ www.belarusembassy.org for up-to-date information. A transit visa usually costs about $15 and must be acquired in advance, not at the border. Border guards have been known to force people off trains and back to where they came from if they don't have a visa.

### Estonia

Between Tallinn and St Petersburg there's one overnight train every second day ($22 one way kupe, 9 hours).

### Buying Tickets

As of 2000, there is no longer a Russian and foreigner's price: the prices were raised, and now everyone pays the same. That means you no longer have to deal with Intourist offices to get your tickets.

Therefore, you can buy tickets at the station from which your train departs (usually no problem, but the line-ups at the Moscow Station, especially in the summertime, can keep you waiting for hours). Trains departing 24 hours or less after ticket purchase can only be bought at the train station.

You can also buy tickets from the Central Train Ticket Office (Map 8; ☎ 162 33 44, nab kanala Griboedova 24). It's open 8am to 8pm Monday to Saturday and 8am to 4pm Sunday.

Signs directing you to the appropriate window are in English. For international destinations, use window Nos 1 to 3 on the left as you enter. You can also book in advance by telephone (☎ 162 44 55).

Another option is buying your tickets at the Central Airline Office. It adds a $2.50 commission, but there's usually not much of a line-up.

Many popular routes within Russia are booked weeks ahead of time in summertime (from St Petersburg, especially all southbound trains!), so get your tickets as much in advance as possible. Sindbad

Travel at the HI St Petersburg Hostel issues Moscow tickets and discounted Helsinki tickets on the spot. It also has a ticket-buying service for those who just can't deal with the folk at the stations (it tacks about $5 onto the ticket price).

## CAR & MOTORCYCLE

See the Getting Around chapter for specific driving tips for St Petersburg.

Driving in Russia is *truly* an unfiltered Russian experience. Poor roads, inadequate signposting (except in St Petersburg's centre) and overly keen highway patrollers can lead to frustration and dismay.

Motorbikes aren't a great idea here. They will undergo vigorous scrutiny by border officials and highway police, especially if you're riding anything vaguely Ninja-ish. Mostly they'll just be personally curious about make, model and price. Motorcycles are almost never seen in the city, where the ones that don't fall into bottomless potholes will attract unwanted attention. If you ever need repairs, parts will be hard to come by.

### Car Rental

Not every car rental agency in neighbouring countries will let you take their cars into Russia. From Helsinki, try Transvell (☎ 0800-8000 7000 toll-free from Finland), which can set you up but for about $90 a day. From Estonia, Avis (☎ 631 59 30, W www.avis.ee, Liivalaia tänav 12, Tallinn) charges an extra $70 for the needed notarised permission, on top of its already stellar prices.

### Departure Tax

A departure road tax of about $10 is collected at the border.

### The Basics

To be allowed to drive your own or a rented car/motorcycle in Russia you'll need to be 18 years old and have a full driving licence. In addition, you'll need an International Driving Permit with a Russian translation of your licence, or a certified Russian translation of your full licence (you can certify translations at a Russian embassy or consulate).

You will also need your vehicle's registration papers and proof of insurance. Be sure your insurance covers you in Russia. Finally, a customs declaration promising that you will take your vehicle with you when you leave is also required.

Speed limits are generally 60km/h in cities and between 80 and 100km/h on highways. Russians drive on the right and traffic coming from the right has the right of way. Children under 12 may not travel in the front seat, and safety belt use is supposedly mandatory. Motorcyclists (and passengers) must wear a crash helmet.

Technically, it is legal to have a blood-alcohol level of up to 0.04%, but driving after any alcohol consumption at all is not suggested.

### Border Crossings

You'll first pass the neighbouring country's border point where you'll need to show your vehicle registration and insurance papers, your driving licence, passport and visa. These formalities are usually minimal for Western citizens.

On the Russian side, chances are your vehicle will be subjected to a thorough inspection by border guards. You pass through customs separately from your car, walking through a metal detector and possibly having hand luggage X-rayed.

### BOAT

If you thought the break-up of Aeroflot was something, wait till you see what's happened to Russian shipping services. Russian shipping services have been seriously curtailed over the past couple of years. There are currently no scheduled passenger ships to and from St Petersburg, but if they start up again, they'll dock at the Sea Terminal (Morskoy Vokzal; Map 6; ☎ 322 60 52) at the west end of Bolshoy pr on Vasilevsky Island.

Baltic Lines (☎ 355 16 16; W www .baltics.ru) has not had regular passenger cruises since 1996, but some day they may revive the route to Stockholm.

Call to check current status – they'll be happy to chat with you as they don't have much else going on. They can book other Scandinavian cruises for you, though. Their US agent (EuroCruises) can be contacted on ☎ 212-366 4747 or (toll-free) ☎ 800-688 3876.

## River Cruises

A great option to prolong your trip and see more of the country is to consider a cruise. In summer, passenger boats ply the rivers and canals between Moscow and St Petersburg. The route follows the Neva River to Lake Ladoga, sometimes up to Valaam, to the Svir River and Lake Onega to Kizhi, the Volga-Baltic canal to the Rybinskoe Reservoir and through some of the Golden Ring along the Volga to Moscow.

The River Terminal (Rechnoy Vokzal; Map 3; ☎ 262 13 18, ☎ 262 02 39, pr Obukhovskoy oborony 195), near metro Proletarskaya (turn right upon exiting and take any tram one stop) sells a wide variety of excellent cruises to Moscow, from five to 14 days long, taking in different routes. Ships make eight- and 12-day trips to Moscow via Valaam, Kizhi, Yaroslavl and many other stops from $250 to $450 all included. They also offer cruises to Kizhi and Valaam; four different boats a day leave to either or both on two to four-day cruises. Prices for these cruises average from $125 to $200. You can buy tickets directly from them.

If you don't get anywhere with the River Terminal staff, get more information on the expansive range of cruises available at Cruise Russia (Map 7; ☎ 164 69 47, W www .cruise-ru.com, Ligovsky pr 87), through which you can book online. It helps to call first, though, as schedules change. Prices are pretty much the same as the River Terminal itself; they all book the same boats in any case. To book through a travel agent, Sindbad or Ost-West could help you out.

## HITCHING

Though the hitchhiking culture is not as ingrained in Russian society as in other countries (the fear of robbery is greater here), you'll always eventually find someone who'll stop their car for you (the desire for financial compensation is greater here). Of-

fering a small sum is usually expected. However, the amazing folk at Russia's Academy of Free Travelling (W www .avp.travel.ru) out of Moscow have literally made a science of figuring out how to travel far and wide for next to nothing, mainly by hitchhiking (they calculate that the average speed you can travel this way in Russia is 55km/h). The fascinating Web site, though all in Russian, will give you details and hints on how to do this. Using the schedule of all suburban trains in Russia, you can combine cheap train with cheaper hitchhiking to get anywhere. If you worry about the possibility or safety of finding a lift in remote Russian areas, the site will assure you once and for all that anything is possible in Russia – the trick is just finding out how to do it.

For more links on all things related to hitchhiking in Russia, see W www.auto stop.ly/links.html#rus.

## ORGANISED TOURS

Although you can advance-book a wide array of tours with (likely much cheaper) Russian-based tour and travel agencies, or do it once you arrive, if you wish to prepare from home, these agencies can do great work for you. In the following tours, prices are always higher for individuals travelling alone.

## The UK

Russian Gateway (W www.russiangate way.fsnet.co.uk) is the leader in British-run tours throughout Russia. It offers ballet tours to Moscow and St Petersburg as well as a host of city tours, plus more adventurous trips to the Russian Far East. Its Moscow–St Petersburg river cruises start at UK£920. It also sells domestic train tickets but at much inflated prices.

Travel For The Arts (☎ 0207-483 4466, fax 0297-586 0639, W www.travelfort hearts.co.uk, 117 Regent's Park Rd, London NW1 8UR) organises luxury 'culture'-based tours to St Petersburg and other European cities for people with a specific interest in opera and ballet. It runs well-organised theme tours starting from UK£1495, including airfare, transfers, half-board and accommodation at the Astoria Hotel. Its five-day White Nights Festival tour costs from UK£650 to UK£995.

## North America

General Tours (☎ 603-357 5033, toll-free ☎ 800-221 2216, 53 Summer St, Keene, NH 03431) is a well-established company offering a wide range of tours, fully and partially guided, including flights, transfers, accommodation with breakfast, city, palace and Hermitage tours. These cost from $1069 to $1329, depending on how many stars you insist your hotel has. Prices are slightly higher in midsummer.

EuroCruises (☎ 212-366 4747 or toll-free in the US ☎ 800-688 3876, 303 W 13th St, New York, NY 10032) is the US agent for Baltic Lines, the Russian company that runs four-day visa-free cruises from Helsinki, which give you two days in St Petersburg and Petrodvorets to quickly see the sights without having to get a visa (you sleep on the boat, see). Tours costs from $419 to $999.

## Australia

Eastern Europe Travel Bureau (☎ 02-9262 1144, fax 9262 4479, e eetb@optus net.com.au, 75 King St, Sydney 2000) does budget tours (airfares not included): Moscow and St Petersburg, eight days from A$845; and three- to five-day tours in St Petersburg cost from A$251 to A$482 (shared twin; singles are more expensive). It also offers visa assistance, organises river cruises and arranges homestays in Moscow or St Petersburg.

Passport Travel, the representative of Red Bear Tours (☎ 03-9867 3888, fax 9867 1055, W www.travelcentre.com.au, 11a 410 St Kilda Rd, Melbourne 3004) can arrange visa invitations, independent travel, language courses, Trans-Siberian Railway

tours and much more, and the low prices show that, unlike many tour operators, it understands what things really cost in Russia and don't try to bleed clients. A Moscow–St Petersburg combined tour costs from US$344. Check out the great Web site.

## Finland

The very helpful and friendly Eurohostel (☎ 09-62 20 47, fax 65 50 44) works closely with the Russian Youth Hostel Association and can help with paperwork and visa support. It can provide bus and train schedules and assist with car rental. It's also on the IBN HI reservations system. It's located just off the Silja Lines port in Helsinki at Linnankatu 9 and is a key source in Helsinki for Russia-related travel information.

RTT Matkapalvelut Travel Agency (☎ 09-65 90 52, Laivasillankatu 14, Helsinki), near the Russian embassy, has a very handy deal on its visa invitations (see Visas in the Facts for the Visitor chapter) and can also book discounted hotel rooms in St Petersburg and help you rent a car.

Finnsov Tours (☎ 09-694 20 11, W www .finnsov.fi, Eerikinkatu 3, Helsinki) offers short package tours from Helsinki to St Petersburg and other Russian cities by train, bus and ship. It has a three-day and two-night train tour to St Petersburg for $330 to $770 (depending on hotel), inclusive of tours, hotel, meals and transport. Bus tours are cheaper. The cost does not include a visa, and there are dozens of rather pricey add-ons.

## Estonia

Luminary (☎ 372-646 6399, e luminary@infonet.ee, Estonia puiestee 7) organises excursions throughout Russia, including a three-day trip from Tallinn to St Petersburg and Petrodvorets for about $55 including accommodation and food.

# Getting Around

St Petersburg's excellent public transport system makes getting around the entire city very simple and inexpensive. An army of buses, trolleys, trams, taxi-buses and express micro-buses (minibuses, vans) serve the centre and outlying areas. The centre, especially Nevsky pr, is best seen on foot.

Getting a copy of a transport map, like the one published by Karta, is a great idea if you'll be using public transport – it shows every bus, trolleybus, tram, metro and even micro-bus route in the city (see Maps in the Facts for the Visitor chapter).

## TO/FROM THE AIRPORT

St Petersburg's airports (Map 3) are at Pulkovo, 17km south of the centre. The cheapest do-it-yourself transport is metro plus bus. From Moskovskaya metro (not Moskovskie Vorota), cross Moskovsky pr (via the underground passageway) and at the bus stop on your left, wait for bus No 39 to Pulkovo-1, the domestic terminal, or bus No 13 to Pulkovo-2, the international terminal, each taking about 15 minutes for the journey. There are also micro-buses (they'll have either No 39 or No 13 on them too) making the journey even quicker. Total expenditure from the centre to the airport: about $0.35. On the bus, you may be charged an extra ticket if you have a large suitcase.

From Pulkovo-2, take bus No 13 to Moskovskaya metro: exit the arrivals terminal, turn left, decline all enthusiastic offers for a taxi ride and wait at the closest of the two bus stops.

Shuttle buses run between the domestic and international terminals, costing about $2.

Taking a taxi from the city is cheaper than from the airport. From the city, hailing down a private car is your cheapest bet – they'll do it for about $6. A registered cab will ask at least $10. If you're coming from the airport, you'll be introduced to the taxi 'Mafia': a bunch of thugs controlling who can park and wait for fares there. If there's a whiff of accent in your speech, they'll ask

$40 to get you into town, then bring it down to $30 if you complain and walk away (that's 20m on to the bus No 13 stop!).

You can also fax in advance one of the car rental agencies (see Car & Motorcycle in this chapter), and they'll pick you up, for about the same as the 'Mafia' would charge (except Astoria Service, ☎ 112 15 83, which could do this for under $20). If you're staying at any of the luxury hotels in town, or if your hotel package includes transfers, you'll be met by bus or minivan.

## TO/FROM THE SEA TERMINAL

The Vasilevsky Island Sea Terminal (Map 6) is on the bus No 7 and trolleybus No 10 routes which leave from near the Hermitage.

## TO/FROM THE TRAIN STATIONS

All train stations are at or near metro stations, and taxis are easily found at each of them. You can walk past the taxi 'Mafia' and hail your own once you reach the main roads (see the boxed text 'Going My Way' later in this chapter).

## METRO

Though less majestic than Moscow's, the St Petersburg metro leaves most of the world's other 'undergrounds' for dead. You'll rarely wait more than two minutes for a train during the day (even at 6am on a Sunday, the wait will be about five minutes); the clock at the end of the platform shows time elapsed since the last train departed. The grandest stations are on Line 1 (see the boxed text 'Metro Fun Facts' later in this chapter). Stations open around 5.30am and close around 12.30am.

Taking the metro is the quickest way around the wider city and tokens (zhetony) cost only R5 ($0.18).

Note that due to a cave-in of a section of a tunnel in 1995 (despite multi-million dollar foreign loans, they're still working to fix it), there is an interruption in Line 1 service north of the city. Lesnaya and Ploshchad Muzhestva

## Metro Fun Facts!

Most tourists see the outside of the Ploshchad Vosstania metro station and think, 'And what museum could that be?'. Welcome to the St Petersburg metro with its themed stations, grand, ornamental (sometime gaudy) decor and endless, streaming escalators.

The first metro line opened on 15 November 1955; planned 15 years earlier, the war delayed construction. At that time, the metro connected Avtovo and Ploshchad Vosstania, and the stations on this stretch are among the most dazzling, designed to impress upon all the glory of the Soviet Union.

Avtovo takes the cake as the most awesome (garish or beautiful, depending on your taste): on the downstairs platform are 46 columns, 30 of which are covered in white marble, 16 in cut, decorative glass. Kirovsky Zavod is a paean to Leningrad's pursuit of technological progress. Dostoevskaya recreates the atmosphere of the writer's time. Ploshchad Muzhestva embodies the mourning and sombre mood of nearby Piskaryovskoe cemetery. Ploshchad Vosstania is a five-star tribute to the revolution.

The metro also doubles as a bomb shelter – note the massive steel plates under the floors or along the walls at the thresholds between the platform and the escalator. These could, in an emergency, close tight shut.

The metro can also be a source of entertainment. A favourite pastime of residents is to stare at the people on the escalator opposite to theirs – there's a fascinating cross-section of society to be gleaned, and observing the facial expressions or interactions between people is like watching a documentary film about life in contemporary Russia. If your mother told you not to stare, you can just relax and listen to the recorded announcements boomed into the station – either advertisements for an exciting linoleum store, or else grandmotherly instructions on how to behave properly in the metro. Give your seat to the elderly; stand on the right on the escalator; make sure your bags don't get in someone's way...

A few fun facts:

- St Petersburg's metro is the world's deepest; the average depth of the stations is 60m below ground.
- At present there are 56 stations connected by tunnels 94.4km long; plans are to eventually add two more lines which would double the overall length.
- The average distance between stations is 1.9km; the longest is almost 3km (between Obukhovo and Rybatskoe).
- In any given hour, between 25,000 and 47,000 people ride the metro.
- About 22,000 sq metres of marble and over 10,000 sq metres of granite have gone into the construction of the metro stations.
- Many of the tunnels between stations are ingeniously formed in a slight 'V' shape, so that trains use the force of inertia gained by going 'downhill' so as to use less energy overall.

are connected by a free shuttle-bus service (Bus No 80). This should affect only those tourists interested in visiting the Piskayovskoe Cemetery or the Kruglye banya.

## Using the Metro

Buy your tokens from the booths in the stations, place them in the entry gates, and walk through. Even cheaper, and more convenient than the tokens are seven, 15 and 30-day multi-ride pass-cards with a magnetic strip which are sold at all metro stations in multiples of 10, 20, 25, 40, 50 or 70 rides. All metro stations have card-reading turnstiles – place your card in the slot and when it comes back out you'll have a green light to proceed if there's sufficient credit left on the card.

To anyone for whom Cyrillic is nothing more than pretty little symbols mixed in with the occasional 'English' letter, getting around the metro can be a bit of an adventure. Some (10) station platforms have outer safety doors, so you can't see the station from an arriving train; also, you can't rely on spotting the signs on the platforms as you pull in. Furthermore, the announcements in the carriages are confusing: just before a departing train's doors close, a recorded voice announces '*Ostorozhno! Dveri zakryvayutsya. Sleduyushchaya stantsia* (name of next station)'. This means 'Caution! The doors are closing. Next station (name of next station).' Just before the train stops at the next station, its name is announced. In case you don't catch these the surest way of getting off at the right station is to count the stops.

Metro stations are mostly identified from outside by big 'M' signs. To exit to the street, follow signs saying 'Выход в город' '*Vykhod v gorod*', meaning 'Exit to the city'. If there's more than one exit, each sign names the street you will come out on. If you need to change to another line, the process is much the same whether the line passes through the same station or through a nearby one linked by underground walkways. The word to look for is 'Переход' '*perekhod*', meaning 'passage-way', often with a blue-background man-on-stairs sign, followed by 'на станцию...' '*na stantsiyu*...' (to ... station) then usually 'к поездам до станций ...' '*ke poezdam do stantsiy ...*' (to trains to ... stations).

## BUS, TROLLEYBUS & TRAM

A R4 ($0.14) ticket *(bilet)* is used on all buses, trolleybuses (electric buses) and trams. You must buy these from a ticketseller on the inside.

Bus stops are marked by 'A' signs (for *avtobus*), trolleybus stops by 'П' (representing a handwritten Russian 'T') on signs by the roadside, tram stops by a 'T' sign over the roadway, all usually indicating the line numbers too. Stops may also have roadside signs with little pictures of a bus, trolleybus or tram. Most transport runs from 6am to 1am.

The following are some important long routes across the city:

• Along Nevsky pr between the Admiralty and Moscow Station: bus Nos 7, 44; trolleybus

Nos 1, 5, 7, 10, 22. Trolleybus Nos 1 and 22 continue out to Hotel Moskva and Alexandr Nevsky Monastery. Trolleybus Nos 5 and 7 continue to Smolny.
• From the Hermitage to the Pribaltiyskaya Hotel on Vasilevsky Island: bus No 7; trolleybus No 10.
• To the Kamenny Islands: tram No 34 from the Baltic Station or Liteyny pr just north of Nevsky pr goes along Kamennoostrovsky pr and ends up on Krestovsky Island. Bus No 10 from the corner of Bol Morskaya ul and Nevsky pr will also get you there.
• From near the Primorskaya metro station bus No 128 runs along both Bolshoy prospekts ending up on the Petrograd Side at the Botanical Gardens.

## CAR & MOTORCYCLE

The best way of getting around the city by road is on a bus. St Petersburg's roads are gnarled, its laws are strange, and the *semper vigilans* eyes of the DPS goons (traffic cops, seen, seemingly, on every city corner), who are empowered to stop you and fine you on the spot, are always on you. Oh, yeah, they can also *shoot* at your vehicle if you don't heed their command to pull over, which is a wave of their striped stick towards your car.

### Driving Tips

See the Getting There & Away chapter for information on national driving regulations and border crossings with your car. Left turns are illegal except where posted; you'll have to make three rights or a short U-turn (this is safer?). Street signs, except in the centre (where they have been sponsored by advertisers), are woefully inadequate and Russian drivers make Italian drivers seem downright courteous! Watch out for drivers overtaking on the inside, which would appear to be the national sport. There are potholes and jagged crevices everywhere – straddle them.

### Rental

Renting a car here is now a pretty simple thing, though as with most simple things in Russia, it's inordinately expensive; following are some agencies offering self-drive and chauffeured vehicles:

**Astoria Service** (Map 7; ☎ 112 15 83, 164 96 22, ul Borovaya 11/13) Rents cars with friendly drivers only for the most reasonable rates – from $3.50 an hour for an old Zhiguli to $12 an hour for a Mercedes (minimum three hours).

**Hertz** (☎ 324 32 42, @ hertz-led@peterlink.ru, Pulkovo-2 airport) Compact Fords for about $420 a week, all included. Transfer service from the airport to the centre for $30.

**Svit** (☎ 356 93 29, Pribaltiyskaya Hotel) Rents Fords with drivers for $20 per hour.

## Fuel

By Western standards, fuel prices are quite low, though residents were faced with sharp price rises in 2000. In early 2001, petrol prices here were about $0.37 a litre for the most popular 92 octane fuel and $0.46 for 95 octane. In addition to state-run filling stations, Neste currently operates over 15 full-service filling stations in and around St Petersburg that charge more for petrol but offer faster service and accept major credit cards. You can get leaded and unleaded fuel at the following places in St Petersburg:

Teatralnaya pl
Aleksandrovsky park
nab reki Fontanki 156
Maly pr (Vasilevsky Island) 68A (Neste)
Pulkovskoe sh 32A & 38 (Neste)
Moskovsky pr 100 (Neste)
Savushkina ul 87 (Neste)

## Parking

In the town's centre uniformed parking attendants charge about $1 to watch your car for you. There are guarded parking lots outside many hotels now – use them when you can. Never leave anything of value, including sunglasses, cassette tapes and cigarettes, in a car. Street parking is pretty much legal wherever it seems to be; it's illegal anywhere on Nevsky pr. Use common sense – avoid parking in dark side streets and isolated areas.

## Emergencies

The law says that when you have an accident you're supposed to remain at the scene until the DPS arrive; in practice, if the damage isn't major, most people would rather leave than add insult (a fine) to injury.

### Raising the Bridges

Many of St Petersburg's main bridges are raised every night when the Neva isn't frozen over to let seagoing ships through. The following schedule (which every year sometimes changes by five minutes here or there) governs the lives of the city's motorists and nighthawks trying to get from one area to another. Watching them raise is also a favourite, romantic activity of locals and foreigners alike.

**Dvortcovy** (Map 6), 1.55am to 3.05am & 3.15am to 4.45am
**Troitsky** (Map 5), 2am to 4.40am
**Leytenanta Shmidta** (Map 6), 1.55am to 4.50am
**Birzhevoy** (Map 4), 2.25am to 3.20am & 3.40am to 4.40am
**Tuchkov** (Map 4), 2.20am to 3.10am & 3.40am to 4.40am
**Liteyny** (Map 5), 2.10am to 4.35am
**Alexandra Nevskogo** (Map 7), 2.35am to 4.50am
**Petra Velikogo** (Map 7), 12.30am to 4.45am

Lenavtotekhnika (☎ 001) is a towing company that will come and get you 24 hours a day. Spas (☎ 327 70 01) will do the same. There are a number of foreign car service centres in town (check *Luchshee V Sankt Peterburge*); they include Chrysler (☎ 591 07 50), Swed-Mobil (Volvo; ☎ 225 40 51) and Laura (Opel, Chevrolet; ☎ 327 54 45).

## TAXI

Official taxis (four-door Volga sedans with a chequerboard strip down the side and a green light in the front window) have a meter that the drivers sometimes use, though you most often pay a negotiated price.

Most often, however, people use unofficial taxis, ie, anything you can stop (see the boxed text 'Going My Way?').

If you can't be bothered with such shenanigans, you can hire a cab with Peterbursky Taxi (☎ 068), New Service (☎ 327 24 00) or Taxi na Zakaz (☎ 100 00 00).

To rent out cars with drivers for longer excursions, see Car & Motorcycle.

GETTING AROUND

## Going My Way?

Like many other elements of Russian life, the process of getting a cab is at once extremely simple and also riddled with complications. Sure there are official taxis in St Petersburg (they're the ones that look like taxis), but no-one uses *those*! They're likely to charge more (especially if they're standing waiting on Nevsky pr) and besides, they're no fun – you don't have to negotiate your fare with them.

By standing on practically any sidewalk in town and sticking your arm out, palm facing down, you can be assured that within less than a minute, a car will stop for you. Usually it's a ruddy little Lada or Zhiguli, but it can be anything – a snazzier car, an off-duty city bus, an army Jeep with driver in camouflage. This is someone who allegedly just happens to be going your way and will do you a favour of dropping you off – just as you'll do the favour of paying him for it.

The driver is most likely someone who drives around a few hours each day trying to supplement his meagre income and bring something extra home to his family. For some, it is the main or only source of income.

So, you've stuck your arm out, a car has stopped. This is where the fun starts. You open the door and shout out your destination, say, '*ulitsa Marata!*'. The driver looks away for a second and shouts back '*skolko?*' (how much?). You bark back a price, and if he's happy with that amount, he'll say, '*sadites!*' (sit down!) at which point you get in and drive off.

It could get more complicated, though. In response to your suggested price, he could answer back a fare 10 or 20 roubles higher, at which point you look away for a second and either say '*davai*' (OK) or '*poyekhali!*' (let's go!) or else a gruff '*nyet!*', slam the door shut and wave another car down.

If you feel that the driver is trying to rip you off because of your accent, shut the door. If there is more than one person in the car, do not get in. And if the driver strikes you as creepy, let him drive on. There'll be another car coming in a flash.

Alternatively, the driver might not ask you for a price and just tell you to get in or not depending on whether he wants to go your way. If that's the case, at the end of the ride, you pay him what you think the fare was worth. The official taxi rate is R8 ($0.28) per kilometre, but a better barometer of an accepted price is time – depending on traffic, if your ride is under five minutes long, R20 to R30 ($0.72 to $1.07) is acceptable. For R50 ($1.80) you can travel for almost 10 minutes and go about 5km. To go from the Hermitage to the Moscow Station, R30 is fine.

Depending on your financial situation, it's best to err on the side of generosity – all things considered, it's still a cheap way to get around, and the extra 10 or 20 roubles will undoubtedly mean more to him than to you.

As a bonus, very often these drivers are personable fellows you wouldn't ordinarily meet on your trip, and chatting with them (about the potholes, Putin, whatever) can be a lot of fun.

## Risks & Precautions

Generally speaking both standard and private taxis are safe. Now and then tales crop up of rip-offs or robberies in taxis. Russian citizens rather than foreigners seem to be the chief victims, but you are advised to take sensible precautions.

The following tips refer to both official and unofficial taxis, though the former are generally safer than the latter.

- Avoid taxis lurking outside foreign-run establishments, luxury hotels etc – they charge far too much and get uppity when you try to talk them down.
- Know your route – be familiar with how to get there and how long it should take.
- Keep your fare money in a separate pocket to avoid flashing large wads of cash.
- Have the taxi stop at the corner nearest your destination, not the specific address, if you're staying at a private residence.
- Check the back seat of the car for hidden friends before you get in.

## BOAT

In this 'Venice of the North' there is surprisingly no scheduled water-based public transport other than tour boats and hydrofoil and ferry services to Petrodvorets, Kronshtadt and Lomonosov. There is also a wide range of river and canal boat cruises, with the possibility of renting out a private boat (see Organised Tours).

## BICYCLE

St Petersburg is a bad place to ride a bike – bumpy, pothole-filled roads and lunatic drivers not accustomed to seeing cyclists make it a dangerous proposition. It's a very nice pastime outside the centre or through the parks, though, particularly throughout the Kirovsky Islands.

One wonderful bicycle ride – wonderful, that is, once you are south of the airport – is to head due south on Moskovsky pr. Once you pass the airport, you're suddenly in lovely countryside. At the turn off (there's a statue of Pushkin and the sign points south to Kiev and east to the town of Pushkin) turn left and you'll get to Pushkin Palace. It's a long (about 25km) ride, but

you can take the *elektrichka* train back to St Petersburg.

Lock your bike before you leave it, preferably with a Kryptonite or other 'U'-type lock and not just a chain and padlock.

If you think biking to Pushkin is a heroic feat, check out Dan Buettner's excellent book *Sovietrek: A Journey by Bicycle Across Russia* (1994). His trek across Russia was completed in 124 days in 1990. The Bicycle Club of Russia (W www.bigfoot.com/~rctc) organises expeditions that you can join

## WALKING

The best way to get around St Petersburg is to combine walking with public transport. Distances are not too taxing but the roads and footpaths are not in the best condition. Even the renovated sidewalks have drainage grooves you can trip over. Bring good, comfortable walking shoes and some foot rub for day's end.

## ORGANISED TOURS
### City Tours

You'll have your pick of them here. Tour buses leave throughout the day (usually until 2pm or 3pm) from the west end of Gostiny Dvor, from outside Kazan Cathedral and from Dvortsovaya Pl. These are either city tours or excursions to Pushkin and Pavlovsk, Petrodvorets or Kronshtadt. The tours usually cost under $4, but are all in Russian.

Eclectica (Map 8; ☎ 275 05 53, e reception@eclectica.spb.ru, W www.eclectica.spb.ru, Ligovsky pr 1, office No 313) has some 200 city theme tours (all the expected plus Pushkin, Catherine the Great, Swedes in Petersburg etc) up its long sleeve, and can give them in different languages, with enough advance notice. They are more geared towards groups, even small ones, and can handle groups of 50 at a time and provides transportation.

Another reliable firm is the City Excursion Bureau (Map 7; ☎ 312 05 27, fax 311 40 19, Sadovaya ul 26/28) at the Apraxin Dvor. It does city and suburb tours for groups of two or three to 30 people in English, German and French. It also offers tours of the Hermitage and Russian Museum ($20

GETTING AROUND

each per group) and to any palace in or outside the city ($12 per group).

For something more exotic, try Monomex Tours (☎ 445 01 59, fax 324 73 22, W www .2russia.com, Zanevsky pr 1) which has experience organising conferences for business groups but also gives intriguingly-titled sociological tours like Russian Child Rearing Practices and Police Enforcement. Check out the Web site for more info.

The Tourist Information Office (see Tourist Offices in the Facts for the Visitor chapter) can also suggest other possibilities.

## Personal Guides

Peter Kozyrev runs the excellent Peter's Tours (☎ 329 80 18, e petertour@ yahoo.co.uk), walking tours which leave the HI St Petersburg Hostel at 10.30am daily. He offers several cool variations, like a Dostoevsky walking tour, a visit to the city's outlying areas, and, more rarely nowadays, a rooftops tour, as well as other custom-made tours depending on your interests. He's ultra knowledgeable and laid-back, but most importantly, his passion for the city is infectious. He usually charges $8 per person for a four to five-hour walk.

Sasha Bogdanov (☎ 322 75 00, 314 57 05) is an affable and eccentric character who offers unique tours of the city. His knowledge of the city is encyclopaedic and his range wide, equally at home with students and the elderly. His speciality is providing alternative experiences of the city, taking people to off-beat nooks and crannies tourists rarely see, to discover the pulse of the contemporary city. His going rate is $20 a day.

## River & Canal Tours

From May to October excursion boats ply the rivers and canals of St Petersburg at all hours of the day. No matter how pressed for time you are, or your aversion for touristy-looking activities, don't leave the city without taking one of these, even if the excursions are most often given in Russian only. It's romantic enough to just look at the scenery.

There are many to choose from – all sizes of boats offering excursions are found at the Anichkov most landing on the Fontanka River, just off Nevsky pr; at the Hermitage No 2 landing just east of the Dvortsovy most; at a small landing on the west side of the Dvortsovy most in front of the Admiralty; at the Dekabristov landing; along the Griboedova Canal, just north of Nevsky pr and one block south near the Bankovsky most; and along the Moyka River at Nevsky pr and one block south.

Prices and frequency range, but you can expect to pay $5 for a 40-minute ride. The cheapest ones leave from in front of the Admiralty ($2 for 30 minutes). The tours are longer from the Anichkov most (about 75 minutes for $7).

Most all boat trips will cruise along the Neva and dip into the city's rivers and canals, passing by the Church on Spilled Blood, and under some of the city's most famous bridges. Some will go further south along the Moyka and Fontanka Rivers. Only the larger boats (which mainly leave from the Dekabristov landing) will have on-board cafes – otherwise bring your own champagne.

There are also plenty of opportunities to use small boats as your own private water taxis. With boats docked along the Griboedova Canal and Moyka River, and near the Hermitage No 2 landing, you haggle your way to being put-putted anywhere you like. Prices may start at $60 an hour, but you can often get down to around $40 an hour or less for a small group. You can do whatever you like on the rides – the drivers have already seen it all.

## Helicopter Tours

Now that aviation restrictions have been loosened, helicopter tours are much more common. You still can't fly directly over the city centre, but you can fly over the Neva, between the Admiralty and the Peter & Paul Fortress and over to Smolny. Baltic Airlines (☎ 311 00 84, 104 16 76) flights leave from the beach in front of the Peter & Paul Fortress on weekends; just show up and wait to join a tour ($35 for 10 to 15 minutes). You can also arrange a parachute jump for $200.

The Hermitage

**S**et in a magnificent palace from which tsars ruled Russia for one-and-a-half centuries, the State Hermitage **(Map 7)** (*Gosudarstvenny ermitazh;* ☎ *311 34 65,* Ⓦ *www .hermitage museum.org, Dvortsovaya nab 34*) fully lives up to its reputation as one of the world's great art museums. You can be absorbed for days by its treasures and still come out wishing for more time.

The enormous collection almost amounts to a history of Western European art, displaying a full range of artists such as Rembrandt, Rubens, Picasso and Matisse, and schools including the Florentine and Venetian Renaissance, impressionism and post-impressionism. There are also prehistoric, ancient classical, Egyptian, Russian and Oriental sections, plus excellent temporary exhibitions. The wealth of the collection itself is limitless – as much as you see in the museums, there's about 20 times more in its vaults. Some famed Fabergé jewels, for example, are only on display during certain temporary exhibitions.

The vastness of the place – five main buildings, of which the Winter Palace alone has 1057 rooms and 117 staircases – and its huge number of visitors (more than three million annually) demand a little planning. It may be useful to make a reconnaissance tour first, then return another day to enjoy your favourite parts.

The State Hermitage consists of five linked buildings along riverside Dvortsovaya nab – from west to east they are the **Winter Palace**, the **Little Hermitage**, the **Old** and **New Hermitages** (sometimes grouped together and called the Large Hermitage) and the **Hermitage Theatre**. The art collection is on all three floors of the Winter Palace and the main two floors of the Little and Large Hermitages. The Hermitage Theatre is open for special events, mainly concerts.

Though the rooms listed in our room-by-room guide should in principle be open during your visit, occasionally some will be closed without warning for maintenance or other mysterious reasons. If the painting you came to Russia to see is inaccessible, ask one of the guard ladies when it is expected to open again.

## History

The present baroque/rococo Winter Palace was commissioned from Rastrelli in 1754 by Empress Elizabeth. Yet it had three predecessors, which all stood near the embankment, between the Admiralty and the tiny Zimnaya Canal. The first was built in 1711, but was replaced by number two, built between 1716 and 1720. Peter the Great died in that one in 1725 (it was situated at the site of the present-day Hermitage Theatre). Empress Anna decided to have another stab at it in the early 1730s, engaging a young Bartolomeo Rastrelli. It was enthusiastically built upon and redeveloped in the 1740s, but (lucky for us) the whims of Empress Elizabeth were still not satisfied.

Elizabeth ordered Rastrelli to give it a final go in 1754, closely supervising the ensuing building's construction and design. Sadly, she didn't survive to occupy it. She was living in a temporary residence specially

**Previous page:** The Hermitage Building
**Photographer:** Steve Kokker

built by Rastrelli for her, a so-called Wooden Hermitage (between present-day Bol Morskaya ul and the Moyka near Nevsky pr) and died there in December 1761, only a few months before the Winter Palace was finally completed.

Catherine the Great and her successors didn't much care for Rastrelli's baroque interiors and had most of the rooms completely remodelled in classical style by the 1830s. They didn't touch the exteriors, however, and left the Jordan Staircase and the Cathedral alone.

The classical Little Hermitage was built for Catherine the Great as a retreat that would also house the art collection started by Peter the Great. At the river end of the Large Hermitage is the Old Hermitage which also dates from her time. At its south end, facing Millionnaya ul, is the New Hermitage, which was built for Nicholas I to hold the still-growing art collection and to turn it into a public museum.

The Hermitage Theatre (where plays would be performed for the imperial family) was built in the 1780s by the classicist Giacomo Quarenghi, who thought it one of his finest works. Rossi later reworked it.

In December 1837, a devastating fire broke out in the heating shaft of the Field Marshals' Hall; it burned for over 30 hours and destroyed a large portion of the interior. Most of the imperial belongings were saved, thrown out of windows or dragged outside to sit in the snow. Nicholas I vowed to restore the palace as quickly as possible, and by using as many as 10,000 exhausted workers at a time, had it pretty much looking like it had before in only 15 months. Architects and designers Stasov and Bryullov headed the operation. Huge furnaces burned day and night inside the palace, raising the temperature to nearly 30°C to dry the paint faster. In winter, workers fell seriously ill, some even dying, from the drastic drop in temperature after leaving the building.

From Catherine's time on, the palace was used as the imperial family's residence (her murdered husband Peter III was its first inhabitant, but only for three months). There were some exceptions: Catherine's son, Paul I, had an entire castle built for himself (the Engineer's Castle) only to be murdered in it after 40 days of occupancy; and Alexander III and Nicholas II both preferred to spend their time at the Anichkov Palace (Nicholas II eventually resided most of the time in the Alexander Palace in Pushkin).

After the February 1917 Revolution, the seat of the Provisional Government under Karensky was placed here, but only for a few months – they were arrested in the Small Dining Room on 26 October 1917. During the revolution, the Winter Palace was taken by the Bolsheviks, however the dramatic storming portrayed in all those Soviet paintings or in Eisenstein's film *October* never occurred. Three shells struck the building, bullet holes riddled the square side of the palace, and a window was shattered on the third floor.

The Bolsheviks renamed the Winter Palace the Palace of the Arts. In November 1918, on the revolution's first anniversary, several thousand participants arrived in the city for a congress of peasants. Most were housed in the Palace of the Arts. In a vulgar show of contempt for the palace's previous owners and all they had stood for, they filled all the bathtubs and many valuable Oriental and Saxon vases with their own excrement.

In 1922, the Winter Palace was officially transferred to the State Hermitage, and before WWII part of it was used to house the Museum of the Revolution. The Soviet period saw the Hermitage transform itself into one of the world's greatest museums.

Throughout the 1990s, the museum has, partially thanks to partnerships with foreign museums and donors, been able to renovate its heating and temperature control system, install a new fire detection system, fit its windows with a thin sheath of UV-filtering plastic, and to begin the first thorough, digitised inventory of its mammoth collection.

There are major plans for further renovation (leaky rooftops and flooded basements need repair, and the main entrance will eventually be moved to the Dvortsovaya pl side of the building), and the museum is now actively promoting itself abroad (see the boxed text 'Hermitage Around the World' in this special section).

Today, the museum receives some three million visitors a year, and now also encompasses the east wing of the General Staff Building, the Menshikov Palace and Peter the Great's Palace.

**Below:** View over the Hermitage

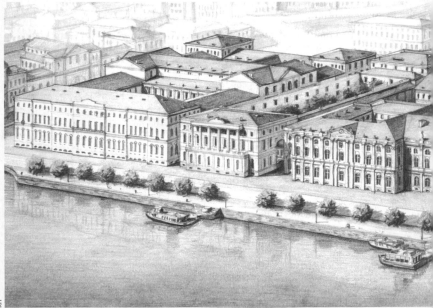

KH

# Admission

The main entrance is on the river side of the Winter Palace. Just inside are four ticket counters, flanking a booth dedicated to the Friends of the Hermitage Foundation.

That the admission price is 20 times higher for a foreigner than for a Russian is just something you'll have to grin and bear. Admission to the Hermitage is just under $11; however, ISIC card-holders and visitors under the age of 17 get in free of charge. Also, foreigners working or residing in Russia (and who can show proof of this) get in for the Russian price – $0.54. Anyone wishing to take photographs must pay an extra $3.60; using your camcorder will cost you another $9.

The museum is open 10.30am to 6pm Tuesday to Saturday and 10.30am to 5pm Sunday. The ticket sale counter closes one hour before closing time.

There are also tickets for $18 which give you access to the Hermitage, the General Staff Building, the Menshikov Palace and the Peter the Great Palace, but the ticket is only valid for one day. It is also possible to visit these other places and simply pay a separate admission.

The queues can be horrendous in summer – try to get there as early as possible to avoid an unpleasant wait. Sometimes, enterprising Russians will 'sell' you their place at the front of the line – you may get a few nasty looks but there's nothing illegal about it.

# Tours & Information

To avoid queues altogether, you can join a tour, which whizzes round the main parts in about 1½ hours but at least provides an introduction to the place in English. It's easy enough to 'lose' the group and stay on till closing time.

The museum's **excursions office** (☎ 311 84 46, 213 11 12; open 11am-1pm & 2pm-4pm) is down the corridor to the right as you enter, up the stairs and straight to the end of the small corridor (don't turn right towards the coat-check).

You can either call in advance (suggested) or show up and hope to be able to arrange a guided tour through the museum in English, German or French, a thematic tour, or to book a place in groups to see the Golden Collection (about $14).

At the top of the Jordan Staircase you can rent a Walkman with recorded tours in English, German, French, Italian or Russian, including a general orientation, and tours of either the Flemish and Dutch collections, 'Impressionism to Picasso', and 'Unknown Masterpieces Revealed'. They cost $3.60 for the general tour; $4.30 for the thematic ones.

You'll trip over all the book stalls and souvenir kiosks set up throughout the museum. You can stock up on Hermitage T-shirts, mugs, calendars, figurines and *palekh* painted boxes – not to mention fine-looking imitation Fabergé eggs and sumptuous chess sets. Books of all kinds are rife, including a *Hidden Treasures Revealed* ($20) and a Hermitage-produced guide to the museum, available in many languages for $14.30.

There's a small cafe on the 1st floor, opposite an educational centre with computer terminals offering a virtual tour of the museum and the opportunity to search for the location of your favourite painting. These are to the right of the Jordan Staircase.

There are several toilets on the 1st floor only – downstairs by the coat-check (old and stinky; you'll think you're at a train station), near the cafe, next to room 99, and by both the State and Council Staircases.

A ticket booth in the basement near the coat-check sells tickets for events at the Hermitage Theatre.

Much of the Hermitage is now wheelchair accessible, though that may entail having you and your wheelchair carried upstairs by museum staff. There are wheelchairs available on site. Note that the invalid entrance is on the square side of the building; there is a special lift there for that purpose. It's best to call in advance and warn them that you're coming, so someone will be there to open the gates. Otherwise, ring the bell and hope for the best.

Note that Russians number their levels in the same way as in the US. There is no 'ground floor' as such – the ground level is known as the first floor. We have followed the Russian/US system as with the rest of this guide.

# Suggested Itinerary

If your time at the Hermitage is limited, the following route takes in the major highlights.

### Winter Palace, 2nd floor

**189:** Malachite Hall; **190-198:** Great State rooms.

### Little Hermitage, 2nd floor

**204:** Pavilion Hall, with its view onto the 'Hanging Garden'.

### Large Hermitage, 1st floor

**107-109:** Ancient Classical Culture, with gorgeous rooms designed by Leo von Klenze. **128:** The jasper Kolyvanskaya Vase.

### Large Hermitage, 2nd floor

**207-215:** Florentine art, 13th to 16th centuries; **217-222 & 237:** Venetian art, 16th century; **229:** Raphael and his disciples; **239-240:** Spanish art, 16th to 18th centuries; **244-247:** Flemish art, 17th century; **249-252 & 254:** Dutch art, 17th century.

### Winter Palace, 3rd floor

**315-333:** Impressionists and post-impressionists; **334:** Vincent van Gogh; **343-349:** Picasso and Matisse.

## Friends of the Hermitage

Since 1997, the Friends of the Hermitage Society (☎ 110 90 05, fax 311 95 24, ⓔ development@hermitage.ru, Ⓦ www.hermitagemuseum.org) has been encouraging membership and donations to help with their restoration and conservation programs.

All memberships allow you access to special events hosted by the Hermitage, either at a reduced cost or for free.

A $100 annual donation will get you a free entry to the Hermitage and Menshikov Palace for a year, plus a 20% discount at their shops; for $200 you can bring a friend along for free as well and get invitations to opening parties; $500 allows you to bring two friends along for free and even more privileges.

See its Web page for more details.

**Right:** Atlas statue

## Hermitage Around the World

Over the last few years, the Hermitage's international visibility has increased exponentially. Not only are more exhibits being toured around the world or loaned to other museums, but bite-sized Hermitages have opened to give a far-away public a taste of the 237-year-old museum.

Hermitage Director Professor Mikhail Piotrovski has made agreements with several museums around the world to ensure greater exposure of the Hermitage's treasures – as well as extra sources of funding. The first fruits of these agreements blossomed with the opening, in November 2000, of the Hermitage Rooms at the Somerset House (W www.hermitage rooms.com) in London.

In this miniature version of the Winter Palace (complete with replica paintings, chandeliers, gilded chairs, vitrines, window panels and blinds and a marquetry floor crafted by Russian specialists) are five galleries and one small corridor. There will be rotating exhibits every 10 months of thematically-linked Hermitage treasures. Computer terminals offer virtual tours of the real thing, and a monitor shows what's happening on Palace Square in real-time. The first exhibit, Treasures of Catherine the Great, was a huge hit with the public.

Next, the Hermitage is set on conquering America – and in one of the least likely settings imaginable for some of the rarest examples of world art and culture: a Las Vegas casino. Only in America, folks! (On second thought, it is probably the most appropriate place for a simulacrum of culture!) From September 2001, visitors tired of the blackjack tables and topless dancers in the Venetian Resort-Hotel-Casino can rest their eyes for a while inside the Hermitage-Guggenheim Museum, a 712-sq-metre structure inside the casino complex built specially to house rotating exhibits from both world-famous museums.

Designed to look and feel like a jewel box, the surroundings will be a mix of classical elegance and modernism – architect Rem Koolhaas (who designed the Kunsthal in Rotterdam) made the walls with Cor-Ten steel, a material previously only used in large-scale modern sculptures. This conforms to the modernist idea that buildings are meant to be a product of their era. It is still a hugely controversial venture, the brainchild of Guggenheim Director Thomas Krens, who has orchestrated many uncommon methods of making art reach the people, and turning a healthy profit in the process; all have set their sights on a cash-heavy tourist influx (over 35 million people a year visit Las Vegas). The Hermitage is set to receive an estimated and much-needed $7 million a year from the venture.

In addition, a partnership was established in early 2001 between the Hermitage and Vienna's Kunsthistorisches Museum that will see future joint exhibits and exchange of art works.

These efforts will undoubtedly introduce St Petersburg's and the Hermitage's splendours to a wider audience and hopefully lead to a greater – not lesser – desire to visit the city itself: Inside Somerset House, we twice heard people saying, after wandering through the replica Hermitage, 'That was just lovely! And now we don't have to go all the way to Russia!'.

# The Collection

Many objects in the Hermitage's collection, which topples the three million mark (only 5% to 10% of the entire collection is ever on display at one time), were obtained thanks to shrewd negotiating and as a result of forced nationalisation (a diplomatic term for state-sponsored looting).

Though Peter the Great had purchased some Rembrandts and other objects of art, the Hermitage's collection really began with Catherine the Great, one of the greatest art collectors of all time. She managed to make some great deals – in 1779, she bought a series of valuable paintings by Poussin and others from the famous Walpole collection in England (Sir Robert Walpole was Britain's first prime minister). She convinced – somehow – his grandson to give her the paintings of her choice (she chose 15 Van Dykes!) in exchange for a large, framed portrait of herself! At the time, this caused a scandal, as the collection had been destined to form the foundation of a national gallery in England.

Six years later, she acquired 250 Roman busts, marbles and reliefs from a director of the Bank of England, and later immediately purchased 1120 important drawings by architect Charles-Louis Clérisseau when she found out that the Emperor Joseph was interested in buying them. She also had thousands of objects commissioned, including furniture, dinner services, portraits, and some 32,000 copies of glass gems.

Nicholas I also greatly enriched the Hermitage's collection, which he opened up to the public for the first time in 1852. But it was the post-revolutionary period that saw the collection increase in size threefold. Many valuable private collections were seized by the state and nationalised, namely those of the Stroganovs, Sheremetevs, Shuvalovs, Yusupovs and the Baron Stieglitz. These considerably swelled the Hermitage's coffers in a matter of years. Most remarkable was the 1948 incorporation of impressionist and post-impressionist paintings from the renowned collections of Moscow industrialists Sergey Shchukin and Ivan Morozov.

However, a number of major works by Rembrandt (15), Rubens and Van Eycks, were sold in the 1920s and 1930s to bolster the cash-strapped new government and to purchase imported machinery.

In 1995, the Hermitage displayed, for the first time, some of the sweetest 'war booty' seen in the 20th century. 'Hidden Treasures Revealed' was composed entirely of art captured from German private collections by the Red Army in 1945, including works by Monet, Degas, Renoir, Cézanne, Picasso and Matisse – almost all of which had previously never been publicly displayed. There was a political debate as to whether the paintings belong back in Germany, but evidently a resolution has been found, as most of these paintings are now on permanent display, in rooms 143-146 under the coy moniker 'French Paintings from the 19th and 20th centuries'.

# Winter Palace, First Floor

**Rooms 1-33 Russian prehistoric artefacts – 11:** Palaeolithic (from five hundred thousand years ago to the 12th millennium BC) and Mesolithic (from the 12th to the 3rd millennium BC); **12:** Neolithic (from the 4th millennium BC to 2400 BC) and Bronze Age (from 2000 to 500 BC), including petroglyphs from 2500 to 2000 BC taken from the north-eastern shores of Lake Onega after archaeological expeditions in 1935; **13:** Bronze Age, western steppes, 4th to 2nd millennium BC; **14:** Bronze Age, southern Siberia and Kazakhstan, 2nd millennium to 9th century BC, fine bronze animals; **15-18:** Culture and art of the Scythians, who lived in what is presently the south of Russia from the 7th to 3rd century BC. There's the stunning Golden Stag, which once formed part of an iron shield – but the best Scythian material is in the Golden Rooms Special Collection; **19 & 20:** Forest steppes, 7th to 4th century BC; **21-23 & 26:** Material from Altai Mountains burial mounds, including **26:** Human and horse corpses preserved for over 2000 years complete with hair and teeth; **24:** Iron Age, Eastern Europe, including Finno-Ugrians and Balts, 8th century BC to 12th century AD; **33:** Southern steppes tribes 3rd century BC to 10th century AD – some fine Sarmatian gold.

**Rooms 34-40 & 46-69 The Russian East – 34-39:** Central Asia, 4th century BC to 13th century AD; **55-66:** Caucasus and Transcaucasia, 10th century BC to 16th century AD, including **56:** Urartu, 8th to 6th century BC, discovered in digs in 1911 and 1916; **59:** Dagestan, 6th to 11th century AD; **66:** 14th-century Italian colonies in Crimea; **67-69:** Golden Horde, 13th to 14th century.

**Room 100 Ancient Egypt** A fine collection, including clay plates from 5000 BC and wooden figurines from about 2000 BC, much of it uncovered by Russian archaeologists; sadly there is no labelling in English except the signs saying 'Please Do Not Touch'.

# Little Hermitage, First Floor

The little staircase at the end of room 100 will bring you into the Little (or Small) Hermitage, which on this floor used to house the palace stables and riding school. Most of it is off-limits, but rooms **101 & 102** have displays of Roman marble.

# Large Hermitage, First Floor

**Rooms 106-131 Ancient Classical culture – 106-109 & 127:** Roman sculpture, 1st century BC to 4th century AD; **107:** The Jupiter Hall (a statue of the god sits near the middle – look for his pet eagle), a sumptuous space, with portraits of sculptors on the walls (can you spot Michelangelo?), and a near-intact ancient Roman sarcophagus; **108:** Architect Leo von Klenze wanted the room to reflect the courtyard of a Hellenistic or Roman house, and so it is filled with Greco-Roman decorative art; **109:** has the *Tauride Venus*, acquired by Peter the Great from Pope Clement XI, and which

# HERMITAGE – FIRST FLOOR ЭРМИТАЖ - ПЕРВЫЙ ЭТАЖ

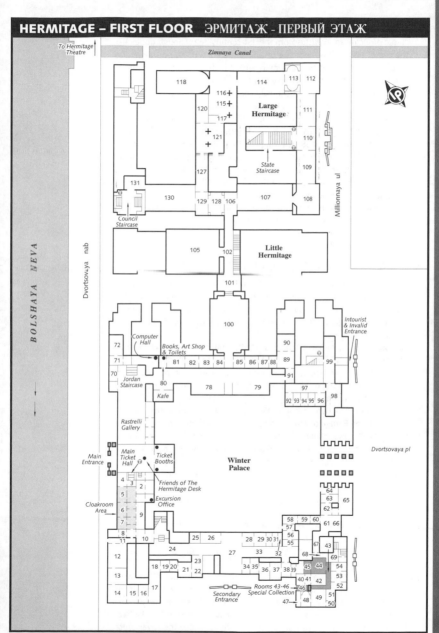

To Hermitage Theatre

*Zimnaya Canal*

118

114

113  112

116 +
115 +

**Large Hermitage**

111

120

117 +

121
+
+

110

*State Staircase*

109

127

131

130

129 128 106

107

108

Council Staircase

105

102

**Little Hermitage**

*Dvortsov-ya nab*

*BOLSHAYA NEVA*

*Millionnaya ul*

101

100

Intourist & Invalid Entrance

90

72

*Computer Hall*

71

*Books, Art Shop & Toilets*

81  82  83  84

85  86  87 88

89

99

70

*Jordan Staircase*

80

78

79

97

98

*Kafe*

92 93 94 95 96

91

*Rastrelli Gallery*

*Dvortsovaya pl*

*Main Entrance*

*Main Ticket Hall*

*Ticket Booths*

**Winter Palace**

*Friends of The Hermitage Desk*

4
3

2

*Excursion Office*

64

63

5

65

62

*Cloakroom Area*

6

9

58  59  60

61 66

7

57

8

56

67

43

11

10

55

68

69

25  26

28 29 30 31

45  44

54

24

27

33  32

53

12

34 35

36  37

38 39

40 41

52

13

18 19 20

21  22

42

51

23

46

49  50

14  15  16

17

Rooms 43-46 Special Collection

47

48

Secondary Entrance

resided in the Tauride Palace until the mid-19th-century; **127:** A great statue of Octavian Augustus from the 1st century AD. Though done near the end of his life, it was a stroke of brilliant, eternal PR to portray him as an omnipotent, young, muscular man, sitting half-naked with a sceptre in one hand and the goddess Victory (Nike) in the other; **111-114:** Ancient Greece, 8th to 2nd century BC, mostly ceramics and sculpture. The beautiful room 111, designed by von Klenze, was initially meant to be used as a library – hence the portraits of famous philosophers high up on the walls; **115-117 & 121:** Greek colonies around northern Black Sea, 7th century BC to 3rd century AD; **128:** The huge 19th-century jasper Kolyvanskaya Vase from Siberia – this is one of the highlights of the museum. The vase, which weighs 19 tonnes, was designed by Avram Malnikov and made by craftsmen of the Kolyvan Lapidary Works in the Altai mountains over 14 years. It took nearly 800 men to position it where it sits now, in a luscious yet subdued room with magnificently subtle lighting; **130 & 131:** Ancient Italy, 7th to 2nd century BC, including Etruscan vases and bronze mirrors. Room 130 is known as the Hall of Twenty Columns, for obvious reasons.

# Large Hermitage, Second Floor

From room **131**, head up the Council Staircase (Sovietskaya Lestnitsa; its name derives from the members of the State Council who most often used it in the 19th century). At the top is room **206** where a marble, Malachite and glass triumphal arch announces the beginning of the Italian section;

**Rooms 207-215 Florentine art, 13th to 16th centuries – 207:** Ugolino Di Tedice's *The Crucifixion* is the earliest example in this collection, from the first half of the 13th century, but Simone Martini's *Virgin of the Annunciation* from either 1339 or 1342 is the room's subtly-crafted standout; **209:** 15th-century paintings, including Fra Angelico; **213:** 15th and early 16th centuries, including two small Botticellis (commissioned by Lorenzo Medici), Filippino Lippi, Perugino; **214:** Russia's only two paintings by Leonardo da Vinci – the *Benois Madonna* (1478) and the strikingly different masterpiece *Madonna Litta* (1490), both named after their last owners. Note also the room's beautiful jasper columns and the doors with tortoise shell and copper inlays; **215:** art by Leonardo's pupils, including Correggio and Andrea del Sarto.

**Room 216 Italian Mannerist art, 16th century** Also a nice view over the little Winter Canal to the Hermitage Theatre.

**Rooms 217-222 Venetian art, mainly 16th century – 217:** Giorgione's *Judith*; **219:** Titian's *Portrait of a Young Woman* and *Flight into Egypt*, and more by Giorgione; **221:** More Titian, including *Dana* and *St Sebastian*; **222:** Paolo Veronese's *Mourning of Christ*.

**Rooms 226 & 227 Loggia of Raphael** Quarenghi's sumptuous 1780s copy of a gallery in the Vatican with murals by Raphael. This was built at the request of Catherine the Great, who so liked what she saw in the Vatican, she decided to build her own (there weren't many souvenirs to take back home then). These copies were done on canvas – note the royal touch

# HERMITAGE – SECOND FLOOR   ЭРМИТАЖ - ВТОРОЙ ЭТАЖ

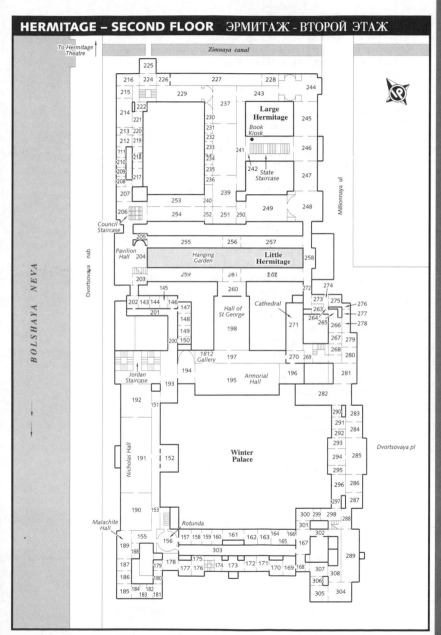

To Hermitage Theatre

Zimnaya canal

225

216 224 226 | 227 | 228 | 244

215 | 229 | 243

214 222 | 237 | **Large Hermitage** | 245

221

213 220 | 230 | *Book Kiosk* | 246

212 219 | 231 232 | 241

111 218 | 233 234 235 236 | 239 | 242 *State Staircase* | 247

210 209 208 217

207 | 253 240 | 249 | 248

206 | 254 252 251 250

*Council Staircase*

205 | 255 | 256 | 257 | 258

*Pavilion Hall* 204 | *Hanging Garden* | **Little Hermitage**

203 | 259 | 261 | 262 | 272 274

202 143 144 | 145 146 | 260 | *Cathedral* | 273 275 276

201 | 147 | *Hall of St George* | 271 | 263 277

148 149 | 198 | 264 265 266 278

200 150 | | 267 279

*Jordan Staircase* | 1812 Gallery | 197 | 268 280

194 | 195 | 196 | 281

193 | *Armorial Hall* | 270 269

192 151 | | 282

| 290 283

191 152 | **Winter Palace** | 291 292 284

*Nicholas Hall* | | 293 294 285 295

| 296 286 297 287

190 153 | | 300 299 298 288

*Malachite Hall* | *Rotunda* | 301 302

189 188 155 156 | 157 158 159 160 161 162 163 164 166 165 167 | 289

187 179 178 | 303 | 307 308

186 180 | 175 177 176 174 173 172 171 170 169 168 | 306

185 184 182 183 181 | | 305 304

*Dvortsovaya nab*

*BOLSHAYA NEVA*

*Millionnaya ul*

*Dvortsovaya pl*

of russification here and there, like the replacing of the Pope's coat-of-arms with the Romanov dynasty's two-headed eagle. The Tyrolese Christopher Unterberger headed a team of artists who drew the murals.

**Rooms 228-238 Italian art, 16th to 18th centuries – 228:** 16th-century ceramics; **229:** Raphael and disciples, including his *Madonna Conestabile* and *Holy Family*, plus wonderful ceramics and decorations, as well as Russia's only Michelangelo, a marble statue of a crouching boy; **237:** 16th-century paintings, including Paolo Veronese and Tintoretto. The high vaults and frieze are decorated with arabesque stucco; **238:** 17th- and 18th-century painters including Canaletto and Tiepolo; also two huge 19th-century Russian malachite vases. 237 & 238 have lovely ceilings.

**Rooms 239-240 Spanish art, 16th to 18th centuries – 239:** Goya's *Portrait of the Actress Antonia Zarate*, Murillo's *Boy with a Dog*, Diego Velazquez' *Breakfast*; **240:** one of El Greco's last paintings, the marvellous *St Peter and St Paul*.

**Room 241 Marble sculptures**, Antonio Canova and Albert Thorwaldsen; **242:** is mainly taken up by the State Staircase, surrounded by walls of yellow marble; **243:** The slightly creepy Knights' Hall; Western European armour and weaponry from the 15th to 17th centuries, featuring four 16th-century German suits of armour atop armoured horses.

**Rooms 244-247 Flemish art, 17th century – 245:** Savage hunting and market scenes by Snyders; **246:** Van Dyck portraits; **247:** A large room displaying the amazing range of Rubens. It includes *Descent from the Cross, Bacchus, The Union of Earth and Water, Portrait of a Curly-Haired Old Man* and *Roman Charity*.

**Rooms 248-252 & 254 Dutch art, 17th century – 249:** The Tent Hall, designed by Leo von Klenze. Landscapes and portraits by Ruisdael, Hals, Bol, Steen (whose *Idlers* is a memorable highlight), and others; **250:** 18th-century Delft ceramics; **254:** 26 Rembrandts ranging from lighter, more detailed early canvases like *Abraham's Sacrifice of Isaac* and *Dana* to *The Holy Family* of 1645, and darker, penetrating late works like *The Return of the Prodigal Son* and two canvases entitled *Portrait of an Old Man*. There's also work by Rembrandt's pupils, including Bol.

# Little Hermitage, Second Floor

**Room 204 Pavilion Hall** A sparkling, airy white-and-gold room with 28 lovely chandeliers, tables, galleries, and columns. The south windows look on to Catherine the Great's hanging garden, the north onto the Neva; the floor mosaic in front of them is copied from a Roman bath. Roman and Florentine mosaics from the 18th and 19th centuries, and the amazing Peacock Clock (James Fox, 1772) – a revolving dial in one of the toadstools tells the time, and on the hour (when it's working) the peacock spreads its wings and the toadstools, owl and cock come to life.

**Room 258 Flemish art, 17th century** This long corridor used to be the only entrance to the Little Hermitage from the Winter Palace – it was along here that Catherine the Great would flee the business of the day to have a rest, accompanied or not.

Room 259 Western European applied art, 11th to 15th centuries
Rooms 261-262 Dutch art, 15th and 16th centuries

# Winter Palace, Second Floor

**Rooms 143-146 French Paintings of the 19th and 20th Century** This is most of what used to be called the Hidden Treasures Revealed exhibit. It boasts oil paintings captured by the Red Army from private collections in Germany, including works by Monet, Degas, Renoir, Cézanne, Picasso and Matisse, almost all never before publicly displayed.

**Rooms 147-189 Russian culture and art – 147-150:** 10th to 15th century; **151:** 15th to 17th century; **152:** Icons, ceramics, jewellery etc from 'Moscow Baroque' period, first half of the 17th century; **153:** Items relating to Peter the Great; **155-166:** Late 17th and early 18th century, including **155:** Moorish Dining Room and **156:** Rotunda, with a bust of Peter the Great and a brass Triumphal Pillar, topped by a Rastrelli-created statue of Peter, which emphasises his harsher, crueller side; **157-first half of 161:** Petrovskaya Gallereya, including lathing machinery used by Peter; **161:** An ivory chandelier that was partly built by the Great Guy himself. It was in this room in 1880 that there was an attempt on the life of Alexander II – a bomb had been set off in the room below, killing 11 soldiers (the tsar had wandered into another room at the time). Khalturin, the young revolutionary who planted the bomb was executed, but got belated tribute for his great deed by the Soviets, who renamed ul Millionaya after him; **162:** Mosaic of Peter by Lomonosov; **167-73:** Mid to end 18th century – spot the bizarre 1772 tapestry image of Australia (**167**); **175-187:** (Start at 187 and work your way back.) Rooms occupied by the last imperial family, now displaying 19th-century interior design, including **178:** Nicholas II's solemn and decidedly scholarly English Gothic library; **188:** Small Dining Room, completed in 1894; **189:** Malachite Hall with two tonnes of gorgeous green malachite columns, boxes, bowls and urns. This may be the most impressive of all the palace's rooms, designed by Bryullov in 1839. The three figurines on the wall represent Day, Night and Poetry. This was where the last meeting of the 1917 Provisional Government occurred, on the fateful nights of October 25–26 1917 (they were soon-after arrested in the Small Dining Room next door).

**Rooms 190-192 Neva Enfilade** One of two sets of state rooms for ceremonies and balls – **190:** Concert Hall for small balls, with an 18th-century silver tomb (1747–52) for the remains of Alexandr Nevsky. This monument is typically Russian in its larger-than-life grandeur. It was commissioned by the Empress Elizabeth; **191:** Great or Nicholas Hall, the palace's largest room, scene of imperial winter balls (5000 guests could be squeezed in here); **192:** The Fore Hall, the site of pre-ball champagne buffets; all are now used for temporary exhibitions.

**Rooms 193-198 Great Enfilade** The second series of state rooms – **193:** Field Marshals' Hall, with its military-themed chandelier and coach, a real crowd-pleaser. This is where the disastrous fire of 1837 broke out; **194:** Peter the Great's Hall, with his none-too-comfy looking oak and silver throne. Better is Jacopo Amigoni's portrait of *Peter I with Minerva*, in which the Emperor looks more pleased with himself than with his date. This room was severely damaged from a Nazi shell during the Blockade; **195:** Armorial Hall, bright and gilt encrusted with chandeliers engraved with the coat-of-arms of all the Russian provinces. Also displays of 16th- to 19th-century Western European silver; **197:** The 1812 Gallery, hung with 332 portraits of Russian and allied Napoleonic war leaders; **198:** St George's Hall or Great Throne Room – once a state room where the Imperial Throne used to sit, its 800 sq metres are now used for temporary exhibitions. The white Carrara marble was imported from Italy and the floors were crafted from the wood of 16 different kinds of trees. Official receptions and ceremonies were held here.

**Rooms 200-202 Western European tapestry, 16th to 19th century**

**Rooms 263-268 German art, 15th to 18th century** Including Dürer and Lucas Cranach the Elder.

**Rooms 269-271 Western European porcelain, 18th century**

**Room 271 Imperial family's cathedral** Many royal weddings took place (here Nicholas II married Alexandra in 1894).

**Rooms 272-289 French art, 15th to 18th century – 272-273:** Tapestries, ceramics, metalwork; **279:** Paintings by Poussin; **280:** Lorrain; **282:** The Alexander Hall, a testament to the victory over Napoleon in 1812 – scenes from the war are painted in bas-reliefs, with a portrait of Alexander I presiding over it all; **284:** Watteau; **287:** Jean-Antoine Houdon's marble statue of Voltaire; **288:** Greuze; **289:** The White Hall, a pleasant space built for Alexander II's wedding, with 18th-century furniture and vases. Bryullov designed this in 1838 using a Roman bath as a model.

**Rooms 298-302 British art, 16th to 19th century – 299:** Reynolds; **300:** Gainsborough's *Lady in Blue*.

**Room 303 'Dark Corridor' containing Western European tapestry, 16th to 18th century** Mainly from Flanders. Follow the confusing trail through 167 and 308 to get to **304:** A wonderful collection of **Western European stone engravings** from the 13th to the 19th century; **305:** The Burgundy Hall, containing English and French Porcelain; **306:** Maria Alexandrovna's bedroom, fit for a princess, with lush red brocatelle (made by Cartier in Paris) used in the curtains and on the walls; **307:** the Blue Bedroom, containing French, Austrian and German porcelain.

**Left:** Soaking up modern masterpieces

Winter Palace: breathtaking any way you look at it

Jordan Staircase sculpture

The baroque Winter Palace and the neighbouring Hermitage buildings overlook the Neva.

Entry to Dvortsovaya ploshchad

Statues of Atlas hold up the roof, while the idle look on.

Jordan Staircase

The facade of the Winter Palace in the evening light

Golden throne and footrest

The classical Hermitage Theatre is thought to be one of Quarenghi's best works.

# Winter Palace, Third Floor

An approximate chronological order in which to view the French art collection is 314, 332-328, 325-315 and 343-350. The staircase beside room 269 on Floor 2 brings you out by room 314.

**Rooms 314-320, 330-332 French art, 19th century**

**Rooms 321-325, 328, 329** Mostly Barbizon School, including Corot, Courbet, Millet; **331:** Delacroix and Vernet.

**Room 315 Impressionists and post-impressionists – 315:** Rodin sculptures; **316:** Gauguin's Tahitian works; **317:** Van Gogh's *The Bush*, Rousseau, Forain, Latour; **318:** Cézanne, Pissarro; **319:** Pissarro, Monet, including *Woman in a Garden* and the wonderful *Waterloo Bridge, Effect of Mist*, Sisley; **320:** Renoir, Degas; **321 & 322:** Corot, Courbet, Rousseau; **333:** Kandinsky

**Room 334 Vincent van Gogh**

**Rooms 334-342 European art, 19th century** Including landscapes by Caspar David Friedrich.

**Rooms 346, 347, 350 French art, 19th to 20th centuries** Bonnard, Vlaminck, Marquet, Leger and others.

**Rooms 343-345 Matisse** 35 canvases in all, including *The Dance*, and *Arab Coffeehouse* which shows his new experimentation with light effects, painted after his trip to Morocco.

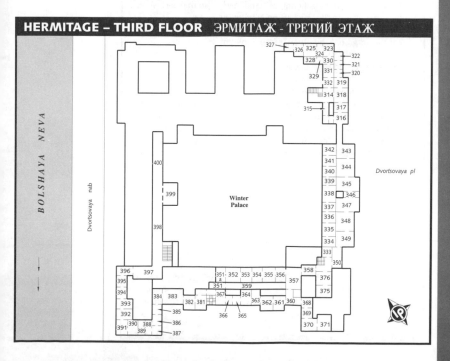

## Guest Rules

If you think you had a hard time getting into the Hermitage (line-ups, organising tours etc), woe to the invited guests of Catherine the Great in her time! The empress herself came up with a list of 'Ten Commandments' to be followed by her personal guests on social events held inside the Little Hermitage, which was built as her retreat (these were hung in the current-day room 258):

1 All ranks shall be left outside the doors, similarly hats, and particularly swords.
2 Orders of precedence and haughtiness, and anything of such like which result from them, shall be left at the doors.
3 Be merry, but neither spoil or break anything, nor indeed gnaw at anything.
4 Be seated, stand or walk as it best pleases you, regardless of others.
5 Speak with moderation and not too loudly, so that others present have not an earache or headache.
6 Argue without anger or passion.
7 Do not sigh or yawn, neither bore nor fatigue others.
8 Agree to partake of any innocent entertainment suggested by others.
9 Eat well of all things, but drink with moderation so that each should be able always to find his legs on leaving the doors.
10 All disputes must stay behind closed doors; and what goes in one ear should go out the other before departing these doors.

These were followed by this warning:

If any member violates the above rules, for each fault witnessed by two persons he must drink a glass of fresh water (ladies not excepted): furthermore he must read aloud a page of the *Telemachiad* (a poem by Frediakovsky). Whoever fails during one evening in three of these articles, must learn by heart six lines of the *Telemachiad*. He who fails in the tenth article must never more re-enter the Hermitage.

Such were the ways the imperial powers amused themselves (a glass of fresh water?).
   The ever-cranky writer Marquis de Custine, while visiting the Hermitage in 1839, was less than amused when he came upon these rules, then hung only in memory of the empress who had died 43 years prior:

Before reading the above, I believed the Empress Catherine possessed a livelier and more pointed wit. Is this a simple pleasantry? If so it is a bad joke, for the shortest jokes are the best. The care which has been taken to preserve the statutes, as though of great value, surprises me not less than the want of good taste which characterises them.

**Rooms 348 & 349 Picasso – 348:** Mainly his blue and Cubist periods; **349:** Cubist and later periods.

**Rooms 351-371, 381-397 Oriental and Middle East culture and art – 351-357, 359-364:** Art of China and Tibet, an excellent collection; **358:** Indonesia; **365-367:** Mongolia; **368-371:** India; **381-382:** One of the world's best collections of Byzantine art – look for the amazing ivory diptych of men fighting beasts from AD 500; **383-387, 391-394:** Iran and Middle East from 3rd to 18th centuries, including the world's largest collection of Sasanide silver (vases, plates, ornamental wine glasses) from the 3rd to the 7th centuries. These were accidentally uncovered near the Ural mountains, where ancient merchants had traded furs for them; **388:** Syria and Iraq 13th to 15th centuries; **389-390:** Egypt from 7th to 15th centuries; **395-397:** Turkey from the 15th to 18th centuries.

**Rooms 398 & 400 Coins** Includes the numismatic collection, boasting over 90,000 coins and medals.

## Golden Rooms Special Collection

To get into this mind-bending display of crafted gold, silver and jewels in rooms 41 to 45 you must either book with a group at hotel concierge desks or with a travel agency, or through the Hermitage's excursion office (see Admission). Prices vary depending on who you book your tour through, but an average would be $10 to $20, and even at these prices places are scarce (and days on which you can enter are limited), so book as soon as you reach St Petersburg.

You'll also need to pass through a special security checkpoint within the museum, and cameras and video cameras are not permitted inside.

The focus is a hoard of fabulously worked Scythian and Greek gold and silver from the Caucasus, Crimea and Ukraine, dating from the 7th to 2nd centuries BC when the Scythians, who dominated the region, and the Greeks, in colonies around the northern Black Sea, crafted the pieces to accompany the dead into the afterlife. There are labels in English.

The treasure was unearthed from graves in the late 19th century. The rest of the collection is European jewellery, precious metals and stones of the 16th to 19th centuries, amassed by tsars from Peter the Great onwards.

## Menshikov Palace

Alexandr Menshikov was a close friend (many now say lover) of Peter the Great. For helping the tsar defeat the Swedes he was made governor general of St Petersburg and given Vasilevsky Island. Peter later took the island back, but in 1707 Menshikov put up one of the city's first buildings, a riverside **palace (Map 6)** *(Dvorets Menshikova; ☎ 323 11 12, Universitetskaya nab 15; separate entry adult/student $6/4; open 10.30am-4.30pm Tues-Sun)* just west of the Twelve Colleges. He effectively ran Russia from here for three years between Peter's death and his own exile. Later, the palace was a military academy and then it went to seed until Lenin suggested it be saved.

Now its lavish interiors are again filled with period art and furniture as a branch of the Hermitage, with an exhibit of 'Russian Culture of the First Third of the 18th century'. Despite the 'Russian culture' theme, there are many lavish objects of foreign origin on display here in a recreation of Menshikov's original surroundings. Impressive are the Walnut Study and the Great Hall, where Peter and Menshikov came up with bizarre ideas and games to entertain the guests. Russian-language tours, which start every 10 minutes, are included in the price.

## The General Staff Building

The impressive, 580m long General Staff Building (Carlo Rossi, 1819–29), which faces the Hermitage on the opposite side of the square, was traditionally the headquarters of the Russian army. Over the years, however, various branches of the military, as well as other offices, a policlinic and cafeteria have occupied parts of the premises. In September 1999, the Hermitage, which had been handed over the east wing of the building, opened several exhibition halls on the third floor. It is now considered to form part of the Hermitage museum.

This wing, accessed via a small door leading out onto the square, has the same opening hours as the Hermitage, and, if you had not already purchased an all-inclusive ticket, a separate admission price: $5.40 for adults, students with ISIC cards free.

The focus here is on decorative arts. The rooms are grand – of course a far cry from the splendour of the Winter Palace, but there's also a sedate quality here not found in the main museum in which to quietly appreciate the works on display. Though the permanent collection has not been definitively mounted yet – it will grow over the coming years – there is presently an exhibit of imperial art: porcelain, tapestries, furniture, vases and metal works with imperial designs. There is also *The Story of Psyche* series (1907–08) of huge paintings, by French painter Maurice Denis. These works, originally commissioned by Moscow businessman IA Morozov for his flat, take up three full halls.

## Peter the Great Palace

Several years ago, the original foundation of Peter the Great's stone and wood Winter Palace was found on the site of the present-day Hermitage Theatre. This is where he died in 1725. Several rooms have been recreated and objects such as a wax figure of Peter have been placed there. If you don't have time for this, you won't have missed much. The gorgeous theatre itself, which would have been worth a detour, is off-limits during the day.

# Things to See & Do

## Highlights

- Leave the Hermitage in awe
- See a ballet at the Mariinsky
- Be startled by the cannon blast at the Peter & Paul Fortress
- Get a whipping in a Russian banya
- Solemnly walk in Dostoevsky's footsteps
- Explore Peterhof and other suburbs
- Stroll through the Summer Gardens
- Count the mosaics on the Church on Spilled Blood
- Boat along the city's canals
- Go ice swimming in the Neva

## WALKING TOURS

Here are a few of the more interesting walks you can take on your own. Each one will introduce you to a different aspect of this multifaceted city. Walk 1 will leave you purring in the wake of so much luxury and imperial beauty. Walk 2 is for Dostoevsky lovers, and Walk 3 will acquaint you with the lesser-known charms of St Petersburg in ambient areas where nothing glitters and everything is falling apart. For more historical and practical details about the sights, refer to the text in the appropriate sections. Each of the walking tours has an accompanying map.

## Walk 1: Imperial Luxury

*Time: about an hour, not counting stops*
The most perfect way of seeing **Dvortsovaya pl** and the **Hermitage** for the first time is to approach it via Bol Morskaya ul. As you turn the corner, behold the **Alexander Column**, with the Hermitage in the background, perfectly framed under the triumphal double arch. If you aren't too ga-ga, grab your camera now.

Keep walking towards the square, keeping your eyes fixed on the column and enjoy the visual magic tricks as the perspective changes the closer you get to the arches' opening. Head north-east to the start of Millionnaya ul, and into the porch covering the south entrance of the New Hermitage. Here was the museum's first public entrance when it opened in 1852. This is one of several buildings in the city that has a facade supported by semi-clad musclemen. A favourite tourist shot is from here looking west towards St Isaac's Cathedral past the Winter Palace – you can usually fit in a few of the Atlantes, or at least a calf or two.

Walking north-east again, make the first right turn and walk along the **Zimny Canal** the short block to the **Moyka River** (glance behind you towards the Neva for another great view). This stretch of the Moyka is lovely: to your right, Nevsky pr is crossed

### IMPERIAL LUXURY

*[Map showing the Imperial Luxury walking tour with labels including: Bolshaya Neva, Dvortsovaya nab, Millionnaya ul, French Consulate, Mars Field, nab Zimney Kanavki, Pervy Zimny most, Court Stables, Large Hermitage, Zimny Canal, Teatralny most, Moyka, Souvenir Fair, Puskin Flat-Museum, Church on Spilled Blood, Dvortsovaya pl, Shvedsky per, Mikhailovsky Gardens, Alexander Column, Volynsky per, Inzhenernaya ul, Triumphal arch, Italyansky most, pl Iskusstv, Nevsky pr Start, House of the Joint Credit Society, Zelyony most, Dom Knigi, Nevsky pr, Stroganov Palace, Nevsky pr, Kazan Cathedral, Kazanskaya pl, Gostiny Dvor, Krasny most, per Serzeya Yulenina, Bankovsky most, Finish, Kazanskaya ul, canal Griboedova, nab kan Griboedova, Muchnoy per. Scale: 0–200–400m, 0–200–400yd]*

**101**

by the **Zelyony most**, and across Nevsky, catch a glimpse of the **Stroganov Palace**. Turn left and walk along the side of the river, past the French Consulate at nab reki Moyki 15. Diagonally opposite you is **Pushkin's last home** at No 12, where the poet died in 1837. The six fluted Corinthian pilasters you see date from the 1770s.

Continue to the next bridge (Bol Konyushenny) where across the street to your right you'll see the former **Court Stables**, dating from Peter the Great's time, but completely redone by Stasov between 1817 and 1823. One of Imperial Petersburg's flashiest streets, Bol Konyushennaya ul (the Russian for horse is 'kon'; hence its name) extends south from here. Turgenev, Rimsky-Korsakov and Chernyshevsky all called this street home.

Continue along the river, looking at the stables from their north side, until you come to a very picturesque ensemble of bridges where the Moyka intersects at right angles with the start of the Griboedova Canal. Count the number of bridges you can spot from here. Across the top of the touristy souvenir kiosk canapes you can see the **Church on Spilled Blood** looming in the foreground. Head towards this, crossing over the **Malo Konyushenny most**, which itself is connected to the pretty **Teatralny most**.

See how much of a foreigner you look like by counting the times you are approached to buy items for 'not many money' as you pass through the souvenir market, then cross over to the church. Circle around the church towards your left and admire the striking Art Nouveau wrought-iron fence of the Mikhailovsky Gardens.

Walk south along the Griboedova Canal until you reach the sweet footpath that crosses the canal. Called the **Italyansky most**, it dates from 1896, but was redesigned in 1955. Its main purpose seems to afford photographers a postcard perfect view of the Church on Spilled Blood. Note the amazing building on the west side of the street at No 13. Originally the **House of the Joint Credit Society** and built in 1890, its richly dressed rizalits and central cupola were placed to give the appearance of a grand palace.

Continue down to Nevsky pr, where the old Singer sewing company building stands regally on the corner (it's the present-day **Dom Knigi**). Cross Nevsky toward the Kazan Cathedral and head to the next bridge, no doubt St Petersburg's most picturesque and most photographed, the Bankovsky most (1826). The cables of this 25.2m-long bridge are supported by four cast-iron gryphons with golden wings.

## Walk 2: Crime & Punishment
*Time: about an hour*

Looking at **Sennaya pl** (the Haymarket) today, it's not hard to imagine that in Dostoevsky's time it was a teeming madhouse, filled with drunks, layabouts and guttersnipes. Though the present-day metro station is built on the site of the former Church of the Assumption (1760s; destroyed in the Soviet period), the major landmarks of the day were seedy pubs and inns. It's doubtful that the major reconstruction that's currently changing the face of the square will change the flavour its traditional denizens have always lent it.

The border between reality and fantasy has been smudged irrevocably here: Petersburgers will point out where Dostoevsky lived as quickly as they will the home of his protagonist Raskolnikov and the old pawn broker. And snatches of the grim reality of slum life in the mid-19th-century can still be had during an hour's walk. The omnipresent stray cats – as permanent a fixture in St Petersburg courtyards as dim light and foul odours – are the gatekeepers to a neighbourhood whose gloominess and squalor has been preserved well enough to make it instantly recognisable, even to Fyodor himself.

**Raskolnikov's Flat(s)** From Sennaya pl, walk north on per Grivtsova, across the canal, and turn left onto Grazhdanskaya ul to the next corner – at Stolyarny per 5 is one of the two possible locations of Raskolnikov's attic. The building bears marble plaques in Russian and German marking the waterline reached by the great flood of 7 November 1824, immortalised in Pushkin's poem, *The Bronze Horseman*. There's a plaque which says something to the effect of 'The tragic fate of the people of this area of St Petersburg formed the foundation of Dostoevsky's passionate sermon of goodness for all mankind'.

Unfortunately, the door to the stairwell is locked. Those who say that this is the place go further, saying that Rodya (the diminutive of Raskolnikov's first name, Rodyon) retrieved the murder weapon from a street-sweeper's storage bin inside the tunnel leading to the courtyard.

From that corner, turn south onto Stolyarny per ('S ... lane', from the book), where at **No 9**, you can enter the building of the second possible, and most likely, address. Walk through the tunnel, turn right and use entrance 2 (up the crumbling stone steps), and walk up four flights until the stairwell ceiling opens upward. Graffiti on the wall sometimes reads, 'Don't Kill, Rodya'. Rodya's flat would be the padlocked attic on the left hand side of the 5th floor. In Dostoevsky's time, there were 18 drinking establishments on nearby Stolyarny per alone!

**Dostoevsky's Flats** Keep going south along Stolyarny per to ul Kaznacheyskaya. Dostoevsky lived in three flats on this tiny street alone: from 1861 to 1863 at **No 1**, and from 1864 to 1867 at **No 7**. It was from this flat that he wrote *Crime and Punishment*. Dostoevsky spent one month living in the faded red building, **No 9**, before moving to No 7.

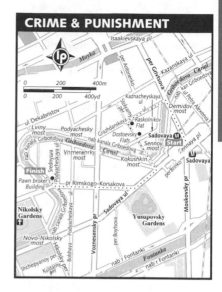

CRIME & PUNISHMENT

One of the two possible locations of Raskolnikov's Flat on Stolyarny per.

**The Murder Route** From whichever flat Raskolnikov lived, he went down Stolyarny per towards the Griboedova Canal. He crossed the **Kokushkin most**, where he would stand and gaze into the canal, deep in thought. Looking at the canal today you'd never guess it used to be very dirty (yes, that was a joke).

Murderer yes, orienteering student no; the route to the pawn broker's house taken by Rodya is circuitous. After you cross the canal, head straight to Sadovaya ul then turn right. Make your first right turn into ul Rimskogo Korsakova. Cross Voznesensky pr, and continue past ul Bol Podyacheskaya and Srednyaya Podyacheskaya; the pawn broker's building sits between there and the canal embankment.

The entrance to the courtyard is a bit north on the embankment, **nab kanala Griboedova 104**. Enter the dank, pot-holed tunnel, and head straight for **entrance No 5** (flats 22–81).

The building's residents are used to people entering the building to get a look. In fact, brass balls at the corners of the iron banisters are there specifically for visitors, and they end just after the 3rd floor, where her flat (74) is on the right-hand side. After the murder, the suspect ran through the tunnel leading to Srednyaya Podyacheskaya.

## Walk 3: Beauty in Decay

*Time: 1½ hours*

While taking in some of the city's most atmospheric ruins in this walk, it would help to keep a Russian proverb in mind: *lamat, nye stroit – golova nye balit!* (break, don't build – then there are no headaches!)

Start at Isaakievskaya pl. Opposite Hotel Astoria at **No 11** is the former German embassy (1911), a stunning building done in solid half-columns of granite blocks. There used to be a stone equestrian ensemble on top of the building that was pushed off the roof during anti-German demonstrations at the outbreak of WWI.

Round the corner onto Bol Morskaya ul. A few steps away is **No 43**, which used to house the Italian embassy; Montferrand built this in 1849 as a mansion for industrialist Demidov. It's now property of Petrovsky Bank, which hasn't done much to repair those glorious but crumbling Atlantes out front, doing their best to keep the whole thing up. Continue down Bol Morskaya ul to the next corner. On the

south-west corner is the **Railroad Workers' House of Culture**. Built in 1878 as the Reformatskaya Church, it was taken apart and rebuilt to be more in keeping with the railroad spirit. As a result, it has an unusual, piecemeal look (the best views are from the other side of the Moyka River).

We're heading further west, but a little detour would be in order – from the House of Culture, head 200m north to Pochtamskaya ul. Scribble 'wish you were here' on a postcard and send it to someone now from the **Central Post Office** at No 9. If you're glad they're not around, then just check out the building's lush neo-classical facade (1782–89). The arch across the street was added in 1859. Inside, it's a turn-of-the-20th-century Style Moderne delight.

Feel free to cruise up and down this ghost-town of a street. The scent of faded glory is strong here; the street is full of **ruined old buildings**, namely No 5 and No 7, which was the post and telegraph building from 1811 to 1917.

Now get back to the Moyka walking along Konnogvardeysky per. Those faded, red Soviet stars you see on rickety metal gates shield your view from several hundred

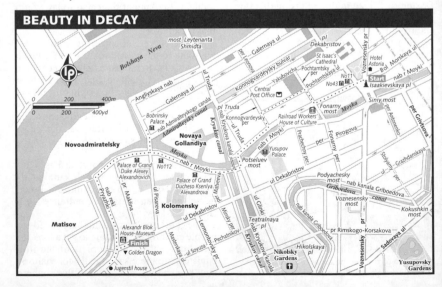

lowly soldiers fulfilling their obligatory military service here. If you loiter here long enough, officers will come out to ask what you're up to, so hurry on to the Moyka, turn right and and walk along the embankment. Opposite you is the **Yusupov Palace** at No 94, where Rasputin enjoyed his last meal. Let your fantasies roam wild until you get to nab Kryukova kanala. Cross the bridge and keep going along the south bank of the Moyka. Across the river is the island **Novaya Gollandiya** (New Holland), one of the city's most mysterious sectors. Except for one day in 2000 when an exhibit of avant-garde art was held there, the island has been closed to the public for the nearly three centuries of its existence.

In Peter's time, it was used for ship-building (its name refers to the place where he learned the trade). It was slowly built up, and in the 1760s to 1780s, the impressive red brick and granite **arch** was constructed, a prime example of early Russian classicism. In 1893, a large basin was built in the middle of the island. Here, experiments were conducted by scientist A Krylov in an attempt to build a boat that couldn't be capsized. In 1915, the navy built a radio transmitter here, the most powerful in Russia at the time, and from which the Soviets broadcasted their first directives. There are plans to turn the island into a giant art exhibition space.

The area has several old palaces, all in a state of charming decay. Moyka 108 used to be the **Palace of Grand Duchess Kseniya Alexandrova** (built in 1833), Nicholas II's sister. **No 112**, a sumptuous building by V Shreter from the 1890s was once considered one of the city's most elite residences. Turn right and over the bridge to the corner of the Anglisky Canal and the Admiralteysky Canal. Here is the **Bobrinsky Palace**, built for the son of Catherine the Great and Count Orlov in the 1790s. It's been left to rot (check out the facade along Galernaya ul); it's now property of the St Petersburg University and houses a theatre department.

Best of all is the romantic shambles that is the **Palace of Grand Duke Alexey Alexandrovich** (1882–85, architect: Mesmakher) at Moyka No 122. The son of Alexander II, he

was also the General-Admiral who bore responsibility for the shabby state of the Russian navy before the war with Japan in 1904. The ghosts of the palace's past greatness can best be felt by entering the courtyard around the corner at Anglisky pr 2 and stroll through the palace's former park grounds. Since 1985, it has been under the (subtle) ownership of the Institute of Russian Literature. While here, check out the beautiful building at Anglisky pr 8–10, which used to house the Dutch consulate.

This district of Kolomna, which stretches south to the Fontanka River, was once full of small wooden houses and was the subject of Pushkin's *Little House in Kolomna* and Gogol's *Portrait*. Continue down to the end of the Moyka River and left along nab reki Pryazhki. Across the tiny river is the desolate Matisov Island, named after a miller who lived in a little village located here in Peter the Great's time – he was favoured by the tsar for his reconnaissance efforts, relaying information about approaching Swedish ships. Now there are factories, a psychiatric hospital and a lovely guest house on it. Explore!

Be sure to check out the **Jugenstil gem** at nab reki Pryazhki 34. At the corner of ul Dekabristov is the **Alexandr Blok House-Museum**. Treat yourself to a nice meal at the Golden Dragon restaurant across the street and call it a day.

## HISTORIC HEART
## Dvortsovaya Ploshchad (Map 8)

From the Nevsky Prospekt/Gostiny Dvor metro, a 10-minute walk along Nevsky pr (or one stop on a bus or trolleybus) brings you to Dvortsovaya pl (Palace Square) where the stunning green, white and gold **Winter Palace** (Zimny Dvorets) appears like a mirage, its rococo profusion of columns, windows and recesses topped by rows of larger-than-life statues. A residence of tsars from 1762 to 1917, it's now the largest part of the **Hermitage** museum (see the special section 'The Hermitage').

On Bloody Sunday (9 January 1905), tsarist troops fired on workers peaceably gathered in the square, thus sparking the

1905 revolution. And it was across Dvort-sovaya pl that the much-exaggerated storming of the Winter Palace took place during the October 1917 Revolution.

The 47.5m **Alexander Column**, designed by Monferrand in 1834, in the square commemorates the 1812 victory over Napoleon and is named after Alexander I. On windy days, contemplate that the pillar is said to be held on its pedestal by gravity alone!

The former **General Staff Building** of the Russian army (1819–29) form an incredible 580m curve around the south of the square in two great blocks joined by arches over Bol Morskaya ul. The arches are topped by a chariot of victory, another monument to the Napoleonic Wars. On New Year's Eve 2000, fireworks set off by some youngsters landed on these mainly wooden statues and caused severe damage. Up to two years of reconstruction are planned.

## The Hermitage (Map 7)

See the special section 'The Hermitage' for a detailed guide to the building and its museums.

## Admiralty (Map 7)

The gilded spire of the old Admiralty across the road from Dvortsovaya pl is a prime St Petersburg landmark. Gorokhovaya ul, Voznesensky pr and Nevsky pr all radiate

---

## Maestro Plays the Blues

A regular fixture of Dvortsovaya pl for the last 20 years is the saxophonist who calls himself Maestro. Each evening throughout of the year (except wintertime), he can be seen – and heard – playing his forlorn, often tuneless music on the pedestal of the Alexander Column. He fills the entire square with notes of melancholy which weave their magic around an array of passersby, from lonely romantics to kids with nothing better to do.

It's a warm autumn night, about 2am, the square grand and eerie in its emptiness, illuminated by street lamps and dim moonlight. Maestro sits on his little wooden stool (he has a bum leg and walks with a cane) facing the base of the column, blowing mournfully into his sax, eyes closed.

In the space of 15 minutes the following events transpire. A pair of lovers walking home arm in arm pause to listen to the music, turn to kiss each other in a slow, drunken gesture, their swaying gently giving way to an awkward waltz. They do a clumsy pirouette, then twirl slowly in the shadows of the Winter Palace before breaking out into laughter and walking away. Then a middle-aged man in a wide-brimmed hat and raincoat, walking with a cane, slowly hobbles his way to the column and stops to listen, closing his eyes. When the tune finishes, he utters with great feeling 'spas-sibo' three times, drops a few coins in Maestro's open sax case and shuffles off.

Next, a young man, bearded and philosophical-looking, saunters up to listen, draws deeply from his pipe and walks on. A few minutes later, three young teens, 14-year-olds maybe, zigzag towards the column, beers in hand. They all stop and loiter nervously – are they waiting for their chance to grab the coins or just self-consciously appreciating the music? Maestro interrupts his playing and turns his head around, as if sensing their presence, and asks them not to stand too closely to the case, please. They slowly, silently back away and walk on, reluctantly.

Maestro likes when people tell him that his music embellishes the square, that it reflects and underscores another spirit of this space, which has hosted not only beauty, elegance and glory over the centuries, but also pain, chaos and blood. He started playing there 20 years ago as a kind of performance piece. It caught on with the locals (though not with the authorities, who only gave him official permission to play in 1997), and now he earns his living this way. Occasionally his young son, who has not yet learned his father's grace and restraint, comes along and runs wildly up to passersby asking for money. Other times, his dog is his companion, a glum Doberman who guards the coins but is more pleasant than the kid.

He usually begins late evenings and quits when the Dvortsovaya most closes around 3am.

outwards from it. This spot was the head-quarters of the Russian navy from 1711 to 1917. Now it houses the country's largest military naval college. In late 2000, funeral services were held here for some of the victims of the tragically sunk *Kursk* submarine, past graduates of the college. Despite the spire's solid gold appearance, it's actually made from wood, and almost rotted through before restoration efforts began in 1996.

The Admiralty was reconstructed between 1806 and 1823 to the designs of Andreyan Zakharov, and with its rows of white columns and plentiful reliefs and statuary it is a foremost example of the Russian Empire style. One feature you can get a close look at is the nymphs holding giant globes flanking the main gate. Its statue-filled gardens (laid out from 1872 to 1874) and fountain (1877) are particularly lovely in summer, where it's a main centre of general merry-making. Busts and statues of Glinka, Lermontov, Gogol, other cultural figures – and Hercules – dot the gardens.

## Museum of Political History Annexe (Map 8)

Across the street is a branch of the Museum of Political History *(☎ 312 27 42, Admiralteysky pr 6/2; admission $2; open 10am-6pm Mon-Fri)* in what was once the grand Fitinhov mansion (1790), later turned into the city administration building which housed police security service offices. Even poor Lenin spent 10 days in a jail cell in the basement. From 1917 to 1918 Felix Dzerzhinsky, founder of the KGB precursor Cheka, set up his All-Russian Extraordinary Commission here, where many people were interrogated, some shot on the premises. In 2001, a small but interesting exhibit opened on the 2nd floor chronicling the history of police repression in Russia, detailed through documents, photos and short video documentaries. The exhibit will be a bit obscure without a guide. For an English tour, call in advance.

## Ploshchad Dekabristov (Map 6)

West of the Admiralty, pl Dekabristov (Decembrists' Square) is named after the first attempt at a Russian revolution – the Decembrists' Uprising of 14 December 1825. Inspired by radical ideas from France during the Napoleonic campaigns, young officers who wanted to introduce constitutional monarchy ineptly set up a protest on the very day of the new tsar Nicholas I's swearing-in ceremony. After repeated attempts by Nicholas to reason with the rebels, they were fired upon. Many officers and bystanders died as a result. Most of the leaders later ended up on the gallows or in Siberia.

The most famous statue of Peter the Great, immortalised as the **Bronze Horseman** by Pushkin, with his mount rearing above the snake of treason, stands at the river end of the square. This statue was sculpted over 12 years for Catherine the Great by Frenchman Etienne Falconet. Its inscription reads 'To Peter I from Catherine II – 1782'. The statue has become a much-debated philosophical symbol of the city and Russia itself. Is the horse charging forward or rearing back? The snake is trampled on, but still alive. This statue has become the main trademark of the new spirit of St Petersburg.

Most of the west side of the square is occupied by the Central State Historical Archives in the former Senate and Synod buildings, built by Rossi between 1829 and 1834. These institutions were set up by Peter the Great to run the civil administration and the Orthodox Church.

**Manege Central Exhibition Hall** *(☎ 314 82 53, Isaakievskaya pl 1; about $1; open 10am-6pm Fri-Wed)*, across the street, used to be the Horse Guards' Riding School (constructed between 1804 and 1807 from a design by Quarenghi). It now has rotating exhibitions.

## St Isaac's Cathedral (Map 7)

The golden dome of St Isaac's Cathedral *(Isaakievsky sobor; ☎ 315 97 32, Isaakievskaya pl; $8/4 adult/ISIC holder; open as museum 11am-6pm Thur-Tues)*, looming just south of pl Dekabristov, dominates the St Petersburg skyline. It is one of the largest domed buildings in the world, and over 100kg of gold leaf was used to cover the 21.8m-high dome.

French designer Ricard de Montferrand began designing the cathedral in 1818. It took so long to build (until 1858) that Nicholas I was able to insist on a more grandiose structure than Montferrand had planned.

Special ships and a railway had to be built to carry the granite from Finland for the huge pillars, which each weigh some 120 tonnes. It was the last neo-classical structure to be built in St Petersburg. There's a statue of Montferrand holding a model of the cathedral on the west facade.

Since 1990, after a 62-year gap, services have been held here on major religious holidays and St Isaac's may return to full Church control before long.

St Isaac's obscenely lavish interior, covering 4000 sq metres with 600 sq metres of mosaics and 16,000kg of malachite, 14 types of marble, is not to be missed. Once inside, look up, way up, to the ceiling painting by Karl Bryullov from 1847, which covers an area of 816 sq metres.

Don't miss the sublime city views from the 43m-high **colonnade** *(kolonnada; adult/ISIC holder $3.20/1.60; open 11am-6pm Thur-Tues)* around the drum of the dome. You need to purchase separate tickets for this.

After you climb the 262 steps, babushkas will try to prevent you from photographing the impressive skyline from up there (something about national security), but people sneak shots all the time.

Be aware that photography is not permitted inside the cathedral.

## St Petersburg History Museum (Map 6)

Along Angliyskaya nab, just past the Leytenenta Shmidta most is the St Petersburg History Museum *(☎ 311 75 44, Angliyskaya nab 44; about $2; open 11am-6pm Thur-Tues)*. Located inside the once-glorious neo-classical Rumyantsev Mansion (1802, reconstruction 1826), the museum focuses on Leningrad after the revolution, and has the city's largest collection of documents related to the Blockade (see the boxed text 'The Blockade of Leningrad' later in this chapter).

## Museum of the History of Religion (Map 6)

This museum *(☎ 314 58 38, excursions ☎ 311 04 95, Pochtamskaya ul 14/5; adult/ISIC holder and children $3.20/1.60; open 11am-6pm Thur-Tues)* used to be inside the Kazan Cathedral and moved into its new home near the Main Post Office, a few blocks south of Angliyskaya nab, in 2000. In nine halls, go through the history and infamies of many religions.

## NEVSKY PROSPEKT (MAP 8)

Even stranger are the things that happen on Nevsky Prospekt. O, don't trust that Nevsky Prospekt! I always wrap my cape more tightly around me when I walk on it…It lies all the time, that Nevsky Prospekt, especially when night thickens upon it, separating the white and pale walls of the houses, when the entire city turns into thunder and sparkle…

**Gogol,** *Nevsky Prospekt*

Though the Soviets tried renaming it 25th of October Avenue in honour of their revolution, the name never stuck. Nevsky pr is and always will be Russia's most famous street, running 4.7km from the Admiralty to the Alexandr Nevsky Monastery, from which it takes its name. The inner 2.5km to Moscow Station is St Petersburg's seething main avenue, the city's shopping centre and focus of its entertainment and street life. Pushing through its crowds is an essential St Petersburg experience, and if you're there on a holiday evening (like City Day), the sight of thousands pouring like a stream down its middle is one you'll not soon forget.

Nevsky pr was laid out in the early years of St Petersburg as the start of the main road to Novgorod and soon became dotted with fine buildings, squares and bridges. At the turn of the 20th century, it was one of Europe's grandest boulevards, with cobblestoned sidewalks, a track down the middle for horse-drawn trams (Russia was the fourth country in the world to have them), on either side of which were wooden paving blocks to muffle the sound of horse-drawn carriages – an innovation that was apparently the first in the world and for which Nevsky pr was dubbed the quietest main street in Europe.

Today, things are a bit noisier. A walk down Nevsky is a walk into the heart of the new Russia: a dizzying mishmash of new and colourful shops, restaurants, bars, art galleries, banks and perfumeries overflowing with locals buzzing to and fro, or stopped to have a gander, workers, beggars, tourists, the new rich elite, people selling their pets and shoes, scamrunners, pickpockets, yahoos and religious fanatics – and all of them are shoving past on their way to the action.

See also Arts and Antiques in the Shopping chapter for a list of art galleries worth visiting – many are along the Nevsky.

## Admiralty End (Map 8)

Inner Nevsky, Mal Morskaya ul and Bol Morskaya ul were the heart of the pre-revolutionary financial district. Between the Admiralty and the Fontanka River, there were 50 buildings; banks were in 28 of these.

Points of interest include Mal Morskaya ul 13, where Tchaikovsky died in 1893. The wall of the school at **Nevsky pr 14** (1939) bears a blue-and-white stencilled sign maintained since WWII. Beginning Граждане! *(Grazhdane!)*, it translates: 'Citizens! At times of artillery bombardment this side of the street is most dangerous!'.

Close to the Moyka, the **Kafe Literaturnoe** is, despite being an over-priced tourist trap, worth peeping into for its Pushkin associations (he had his last meal here). Across the Moyka, Rastrelli's green **Stroganov Palace** *(☎ 219 16 08, Nevsky pr 17; adult/student $8/4; open 10am-5pm Tues-Sun)* has kept most of its original baroque appearance. It was built between 1752 and 1754. The Stroganovs were a prominent family in pre-revolutionary Russia and were noted art collectors (and yes, if you absolutely must know, their chef *did* create a certain beef dish). Inside there is a gallery of wax figures of the Romanov family, and an exhibition of Russian decorative and applied arts from the Russian Museum's collection.

## Kazan Cathedral Area (Map 8)

A block east of the Moyka, the great, 111m-long colonnaded arms of the neo-classical Kazan Cathedral *(Kazansky sobor; ☎ 311 48 26; admission free; open 11am-6pm daily)* reach out towards the avenue. Andrey Voronikhin, a former serf, built the cathedral between 1801 and 1811 and his design was influenced by St Peter's in Rome. His original plan was to build a second, mirror version of the cathedral, opposite it on the other side of Nevsky. The square in front of it has been a site for political demonstrations since before the revolution.

The cathedral now holds daily services (at 9am and 6pm), and it is free to wander through and gaze up at the daunting 80m high dome. The two statues out front are of the victorious Napoleonic War Field Marshall Mikhail Kutuzov (whose remains are buried inside the cathedral) and his friend and aide Mikhail Barclay de Tolly.

Across Nevsky pr, tucked in a recess between Bol and Mal Konyushennaya is the lovely **Lutheran Church** (1830s). Distinguished by a four-column portico and topped with a discreet cupola, this was turned into a swimming pool in the 1950s (the high diving board was placed in the apse) – but is that worse than using it to store vegetables, as it had been since the 1930s? Restoration is, needless to say, still under way, but the church is open to visitors. Check out the photos from its chlorine era just inside.

Opposite the cathedral, St Petersburg's biggest bookshop, **Dom Knigi**, is topped by the globe emblem of the Singer sewing machine company, which constructed the building between 1902 and 1904. The building also housed the American consulate for a few years prior to WWI. Just behind the Kazan Cathedral, a bit south of the central train ticket office, sits the **Bankovsky most** (1825–26), one of St Petersburg's loveliest bridges. Suspended by cables emerging from the mouths of golden-winged griffins, the wooden bridge affords a splendid view north up the Griboedova Canal past Nevsky pr to the Church on Spilled Blood.

In the next block of Nevsky pr, pavement artists cluster in front of the **Central Art Salon**, and offer to paint your portrait or caricature.

THINGS TO SEE & DO

## The Blockade of Leningrad

Though it is one of the most significant events in the history of all war, the Siege of Leningrad is little-known by most visitors to the city. While other battles get pages in history books or dramatic re-enactments on *Discovery Channel*, this one gets little attention. Perhaps the human tragedy involved is beyond the scope of page or screen to convey.

After the war began on 22 June 1941, Leningraders knew the Germans were fast approaching: many residents fled; art treasures and precious documents from the Hermitage and other museums were shipped out by the train-full; factories were evacuated and relocated to Siberia; historical sculptures were buried or covered with sandbags. Yet no-one could possibly have predicted the suffering the city was to witness. From 8 September 1941 to 27 January 1944 (872 days), Nazi troops choked the city. Their plan, as indicated in a secret directive, was to 'wipe the city of Petersburg from the face of the earth'. A fragile 'Road of Life' across frozen Lake Ladoga was the only (albeit heavily bombed) lifeline the city had for provisions and evacuations.

Food was practically nonexistent in the city, and at one point rations were limited to 175g of sawdust-leaden bread a day. People ate their dogs and cats, even rats and birds disappeared from the city. A fallen horse would be butchered in minutes and carried home in pieces by starving citizens. The paste behind wallpaper was scraped off and eaten, leather army belts were cooked until chewable. Cannibalism started in the shelters for refugees from the neighbouring towns; without ration cards, they were among the first to die, and strange-flavoured meat went on sale at the Haymarket. People exchanged precious jewels and antiques for a loaf of bread. The exhausted and starved literally fell over dead on the streets. There were periods when over 30,000 people died of hunger each day.

More than 150,000 shells and bombs dropped on the city, the effects of which are still visible on some buildings (notably on the west wall of St Isaac's Cathedral and the north-west corner of Anichkov most). Still, life went on. Concerts and plays were performed in candlelit halls, lectures given, poetry written, orphanages opened, brigades formed to clean up the city. Most famous was the 9 August 1942 concert of Shostakovich's 7th Symphony by the Leningrad Philharmonic, nationally broadcasted by radio from the besieged city. According to survivors, random acts of kindness outnumbered incidents of robbery and vandalism, and lessons learned about the human spirit would remain unforgotten for a lifetime. From a poem by Olga Berggolts, written after the blockade was lifted:

In mud, in darkness, hunger, and sorrow, where death, like a shadow, trod on our heels, we were so happy at times, breathed such turbulent freedom, that our grandchildren would envy us.

For a detailed, harrowing description of the siege, read Harrison Salisbury's *The 900 Days*. Otherwise, a visit to one or all of these sites would greatly enrich your understanding of its history.

### Museums

**St Petersburg History Museum (Map 6)** *(☎ 311 75 44, Angliyskaya nab 44; admission $2; open 11am-5pm Thur-Tues)*. Housed in the majestic Rumyantsev Mansion (1826), this reflects St Petersburg since the October 1917 Revolution, but its main focus is the blockade. It has the city's largest repository of documents from the time, displayed in a large exhibit.

**Blockade Museum (Map 5)** *(☎ 275 72 08, Solyanoy per 9; admission $1; open 10am-4pm Thur-Tues)*. This museum opened just three months after the blockade was lifted and boasted 37,000 exhibits, including real tanks and airplanes. But three years later, during Stalin's repression of the city, the museum was shut, its director shot, and most of the exhibits destroyed or redistributed. Only during 1985's *glasnost*, an attempt was made to once again gather documents to reopen the museum; this happened in 1989. The displays contain donations from survivors, propaganda posters from the time, and an example of the sawdust-filled tiny piece of bread Leningraders had to survive on. English excursions are available if booked in advance.

# The Blockade of Leningrad

**Monument to the Heroic Defenders of Leningrad (Map 3)** (☎ 293 60 36, Pl Pobedy; admission free; open 10am-6pm Thur-Tues). This is one of the city's must-see exhibits. Centred around a 48m-high obelisk (if arriving from the airport, it makes a striking introduction to the city), the monument (unveiled in 1975) is a sculptural ensemble of bronze statues symbolising the heavy plight of defence, and eventual victory. The frontline was only 9km from this spot. On a lower level, a bronze ring 40m in diameter symbolises the city's encirclement; a very moving sculpture stands in the centre. Haunting symphonic music creates a sombre atmosphere to guide you downstairs to the underground exhibition in a huge, mausoleum-like interior. Here the glow of 900 bronze lamps create an eeriness matched by the sound of a metronome (the only sound heard by Leningraders on their radios throughout the war save for emergency announcements), showing that the city's heart was still beating. Large bronze sheets form the *Chronicle*; changed daily, these are engraved with the events in Leningrad on each day of the blockade. Twelve thematically assembled showcases feature items from the war and siege. An electrified relief map in the centre of the room shows the shifting front lines of the war. Ask to see the two seven-minute documentary films, played on large screens at the touch of a button. From metro Moskovskaya, it's a 10-minute walk south.

## Piskaryovskoe Cemetery (Map 3)

Some half a million Leningraders are buried in mass graves in this cemetery (☎ 247 57 16, Nepokoryonnykh pr; admission free; open 10am-6pm daily). Bodies were dragged here on little sleds by relatives, or brought here from collection points around the city. This is a sobering place; here you'll understand the Russian obsession with that war. There are 186 raised mounds marked only by simple plaques engraved with a year and either a red star or hammer and sickle (indicating a military or civilian grave mount). At the entrance is an exhibit of photographs that need no captions. It's about 35 minutes from the centre on public transport. From metro Ploshchad Muzhestva turn left, cross pr Nepokoryonnykh and take bus No 123. It's the 6th stop.

## Outside the City

The **Breakthrough of the Blockade Museum** (☎ 262 207 62; admission free; open 10am-6pm Tues-Sun) is located in the village of Marino near the town of Kirovsk. It displays a large diorama painting of the breaking of the siege. Take bus 565 or 575 for about 30 minutes from metro Ulitsa Dybenko. The **Sologubovka German Military Cemetery** (admission free; open daily) is the result of an ongoing project to give the some 100,000 German soldiers who died in the area a proper final resting place. About 20,000 war dead have been placed already; the goal is to bury up to 80,000 here. A nearby orthodox church is being restored to house an exhibition and to serve as a gesture of reconciliation. Every November, a German delegation holds memorial services here. The village of Sologubovka can be reached by electric suburban train from Moscow Station in the direction of Budogoshe. It's almost a two-hour trip east of the city.

**Monument to the Heroic Defenders of Leningrad**

STEVE KOKKER

## Griboedova Canal to The Fontanka River (Map 8)

This section of Nevsky is the busiest. Standing proud as a peacock on the corner of Nevsky and Mikhailovskaya ul is the **Grand Hotel Europe**, built between 1873 and 1875, redone in Style-Moderne in the 1910s and completely renovated from 1989 to 1991. It is one of the city's architectural gems, boasting shameless splendour: marble and gilt, sweeping staircases and antique furnishings. If you're feeling wicked, you can lounge about in the atrium (or visit the nicest toilets in the city, the reason many strained-faced tourists come here in the first place) and you don't even have to buy one of its $4 cups of coffee.

Tucked in a recess near Mikhailovskaya ul, is the **Armenian Church of St Catherine** (1771–80). The Soviet regime deemed it reasonable to bash the place to bits and install a 2nd floor, which blocked the view of the cupola. The renovation is still under way, but the church is open to visitors.

Diagonally across Nevsky, the arcades of **Gostiny Dvor** department store stand facing the clock tower of the former **Town Duma** on Dumskaya ul, seat of the pre-revolutionary city government. One of the world's first indoor shopping malls, the 'Merchant Yard' dating from between 1757 and 1785, stretches 230m along Nevsky (its perimeter is over 1km long), and is another Rastrelli creation. St Petersburg's equivalent of Moscow's GUM, Gostiny Dvor got a facelift in the late 1990s and the inside is now quite fashionable. On weekend afternoons, you can watch the traditional spectacle of lunatic-fringe political groups proselytising their important messages out front. It's the Hyde Park Corner of St Petersburg; in other words, get your Stalin calendars here.

On the other side of Nevsky, in the arcade at No 48, the **Passazh** department store is pretty (notice the glass ceilings) and packed with pricey goods, but the atmosphere is a bit anaemic. Downstairs in the basement is a well-stocked supermarket.

The **Vorontsov Palace** (1749–57) on Sadovaya ul, opposite the south-east side of Gostiny Dvor, is another noble town house by Rastrelli. From 1810 it was the most elite military school in the empire. It's still a military school for young cadets; on weekends you can watch mothers pass food parcels to their sons through the wrought-iron front gates.

A very pleasant street is the newly pedestrianised Mal Sadovaya ul. A number of statues and sculptures have been placed here (see the boxed text 'Not Size That Counts'), including a marble ball with a fountain underneath which makes it spin forever, and a metal/LED stand which counts down the days and minutes to the city's 300th birthday.

At Nevsky pr 56 is the **Yeliseevsky Food Shop**, the most sumptuous 'grocery store' you may have ever seen. Built in Style Moderne between 1901 and 1903, it is decorated with sculptures and statues on the outside, and a gorgeous mirrored ceiling and stained glass windows on the inside.

## Around Ploshchad Ostrovskogo (Map 8)

An enormous **statue of Catherine the Great** (1873) stands amid the chess, backgammon and sometimes even mahjong players that crowd the benches here. At the Empress' heels are renowned statesmen of the 19th-century, including her lovers Orlov, Potyomkim and Suvorov.

This airy square, commonly referred to as the Catherine Gardens, was created by Carlo Rossi in the 1820s and 1830s, and its west side is taken up by the lavish **National Library of Russia**, St Petersburg's biggest with some 31 million items, nearly a sixth of which is in foreign languages. Rossi's **Pushkin Theatre** (formerly the Alexandrinsky) at the south end of the square is one of Russia's most important. In 1896 the opening night of Chekhov's *The Seagull* was so badly received here that the playwright fled to wander anonymously among the crowds on Nevsky pr.

Behind the theatre, on ul Zodchego Rossi, is a continuation of Rossi's ensemble. It is proportion deified: the buildings are 22m wide, 22m apart and 220m long. The **Vaganova School of Choreography**

Best view in town: St Petersburg from the dome of St Isaac's Cathedral.

Old Admiralty's golden spire is a St Pete landmark.

Russian Empire on show: Zakharov's Admiralty

The ice-blue Smolny Cathedral

Vosstania ploshchad lauds 'Leningrad – Hero City'

Alexandr Nevsky Monastery

Bolshoy zal: St Petersburg Philharmonic's home

A spring clean for the St Petersburg Mosque

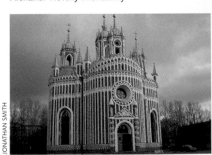

The candy-striped, psuedo-Gothic Chesma Church

Rimsky-Korsakov Conservatory

## Not Size That Counts

You've been walking open-jawed around St Petersburg, feeling dwarfed by the Herculean proportions of the buildings, monuments and statues. *Is there anything small in this country?*, you may well be asking yourself. Yes! Besides people's salaries, there are tiny things here, and their petiteness makes a nice respite from the colossal grandeur of everything else.

St Petersburg's smallest statue, nicknamed **Chyzhik** (Map 7), is at the Inzhenerny most over the Moyka where it flows into the Fontanka, just east of the Summer Gardens' main entrance. The notoriously carousing and fun-loving students of the 19th-century Engineering Institute nearby came up with a popular ditty: *Chyzhik, pyzhik, gde tyi byl? Na Fontanke, vodku pyl!* (Little birdie, where have you been? Down at the Fontanka, drinking vodka!). This charming ode to the studying habits of St Petersburg's civil engineers inspired a charming little monument by Rezo Gabriadze that's exceptionally easy to miss: a little bird perched just above the river. You can see it best from the southwest side of Inzhenerny most. It's good luck to throw coins: if it lands on the bird's perch you'll get a wish fulfilled (and it's appreciated by the kids who hang round with magnets and gum at the end of string fishing for coins!).

Three other wee statues are along the pedestrian Mal Sadovaya ul (Map 8). Walk up from Nevsky pr about 20m, then look up on either side of the street – perched on the ledges of the buildings' 2nd floors are a small **black cat** (a male, done by a female sculptor, L Domrachyova) and a 33cm-tall **white cat** (female, done by a male sculptor, V Petrovichev). Both were placed in January 2000. They stand opposite each other, destined never to meet.

Just up the street a bit, and into the courtyard of house No 3 you'll find the fun metallic **Mutt** (1999), a 70cm-high composition of artist V Sivakov's dearly departed doggie. The walls surrounding the statue are covered in graffiti – people were meant to scribble their testaments of love to the dog who used to brighten up this courtyard, but instead the graffiti is of the Misha loves Masha, or Offspring Iz Kool variety.

There's another statue on Mal Sadovaya ul, near the puttycats, of a photographer (this one's life-size). Placed in 2001, this bronze, amiable work is in honour of old St Petersburg's most famous photographer Karl Bulla. His stunning – documentary, but poetic and evocative – images of the early 20th century St Petersburg comprise the bulk of published photos from that period.

---

situated here (at No 2) is the Kirov Ballet's training school, where Pavlova, Nijinsky, Nureyev and others learned their art.

The **Anichkov Palace** (1741–50) is the city's second palace, between pl Ostrov-skogo and the Fontanka (its main facade faces the river, and was once joined to it by a canal). It was also twice a generous gift for services rendered – Empress Elizabeth gave it to her favourite Count Razumovsky, and later Catherine the Great presented it to Potyomkin. A slew of architects, including Rastrelli and Rossi, worked on it. It became the city's largest Pioneer Club headquarters after 1936 and to this day houses over 100 after-school clubs for over 10,000 children. Today there's a small museum (☎ 310 43 95, *palace* ☎ 310 84 33, **W** *anichkov-dvorets.spb.ru;*

*admission $2; open 10am-5pm Mon-Fri)* inside, where worthwhile and relaxed tours of the charming palace and grounds can be organised. Otherwise, the palace, as a children's club, is off-limits to casual tourists.

### From Fontanka River to Ploshchad Vosstania (Map 8)

Nevsky pr crosses the Fontanka on the **Anichkov most**, with famous 1840s statues (sculpted by the German P Klodt) of rearing horses at its four corners. They symbolise man's struggle with and eventual taming of nature. To witness pure artistic revenge, put prudery aside and take note of the southwestern horse's genitals: unlike his anatomically correct companions, his naughty bits are in the image of the sculptor's unfaithful wife's lover (another version has it that it's Napoleon's profile).

A photogenic baroque backdrop is provided by the (currently rather faded) red 1840s **Beloselsky-Belozersky Palace**. The palace was formerly a home of Communist Party officials and is now the **Historical Museum of Wax Figures** *(☎ 312 36 44, Nevsky pr 41; adult/student $4/2; open noon-6pm daily)*, which is a hoot; if you ever questioned the legitimacy of the 'body' in Lenin's tomb in Moscow, you'll know for sure after you see this. There are two displays: 'Russia from the 7th to 18th Centuries' and 'From Alexander to Putin'.

Between the Fontanka and Moscow Station, Nevsky pr has fewer historic buildings but heaps more chi-chi shops, restaurants and cinemas.

Marking the division of Nevsky pr and Stary (old) Nevsky pr is **Ploshchad Vosstania** (Uprising Square), whose landmarks are the giant granite pillar with the Commie star, the Moscow Station, and the animation screen atop the building next to the station. Note the writing on top of the Hotel Oktyabrskaya across from the station: ГОРОД-ГЕРОЙ ЛЕНИНГРАД (Hero City Leningrad); several cities were conferred a hero status for their heroism, stoicism, and losses during WWII.

Stary Nevsky juts off the square at a 45° angle and heads south-east to the Alexandra Nevskogo most. It's charm is in its relative desolation and laid-back mood.

## Akhmatova Museum (Map 8)

Across the Fontanka, north of Nevsky pr, the yellow **Sheremetev Palace** (1750–55) houses two lovely little museums. In the palace itself, accessed via nab reki Fontanki 34 is a branch of the **Museum of Theatrical and Musical Arts** *(☎ 272 44 41; nab reki Fontanki 34; admission $1.50; open noon-6pm Wed-Fri, noon-4pm Sat-Sun)* which has a collection of musical instruments from the 19th and 20th centuries, some beautifully decorated. The Sheremetev family was famous for the concerts and theatre they hosted at their palace, which was a centre of musical life in the capital in the 18th century.

Behind the palace is the **Akhmatova Memorial Museum** *(☎ 272 22 11, nab reki Fontanki 34; adult/student $2/0.60; open 11am-5.30pm Tues-Sun)*. It is more easily accessed via the courtyard at Liteyny pr 53. Anna Akhmatova was a deeply-loved poet and popular figure in the early 20th century (see Arts in the Facts about St Petersburg chapter), when it was rumoured that she was having an affair with the equally beloved Alexandr Blok. After the revolution, her fate turned sour and she lived through the arrest and execution of her husband, the arrest and exile of her second husband, and two arrests and exile of her son; a direct appeal to Stalin got her son released the first time, but after the second arrest, the official tide had turned against her and her cries were left unheard. Her son languished in Kresty prison, where Akhmatova stood for hundreds of hours, waiting to pass him food.

Her old apartment is on the 2nd floor and is filled with mementos of the poet and correspondence with Pasternak. There's a contemplative, peaceful atmosphere to the flat. Downstairs is a bookshop and video room where you can watch Russian-language documentaries on her life while drinking tea or coffee. It also sells audio tapes of Akhmatova's works read by famous Russian actors. There's another Akhmatova museum in Pushkin (see the Excursions chapter).

## GUVD Museum (Map 7)

For police enthusiasts, there's a great but little-known GUVD Museum *(☎ 279 42 33, ul Poltavskaya 12; group tour about $2, individual tour about $10; open 10am-5pm Mon-Fri)*, which chronicles the history of criminality and law enforcement by the Ministry of Internal Affairs in Leningrad/St Petersburg. This balanced, fascinating exhibit, featuring photos, costumes and weapons in several large halls, will acquaint you with interesting titbits about gang bosses and the Mafia's reign of terror in the 1920s through the fight to control illegal abortions and alcohol production. You'll need to get a guided tour for this, booked in advance. If you understand Russian, you can join an already-arranged group; if not, bring along a translator. A booked tour will cost about $10, but if you just join another group, it will cost about $2.

If this doesn't whet your KGB whistle, take a chilling walk out front of the ex-**KGB headquarters** (and current Interior Ministry headquarters), commonly referred to as the Big House *(Bolshoy Dom)* at Liteyny pr 4. It's a fierce-looking block of granite built in 1932, and where much unpleasantness transpired.

### Alexandr Nevsky Monastery (Map 7)

The working superior monastery *(lavra; ☎ 274 04 09, 179/2 Nevsky pr; admission free)* with the graves of some of Russia's most famous artistic figures, is entered from pl Alexandra Nevskogo opposite the Hotel Moskva. It was founded in 1713 by Peter the Great, who wrongly thought this was where Alexandr of Novgorod had beaten the Swedes in 1240. In 1797 it became a lavra. Today it is open to the public and, sadly, the courtyard is filled with homeless beggars.

You can wander freely around most of the grounds, but you must buy tickets from the kiosk on your right after entering the main gates to enter the **graveyards** *(☎ 271 26 35; admission $1; open 11am-6pm Fri-Wed Mar-Sept, 11am-3.30pm Fri-Wed Oct-Feb).*

The **Tikhvin Cemetery** (Tikhvinskoe kladbishche), on the right as you enter, contains the most famous graves. In the far right-hand corner from its gate, a bust of Tchaikovsky marks his grave. Nearby are Rubinshteyn, Borodin, Mussorgsky, Rimsky-Korsakov (check out his wild tomb!) and Glinka. Make a right after entering and you'll reach the tomb of Dostoevsky.

The **Lazarus Cemetery** (Lazarevskoe kladbishche), facing the Tikhvin across the entrance path, contains several late great St Petersburg architects – among them Stasov, Voronikhin, Quarenghi, Zakharov and Rossi. Scholar Mikhail Lomonosov is also buried here.

Across the canal in the main lavra complex, the first main building on the left is the 1717–22 baroque **Annunciation Church** (Blagoveshchenskaya tserkov), now the

City Sculpture Museum *(☎ 274 25 17; admission $0.80; open 11am-5pm Fri-Wed)* which features a large collection of the original models and designs for the city's sculptures and monuments.

About 100m further on is the monastery's 1776–90 classical **Trinity Cathedral** *(Troitsky sobor; ☎ 274 16 12; open for worship from 6am Sat, Sun & holidays, closed for cleaning 2pm-5pm; early liturgy from 7am, late liturgy from 10am, all-night vigils from 6pm).* Hundreds crowd in here on 12 September to celebrate the feast of Saint Alexandr Nevsky. His remains are in the silver reliquary by the main iconostasis. Behind the cathedral is the **Nicholas Cemetery** *(open 9am-9pm summer, 9am-6pm winter),* a romantically overgrown field where many of the cathedral's priests are buried.

Opposite the cathedral is the St Petersburg **Metropolitan's House** (1775–78), residence of Metropolitan Vladimir, the spiritual leader of St Petersburg's Russian Orthodox community. In the surrounding grounds is a smaller cemetery where leading communist (and atheist!) party officials and luminaries are buried. On the far right of the grounds facing the canal is St Petersburg's **Orthodox Academy**, one of only a handful in Russia (the main one is at Sergiev Posad).

### NORTH OF NEVSKY PROSPEKT
### Russian Museum (Map 8)

The former Mikhailovsky Palace, now the Russian Museum *(Gosudarstvenny Russky muzey; ☎ 311 14 65, Inzhenernaya ul 4; adult/student $6/3, open 10am-5pm Wed-Mon)* houses one of the country's two finest collections of Russian art (the other is in Moscow's Tretyakov Gallery). If your time in the city is limited and you think only the Hermitage is a must-see, try your utmost to accommodate some time for this gem of a museum; your appreciation of Russian culture will be much deepened by it.

The palace was designed by Carlo Rossi and built between 1819 and 1825 for Grand Duke Mikhail (brother of Tsars Alexander I and Nicholas I) as compensation for not being able to have a chance on the throne.

## The Russian Museum (A Room-by-Room Tour)

### Mikhailovsky Palace, Second Floor

**Rooms 1-4:** 12th- to 15th-century icons. Apostle Peter and Apostle Paul by students of Andrey Rublyov are particularly good. **Rooms 5-9:** 17th- to 18th-century sculpture, portraits and tapestries, and Rastrelli's pompous *Anna Joannovna and an Arab boy* (7). **Rooms 10, 12, 13, 14, 17:** Late-18th-century, early-19th-century paintings and sculpture; **11:** The White Hall, the most ornate in the palace, with period furniture by Rossi, and where Strauss and Berlioz, as guests, performed concerts; **14:** Karl Bryullov's *Last Day of Pompei* (1827-33), which was in its time the most famous Russian painting ever; Pushkin, Gogol, Herzen and other writers rhapsodised over it, and there were queues for months to see it. Petersburgers saw it as a doomsday scenario of their own city, which had a few years earlier been damaged in a huge flood. **Room 15:** Big 19th-century canvases mainly by graduates of the official Academy – Aivazovsky's Crimea seascapes stand out, most frighteningly *The Wave*. Here is Ivanov's most famous work, *Christ's Appearance to the People*.

### Mikhailovsky Palace, First Floor

**Rooms 18-22:** 19th-century works focusing (19) on the beginnings of the socially aware 'Realist' tradition and including (21) spectacular works by Semiradsky and Flavitsky, including his gigantic *Christian Martyrs in Colosseum.* **Rooms 23-38:** Peredvizhniki and associated artists including (25): Kramskoy; **26:** Nikolai Ge, including his fearsome *Peter I prosecuting Tsarevich Alexey in Peterhof*; **27:** Shishkin and **31:** KA Savitsky's *To The War*; **32:** Poleneov, including his Christ and the Sinner. **Rooms 33-35, 54:** A permanent exhibition of the work of Repin, probably Russia's best-loved artist; 33 has portraits and the incomparable *Barge Haulers on the Volga*, an indictment of Russian 'social justice'; and 54 contains the massive Meeting of the State Council, Repin's rendering of the meeting at the Mariinsky Palace on 7 May 1901 (it's full of tsarist hot shots; there's a scheme in the room to help you tell who's who). **Rooms 36-37:** Russian history, portraits by Surikov, a national revivalist and Mikhail Mikeshin's model of the Millennium of Russia (36). **Room 38:** Historical works by Vasnetsov including *Russian Knight at the Crossroads* and other 'sketches' for his mosaics. **Room 39:** Popular 19th-century painter Malyavin's depictions of Russian mothers and maidens. **Rooms 40-41:** Unforgettably stunning landscapes by Kuindzhi. **Rooms 42-47:** Works by Levitan and other late-19th-century painters, and **45:** Ryabushkin on pre-Peter the Great 17th-century Russian history, includes the very telling and humorous *Yedut*, or *They Are Coming*, depicting the perturbed-looking reception committee for the first foreigners allowed in Russia. **Room 48:** Antakolski sculptures. (Exits straight ahead lead to 10 halls of Russian folk art, including handicrafts, woodwork, carvings, pottery, toys etc; exits to the right lead to the Benois building.) **Room 49:** A long corridor that houses temporary exhibitions. **Rooms 50-53:** Closed storage area. **Rooms 55-59:** Sculptures (18th-20th centuries) including sensitive works by Matveev and Shubin. **Rooms 60-65:** Temporarily closed for repairs.

### Benois Building, Second Floor

**Rooms 66-79:** 20th-century art, including (66) Vrubel, with his epic *Russian Hero and Venice*, and Artemiy Ober's terrifying bronze *Calamity*; **67:** Nesterov's religious paintings of the history of the Orthodox Church; Konenkov sculptures and Vasnetsov's *The Entombing*; **70, 71:** Serov, portraits of Russian aristocracy and other high-rollers; Trubitskoy sculptures of same including Isaak Levitan and Children; **72:** Impressionists Korovin, Grabar and Serebryakova; Trubitskoy's *Moscow Carriage Driver* and Boris Kustodiev's *Holiday on the Volga*; **73:** Kustodiev's paintings of stereotypical Russians; **74:** The Rerikh Room. **Rooms 75-79:** Russian avant-garde, symbolism, neoclassical works by Saryan Kuznetsov, Petrov-Vodkin, Grigoriev, Shukhaev, Altman, Lenturov etc, including Petrov-Vodkin's famous *Mother* (1915) (78). **Rooms 81-105:** Halls for rotating exhibitions. **Rooms 106-133:** Temporarily closed.

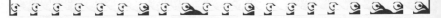

# RUSSIAN MUSEUM РУССКИЙ МУЗЕЙ

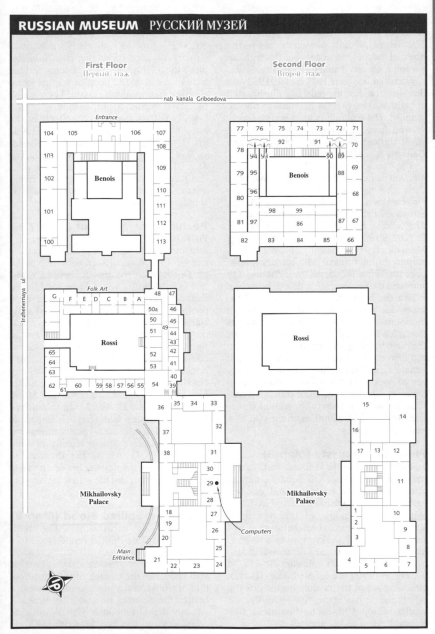

**First Floor**
Первый этаж

**Second Floor**
Второй этаж

The museum was founded in 1895 under Nicholas II, and opened three years later. The Benois building, now connected to the original palace and accessible through an entrance on nab kanala Griboedova, was constructed between 1914 and 1919. Note that the facade of the palace is illuminated at night, making that the best time to photograph it. The building is most impressively viewed from the back, during a late-night stroll through the pleasant **Mikhailovsky Gardens** behind it.

The museum currently boasts over 400,000 items in its collection and now owns three other city palaces where temporary exhibitions are also held: the Marble Palace, the Strogonov Palace and the Engineer's Castle. They also have grandiose plans for the future: In 2002, all 8.7 hectares of the already lovely Mikhailovsky Gardens will be redesigned according to the original 19th-century plans; once funding is found, the moat that used to surround the Engineer's Castle will be redug.

See the boxed text 'The Russian Museum' for a straightforward walk through the rooms. The museum's main entrance is through a tiny door on the far right side of the main building, off Inzhenernaya ul. You can also enter via the Benois wing off nab kanala Griboedova. English guided tours can be booked on ☎ 314 44 48. You can also become a member of the Friends of the Russian Museum society for annual donations from $50 to $2000, entitling you to a range of privileges.

### Ploshchad Iskusstv (Map 8)

Just a block east of the Griboedova Canal is the quiet pl Iskusstv (Arts Square), named after its cluster of museums and concert halls. A **statue of Pushkin**, erected in 1957, stands in the middle of the tree-lined square. The square, and Mikhailovskaya ul which joins it to Nevsky pr, were designed as a unit by Rossi in the 1820s and 1830s.

The **Brodsky House-Museum** (☎ 314 36 58, pl Iskusstv 3) is a former home of Isaak Brodsky, one of the favoured artists of the revolution. It has some 800 lesser-known works by top 19th-century painters like Repin, Levitan and Kramskoy.

The **Museum of Ethnography** (☎ 313 44 20, Inzhenernaya ul 4/1; adult/student $3.50/1; gold & jewellery exhibition $3.25/1.60; open 10am-6pm Tues-Sun) displays the traditional crafts, customs and beliefs of the over 150 peoples who make up Russia's fragile ethnic mosaic. There's a bit of left-over Soviet propaganda going on here, but it's a marvellous collection: the sections on Transcaucasia and Central Asia are fascinating, with rugs and two full-size yurts (nomad's portable tent-house). The Special Storeroom has some great weapons and rare devotional objects. A guide makes a lot of difference to how much you understand on your visit.

### Pushkin Flat-Museum (Map 7)

Pushkin's last home (he only lived here for four months) is beside one of the prettiest curves of the Moyka River, north of Nevsky pr. This is where the poet died after his duel in 1837. His killer was a French soldier of fortune, Baron d'Anthes, who had been publicly courting Pushkin's beautiful wife, Natalia. The affair was widely seen as a put-up job on behalf of Tsar Nicholas I, who found the famed poet's radical politics inconvenient – and who, rumour has it, may himself have been the one really stalking Natalia. The little house is now the Pushkin Flat-Museum (☎ 311 35 31, nab reki Moyki 12; adult/student $2.50/1.25) and includes a Russian-language tour (English tours can be arranged in advance). The apartment has been reconstructed to look exactly as it did in the poet's last days. For the morbid among you, on display are his death mask, a lock of his hair, and the waistcoat he wore when he died.

### Church on Spilled Blood (Map 8)

A church by any other name… The multi-domed Church on Spilled Blood (☎ 315 16 36, Konyushennaya pl; adult/student $8.50/3.60; open 11am-6pm Thur-Tues) is also known as the Church of the Resurrection of Christ, and various combinations of both of these names are also often heard. It sits on the Griboedova Canal north of Nevsky pr and was built between 1883 and

1907 on the spot where Alexander II, despite his reforms, was blown up by the People's Will terrorist group in 1881 (that explains the gruesome name).

It's now most commonly known as the church that took 24 years to build and 27 to restore. In August 1997, with much fanfare, it finally opened its doors after painstaking work on the 7000 sq metres of mosaics by over 30 artists which line the walls inside. On the very spot of the assassination is a marble bust *Shatrovy Cen* of Alexander (some tourists have mistaken this for a bust of Stalin!). However, the exterior is endlessly more impressive than the interior (especially considering the hefty price of admission). If your budget's tight, stick to gawking at the candy-cake Russian Revival style marvel, the only one of its kind in the city.

A few facts: There are 20 granite plaques on the facade which record, in gold letters, the main events of Alexander's reign, the steeple is 81m high; the mosaic panels about half-way up detail scenes from the New Testament; and the 144 mosaic coats of arms each represent the provinces, regions and towns of the Russian Empire of Alexander's time, which all joined in mourning the death of the tsar.

## Mars Field (Map 5)

The Mars Field (Marsovo pole) is the open space south of the Troitsky most, about a kilometre north of Nevsky pr along Sadovaya ul. Don't take a short cut across the grass – you may be walking on graves from the October 1917 Revolution, the civil war, or of later communist luminaries also buried here. The field is so named because it was the scene of 19th-century military parades. An **eternal flame** burns for the victims of the revolution and ensuing civil war.

Between the field and the Neva is the **Marble Palace** *(☎ 312 91 96, Millionnaya ul 5; adult/student $5.40/2.70; open Wed-Mon 10am-5pm)*. It was built between 1768 and 1785 as Catherine the Great's gift to Grigory Orlov for putting a Moscow rebellion down. It's an architectural gem by Rinaldi, who used 36 kinds of marble, and was pained to make them bleed seamlessly into

one another. Formerly the Lenin Museum, it is currently a branch of the Russian Museum featuring rotating exhibitions of modern art and a permanent exhibit on foreign artists who were active in Russia in the 18th and 19th centuries.

A monstrous but amusing **equestrian statue** of Alexander III stands plumply outside; it became the butt of many jokes after it was erected in 1909 (originally outside the Moscow Station). Even son Nicholas II thought of shipping it off to Irkutsk, but when rumours started that he wanted to send his dad into Siberian exile, he changed his mind. Sculptor Paolo Trubetskoy said of his work, 'I don't care about politics. I simply depicted one animal on another'.

## Summer Garden (Map 5)

Central St Petersburg's loveliest and oldest park, the Summer Garden *(Letny Sad; ☎ 314 03 74; adult/child & student $0.55/free; open 9am-10pm daily May-Oct; 10am-6pm daily Oct-mid Apr; closed mid to end Apr)* is between the Mars Field and the Fontanka. You can enter at the north or south ends.

Laid out for Peter the Great with fountains, pavilions and a geometrical plan to resemble the park at Versailles, the garden became a strolling place for St Petersburg's 19th-century leisured classes. The fountains were powered by a canal dug from the Ligovsky Canal, which once flowed along present-day Ligovsky pr. The flood of 1777 destroyed them. Though changed since that era, it maintains a formal elegance, with thousands of lime trees shading its straight paths and lines of statues.

The modest, two-storey Summer Palace in the north-eastern corner was St Petersburg's first palace, built for Peter between 1704 and 1714, and is pretty well intact. Little reliefs around the walls depict Russian naval victories. Today it's open as a museum *(Muzey Letny Dvorets Petra I; ☎ 314 04 56; adult/child & student $1.80/0.60; open 11am-7pm Wed-Mon early May-early Nov)*. Many rooms are stocked with early-18th-century furnishings. Behind the glass cupboards inside the Green Room, on the 2nd floor, is where Peter used to keep those sweet mutants which now wow the crowds at Kunstkammer.

A much greater Summer Palace used to stand across the canal from the south end of the Summer Garden. But Rastrelli's almost fairy-tale, wooden creation for Empress Elizabeth was knocked down in the 1790s to make way for the bulky, brick Engineers' Castle of Paul I. The son of Catherine the Great, he was born in the wooden palace and wanted to build his own residence on the same spot. But this erratic, cruel tsar only got 40 days in his new abode before being assassinated by plotters. In 1823 it became a military engineering school (hence the name), whose most famous pupil was Fyodor Dostoevsky. One wing is now owned by the Russian Museum, who stage occasional exhibitions.

## Museum of Decorative & Applied Arts (Map 5)

Otherwise known as the Stieglitz Museum (☎ 273 32 58, Solyarnoy per 13; adult/student $3/1.50; open 11am-5pm Tues-Sat) this is further north, in the block opposite the east side of the Summer Gardens. This is one of the most impressive museums in the city, full stop. In 1878, the millionaire Baron Stieglitz founded the School of Technical Design and wanted to surround his students with world-class art to inspire them. He began a collection which was continued by his son and was to include a dizzying, unique array of European and Oriental glassware, porcelains, tapestries, furniture and paintings. It eventually grew into one of Europe's richest private collections. Between 1885 and 1895, a building designed by architect Messmacher was built to house the collection, and this building also became a masterpiece. Each hall is decorated in its own, unique style, including Italian, Renaissance, Flemish and baroque. The Terem Room, in the style of the medieval Terem Palace of Moscow's Kremlin, is an opulent knockout.

After the revolution, the school was closed, the museum's collection redistributed to the Hermitage and Russian museums, and most of the lavish interiors brutally painted or plastered over, even

destroyed (one room was used as a sports hall). The painstaking renovation continues to this day, despite receiving no funding from the Ministry of Education under whose direction it falls, being connected to the Applied Arts School next door. This would be the perfect direction for any philanthropic art lovers' extra cash.

The objects on display are simply breathtaking, from medieval handcrafted furniture to a rare collection of 18th-century Russian tiled stoves to the contemporary works of the students of the arts school. Their surroundings merely match their magnificence.

## SMOLNY REGION (MAP 5)
### Tauride Gardens

The former Tauride Gardens, now the City Children's Park, is a lovely place for a stroll, and there are some rusty rides for the kiddies. The view across the lake at the fine Tauride Palace (Tavrichesky dvorets), built between 1783 and 1789 for Catherine the Great's lover Potyomkin, is a fine sight.

The palace, in the park's north-eastern corner, takes its name from the Ukrainian region of Crimea (once called Tavria), which Potyomkin was responsible for conquering (the palace was a thank you for that acquisition). Paul I turned the place into a barracks, which ruined most of the lavish interiors (soldiers have a way of doing that). Between 1906 and 1917 the State Duma, the Provisional Government and the Petrograd Soviet all met here; in the 1930s it housed the All-Union Agricultural Communist University(!). Today it's home to the Parliamentary Assembly of the Member States of the CIS and you can't go in. The gardens are a block-and-a-half east of Chernyshevskaya metro.

Just east of the gardens, on Shpalernaya ul is one of the last remaining **statues** of Felix Dzerzhinksy, founder of the infamous Cheka, KGB predecessor.

## Flowers Exhibition Hall

One of the finest ways to escape momentarily from a St Petersburg winter is to head for the Flowers Exhibition Hall (☎ 272 54 48,

*Potyomkinskaya ul 2; admission $1; open 11am-7pm Tues-Wed & Fri-Sun)*, an indoor tropical paradise just north-west of the City Children's Park. Dig the 'monster tree' to the right of the entrance. It has a wishing well, and there's a flower-selling stall at the front of the building. There's a florist next door, and one diagonally across the street as well.

### Smolny

About a kilometre east of the Tauride Gardens, the **cathedral** *(pl Proletarskoy diktatury 3)* at Smolny is one of the most fabulous of all Rastrelli's buildings, and the Smolny Institute next door was the hub of the October Revolution. Trolleybuses Nos 5 and 7 via much of Nevsky pr end up here.

The ice-blue cathedral is the centrepiece of a convent mostly built, to Rastrelli's designs, between 1748 and 1757. His inspiration was to combine baroque details with the forest of towers and onion domes typical of an old Russian monastery. There's special genius in the proportions of the cathedral (it gives the impression of soaring upwards), to which the convent buildings are a perfect foil. The interior is a disappointingly austere plain white. Inside is a small **art gallery** *(☎ 278 14 61; adult/student $4/2; open 11am-5pm Fri-Wed)* hosting temporary exhibits and it's possible to climb one of the 63m belfries with a guide (the views are stupendous).

The **Smolny Institute** *(☎ 276 14 61, pl Proletarskoy Diktatury 3; open 10am-6pm Mon-Fri by appointment only)*, built by Quarenghi between 1806 and 1808 as a school for aristocratic girls, had fame thrust upon it in 1917 when Trotsky and Lenin directed the October Revolution from the headquarters of the Bolshevik Central Committee and the Petrograd Soviet which had been set up here. In its Hall of Acts (Aktovy zal) on 25 October, the All-Russian Congress of Soviets conferred power on a Bolshevik government led by Lenin, which ran the country from here until March 1918. In 1934, Leningrad Party chief Sergei Kirov was assassinated here, sparking Stalin's notorious purges.

## SOUTH & WEST OF NEVSKY PROSPEKT
### Sennaya Ploshchad Area (Map 7)

This teeming market square, dominated by what seems to be a permanent exhibition of construction equipment, is the gateway to Dostoevskyville. The peripatetic Dostoevsky, who occupied around 20 residences in his 28-year stay in the city, once spent a couple of days in debtors' prison in what is now called the **Senior Officers' Barracks**, just across the square from the Sennaya Pl metro station. Dostoevsky had been thrown in there by his publisher, for missing a deadline ('Had we but thought of it...' – Tony Wheeler). At the site of the metro station there was once a large cathedral that dominated the square.

See Walking Tours earlier in this chapter for more Dostoevsky-related information.

And due west of the square along Sadovaya ul is the charming **Yusupovsky Gardens**, a hugely pleasant park with a big lake in the middle.

### Vladimirskaya Ploshchad Area (Map 7)

Around Vladimirskaya pl is the indoor **Kuznechny Market** *(Kuznechny per 3; open 8am-4pm daily)* – St Petersburg's best stocked – note the 1920s worker statue on its facade. There are also a few museums and a smattering of eateries and shops, all on a backdrop of what is one of the city's liveliest areas. The onion-domed working **Our Lady of Vladimir Church (Map 8)** (1761–69) with its 1783 three-tiered belfry by Quarenghi dominates the square. It's one the city's prettiest churches, a fascinating place to be on Easter eve. Around it, there's an unofficial market of people selling vegetables from their dachas, or items from their homes. They're regularly dispersed by the police but reappear the instant the cops turn their backs.

Dostoevsky wrote most of *The Brothers Karamazov* in a flat just past the market, and died there in 1881. It's now a small and worthwhile **Dostoevsky Museum** *(☎ 164 69 50, Kuznechny per 5/2; adult/student $1.20/0.60; open 11am-5.30pm Tues-Sun)*.

It includes a Dostoevsky city map, illustrations for his books published in his time, and his personal library (heavy on medicine and philosophy), which provides insight into his world view. Every Sunday at noon there's a screening of a film version of one of the master's works. See its Web site at **W** www.md.spb.ru. There's also a fabulously lugubrious **statue** of the writer which was unveiled and consecrated in 1997, standing directly outside the Vladimirskaya metro.

The **Arctic & Antarctic Museum** (☎ 113 19 98, ul Marata 24A; adult/student $1.50/0.60; 10am-5pm Wed-Sun) focuses on Soviet polar explorations, ratty taxidermy exhibitions and objects from Willem Barents' Arctic expeditions. If the building looks like a church, it's because it used to be an Old Believer's Church of St Nicholas, built in 1838.

There's a charming **Rimsky-Korsakov Flat-Museum** (☎ 113 32 08, Zagorodny pr 28; about $1; open 11am-6pm Wed-Sun), lovingly recreated to look as it did when he spent the last 15 years of life in it (he died in 1908). The composer's tradition of holding concerts on Wednesday evenings continues to this day.

Zagorodny pr continues past Pionerskaya pl, the stage of Dostoevsky's 1849 mock execution (see the boxed text 'Dostoevsky' in the Facts about St Petersburg chapter). A bit further along is the Vitebsky Station, the site of Russia's first train station. A wooden, then stone station was replaced in 1904 by this asymmetrical Art Nouveau version with a glass cupola.

## Teatralnaya Ploshchad Area (Map 6)

Known throughout the world during the Soviet reign as the Kirov, the **Mariinsky Theatre** (☎ 114 12 11, **W** www.mariinsky.spb.ru, Teatralnaya pl; tour $10; box office open 11am-7pm daily) resumed its original name in 1992, though the ballet company still uses the name Kirov. Built in 1859, the Mariinsky has played a pivotal role in Russian ballet ever since. Outside performance times you can usually wander into the theatre's foyer, and maybe peep into its lovely auditorium. To organise a full tour fax a request

to Dr Yuri Schwartzkopf at ☎ 314 17 44, and call back for an answer. Check out their colourful Web site.

The **Rimsky-Korsakov Conservatory** faces the Mariinsky. Bus Nos 3 and 22 from Nevsky pr serve Teatralnaya pl, which has been a St Petersburg entertainment centre since fairs were held here in the mid-18th-century. Surrounding it is an area of quiet canals and side streets.

North-east of Teatralnaya pl, before it twists south-west, the Griboedova Canal runs under yet another beautiful beast-supported suspension bridge, the **Lviny most**, with chains emerging from the mouths of lions.

The delicate Kryukov Canal flows behind the Mariinksy. It's a pleasant, two-block walk south along the canal to the baroque spires and domes of **St Nicholas' Cathedral** (1753–62), rising among the trees at the bottom of ul Glinki. Nicknamed the Sailor's Church (Nicholas is the patron saint of sailors), it has many 18th-century icons and a fine carved wooden iconostasis. A graceful bell tower overlooks the canal, crossed by the Staro-Nikolsky most (from this bridge, you can see at least seven bridges, more than from any other spot in the city). South along this canal and across a footbridge over the Fontanka is blue-domed **Troitsky Cathedral** on Izmailovsky pr, Stasov's impressive 1828–35 classical edifice.

The flat where Alexandr Blok spent the last eight years of his life is now the **Alexandr Blok House-Museum** (☎ 113 86 33, ul Dekabristov 57; adult/student $1/0.50; open 11am-5pm Thur-Tues). The exhibitions are spread out over several rooms, and show how the poet lived, and where he died (his death mask is there, as well as a drawing of Blok on his deathbed, drawn on the last page of the poet's pad). There are regular chamber concerts performed here, worthwhile especially for the subdued charm of the flats – and the lovely views out onto the Pryazhka River.

## Yusopov Palace (Map 7)

Most tourists know it as the place where Rasputin got the worst case of upset tummy

Rasputin – don't eat the cookies!

## SOUTH OF THE CENTRE
### Ekateringoff Park (Map 6)

Just west of metro Narvskaya, along ul Perekopskaya is the sprawling Ekateringoff Park, built up in Peter the Great's time. He had a magnificent two-storey wooden palace built here for his wife Ekaterina in 1711 (and people say he was cruel!). It survived two centuries as a dwelling house and later as a museum, but was completely destroyed by fire in 1924 after the Soviets had turned it into a party house for young workers (now, how could *that* have happened?). It stood at the far west end of the park, on the banks of the little Ekateringofka River. The park, which was laid out by Monferrand in the 1820s, was later named after the 30th anniversary of the Communist Youth League (a super kitsch statue remains). Today it's a pleasant place for a stroll. There's a children's playground too.

On your way, check out the **Narva Triumphal Gates** (1827–34), just outside the metro. Standing proudly at one of the city's old gates, this 12-columned monolith designed by Stasov as a tribute to the defeat of Napoleon, is crowned with an angel of victory and decorated with an assembly of valiant warriors. There are two staircases inside leading up to an exposition hall, but the place has been closed for years.

### Moskovsky Prospekt (Map 3)

Moskovsky pr, running straight south from Sennaya pl is the start of the main road to Moscow. The iron **Moscow Triumphal Arch**, 3.5km out, looking very like Berlin's Brandenburg Gate but somewhat less than grand in its surroundings, was built by Stasov in 1838 to mark victories over Turks, Persians and Poles. It was demolished in 1936 then rebuilt between 1959 and 1961. Local legend has it that the gate is built on the spot where travellers entering the city in the earliest days had to show that they had brought bricks or stones with them to be used in the construction of buildings.

A couple of kilometres further south, east off Moskovsky pr on ul Gastello, is **Chesma Palace** (now off-limits), built for Catherine the Great to rest en route to Tsarskoe Selo

in his life: the Yusupov Palace (☎ *314 98 83, nab reki Moyki 94; adult/student $4/2, with separate $3/1.50 tickets to visit the cellar rooms where Rasputin had his last meal; open 11am-4pm daily, but advance reservations are required)*. In 1916 Rasputin, invited here to dinner by Prince Felix Yusupov and friends, was filled with poisoned food, cakes, cookies and drink. After he ate and drank all this and was happily licking his fingers, the Yusupov gang shot ol' Raspy repeatedly. But like a tsarist-era Terminator, he refused to die, and when Yusupov knelt over him, Rasputin grabbed him by the throat! At that point, Yusupov did what any sane man would do: he ran like hell. When he returned with reinforcements, they found Rasputin had dragged himself outside. They shot him a few more times, beat him with sticks for good measure, and stuffed him through the ice of the frozen river. Apparently, after all the abuse, Rasputin ended up dying of drowning – water was found in his lungs.

The palace was built by de la Mothe in the 1760s, and the interiors, redecorated later, are sumptuously rich, many halls painted in different styles and decked out in gilded chandeliers, silks, frescoes, tapestries and fantastic furniture.

## Long Live Soviet Symbols!

Some tourists are surprised to see that not every last symbol of the Soviet Union has been relegated to the dustpan of history; there are quite a few grand old commie statues and plaques around town (but no, the bust inside the Church on Spilled Blood is *not* of Stalin, as the odd tourist – the very odd one in fact – sometimes mistakes Alexander II for).

The granddaddy of them all, the **statue of Vladimir Ilyich Lenin (Map 3)**, can best be seen, all 16m of him, on Moskovsky pr near the Moskovskaya metro station, where he looks like he's decided to splurge on a taxi instead of using public transport. Another impressive one is in front of Warsaw Station **(Map 6)**, standing ominously at the end of Izmailovsky pr. Others are situated at Finland Station **(Map 5)**, along both Bolshoy prospekts on Vasilevsky Island **(Map 6)** and on the Petrograd Side **(Map 4)**, in the Tauride Gardens **(Map 5)**, and by the Smolny Institute **(Map 5)**. The most evil-looking Lenin is a bronze bust sitting on a slab of Ukrainian red marble at the far end of the metro platform inside Kirovsky Zavod Station – he's obviously miffed that no-one seems to notice him there. There are also dozens of plaques around town on buildings where he as much as stepped in the doorway or made a pronouncement.

There's a great 16m-high **statue of Kirov (Map 6)**, the Leningrad Party boss who was assassinated in 1934, just south of Narvskaya metro on pr Stachek, and one of Dzerzhinsky, founder of the Soviet secret police (the Cheka, forerunner to the KGB) right near the Smolny **(Map 5)** (the city's second statue of him can be seen by peeking through the main gates of the Admiralty – the off-limits military naval academy inside is named after him).

On buildings around town, you'll see murals recounting worker rebellions, hammers and sickles and other Soviet emblems (there's even one building built in the shape of a sickle, a 1925–27 school, at pr Stachek 5 **(Map 6)**. To catch a glimpse of a real Soviet rarity these days – Stalin himself – look at the fading relief on the **statue (Map 6)** commemorating the Communists Youth League in Ekateringoff Park.

(now Pushkin). More interesting is the red-and-white 18th-century Gothic shocker, the **Chesma Church** (☎ *443 61 14, ul Lensoveta 12; admission free; open 10am-7pm daily)*. With long, vertical white stripes giving the impression that it's rising straight up from the earth like a mirage and shooting upwards. This church was designed by Y Felten (who also did the Church of St Catherine on Vasilevsky Island) and built between 1777 and 1780 in honour of the Battle of Çesme (1770) when the Russian fleet sailed from the Baltic to the Aegean to beat the Turks.

Just south is the wide but chilly **Moskovskaya pl**, which was intended under a 1930s plan to become the centre of St Petersburg, replacing the old tsarist centre. In a testament to the residents' stubbornness during Stalin's terror, this plan was universally ignored. Moskovsky pr ends a few hundred metres further on at pl Pobedy,

where the **Monument to the Heroic Defenders of Leningrad**, commemorating WWII and the siege, makes a striking first impression on entering St Petersburg (see the boxed text 'The Blockade of Leningrad' earlier in this chapter for details).

Just south of the Pulkovo airports, lies the **Pulkova Observatory** (☎ *106 71 63, ask for Valery Fomin,* W *www.gao.spb.ru; group tours $2 a person, minimum $20, but flexible with individuals; museum hours 9am-5pm Mon-Fri, but hours are flexible)*. For a short time at the beginning of the 20th century, the observatory, founded in 1839, was considered the astronomical capital of the world for the quality and scope of its research. The WWII frontline was only one mile to the south and many buildings suffered damage at that time. The hill on which the observatory stands is the region's highest-elevated point; from here the Nazis used to shell the easily-viewed city. Tours of the museum and arranged evening visits to star search are possible with advance arrangement. Group tours include a peek through the telescopes (the largest being 65cm; there's also a solar telescope). For more information on the observatory's pitiful financial state, see Ⓦ www.geocities.com/soho/workshop/5604/pulkovo. Bus No 55 south from metro Moskovskaya stops right at the observatory. It's a wonderful place that's greatly in need of attention and money.

### Kanonersky Island (Map 3)
An original option for a day's walk or picnic is to head to the remote, grassy tip of this island in the south-west of the city to watch the big boats head out into the Gulf of Finland. This island once served as part of the city's defence, a shooting training ground, and since 1883 a ship repairing factory has been located on it. Taking taxibus No 115 ($0.25, 25 minutes) outside Sadovaya ul 39 (at Sennaya pl), you get to go under the only tunnel linking two islands in the city. After the last stop, continue walking another 40 minutes to the very tip of the island. You'll need good shoes, as there's a bit of climbing over rocks involved, but the views are well worth it. Hardly anyone makes it out here.

### VASILEVSKY ISLAND
The oldest parts of Vasilevsky Island are its eastern 'nose', the Strelka (Tongue of Land), where Peter the Great first wanted his new city's administrative and intellectual centre, and the embankment facing the Admiralty. In fact, the Strelka became the focus of St Petersburg's maritime trade, symbolised by the white colonnaded **Stock Exchange**. The two **Rostral Columns**, archetypal St Petersburg landmarks, are studded with ships' prows and four seated sculptures supposedly representing four of Russia's great rivers, all reachable from this point: the Neva, the Volga, the Dnieper and the Volkhov. These were oil-fired navigation beacons in the 1800s (on some holidays gas torches are still lit on them). The area remains an intellectual centre, with the St Petersburg State University, the Academy of Arts and a veritable 'museum ghetto'.

The Strelka also has one of the best views in the city: you look left to the Peter & Paul Fortress and right to the Hermitage, the Admiralty and St Isaac's Cathedral.

### Museums near the Strelka (Maps 4 & 6)
The Old Stock Exchange is now the **Central Naval Museum (Map 4)** (☎ 218 25 02, Ⓦ www.museum.navy.ru, Birzhevaya pl 4; adult/student $2.25/1.10; open 10.30am-5.30pm Wed-Sun). This is a grand, expansive museum full of maps, excellent model-ships, flags and photos of and about the Russian navy up to the present day – a must for naval enthusiasts. Also on display is Botik, Peter's first boat, a pre-turn-of-the-20th-century submarine (a two-seater!) and some big oars.

To the north is the old Customs House, topped with statues and a dome. It is now called **Pushkin House (Map 4)** (Pushkinsky dom; ☎ 328 05 02, nab Makarova 4; guided tours $2 per person, minimum $10 total; open 10am-4pm Mon-Fri), and is home to the **Institute of Russian Literature** and a **Literary Museum** with exhibits on Tolstoy, Gogol, Lermontov, Turgenev, Gorky and others. The archives contain the richest collection of medieval Russian manuscripts in the world. They're not warm to people off the streets; call in advance to book a tour in English or Russian.

To the left (south) of the exchange is the **Museum of Zoology (Map 6)** (☎ 218 01 12, Universitetskaya nab 1/3; adult/student $0.75/0.35, free Thur; open 11am-6pm Sat-Thur), reputed to be one of the biggest and best in the world, with incredibly life-like stuffed animals from around the world. There are some 40,000 animal species on display in realistic dioramas, including wild camel, a gigantic ram, mammoths and an extinct southern elephant. One of the highlights is a complete woolly 44,000-year-old mammoth thawed out of the Siberian ice in 1902.

### Museum of Anthropology & Ethnography (Kunstkammer; Map 6)
This blue-and-white building with the steeple was the city's first museum, founded

in 1714 by Peter himself. In contrast to the State Museum of Ethnography, this museum (☎ 218 14 12, Universitetskaya nab 3, entrance around the corner on Tamozhyonny per; admission $1.50; open 11am-6pm Fri-Wed, last entry 4.45pm) is about peoples outside the former USSR, with wonderfully kitsch dioramas and displays on the cultures of Asia, Oceania, Africa and the Americas, including rare objects from around the world. The old anatomy theatre in the building's centre is the big draw, with selections from Peter's original *Kunstkammer*. While this translates from German to 'art chamber', the bloodthirsty crowds are really here to see Peter's collection of 'curiosities', notably a ghoulish collection of preserved freaks, two-headed mutant foetuses and body parts. The heart of Peter's giant man-servant 'Bourgeois', is also on display. It's fun for the whole family!

## Twelve Colleges (Map 6)

West of the Anthropology Museum and marked by a statue of scientist-poet Mikhail Lomonosov (1711–65) is Mendeleevskaya linia and the skinny, 400m-long Twelve Colleges building. One of St Petersburg's oldest buildings, it was meant originally for Peter's government ministries, and is now part of the university, which stretches out behind it. Inside is the **Mendeleev Museum** (☎ 328 97 44, Mendeleevskaya linia 2; admission $1; open 11am-4pm Mon-Fri), dedicated to the father of the periodic table of elements, chemist and eclectic inventor Dimitry Mendeleev. His cosy study has been lovingly preserved.

## Academy of Arts Museum (Map 6)

The Russian Academy of Arts Research Museum (☎ 213 64 96, excursions ☎ 213 35 78, Universitetskaya nab 17; adult/student $2/1, excellent Russian-language excursions $5; open 11am-6pm Wed-Sun) doesn't get many visitors but is well worth exploring. It's easy to spot – look for the two imported Egyptian **sphinx monuments** outside, said to be about 3500 years old. Boys would live in this building from the

age of five until they graduated at age 15 – it was an experiment to create a new species of human: the artist. It mostly worked; many great Russian artists were spawned here, including Ilya Repin, Karl Bryullov and Anton Losenko. But the academy's conservatism (it was founded on the idea that art must serve the state) lead to the founding of the Wanderers in 1863 (see Painting & Sculpture in the Facts about St Petersburg chapter) when 14 students left the academy to found the new movement.

Inside are works by academy students and faculty since its founding in 1757, including many studies, plus temporary exhibitions. Make sure to visit the 3rd floor, and the models for the original versions of Smolny, St Isaac's, and the Alexandr Nevsky Monastery, and take a peek into the fabulous old library – you'd think you were in Oxford.

A short walk away, opposite the Andreevsky Market, is **Apteka #13** (☎ 323 13 18, 7-ya linia 16; open 8am-8pm Mon-Fri, 8am-5pm Sat & Sun). Built in 1902 in Style Moderne, the gorgeous interiors will blow away your notion of a drugstore; pharmaceutical tools, jars and porcelain from the 17th and 18th centuries are on display.

## Geological Museum (Map 6)

With over one million exhibits, prehistoric rock and dinosaur fragments, animal sculls and mammoth tusks, the Geological Museum (☎ 312 53 99, excursions ☎ 328 92 48, Sredny pr 74; admission free; open 10am-5pm Mon-Fri) is more than just a collection of impressive rocks and gems (though it's that too – check out the mesmerisingly blue charoyite, and the 1.5m-long crystal from the Altai mountains). To see all the fantastic pieces here, you'd have to walk 3.5km! The real tourist draw is a huge map of the Soviet Union made entirely of precious gems. The winner of the Paris World Exposition Grand Prix in 1937, this 26.6 sq metre, 3½ ton mosaic took over 700 people to create, combining amethysts, diamonds, granite, rubies and other gems from 500 different places in the USSR. It later sat in the Hermitage's St George's Hall for 34 years. There's also a precious gem hammer and sickle nearby, which much more effectively reflects whatever glory of those days existed than those on souvenir pins and rusty metal plaques. It's a great museum.

## D-2 Submarine Museum (Map 6)

Opened as a fun, unique museum, the People's Will D-2 Submarine *(Nadorovolets; ☎ 356 52 77, Shkipersky protok 10; admission $4; open 11am-5pm Tues-Sun)* is one of the first six (diesel-fuelled) submarines built in the Soviet Union. It was in action between 1931 and 1936, and proudly sank five German ships. The tour you're obliged to take (in Russian) will take you through the charming sub to see how the crew of 53 lived and worked. The periscope still works!

## Churches

Vasilevsky Island has its share of churches with odd present or past functions. The **Church of St Catherine (Map 4)** (Tserkov Yekateriny, 1771) at Bolshoy pr 1, is now a sound studio (with purportedly the best acoustics in the city) owned by the record company Melodia.

The **Temple of the Assumption (Map 6)** *(Uspenskoe Podvore Optina Pustin; ☎ 321 74 73, cnr nab Leytenanta Shmidta & 15-ya linia; open daily)* is a stunning neo-Byzantine church (1895), built on the site of a previous monastery by architect V Kosyakov. It was closed in 1934, and from 1957 turned into the city's first – and very popular – year-round skating rink! This is one of the best places to see the process of church reconstruction – the scale of destruction, despite having been in repair since 1991, is still visible. The 7.7m, 861kg metal cross on the roof was only replaced in 1998.

Even more intriguing, near the far west end of Bolshoy pr, on the grounds of what has always been a military training school is the **Church of Mother of God the Merciful (Map 6)** (Miluyoushchi Bozhe Materi; 1889–98), also by Kosyakov (who also built the Naval Cathedral in Kronshtadt). The Soviets converted it into a surreal training base for future submariners and for life-saving exercises. The neo-Byzantine

exterior is more or less intact, but the interior has been completely gutted, and there is now metal scaffolding and a 26m-high tube filled with 333 tons of water, in which young divers practise their craft. As an ironic, blasphemous reference to the religious purpose the space used to serve, the students have suspended an old orange diving suit in mid-air, looking somewhat like Christ on the cross. The church is located on a closed military base and is not open to the public; don't even hope for access.

## PETROGRAD SIDE

Petrograd Side (Petrogradskaya storona) is a cluster of delta islands between the Malaya and Bolshaya Neva channels. On little Zayachy Island, Peter the Great first broke ground for St Petersburg and built the Peter & Paul Fortress. The rest of this fabulous area has sparkling architecture (just stroll up Kamennoostrovsky pr for a Style Moderne treat), a happening main street (Bolshoy pr) and lots of refreshingly uncrowded, green areas.

### Peter & Paul Fortress (Map 5)

Founded in 1703, the Peter & Paul Fortress *(Petropavlovskaya krepost; ☎ 238 45 40; free entry to the grounds, but admission to all buildings costs adult/student $3/1.50; open 10am-6pm Thur-Mon, 10am-4pm Tues)* – see the Peter & Paul Fortress map for more detail – is the oldest building in St Petersburg. Peter planned it as a defence against the Swedes but defeated them before it was finished (the bottom of the Neva rises in front of it, so banked ships could easily be fired upon). In fact, it has never been utilised in the city's defence – unless you count incarceration of political 'criminals' as national defence.

Its main use up to 1917 was as a prison; one of its first inmates was Peter's own son Alexey, whose torture Peter is said to have personally overseen. Other famous residents were Dostoevsky, Gorky, Trotsky, Bakunin, and Lenin's older brother, Alexandr. The entrance to the fortress is on the eastern side of the island, and most worth seeing are the **SS Peter & Paul**

**THINGS TO SEE & DO**

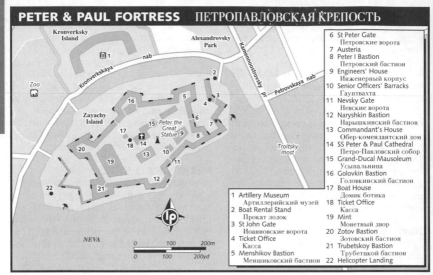

**PETER & PAUL FORTRESS** ПЕТРОПАВЛОВСКАЯ КРЕПОСТЬ

6 St Peter Gate
Петровские ворота
7 Austeria
8 Peter I Bastion
Петровский бастион
9 Engineers' House
Инженерный корпус
10 Senior Officers' Barracks
Гауптвахта
11 Nevsky Gate
Невские ворота
12 Naryshkin Bastion
Нарышкинский бастион
13 Commandant's House
Обер-комендантский дом
14 SS Peter & Paul Cathedral
Петро-Павловский собор
15 Grand-Ducal Mausoleum
Усыпальница
16 Golovkin Bastion
Головкинский бастион
17 Boat House
Домик ботика
18 Ticket Office
Касса
19 Mint
Монетный двор
20 Zotov Bastion
Зотовский бастион
21 Trubetskoy Bastion
Трубецкой бастион
22 Helicopter Landing

1 Artillery Museum
Артиллерийский музей
2 Boat Rental Stand
Прокат лодок
3 St John Gate
Иоанновские ворота
4 Ticket Office
Касса
5 Menshikov Bastion
Меншиковский бастион

**Cathedral**, with its landmark needle-thin spire, and the **Trubetskoy Bastion**.

The cathedral, though plain on the outside, is radically different from traditional Orthodox churches. Don't miss its magnificent baroque interior. All of Russia's pre-revolutionary rulers from Peter the Great onwards (except Peter II and Ivan VI) are buried here. Nicholas II and his family – minus Alexey and Maria – were the latest, controversial additions (see the boxed text 'Reburying the Past'). Peter I's grave is at the front on the right. The 122.5m-high bell tower remains the city's tallest structure.

Between the cathedral and the **Senior Officers' Barracks** is a **statue** of a seated Peter the Great, with somewhat interestingly proportioned head and hands (rub his right forefinger for good luck!).

In the fort's south-west corner are reconstructions of the grim cells of the Trubetskoy Bastion, where Peter supervised the torture to death of his son. The cells were used by later tsars to keep a lid on original thinking in the empire.

In the south wall is **Nevsky Gate**, a later addition (1787), where prisoners were loaded on boats for execution or exile elsewhere. Notice the plaques showing water levels of famous floods. Outside are fine views of the whole central waterfront. Along the wall to the left, throughout the year on sunny days, you can witness a motley crew of sunbathers (standing's said to give you a *proper* tan), and around the corner, further towards the Troitsky most in winter you can people engaging in ice swimming (see Activities). Regular sun-tanning goes on at the beach facing the Neva.

At noon every day a cannon is fired from **Naryshkin Bastion**, scaring the daylights out of tourists. The **Commandant's House** is an exhibition on the history of the St Petersburg region from medieval times to 1917. The **Engineers' House** has a museum with rotating exhibitions.

To get there, it's a pleasant walk across the Troitsky or Dvortsovy mosts, or across Alexandrovsky Park from metro Gorkovskaya.

### Behind the Fortress (Map 5)

Across the moat, in the fort's original arsenal, is the **Artillery Museum** (☎ 232 02 96, *Alexandrovsky park 7; adult/student $3/1.50; open 11am-6pm Wed-Sun*), which chronicles Russia's military history. It's a great place if

The lavish National Library of Russia

Keeping an eye on the time

Capitalism rules – a Nevsky prospekt billboard trumpets the wares of a local fur salon.

Whatever happened to *Pravda*?

The Lutheran Church is returning to its former use and glory.

JONATHAN SMITH

The *Bronze Horseman* at sunset

GRAHAM BELL

The Kirov Ballet rules the dance world from its headquarters.

GEORGI S SHABLOVSKY

A yacht on the Neva follows the route Peter took 300 years ago.

STEVE KOKKER

A little greenery at St Pete's second palace, Anichkov Palace

JONATHAN SMITH

Statue of Catherine the Great

## Reburying the Past

On 17 July 1998, in a controversial ceremony partially snubbed by the Church and the State, the remains of Tsar Nicholas II, his wife, three of his five children, their doctor and three servants were buried in the Romanov family crypt at the SS Peter & Paul Cathedral within the fortress of the same name. A 19-gun salute bid them a final farewell. The ceremony was contentious for many reasons – political, religious, scientific and financial.

While President Boris Yeltsin and then-General Alexander Lebed were in attendance, together with many Romanov family members, other politicians downplayed the event, and Patriarch Alexey II held his own, rival service in Sergiev Posad, outside Moscow, with a few renegade Romanov descendants in attendance.

The burial, which Yeltsin called an expiation of Russia's common guilt, set off touchy debates on monarchism (to be or not to be?) as a potential solution to the country's state of turmoil (most say: 'not to be'). It also raised debate about the authenticity of the royal remains, despite tests and DNA analyses done since they were unearthed in 1991 which 'prove' they are the royal family's.

After the execution of the Romanovs in Yekaterinburg in July 1918 by a firing squad estimated at 11 men, the bodies were dumped down a mine shaft 30km away. Grenades were tossed in after them in an unsuccessful attempt to collapse the mine. The bodies were then dragged out, doused unevenly with acid and buried quickly in a swamp – all except for two of the children, Maria and Alexey whose remains were allegedly burned and disintegrated completely. The Dom Ipateva, in which the Romanovs had been held and killed, was destroyed in 1977 by the then head of the city's Communist Party, one Boris Yeltsin, on, he says, orders from the Politburo.

The burial of the nine bodies provided an at-best partial closure to an 80 year-old tragedy. Plans by the Orthodox Church to canonise the tsar and his family within a few years do little to alleviate dissatisfaction felt on all sides. Yet many see the burial as a proper step towards finally settling Russia's restless soul – the next, last, and most important, say the superstitious, is to move that waxy-looking bloke off of Red Square and place him by his dear old mum in St Petersburg.

you like weapons: it seems to have one of everything right back to the Stone Age. It also has Lenin's armoured car, which he rode in triumph from Finland Station.

Behind the museum is **Alexandrovsky Park**, a neat hang-out in summer but too close to traffic and thronged with people to be peaceful. There's still lots to do here. The **St Petersburg Zoo** (☎ *232 48 28, Alexandrovsky park 1; adult/child $1.20/ 0.30; open 10am-7pm daily summer, 10am-4pm Tues-Sun winter),* is full of miserable animals and happy kids. The lack of funds are pitifully evident, but all things considered, it's pretty well-kept. It's the world leader in polar bear births (since 1993, over 100 have been born here). Right near the zoo is a large **amusement park**, complete with ferris wheel, bumper cars, petrol-powered go-carts, small roller coasters and the like; rides cost about $0.30, go-carts $0.75 for 10 minutes.

The **Planetarium** *(☎ 233 53 12, Alexandrovsky park 4; shows $0.70-1.50; open 10.30am-6pm Tues-Sun)* has cool 50-minute shows throughout the day.

## Mosque (Map 5)

East of the park across Kamennoostrovsky pr is a working mosque (1910–14), modelled on Samarkand's Gur Emir Mausoleum where Timur (Tamerlaine) is buried. Its fluted azure dome and minarets have emerged from a painstaking renovation and are stunning. Entering is difficult: *jamat* (congregation) members are highly protective of their mosque, which is a serious place of worship and decidedly not a tourist attraction. Women without a *keemar* (head covering) may not be admitted at all; men need to look neat, dress in long pants and preferably a collared shirt and politely ask the guard for entry: saying you're a student of religion or architecture is best. If you are asked in, remove your shoes at the stairs (and hope your socks are clean – dirty socks, like dirty feet, may be an insult to the mosque) and do not talk inside. Forget photography. To enter, walk through the gate at the north-east side.

## Museum of Political History (Map 5)

East of Kamennoostrovsky pr is the Kshesinskaya Palace containing the wonderful Museum of Political History in Russia (☎ 233 72 20, ul Kuybysheva 4; adult/student $2/1, English guide $6; open 11am-5pm Sun-Thur). The Bolsheviks made it their headquarters, and Lenin often gave speeches from the balcony of this elegant Art Nouveau palace (1904) that once belonged to Mathilda Kshesinskaya (see the boxed text 'Monarchs of the Ballet World' in the Facts about St Petersburg chapter), famous ballet dancer and onetime lover of Nicholas II in his pre-tsar days. Go in to see the house itself, the best Soviet kitsch in town (including porcelain with workers' slogans and a watch for astronauts), and some incredibly rare satirical caricatures of Lenin published in magazines between the 1917 revolutions (the same drawings a few months later would have got the artist imprisoned, or worse).

## Peter's Cabin (Map 5)

In a patch of trees east of the fortress is a little stone building known as Peter's Cabin (Domik Petra; ☎ 232 45 76, Petrovskaya nab 6; adult/student $0.80/0.40; open 10am-5pm Wed-Sun). This is St Petersburg's oldest surviving structure, a log cabin built in three days in May 1703 for Peter to supervise the construction of the fortress and city. During Catherine the Great's time, the house was protected by a brick layer. It feels more like a shrine than a museum.

## Cruiser *Aurora* (Map 5)

In the Nevka opposite the Hotel St Petersburg is the *Aurora (Avrora;* ☎ 230 84 40, Petrovskaya nab; admission free; open 10.30am-4pm Tues-Thur & Sat-Sun), a mothballed cruiser from the Russo-Japanese War, built in 1900. From a downstream mooring on the night of 25 October 1917, its crew fired a blank round from the forward gun, demoralising the Winter Palace's defenders and marking the start of the October Revolution. During WWII, the Russians sank it to protect it from German bombs. Now, restored and painted in pretty colours, it's a living museum that swarms with kids on weekends. It's possible to see the crew's quarters.

## Kirov Museum (Map 5)

Sergei Kirov, one of Stalin's leading henchmen after whom countless parks, plazas, squares and a town are named, spent the last days of his life at this decidedly unproletarian apartment before his murder sparked a wave of deadly repression in the country. It is now a museum (☎ 346 02 89, Kamennoostrovsky pr 26/28; admission $0.25; open 11am-6pm Thur-Tues). The apartment is a quick journey back to the days of Soviet glory, including choice examples of 1920s technology and books (20,000 of them). Don't miss the Party leader's death clothes, hung out for reverence: The tiny hole in the back of his cap was where he was shot (blood stains intact!), and the torn seam on his jacket's left breast was where doctors tried to revive his heart. In another part of the museum is a brilliant, lively exhibit on childhood during the Soviet era.

## Sigmund Freud Museum of Dreams (Map 4)

One of the most unique exhibits in the country, itself conceptual and based on abstractions and ideas, not artefacts, the museum (☎ 235 28 57, Ⓦ www.freud.ru, Bolshoy pr 18A; without/with tour $1/4.50; open noon-5pm Tues & Sun) is an outgrowth of the Psychoanalytic Institute which houses it. It aims to stimulate your subconscious via projection as you struggle to read the display symbolising what Freud himself would have dreamt of in a dimly-lit, ambient hall. Illustrations to Freud's patients' dreams and other quotations line the small, eccentric, innovative museum.

## Botanical Gardens (Map 5)

This quiet jungle in eastern Aptekarsky (Apothecary) Island, just north-east of the Petrogradskaya metro station and across the Karpovka Canal, was once a garden of medicinal plants which gave the island its name.

The botanical gardens (*☎ 346 36 39, ul Professora Popova 2; grounds free, greenhouse under $1; open 11am-4pm Sat-Thur)* contains 26 greenhouses on a 22-hectare site and is one of St Petersburg's loveliest strolling grounds and most interesting places to visit – and not just for botanists. The gardens, founded by Peter himself in 1714, offer a variety of excursions to their stunning collection, all the more impressive considering that 90% of the plants died during the war (those 'veterans' that survived have a war medal pinned onto them!).

At the turn of the 20th century, these were the second biggest botanical gardens in the world, behind London's Kew Gardens. A highlight is their tsaritsa nochi *(Selenicereus pteranthus)*, a flowering cactus which blossoms only one night a year, usually in mid-June. On this night, the gardens stay open until morning for visitors to gawk at the marvel and sip champagne.

## Television Antenna (Map 5)

The Leningrad Radio-Tele Broadcasting Centre's antenna (*☎ 234 78 87, Aptekarsky Island; from $4; open 10am-5pm Tues-Sat)*, at the northern end of Petrograd Side, is open for excursions to its 50,000-watt transmitter tower. It stands 310m over the city, and visitors can access the 200m high observation deck.

It's a great place to bring kids; it offers excellent views of the entire city and environs. Individual or group tours can be arranged any time, but there's one fixed every Saturday at 2pm. It costs $4 per person if in a group of 10 or more; $30 for a group of under six persons. To reach the TV Antenna from Petrogradskaya metro, take trolleybus No 31 (or buses No 10, 71 or 128) north for two stops. Walk down to the Kantemirovsky most, turn right and walk to the gates facing the river.

## KIROVSKY ISLANDS (MAP 4)

This is the collective name for the outer delta islands of Petrograd Side – Kamenny, Yelagin and Krestovsky. Once marshy jungles, the islands were granted to 18th- and 19th-century court favourites and developed into elegant playgrounds. Still mostly parkland, they're leafy venues for picnics, river sports and white nights cavorting; the city's oasis.

## Kamenny Island

This island's charm, seclusion and turn-of-the-20th-century dachas (now inhabited by the wealthy, or by the St Petersburg mafiagentsia), combined with winding lanes and a series of canals, lakes and ponds, make a stroll here pleasant at any time of year. At the east end of the island the **Church of St John the Baptist** (1776–81) seems to have found better use as a basketball court. Behind it the big, classical **Kamennoostrovsky Palace**, built by Catherine the Great for her son, is now a weedy military sanatorium.

The island also boasts a **government retreat**, used by the president when he's in town and by other big wigs when he's not. Look for the **tree**, said to have been planted by Peter the Great, almost blocking nab reki Krestovki in the south part of the island near the Maly-Krestovsky most. There are also many splendid estates, like the neoclassical **Polovtsov Mansion** along Teatralnaya alleya in the northern end.

Nearby is the ungainly, though sweet, wooden **Kamenny Island Theatre**, first put up in the 1820s, and a footbridge to Yelagin Island. The **Danish Consulate General** has, hands-down, the best diplomat property in town: a massive dacha on Bolshaya alleya, towards the centre of the island.

Kamenny Island is a short walk south of metro Chyornaya Rechka (turn right as you exit, cross the bridge and you're there), or can be accessed by walking north about 15 minutes from metro Petrogradskaya.

## Yelagin Island

This island's centrepiece is the **Yelagin Palace** (1818–22), built by Rossi for Alexander I's wife, Empress Maria. Rossi also landscaped the entire island for her.

The palace is to your right as you cross the footbridge from Kamenny Island.

The very beautiful restored interiors of the main house (☎ *430 11 31; 1 Yelagin ostrov; adult/student $2.80/1.40; open 10am-6pm Wed-Sun)* include old furnishings on loan from the Grand Europe and Astoria hotels; don't miss the stupendous 1890s carved-walnut study ensemble from Europe and the incredible inlaid-wood floors. Other nearby estate buildings sometimes have exhibitions, too.

The rest of the island is a lovely network of paths, greenery, lakes and channels – you can rent rowing boats at the northern end of the island – and a plaza at the west end looking out to the Gulf of Finland. Sunsets are resplendent from here. It's all now the Central Park of Culture & Rest (still named after Kirov), 2km long and pedestrian only. Several small cafes are open in summer.

## Krestovsky Island

Krestovsky Island, the biggest of the three Kirovsky islands, consists mostly of the vast **Seaside Park of Victory** (Primorsky Park Pobedy), also pleasant for a walk dotted with sports fields and the 100,000-seat **Kirov Stadium**.

Bus No 71 from metro Petrogradskaya goes the length of Krestovsky Island to Kirov Stadium. Trolleybus No 34 from near metro Petrogradskaya terminates on Krestovsky near the footbridge to Yelagin.

## Buddhist Temple

From Yelagin Island a footbridge crosses north to the mainland. There, at Primorsky pr 91 by Lipovaya alleya, is a Buddhist *datsan* (temple). Russia's Buddhist community is centred in the Buryatia Republic in Siberia. A neglected but handsome and richly coloured three-storey building with walls sloping in Tibetan style, it was built between 1909 and 1915 at the instigation of Pyotr Badmaev, a Buddhist physician to Tsar Nicholas II.

See Religion in the Facts about St Petersburg chapter for more details. Services are held at 9am daily.

To reach the datsan, take any tram or trolleybus west from metro Chyornaya Rechka to the Lipovaya alleya stop.

## VYBORG SIDE

Peter the Great had no apparent interest in the far side of the Neva, and today, beyond the embankment and Finland Station, among the factories and railway lines, there are few attractions.

### Finland Station (Map 5)

The Finlyandsky Vokzal is where, in 1917, Lenin arrived after 17 years in exile abroad (having ridden in a sealed railway carriage through Germany, Sweden and Finland) and gave his legendary speech from the top of an armoured car to a crowd who had only heard of but never seen the man, in the square where his statue now stands. After fleeing a second time he again arrived here from Finland, this time disguised as a rail fireman, and the locomotive he rode in is displayed on the platform. It's not really the same station, having been rebuilt following WWII. The Ploshchad Lenina metro station is next door.

### Kresty Prison (Map 5)

Kresty is St Petersburg's main holding prison; if you're busted here, Kresty's where they take you to await whatever it is that awaits you. You wouldn't want to find out: Originally opened in 1892 with 1150 individual cells (later reconstructed and designed to hold 2065 inmates), now close to 10,000 poor buggers call it 'home'. Six-bed cells hold 10 to 15 people, sleeping in rotation.

Tours are possible of the prison and small **museum** (☎ *542 68 61,* ☎ *542 47 35, Arsenalnaya nab 7; admission $9; tours noon, 1.30pm & 3pm Sat & Sun)*. This definitely constitutes a unique day out in the city. You'll be led through the church on the premises, through some of the holding areas, into the inner courtyards where you'll get cat-called by the inmates peeking at you through slats in their cells, and into a great little museum where you'll learn about the past residents (like Trotsky and the entire Provisional government from 1917). There are also art objects made by prisoners with lots of time on their hands.

Most impressive is a beautiful chess set with a cops and robbers motif made entirely from glazed bits of hardened, chewed bread. Bring your passport and leave your camera at home.

If you opt out of the tour, on any given day you can see inmates' friends and family members lining Arsenalnaya nab and communicating with their incarcerated dear ones. Wives and girlfriends move their arms in what may look like intricate dance moves, but what is in fact a crude code, known to inmates and prison guards alike.

The prisoner makes himself known by holding an article of clothing out the window (only their hands are visible, stuck through slats or holes in the steel mesh). When the friend down on the street identifies their man, they start waving their arms about, tracing Cyrillic characters in the air. The prisoner waves up and down to signal 'I understand', and side to side to signal 'repeat'. After five minutes of waving, one can clearly discern the message, 'I-c-a-l-l-e-d-M-i-s-s-h-a'!

The inmates have a better way of communicating. Notice all those bits of folded newspaper littering the sidewalk? It's not trash – Russians are neater than that. These have all been flown over from inside the prison with a blow-pipe, with a written message folded inside. If you see one of these flying towards you, duck – they fly quick and painfully. Police regularly patrol the embankment and will shoo you away if they think you're lingering.

### Piskaryovskoe Cemetery (Map 3)

It's a worthwhile trip out here to the sobering but pretty grounds where under a million victims of the Leningrad blockade are buried. See the boxed text 'The Blockade of Leningrad' earlier in this chapter.

## ACTIVITIES

For ballet, theatre, bars and discos, see the Entertainment chapter; for special events listings while you're in town, check the *St Petersburg Times* and *Pulse*.

### Banya

Tired? Frustrated by Russian bureaucracy? A good beating may be all you need – or all you need to give! Here are a few of the better *banyas* (bathhouses; see the boxed text 'The Theatre of Pain' for correct banya etiquette):

**Kruglye Bani (Map 3)** (☎ 550 09 85, *Karbysheva ul 29A; regular/lux class $0.40/2.75; open 8am-9pm Fri-Tues*) Expats meet here on Wednesday nights, 9pm and enjoy a co-ed lux banya ($3). The banya is opposite metro Pl Muzhestva – look for the round building.

**Mitninskaya Banya (Map 7)** (☎ 271 71 19, *ul Mitninskaya; admission $0.80; open 8am-10pm Fri-Tues, last entry 8.30pm*) This is the last banya in the city to be heated with a wood furnace, just like in the country! Experts swear by it. You'll see lots of tattooed bodies here.

**Nevskie Bani (Map 8)** (☎ 311 14 00, *ul Marata 5/7; regular/lux class $1/4*) A church was torn down to build this. Despite renovations it's not the best, but conveniently located. Mayakovskaya is the closest metro station.

### Rowing Boat Rental

In summer, a lovely way to while away a day is paddling through the canals and lakes on Yelagin Island (rent them near the bridge at the northern end which leads to Primorsky pr). See the section on Yelagin Island (under Kirovsky Islands). There are also rowing boat rentals (about $4 an hour) at the northern end of the moat around the Peter & Paul Fortress.

### Yachting

A great summer's day out is to head out into the Gulf of Finland to see how quickly St Petersburg seems to disappear into the water line. The options are many, and you won't regret doing something 'outside' the city. If you plan on bringing your own vessel into St Petersburg, see W http://sailing.dkart.ru for incredibly detailed information on custom points, anchorage sites, naval charts and full descriptions of docks and ports in the St Petersburg area.

Yachts and other boats can be rented at negotiated rates from private captains at the **Sea and River Yacht Club (Map 4)** (☎ 235 01 11, *nab Martynova 92 Krestovsky*

## The Theatre of Pain

For centuries travellers to Russia have commented on the particular (in many people's eyes, peculiar) traditions of the *banya*. The closest English equivalents to this word, 'bathhouse' and 'sauna', don't quite sum it up. To this day, Russians (though more men than women seem to go to city public banyas) make it an important part of their week. You can't say you've *really* been to Russia unless you've visited one.

The banya's main element is the *parilka*, or steam room, which can get so hot it makes the Finnish sauna look wussy in comparison. These rooms are heated by furnaces which heat rocks, onto which water is poured using a long-handled ladle-like implement. Often, a few drops of eucalyptus or pine oil is added to the water. After a burst of scalding steam is released into the room from the burning rocks, everyone stands up, grabs hold of a tied bundle of birch branches (the *venik*) and well, beat themselves or each other with it.

Though it may sound sadomasochistic (and there are theories tying this practice with other elements of masochism in Russian culture) or at the very least painful, the effect is pleasant and, er, cleansing. Apparently, the birch leaves (sometimes oak or, agonisingly, juniper branches are used) and their secretions help rid the skin of toxins.

Banya has a deep tradition in Russian culture ever since it emerged from ancient Novgorod (the Kievan Slavs would make fun of their northern brothers for all that steamy whipping). In folk traditions, it has been customary for bride and groom to take separate banyas the night before their wedding with their friends; the banya itself became the bridge to marriage; a modern version of this custom is depicted humourously in every Russian's favourite film, *Ironia Sudba* (Ironic Fate). Husband and wife would also customarily bathe together after the ceremony. Midwives used to administer a steam bath to women during delivery, and it was not uncommon to give a hot birch mini-massage to the newborn.

There are also many folk proverbs associated with this tradition, including 'the venik is everyone's master' and 'the banya is a second mother'. The banya, in short, is a place for physical and moral purification.

St Petersburg has dozens of public banyas; they've existed in the city since Peter the Great himself could be seen running frightfully naked into the snow by the banks of the Neva after a good

---

*Island; open 9am-6pm Mon-Fri)*. The **Baltic Shipping Company Yacht Club (Map 5)** *(☎ 235 39 35, ☎ 230 75 85)* at the same place also arranges tours to lakes Onega and Ladoga. **Sunny Sailing (Map 5)** *(☎ 279 43 10, e sunny@sailing.spb.ru, ul Vosstania 55)* is a recommended agency that organises yacht cruises in the Gulf of Finland.

### Beaches

On a hot summer day, no-one wants to stay in the city – see how quick it empties out. If you're stuck in the centre, head to the Peter & Paul Fortress and try to find an extra few centimetres to squeeze into onto the tiny beach (only for the luxury of swimming in the dirty Neva). Otherwise, the lakeshore directly west of metro Ozerki is a more pleasant option. Best still, hop on an elektrichka

from Finland Station to Sestroretsk (Map 2) and follow the hordes 10 minutes through the forest to a long and sprawling beach along the Gulf of Finland.

### Skating & Skiing

There's **ice skating** (with skate rental) at the **Yubileyny Sports Palace (Map 4)** *(☎ 119 56 01, Dobrolyubova pr 18, Petrograd Side; skate & rental $5)* and at the **SKA Palace of Sports (Map 4)** *(Dvorets Sporta SKA; ☎ 237 00 73, Zhdanovskaya nab 2; skate & rental $5)*. Both are closest to metro Sportivnaya.

Russians are avid cross-country skiers, and larger sporting goods shops carry skis and equipment, usually for about half the price you'd pay back home. A popular cross-country skiing destination (for the day) is Toksovo (Map 2), a small town north of the

## The Theatre of Pain

soaking. The modern tradition goes something like this: Usually at the same time every week, people head out to their favourite banya where they meet up with the same people they see each week (the Western equivalent would be meeting your work-out buddies at the gym). Many bring along a thermos filled with tea mixed with jams, spices and heaps of sugar (failing this, a few bottles of beer and some dried fish will do nicely).

After stripping down completely in the sex-segregated changing room and wishing 'S lyokogo para' (something of the order of 'May your steam be easy!') to your mates, you head off into a dry sauna first – just to get the skin nice and hot – then it's into the parilka. After the birch branch bit (best experienced lying down on a bench while someone administers the 'beating'), you run outside and, depending on your nerve, plunge into an ice-cold pool, the barreyn. With your eyelids now draped back over your scull, you stammer back into the changing room to hear your mates say 'S lyogkim parom' ('Hope your steam was easy!'). Then you drape yourself in sheets and discuss world issues before repeating the process (most banya experts go through these motions from five to 10 times over a two-hour period).

To experience the banya with other foreigners who know the intricacies of banya rituals even better than most Russians (the phrase 'more Catholic than the Pope' comes to mind), head over to the downstairs luks section of the Kruglye Bani (see the Banya section in this chapter for details) on Wednesday nights from 9pm to midnight. Each week, foreigners working and living in St Petersburg meet there to analyse the Russian plight ('It's such a big, rich country, and yet people live so poorly!') or gripe about their home country ('People are just so materialistic there!'). It's a co-ed crowd, so rent a sheet to drape around you for an extra 20 roubles. It feels a bit like an FKK outing, but it'll give you a good introduction to banya life. And the heated outdoor pool under the stars is a dream.

city, reachable by *elektrichka* from Finland Station. People also head to the grounds surrounding the Pulkovo Observatory.

### Ice Swimming

Every day all year round, people come to the Peter & Paul Fortress for a dip in the waters of the Neva. In winter, when it's frozen over, a 10m-long hole in the ice receives many guests who like to start their day this way. Don't snicker – a look at these people's healthy, ruddy complexion and physique will make you ashamedly think, 'and I start my day with coffee!?'. The scene of all this health is the south-eastern corner of Zayachy Island, where it's least windy. Look for the painted blue walrus on the fortress wall (the slang for ice-swimmers is 'walrus' in Russian).

### Sporting Activities & Events

Russians don't begin casual conversations with, 'So, like, where do you work out?'; gym culture here is minimal. Still, Russians are very active in recreational sports – check out *Lutshee V Sankt Peterburg* under Sports Clubs for a complete list. There are gyms at all the major hotels (prices are exorbitant), aerobic centres for women have become quite popular, and weight rooms have sprung up in many corners of the city (mainly, so far, for the likes of bodyguards and thugs).

The best sports complex in the city is called (you'll never guess) **Sports Complex (Map 5)** (☎ 238 16 32, *Kronverksky pr 9A; admission $3.50 for 90min; open 7am-11pm daily*). The 25m pool, under a glass roof, is heavenly, and you can get in without the usually required medical certificate if you look clean. There's a weight room, and clubs for every sport imaginable meet there. It's also a good source of information for spectator sporting events in the city.

Zenith, St Petersburg's football team, was a sorry lot in the mid-1990s and deserved all those nasty slurs by Spartak (Moscow's team) fans. But under coach Anatoly Davydov's leadership, they won the 1998 Russian Cup, and made it to the nationals in 2001. They usually play at the **Petrovsky Stadium** *(Petrovsky ostrov 2,* ☎ *119 57 00),* near metro Sportivnaya, where you can spy their rowdy legion of loyal fans who after a game deafen pedestrians all over town with rally cries, no matter the results. Tickets can often be purchased at any Teatralnaya Kassa or at the stadium where the game is being held; posters are often plastered all over town well beforehand. Ticket prices vary from about $2 to $10.

### Billiards & Bowling
You'd have to try real hard not to trip over all the billiards places in the city. The city's premier pool and bowling hall is in a beautifully converted Dom Kultury.

**Leon (Map 6)** *(☎ 114 06 39, ul Dekabristov 34; bowling $4-12/hr, billiards $1-4/hr; open 24 hours).* Eight ten-pin lanes (under a chandelier) can be rented, and more than 20 billiard tables (three sizes) are in a luscious, grand space. Prices vary depending on time of day.

Another bowling-billiards combo is in the huge **Akvatoria (Map 5)** *(☎ 245 20 30, Vyborgskaya nab 61; open noon-6am daily).* There's also great billiards inside the cinema **Barrikada (Map 8)** *(☎ 312 53 86, Nevsky pr 15).*

At the Dvorets Molodyozhy there's not only a hotel, billiards and bowling halls, a pool and work-out room, but also **Q-Zar (Map 4)** *(☎ 234 11 14; bowling $4-12/hr and billiards $1-4/hr depending on time and day; open 2pm-11.30pm Mon-Fri, noon-5am Sat-Sun)* a laser-gun labyrinth Quazar game which can be rented in 15-

minute blocks to groups of up to 40 hotshots ($2.50).

### Bunjee Jumping
You can plunge waist-deep into one of the cluster of lakes to the west of metro Ozerki in summertime, though the opening hours are erratic and unpredictable. A free-fall (with or without instructor) costs about $35.

### Frisbee
There are team games of 'ultimate Frisbee' year-round, at 3pm every Sunday and at 9pm Monday in a field near Lesnaya metro station (though in winter it's sometimes held inside, sometimes in the snow); call George on ☎ 552 40 37 or ⓔ frisbee@neva.math.spb.ru for more information.

### Hash House Harriers
A 'drinking club with a running problem', the HHH was invented by energetic British soldiers in 1938 in Malaysia, and has since spread to British consulates all over the world. The runs, during which groups go in search of hidden objects, are usually 5km or less, followed by serious 'down-down' chug-a-lug sessions and a trip to the banya. It can be great fun in a football-hooligan sort of a way. They meet at 1pm every second Sunday – bring running gear. Contact Sarah Powell on ☎ 325 60 36, or fax inquiries to 315 64 34.

## COURSES
The *St Petersburg Times* advertises many private tutors and classes, but the **Herzen State Pedagogical University** *(☎ 311 60 88,* ⓔ *ssm@herzen.spb.ru,* Ⓦ *www.herzen.spb .ru, Kazanskaya ul 6)* **Map 8** runs excellent courses on a range of subjects for all levels, from two weeks to graduate programs several years long, 20 hours a week, for $4 to $7 an hour in groups of two to eight.

***Liden & Denz*** *(☎ 325 22 41,* Ⓦ *www.lidenz .ru, Transportny per 11)* **Map 7** offer well-structured courses costing from $650 for a two-week intensive.

# Places to Stay

Independently booking a hotel room is no problem here – you can even be spontaneous and just walk in off the street and get one! You'll often get a better rate if booking through a travel agent or the Tourist Information Centre. They can also help you rent an apartment, a better option if staying longer.

## PLACES TO STAY – BUDGET

### Camping

Slim pickings. The only camping ground is far from the centre, unsafe and poorly equipped.

*Motel-Camping Olgino* (☎ 238 36 71, *Primorskoe sh 59*) **Map 3** Beds in tiny cabins $18, a two-room 'luxury' $30. No tent space. Full of hard-drinking clientele, this unsavoury place is 18km out of the city, a 20-minute ride on bus No 210 or 110 from metro Staraya Derevnya.

### Hostels & Student Accommodation

For details on how to get to the hostels, see the boxed text 'To the Hostels!'.

*HI St Petersburg Hostel* (☎ 329 80 18, *fax 329 80 19,* e *ryh@ryh.ru,* w *www .ryh.ru, 3-ya Sovetskaya ul 28)* **Map 8** Metro: Ploshchad Vosstania. Dorm bed $19, doubles per adult/ISIC holder/HI member $24/18/17; all including breakfast, about 20% cheaper from Nov-Mar. This is Russia's first (and to date its only) Hostelling International (HI) member hostel. It's a five-minute walk north-east of Moscow Station, and rooms are clean and comfortable. Staff is preternaturally friendly. The Sindbad Travel Agency is conveniently on the 1st floor. Dorm beds are in rooms with three to six beds, and there's a kitchen for guests' use. Reserve by fax or email.

*Holiday Hostel* (☎/*fax 542 73 64,* e *info@hostel.spb.ru, ul Mikhailova 1, 3rd floor)* **Map 5** Dorm bed $12, for 1 person in double room $15; tourist visa invitation $30. Its location has its pros and cons. The

pro is definitely the river view in summer – the rooftop cafe offers the classic panorama of the Peter & Paul Fortress against the backdrop of raised drawbridges. But there's not much out this way. Still, being so close to the Kresty Prison has its exotic side (see the Things To See & Do chapter).

The hostel is clean and fun, staff are friendly and efficient. From Finland Station (metro Ploshchad Lenina) make a left, walk to Mikhailova ul, turn right and cross the street; the entrance to the yard is on the left (you'll see the big red-brick prison wall), the hostel's entrance is in the south-west corner of the courtyard. There's a kitchen for guests' use.

*Petrovskogo College Student Hostel* (☎ 252 75 63, *fax 252 40 19, Baltiskaya ul 26)* **Map 6** Bed in a double or triple $6. Not near the centre, but it's your cheapest option by far. It's inside a grey, dour college, so by day it's full of swarming students. The rooms are also mainly filled with out-of-town students. Passable showers and toilets are shared between four rooms. There's a cafeteria on the premises. You must call and reserve in advance, as it's often full.

*Herzen Institute Student Dormitory* (☎ 314 74 72, *fax 314 76 59, Kazanskaya ul 6)* **Map 8** Bed in a single/double $18/16, with shared toilet $13, lux $71. The location is a dream – just 120m behind the Kazan Cathedral. The rooms are sparse but decent – and the location (did we mention this?) is perfect! Remember that they cannot register your visa, and, if you're staying in the country for more than three days, you'll have to find alternate ways of doing this (see Visas in the Facts for the Visitor chapter). Availability is tight, especially in summer.

### Hotels – City Centre

*Oktyabrsky Filial* (☎ 277 72 81, *fax 315 75 01, Ligovsky pr 43/45)* **Map 8** Singles/doubles from $10-28. This place has the best deals in town, hands down, even cheaper than the hostels. Affiliated with the

## To the Hostels!

For those who want to make it to the hostels via public transport, here are some succinct pointers to get you there efficiently. If you take a taxi, the rides should never be more than about $5 (see Taxi in the Getting Around chapter).

If you're arriving at the Baltic or Warsaw Stations, to get to the HI St Petersburg Hostel, take the metro (see the boxed text 'Metro Fun Facts!' in the Getting Around chapter) at the Baltic Station, on the right-hand side platform after descending the escalator, to the fourth stop, Ploshchad Vosstania (Площадь Восстания). From there, it's a five-minute walk (refer to Map 8). To get to the Holiday Hostel, just stay on the same metro an extra two stops, to Ploshchad Lenina (Площадь Ленина), located at Finland Station. Head towards the water and turn left (see Map 5).

For the Petrovskogo College Student Hostel, either take an unscenic 25-minute walk (exit Baltic Station, turn left to the first street, Shkapina ul, follow it past the railway tracks and at the first crossing, Baltiskaya ul, turn right and continue one and a half blocks) or hop on the metro on the left-hand side of the platform and get off at the next stop, Narvskaya (Нарвская). From the metro, walk left (south), down pr Stachek to Baltiskaya ul (the big Kirov statue will let you know you're there), turn left and continue 300m.

If you arrive at Moscow Station, you're on pl Vosstania, so you're within walking distance of the HI St Petersburg Hostel and two metro stops north on Line 1 (usually indicated in red) is the Holiday Hostel. To get to the Petrovskogo hostel, take metro Line 1 south to Narvskaya, the fifth stop.

If you arrive at Finland Station, you're within walking distance of the Holiday Hostel, two stops away from Ploshchad Vosstania metro (and hence the HI St Petersburg Hostel) and seven stops away from Narvskaya metro and the Petrovskogo hostel.

If you arrive at Pulkovo airport, don't believe the taxi mafia that it will be 'little money' to the centre and take Bus No 13 to Moskovskaya metro (see To/From the Airport in the Getting Around chapter). Then head to Tekhnologichesky Institut (Технологический Институт) station, get off and cross the platform, hop onto the Line 1 metro and go another three stops to Ploshchad Vosstania (or two stops in the other direction for the Petrovskogo hostel).

Finally, with the money you saved yourself on the cab fare, buy yourself a beer and congratulate yourself for having made it there.

nearby Oktyarbrsky Hotel (see Mid-Range), this is its poorer, run-down brother, directly opposite Moscow Station. It may look like the kind of seedy place usually found opposite railway stations, and while it's definitely not for the spoiled, it's clean, friendly, convenient and atmospheric. There are about a dozen different types of rooms to choose from, with or without bath, fridge or breakfast.

If there are three or four of you, ask for their gigantic, bright triples (like #364 and #376). Late at night, prostitutes hang out on the street outside, but the area is pretty safe. When reserving, specify your interest in the 'Filial'.

**Hotel Kievskaya** (☎ 166 58 11, fax 166 53 98, Dnepropetrovskaya ul 49) **Map 7**

and **Kievsky Filial** (same ☎ & fax, Kurskaya ul 40) **Map 7** Both have singles/doubles with shared facilities $6/10, with toilet and breakfast $14/22. These sister hotels within a block of each other (the better one is the Filial) will do in a pinch but are in a boring neighbourhood near the bus station, though Moscow Station is a three-stop ride along Ligovsky pr on anything but Bus No 14.

**Bolshoy Teatr Kukol Hotel** (☎ 273 39 96, fax 272 83 61, ul Nekrasova 12) **Map 8** Doubles including breakfast $21. This is a great option if you can get a place – central, friendly, cosy and clean. You can book directly or via the HI St Petersburg Hostel. (Yes, the name does mean Big Puppet Theatre Hotel…the theatre's next door.)

## Hotels – Petrograd & Vyborg Sides

*Dvorets Molodyozhy (Palace of Youth;* ☎ *234 32 78, fax 234 23 61, ul Professora Popova 47)* **Map 4** Singles $35, doubles $38-104, triples $45 with breakfast. It's in a very quiet location, but bus No 10 to Nevsky pr doesn't come by often, and it's a 20-minute walk to metro Petrogradskaya. It's big and Soviet-modern outside, plain inside, though the place is an entertainment emporium with bowling, billiards, laser-gun, sauna, pool and concert hall on premises. A tough-guy crowd naturally follows in this wake.

*Hotel Vyborgskaya (*☎ *246 91 41, fax 246 81 87, Torzhovskaya ul 3)* **Map 3** Metro: Chyornaya Rechka. Singles/doubles with breakfast and private bath $30/43. This pleasant place is on the mainland, north of Kamenny Island. Head left out of the metro, then follow the main road over the little bridge. The hotel is to your right. Not many tourists use this place, but all things considered, it's a good option.

## PLACES TO STAY – MID-RANGE
## City Centre

*Hotel Oktyabrskaya (*☎ *277 63 30, fax 315 75 01, Ligovsky pr 10)* **Map 8** Singles $38-49, doubles $54-72, triples $55-75, two-room apartments $61-163. Smack on pl Vosstania, it has seen plenty of upgrading in recent years and is the best bet for your money in the centre. It offers a full range of services, including visa support. Rooms are five times cheaper than at the nearby Nevskij Palace, but the comfort level is not hugely less, if you aren't too precious. A popular suite overlooking pl Vosstania is #539 ($98).

*Hotel Rus (*☎ *273 46 83, fax 279 36 00, Artilleryskaya ul 1)* **Map 7** Metro: Chernyshevskaya. Singles/double with bath $57/80. This large, Soviet-style place is nevertheless popular. The sauna has a little swimming pool.

*Hotel Neva (*☎ *278 05 35, fax 273 25 93, ul Chaikovskogo 17)* **Map 5** Singles $28-39, doubles $46-64. A bit farther out, this hotel is near the former KGB headquarters and was once a bordello (could there be a con-

nection?). Rooms are basic, a bit melancholic, but travellers never have a bad report about it. Buses and trolleybuses run frequently down to Nevsky pr (a seven-minute ride).

*Hotel Moskva (*☎ *274 30 01, fax 274 21 30, pl Alexandra Nevskogo 2)* **Map 7** Metro: Ploshchad Alexandra Nevskogo. Singles/doubles $80/96. This monstrous, three-star place is a package-tour haven. Efficient service to be sure, but the place has a creepy, unfriendly, disorienting feel. If you must be here, try for a room at the back where it's quieter (unless you want to be nearer to Dostoevsky's grave, across the street).

*Matisov Domik (*☎ *219 54 45, fax 219 74 19, nab reki Pryazhki 3/1)* **Map 6** Singles/doubles/lux $38/57/84. This is a wonderful option if you don't mind not being smack in the centre (it's a 10-minute walk west of Mariinsky Theatre). The area is quiet and evocative (see Walk 3 in the Things to See & Do chapter), and this family-run place has 24 super-clean rooms in a villa-style atmosphere, all with phone, TV, free soft drinks and breakfast included. There is also a sauna for guest use ($14 per person). From the Mariinsky, walk west on ul Dekabristov, up to the canal. Cross it, turn right and the hotel is 200m ahead.

## Vyborg Side

*Hotel St Petersburg (*☎ *542 81 49, fax 542 90 64, Pirogovskaya nab 5/2)* **Map 5** Metro: Ploshchad Lenina. Singles/doubles $77/97, with no river view $50. This big three-star hotel opposite the Cruiser *Aurora* has front rooms with amazing views over the Neva towards the Hermitage but traffic noise if you open the windows. It's not a bad deal. It's a 15-minute walk to the nearest metro.

## Vasilevsky Island

*Pribaltiyskaya Hotel (*☎ *356 01 58, fax 356 44 96,* e *market@pribalt.spb.su, ul Korablestroyteley 14)* **Map 6** Singles/doubles including breakfast and transport to/from city centre $140/160. This behemoth on the Gulf of Finland is popular with package-tour groups and has big, clean rooms with stunning views of the Gulf of Finland (ask). If you request a discount – and have a good reason for asking – you'll probably get it. There's a bowling alley, billiards hall and sauna on the premises, and a small beach nearby. All in all not a bad place.

*Hotel Morskaya* (☎ 322 60 40, fax 322 60 55, pl Morskoy Slavy 1) **Map 6** Singles/doubles including breakfast $50/70. Located right at the Sea Passenger Port, this is a good place if you'll be doing lots of boating activities. Otherwise it's concrete and drab. A bowling alley, billiards hall and fantastically well-equipped sports shop brighten things up.

## South & East of the City Centre

*Hotel Neptune* (☎ 210 18 11, fax 324 46 11, e hotel@neptun.spb.ru, nab Obvodnogo kanala 93A) **Map 7** Singles/doubles from $90/120. This hotel, managed by Best Western, is in a pretty odd location, but its rooms are upscale, and the workout room is nice. It's about a 10-minute walk to metro Pushkinskaya.

*Hotel Pulkovskaya* (☎ 123 51 22, fax 123 58 56, pl Pobedy 1) **Map 3** Metro: Moskovskaya. Singles/doubles $115/135. Staying at this Finnish-built hotel, 8km south of the centre, has the main advantage of being close to the airport, 15 minutes away by bus No 13. A taxi ride in a private car to the airport from here costs $5. It's a pretty anonymous place, but a step above other Intourist giants, with comfortable rooms, good service, and decent restaurants and lobby bar. It's about a half-hour metro ride to the centre.

## PLACES TO STAY – TOP END
## City Centre

If you get accustomed to a certain level of luxury visiting St Petersburg's palaces, it may be a shock to your aesthetics senses shlepping back to your cheapo hotel. It only takes an extra $300 a day or so to bring an imperial level of elegance to your sleeping quarters. The top hotels here are truly sumptuous.

*Grand Hotel Europe* (☎ 329 60 00, fax 329 60 01, e res@ghe.spb.ru, w www.grand hotel-europe.com, Mikhailovskaya ul 1/7)

**Map 8** Singles/doubles from $295/335, varied suites $390-2350 (+20% tax), about 10% higher in May and June. There are weekend discounts, and nonsmoking floors. Some rooms are spectacular (though smaller than you'd think), and the original, breathtaking Art Nouveau interiors (fashioned in 1905), and eclectic facade (1873–75), still manage a touch of restraint despite the bravura. There are shopping arcades in the lobby, several bars and restaurants, and a harpist on the mezzanine. Your breakfast (not included in your room price!) will cost you a sweet $27.50.

*Hotel Astoria* (☎ 313 57 57, fax 313 51 33, e reserv@astoria.spb.ru, w www.rf hotels.com, Bol Morskaya ul 39) **Map 7** Singles/doubles from $275/335, apartments $480, suites $1000-1700; all including buffet. This is the very essence of class and old-world glory, and as such tends to suit an older, rarefied clientele. Actually two hotels in one, the old wing, named the Astoria, is a five-star treat with Art Nouveau and classical interiors. Each room has its own look and feel, and most have original period antique furniture. The dining hall on the main floor is a true wonder to behold; it's easy to see why Hitler wanted to hold his victory celebration here.

*Hotel D'Angleterre* (☎ 313 57 57, fax 313 51 33, e reserv@astoria.spb.ru, w www.rf hotels.com, Bol Morskaya ul 39) **Map 6** Doubles/suites including buffet from $255/295. The administration in this wing is the same as the Astoria's even if under another name. Less grand with a four-star rating, but still very elegant. Romantics will like to know that poet Sergei Esenin hanged himself on the 2nd floor; it's the room whose balcony is closest to the left-hand corner when facing the hotel.

*Sheraton Nevskij Palace Hotel* (☎ 275 20 01, fax 301 75 24, Nevsky pr 57) **Map 8** Singles/doubles/suites from $290/315/440. This one caters to a business clientele, and its total lack of warm atmosphere attests to this. Corridors go on forever, like in *The Shining*, and rooms are excellent, of course, but forgettable. The presidential suite (where Prince Andrew and Ringo

Starr once slept, though on separate occasions) is a stunner, though for $1900 a day it should be! One of the city's best restaurants, the Landskrona is in the hotel (see Places to Eat).

## OTHER ACCOMMODATION
### Homestays
***Host Families Association*** *(HOFA;* ☎*/fax 275 19 92,* 🇪 *alexei@hofak.hop.stu.neva.ru,* 🆆 *www.spb.ru/homestays, Tavricheskaya ul 5/25)* **Map 7** B&B in a central location: singles $30-85, doubles $50-120. Reliable and established (since 1991), it can place you in English-speaking families throughout Russia and the former Soviet Union. Service options range from simple B&B to guided tours and ticket booking, though these extras are relatively pricey. It charges $30 to $50 for an invitation and registration.

You can also rent a room in a private flat for about $10 a night by going with one of the older women who approach travellers arriving off major trains at Moscow Station. You'll have to use your judgement about who to trust (many really are honest folk in need of extra cash) and establish how far from the city centre their place is before accompanying them (ask to see it on a map).

### Apartment Rentals
If you luck out and find a good apartment to rent, you may never stay in a hotel again.

For privacy and getting a better taste of Russian life, this is the best option, but it's tricky to get a good flat at a good price. If you have trustworthy Russian friends, ask them about available flats (someone's aunt is always willing to move out for you to make some extra cash, usually $15 to $20 a day). Ost-West Kontaktservice (see Travel Agencies in the Facts for the Visitor chapter) can also find you a central flat with reliable landlords for about $30 to $50 a day. Otherwise, it's best to avoid the ads in the local papers – there are dozens of ways to get ripped off renting a flat (the methods involved are mind-boggling) and while many offers may be genuine, it's not worth the risk.

Another recommended and easy option is using Apartment City at 🆆 www.apartment.spb.ru. It has flats for $30 to $80 a day, and the site gives you virtual tours of the flats for rent, with all the details.

PLACES TO STAY

# Places to Eat

The choice of dining in St Petersburg – from super cheap to very fine, from borscht to eel in orange sauce – is enormous. In fact, eating out is likely to be a highlight of your stay, and you don't have to have pay much for the pleasure. See the Language chapter for food-related terminology.

One trend that has emerged is a tendency for restaurants, bars and cafes to try to be all things at once. That's why seafood restaurants will also have 20 meat dishes and a topless floor show to boot. Or a traditional Russian restaurant will also specialise in French and Chinese cooking. The 'eating out' and entertainment worlds here cast their nets wide. Therefore, many places listed under Cafes will have some of the city's best food. Approach eateries with the same general rule as everything else in Russia: Never judge by appearances!

## FOOD

Food is of course important in any culture, but in Russia it takes on soulful dimensions. An invitation to any Russian home will likely centre around a table cluttered with bowls of all shapes, each filled to the brim with salads of all kinds, boiled potatoes and sauces. The less empty space on a table, the more hospitable your host will feel. Meat will figure principally in the scenario (you'll think that there must be a passage in the Russian Constitution that states that a meal is not a meal without meat). You'll be expected to shovel down plate-fulls in between toasts.

Breakfast places are few and far between in Russia, but in a hotel or homestay it usually means a help-yourself buffet spread with jams, cold meats and boiled eggs. Given a choice, Russians will opt for a heavy mid-afternoon lunch and a lighter supper, though dinners are known to go on and on. As a guest in someone's home, it's good form to continually nibble until the wee hours.

Appetisers *(zakuski)* figure prominently in any main meal, and these can sometimes match the main meal in excellence. You

should, of course, try the caviar. The best, most expensive is black (sturgeon) caviar (this is getting more rare every year due to depleting stocks resulting from horrendous overfishing). Cheaper and saltier is red (salmon) caviar.

Soups are a big highlight of any meal. Many Russians don't consider a meal complete without it, and rightly so considering how tasty many of them are. There are dozens of varieties, most served with a dollop of sour cream, some of them thick enough to stand your spoon in (Russians are understandably aghast at the notion of pee-thin canned soups that pass for the real thing in the West).

Don't miss the cuisine of the country of Georgia, with truly succulent, unique and spicy dishes that do unforgettable justice to meat and vegetables.

St Petersburg is getting easier for vegetarians – the newer restaurants and even some of the older ones have caught on with salad bars and vegie dishes. Café Idiot and Troitsky Most (see later in the chapter) are dedicated vegetarian restaurants; the Idiot is one of the city's coolest places to hang out.

The new wave of chi-chi sandwich shops like Bon Jour and Minutka (formerly Subway) have begun offering all-vegie sandwiches, so in a pinch, head for one of these. The otherwise dreadful St Petersburg branch of Patio Pizza has a tremendously good all-you-can-eat salad bar for about $8; Pizza Hut's salad bar is $5.

## DRINKS

'Drinking is the joy of the Rus. We cannot live without it.' With these words Vladimir of Kiev, the father of the Russian state, is said to have rejected abstinent Islam on his people's behalf in the 10th century. And who wouldn't want to bend their minds now and then in those long, cold, dark winters? Russians sometimes drink vodka in moderation (and many never touch the stuff), but quite often it's tipped down in swift shots, with a beer to follow, with the aim of getting legless.

The *average* Russian drinks more than 12L of pure alcohol a year – equivalent to over a bottle of vodka a week – and men drink much more than women.

You'll be expected to toss back vodka shots *do dna* – to the end. Not cleaning out your shot-glass is an insult to the toast that preceded. This can initially be fun as you toast international friendship etc, but vodka has a knack of creeping up on you from behind and if that happens after you've started tucking into steak, chips and fried egg, the consequences can be appalling. A slice of heavily buttered bread before each shot, or a beer the morning after, are reckoned to be vodka antidotes.

Refusing a drink can be very difficult. Russians may continue insisting until they win you over, especially on train rides. If you can't manage to stand firm, pour the shots yourself, giving yourself less than your companion, or *try* politely refusing. If you're really not in the mood, the only method of warding off all offers (as well as making them feel quite awful) is to say 'Ya alkogolik' ('alkogolichka' for women) – 'I'm an alcoholic'.

## Alcoholic Drinks

You can buy it everywhere. Kiosks, shops, bars, restaurants – you name it. Be very suspicious of kiosk spirits. There's a lot of bad cheap stuff around that can make you ill. Never buy booze from little old ladies at the train stations. Err on the side of caution. Hundreds of Russians die every year from tainted spirit (though in St Petersburg the problem is rare).

Drinks are most often served in 50g (50ml) or even 100g shots (none of those fey Euro 4cl shots here!).

**Vodka** Vodka is distilled from wheat, rye or occasionally potatoes. The word comes from *voda* (water), and means something like 'a wee drop' (something must have definitely been lost in the translation to Russian!). Its flavour (if any) comes from what's added after distillation. Though Stolichnaya is

Russia's most famous brand, don't get excited when you see how cheap the stuff is here – what you're used to abroad is made for export and is way better than the domestic version; locals consider it to be an inferior brand. Pyati Zvyozdichnaya and Sankt Peterburg are two brands most say are winners. Tastier and more colourful are Pertsovka (pepper vodka), Starka (with apple and pear leaves), Limonnaya (lemon vodka), and especially Okhotnichya (Hunter's), which has about a dozen ingredients, including peppers, juniper berries, ginger and cloves.

Supermarket and liquor store prices range from $2.50 to $4.50 for a half-litre of regular brands, more for flavoured, and Western prices for imports.

**Beer** Beer is hugely popular in Russia, and St Petersburg's distilleries make some of the tastiest brands in the country (see the boxed text 'Hops to It!' listing different brands). It is almost always sold in bottles. The idea of twist-off caps still seems to be anathema to Russians, some of whom delight in peeling off bottle caps with their teeth, to the great amusement of both their friends and dentists.

**Sparkling Wine, Wine & Brandy** The post-war contract with France for permission to use the terms 'champagne' and 'cognac' have run out, so the bottle with the sweetest pop is no longer Sovietskoe Shampanskoe (though a few bottles may be left) but Sovietskoe Igristoe (Soviet Sparkling). It comes in very dry *(bryut)*, this is really rare – Russians have a sweet tooth and rarely buy this; dry *(sukhoe)*; semidry *(polusukhoe)*; semisweet *(polusladkoe)*; and, sweet *(sladkoe)*. Anything above dry is sweet enough to turn your mouth inside out. A 750g bottle is about $8 in a restaurant and $3 in a supermarket, kiosk or liquor store. The most popular wines – usually distinguished merely as sweet and semisweet – come from Georgia and Moldova.

Armenian Brandy (you'll still see it being called cognac) is also popular. Bely Aist (White Stork) and Ararat are quite nice on cold, snowy evenings.

## Hops to It!

The choice of local beer can be daunting. Here's a little guide to help you focus.

**Baltika** This has been the market leader throughout the 1990s, and while they still sell more than other brands, the tide has changed and people no longer tout it as great beer. It is 75% owned by Baltic Beverages Holding, a Scandinavian company that poured $45 million into Baltika for no noticeable effect. Baltika makes 12 different kinds of beer. No 3 is the most popular, a light beer; No 10 has a natural aroma of almond and basil; No 7 is also fine, but only found in bars; Medovoe is made with a taste of (supposedly) honey.

**Stepan Razin** In the last few years, this has proved itself a strong contender for king of the crop, though the local brewery has existed in some form or another for over 200 years. There are 11 different kinds to choose from: Spetsialnoe is very light at 3.6%, very pleasant; Admiralteyskoe is a light Pilsner; Kalinkin, in honour of the company's old name, is a pretty hefty 7%; Zolotoe is probably the best, with a nice aroma of malt and hop.

**Nevskoe** Brewed by the now Finnish-owned Vena (established in 1872), they are novel for selling beer in cans (the idea has never really caught on here) and stand out for having nicely designed labels. Their Porter won first prize at a Danish beer contest in 1998. Also good are Originalnoe (which won second prize in a British beer contest) and Svetloe (no prizes so far, but it only came out at the end of 2000).

**Bochkaryov** A newcomer on the scene (born in 1999), it has already muscled in with the bigger boys with its tasty Svetloe (light), Tyomnoe (dark) and the very light and airy Beli Nochi. They also have five other varieties.

**Kvas** Kvas is fermented rye bread water, dispensed in some marketplaces from big wheeled tanks for $0.30 a glass. You don't want to know what's swimming on the bottom of those tanks, so better buy the bottled version from kiosks or supermarkets. It's mildly alcoholic, tastes not unlike ginger beer, and is cool and refreshing in summer.

*Khmelnoi* is a hop-based drink brewed from honey, fantastically delicious and is popping up on more and more restaurant menus.

## Nonalcoholic Drinks

There's a large selection of foreign and domestic soft drinks and mineral water. In cafes, best ask for some mineral water *mineralnaya voda* which comes carbonated *s gazom* or still *bez gaza*, or for juice *sok*. *Limonad* is a fizzy drink apparently made from industrial waste and tasting like mouthwash.

There are also many popular dairy products and yogurt-like drinks. *Kefir* is popular at breakfast and *Bifolaif* is a great-tasting, flavoured yogurt drink.

**Tea & Coffee** The traditional Russian tea-making method is to brew an extremely strong pot, pour small shots of it into cups and then fill them with hot water from the *samovar*, an urn with an inner tube filled with hot charcoal. The pot is kept warm on top of the samovar. Modern samovars have electric elements, like a kettle, instead of the charcoal tube. Putting jam (instead of sugar) in tea is quite common, and you'll often be served a side dish of yummy homemade jams.

Coffee comes in small cups and unless you buy it at kiosks and stand-up eateries, it's usually good. Cappuccino and espresso are now common, even in Russian-run places – but make sure the cappuccino isn't the powdered kind.

Malaya Neva laps up against St Petersburg's waterfront.

Reflecting on Smolny Cathedral

Rowers pass Yelagin Palace along one of the island's scenic channels.

Summer Gardens statue

The stylish Anichkov most crosses the Fontanka.

JONATHAN SMITH

The meandering Moyka

STEVE KOKKER

The stone Church of Our Lady of Assumption

STEVE KOKKER

Winter's freeze produces a little more walking space across the Neva.

JONATHAN SMITH

Statues at the base of the Rostral Columns

JONATHAN SMITH

Grand Hotel Europe

## PLACES TO EAT – BUDGET
### Self-Catering
**Food Shops & Supermarkets** *Yeliseevsky Food Shop* (☎ *311 93 23, Nevsky pr 56*) **Map 8** Open 9am-9pm Mon-Sat, 9am-7pm Sun. This is perhaps Russia's most beautiful, if not most famous, food shop. A turn-of-the-20th-century food court, the place has now been restored to its Art Nouveau splendour, with stained-glass windows and chandeliers. The left-hand entrance leads to the most impressive hall; the prices here are higher than in other shops, but the choice is good and it's worth visiting just to admire the place.

*Supermarket* (☎ *312 47 01, Nevsky pr 48*) **Map 8** Open 10am-10pm daily. In the basement of Passazh shopping centre, this is sure to stock that special whatever you've been craving since you left home.

*Babylon Supermarket* (☎ *233 35 18, Maly pr 54/56, Petrograd Side*) **Map 4** Open 24 hours. There's a terrific selection of exotic (for Russia) fresh vegies, like fresh ginger root and avocado, and an awesome bakery. It takes credit cards.

*Kalinka Stockmann's* (☎ *542 22 97, Finlyandsky pr 1*) **Map 5** Open 9am-10pm daily. This is a good place to buy decadent Western luxuries to cook up at the nearby Holiday Hostel.

There are dozens of 24-hour supermarkets dotted all over the city. One good central one is *Dzinn* (☎ *164 10 80, ul Marata 16*) **Map 8**.

**Markets** These are fascinating venues to visit, and not only for the choice of exotic and fresh produce (the meats are so fresh, in some cases they're still in the process of being hacked off the carcass). They teem with life (human, that is) – from the mostly southern vendors trying to tip the scales in their favour (bargaining, even if the price is marked, is encouraged) to the customers being beckoned to try the honey and dairy products (the only free things there).

*Kuznechny* (*Kuznechny per 3*) **Map 7** This is one of the liveliest and most central (and most expensive) of the markets. Considered the best.

*Maltsevsky* (*ul Nekrasova 52*) **Map 8** This is the other lively and central market.

*Sytny* (*Sytninskaya pl 3/5*) **Map 5** This smaller market is behind Alexandrovsky Park and up towards Kafe Tbilisi.

*Polyuostrovsky* (*Polyuostrovsky pr 45*) **Map 5** This market has a fur (and cruel pet) market out back, where you can buy great hats. Get off at the Ploshchad Lenina metro station, then take tram No 6 or 90, or bus No 33, 37, 106 or 107.

*Andreevsky* (*Bolshoy pr 18*) **Map 6** This is a less expensive but no less interesting market. Along 6-ya linia is a junk market.

*Torzhovsky* (*Torzhovskaya ul 20*) **Map 3** Kind of decrepit, but it'll do the trick.

**Bakeries** You don't have to go too far in St Petersburg to find a great slice. Here are a few of the best places for breads and pastries.

*Wendy's Baltic Bread* (☎ *275 64 40, Grechesky pr 25*) **Map 8** The city's baker paradise with by far the city's widest selection of fresh-baked breads, cakes, tortes, eclairs, croissants filled with ham and cheese, and delicious pizzas.

*Bushe* (☎ *312 35 78, Razyezzhaya ul 13*) **Map 7** Open 10am-9pm daily. A close second in terms of paradise. Pumpkin bread is just one of their selected fresh breads, and the entire line-up of filled croissants is too yummy to put into words. Frothy milkshakes will keep the kid in everyone happy.

*Sever* (☎ *311 25 89, Nevsky pr 44*) **Map 8** Open 10am-9pm Mon-Sat, 10am-8pm Sun. A legend in the city, crowded at any time, and chock-full of cookies and oddly-coloured pastries.

### Fast Food
You may never crave a Big Mac again after sampling the Russian concept of 'fast food' – and with the great choice available, you don't need to bloat up on KFC grease just to save pennies. In addition to these places, there are *blinnayi* (pancake houses), *bistros* (fancy cafes), *kafe morozhenoe* (ice-cream restaurants), *kafeterii* (cafeterias), *stolovayi* (canteens) and *bufety* (stand-up snack bars) are all over the place. Generally at such

places, a meal with entree and dessert will cost under $5.

*Laima* (☎ *232 44 28, kanala Griboedova 14,* **Map 8**; ☎ *315 55 45, Bolshoy pr 88, Petrograd Side,* **Map 5**). Both open 24 hours. The leaders in this field, both places offer to whip up fresh food of very high quality (the management also runs several restaurants). Their huge menu includes about 20 salads, soups, stuffed peppers, chicken and fish fillets, kebabs, freshly squeezed juices and milkshakes – with no meal more than $3. Everything is served in spotlessly clean surroundings (and with real cutlery!). Ask for the English menu.

*Orient* (☎ *277 57 15, Suvorovsky pr 1/8,* **Map 8**; ☎ *314 64 43, Bol Morskaya ul 25,* **Map 8**). Both open 24 hours. Again, a large and varied menu, and quality very decent. The Suvorovsky pr location is pay-by-weight, fully buffet-style (the first of its kind here), with meat, fish and pasta dishes, a salad and dessert bar – perfect for HI St Petersburg hostellers returning from late-night jaunts.

*Bistro Samson* (☎ *311 19 68, Kamennoostrovsky pr 16*) **Map 5** This is a decent option of a similar genre on the Petrograd Side.

*Teremok* (*near cnr Italyanskaya ul and Mal Sadovaya ul*) **Map 8** Open 10.30am-11pm. This unassuming little kiosk is the locus of some of the most mouth-watering blinys in town. Perfect on cold days, but a treat any time. Made in front of you, they come stuffed with ham and cheese ($1), jams, or a cheese-caraway mix ($0.80) that's pure heaven.

*Kolobok* (☎ *275 3865, ul Chaikovskogo 40*) **Map 5** There is a variety of decent-tasting traditional Russian dishes on offer, most of which can be pointed to.

You'd be better off avoiding the *Fiesta* and *Galeo* bistro chains, or any place named simply 'Bistro'.

For dirt-cheap fill-ups (three-course meals for about $3), there are several atmospheric choices.

*Stolovaya No 5* (*ul Dostoevskogo 6*) **Map 7** Open 11am-5pm Mon-Sat. Their cafeteria fare includes a good meat stew (*zharkoe*)

and borscht, and if you get there in the late afternoon you can sit with blood-stained lady butchers from the nearby Kuznetchy market enjoying a shot of vodka.

*Café Stolovaya* (*nab reki Fontanki 40*) **Map 8** They serves similar fare, with beer on tap. You don't want to use the bathroom, though.

If this choice still leaves you wanting, you can always rely on the tried and true (if you trust edible plastic and nutrient poor foods, that is!): *McDonald's* (☎ *314 68 58, Bol Morskaya ul 11/6,* **Map 8**; ☎ *234 92 63, Kamennoostrovsky pr 39, Petrograd Side,* **Map 5**; ☎ *113 47 32, Sennaya pl 4,* **Map 7**; ☎ *323 15 79, Sredny pr 29A, Vasilevsky Island,* **Map 4**).

Other burger and cholesterol joints in town include the Finnish *Carrols* (☎ *279 17 36, ul Vosstania 5*) **Map 8**, the German *Grillmaster* (☎ *110 40 55, Nevsky pr 46*) **Map 8**, and the American *KFC* (☎ *279 61 36, Nevsky pr 96*) **Map 8**.

*Minutka* (☎ *325 82 24, Nevsky pr 20*) **Map 8** This restaurant serves up Subway-style sandwiches.

## Cafes

These are great hang-outs with mixed Russian and international cuisine, distinguished by the relaxed, low-key atmosphere.

*Staroe Kafe* (☎ *316 51 11, nab reki Fontanki 108*) **Map 7** Soups and entrees $3-4, main course average $6. Open noon-11pm daily. This is what you'd call a 'real find'! This tiny, dimly-lit, red brick and wood space throws you back a century or so: an old upright piano sits in the corner with ancient, crumpled sheet music sitting atop (played after 7pm daily), canned 1920s blues wafts through the air, with old samovars, copper pots, tarnished brass candleholders, musty books all around. The food is decent and so are the drinks (watch the prices – some wines are stellar), but the ambience is the real prize here.

*Sunduk* (☎ *272 31 00, Furshtadskaya ul 42*) **Map 5** Main courses $3-7. One of the most highly recommended places in town! For years, it was the cosiest grotto space with good food and the funkiest bathrooms in the city. Now they've quadrupled their space while retaining the cosiness. Meals are decent, the menu varied, but you don't come here for cuisine – it's the atmosphere that'll keep you lingering. Live music nightly after 8.30pm, though it can get deafening.

***Depo*** *(☎ 277 44 51, Goncharnaya ul 14)* **Map 8** Main meals $4-7. This is just one of those great hang-outs. Nothing extraordinary about the (tasty) food (meat, fish and vegetable dishes available), but the decor – train and train station-themed, with an ironic wink – is light and happy. It's the kind of place where you don't notice time passing by.

***Stroganov Yard*** *(☎ 315 23 15, Nevsky pr 17)* **Map 8** Buffet – lunch $6, supper $9. A popular, spacious hang-out in the courtyard of the Stroganov Palace, you feel like you're in an outdoor cafe because of its glass walls. You can order from a full and varied menu or do what most do – enjoy one of the city's few buffet tables. As an unneeded novelty, each table is hooked up with a phone – if you see someone you fancy, just ring them up and try not to sound too corny. Many come just for one of the exotic cocktails ($5 to $7).

***Kafe Literaturnoe*** *(☎ 312 60 57, Nevsky pr 18)* **Map 8** Entrees $3-7, main courses $5-15. We list this place because it's in so many other guidebooks you might wander in thinking it's a good place. It may have had its day back in Pushkin's time (his last meal was eaten here) but today it's little more than a tourist trap with old-style decor and classical music concerts.

## Coffee Houses

A relatively recent explosion of Western-style coffeehouses has resulted in several excellent places to hang out and get wired.

***Idealnaya Chaska*** *(☎ 251 23 44,* W *www .chashka.ru, Nevsky pr 15, 112 & 130,* **Map 8***; Kirochnaya ul 19,* **Map 5***)* Open 9am-11pm daily. This company opened the city's first Western-style coffee house in 1998 and is opening new branches seemingly every month. There are dozens of different coffees to choose from, including tasty cocktails with lemon and orange juice and

spices. The garlic-honey coffee is a real eye-opener. The Nevsky pr 15 branch is the biggest and most popular.

***Café Rico*** *(☎ 164 72 14, Nevsky pr 77/1, enter on Pushkinskaya ul)* **Map 8** Cool, comfortable, Spanish decor and slightly over-priced but good coffee and coffee cocktails.

***Café Marco*** *(☎ 234 13 28, pl Lva Tolstogo 1)* **Map 5** Open 8am-11pm daily. The usual delicious coffee, plus alcoholic coffee cocktails, salads and cakes in a rather cramped setting. They also sell coffee beans.

## Ice Cream

Russians take ice cream seriously, and even in winter blizzards you'll see them indulging – outside, that is. St Petersburg produces some of the finest ice cream in Russia (much tastier than you'll find on Moscow streets), and it's highly recommended to try one of the ice-cream bars on sale at push-cart freezers all over the city. Baltisky and Bely Nochi are particularly good ones.

***Baskin Robbins*** *(☎ 164 64 56, Nevsky pr 79)* **Map 8** You can try the usual 31 (locally produced) flavours in this and other locations in the city.

***Sladkoezhka*** *(☎ 272 18 52, Zakharevskaya ul 25)* **Map 5** This is a slick ice-cream cafe and pastry shop with several branches throughout the city.

***Gino Ginelli's*** *(☎ 312 46 31, nab kanala Griboedova 14)* **Map 8** Open 10am-midnight daily. This is an Italian ice and ice-cream place, perfectly placed for your summer strolls.

## PLACES TO EAT – MID-RANGE
### Russian

*Bliny Domik* (☎ *315 99 15, Kolokolnaya ul 8)* **Map 8** Breakfast $3, lunch $5, dinner $7. Open 8am-11pm daily. A little slice of heaven! It may take you an hour to read their (English) menu, but that's only because it's so imaginatively comprehensive. Of course, *bliny* (leavened pancakes; $1 to $2) are the attractions here (stuffed with everything possible), but they have many vegetarian delights (spicy eggplant salad for $1.50), cheese or meat fondue ($11 to $14 for two), herbal tea concoctions (one for the libido!), a full breakfast menu – and all using low cholesterol oil! Set up like a country home, this is one of the more pleasant places to eat, and the food never disappoints.

*U Tyoshi Na Blinakh* (*Zagorodny pr 18)* **Map 7** Full course meal $4-6. Open 24 hours. The name means 'At Mother-in-Law's for Pancakes', and indeed bliny are their specialty, but there are other Russian traditionals like *golubtsy* (meat rolled in cabbage) in a buffet-style display easy to point to. You won't break into a folk dance in rapture at the quality, but there's enough here for a tasty, hearty meal.

*Propaganda* (☎ *275 35 58, nab reki Fontanki 40)* **Map 8** Entrees $4-7, main course $9-18. Very popular with tourists and enjoying a good reputation among locals too is this paean to the Soviet glory days. The kitsch here is quite stylised – kind of designer Soviet – but it seems to have struck a chord. Food is fine, though overpriced. Hamburgers (about $5) are a big draw here, as is the lunch buffet ($7).

*Na Zdorovye* (☎ *232 40 39, Bolshoy pr 13, Petrograd Side)* **Map 4** Soups and entrees $3-7, main course $6-11. Open noon-11pm Tues-Sun. It's all about nostalgia here, but the owners couldn't decide which kind, Soviet or Russian folk, so it's a heady mix of both. The decor is a colourful mini museum of old objects culled from nearby villages and Soviet-era posters and soft-drink machines. As if a group of Marxist-Leninst extremists set up shop in a village *izba* (wooden cottage). The menu, too, is a combo of traditional Russian and Soviet cuisine, a mix admittedly half

effective. Their homemade juices are quite nice. It's fun and novel, but you get the sense that they're trying just too hard.

*Kotletnaya* (☎ *318 40 50, per Grivtsova 7)* **Map 8** Meals $3-6. In the heart of Dostoevsky land sits this ironic nod to Soviet life. Its cafe-style interior is filled with Soviet relics (a submarine telephone, propaganda posters) and objects of cultural importance (Soviet pressings of Beatles vinyls), but the decor retains a subtle touch. The menu's main attractions are its *kotlets*, patties made with meats and sauce fillings. A fun place.

*Kalinka Malinka* (☎ *314 26 81, Italyanskaya ul 5)* **Map 8** Entrees $3-6, main course $5-10. Often filled with tourist groups rushing through a meal on their way to the theatre (it's located on pl Iskusstv) but there's good food here in an atmosphere that seems at once classy and downscale. They run the gamut from *pelmeni* (meat dumplings) and bliny to Chicken Kiev ($6) and other Russian favourites. Folk music starts daily at 8pm.

*Staraya Derevnya* (☎ *431 00 00, ul Savushkina 72)* **Map 4** Soups and entrees $2-5, main course $8-14. This first-rate family-run traditional Russian restaurant has enjoyed a solid reputation for many years and is worth going out of your way for (from metro Chyornaya Rechka, take any tram three stops or grab a taxi). Service is great, and because it's small, it's very intimate and cosy – make reservations. Their beef with plum and nut sauce ($9) and ham in apple sauce ($8.50) are winners.

### Caucasian

*Cheburechnaya* (☎ *277 53 85, ul Vosstania 13)* **Map 8** Main dishes average $4. You'd never guess from its unassuming, hole-in-the-wall look, but some of the city's best Georgian food is made here. No-one else does thick, spicy Georgian *selyanka* (soup; $3.75) as deliciously as they do, and the mushrooms and potatoes in cream sauce ($2.50) is a melt-in-your-mouth pleasure.

*Pirosmani Restaurant* (☎ *235 46 66, Bolshoy pr 14, Petrograd Side)* **Map 4** Soups and entrees $3-6, main courses average $8. Open noon-11pm daily. Here's excellent Georgian food in a unique setting. The rear wall of the restaurant is a psychedelically sculpted tribute to the Georgian artist's work, and there are rivers flowing through the restaurant, which is designed to resemble a Georgian mountainside village. It has a well-earned high reputation, and is worth a trip.

*Kafe Tbilisi (☎ 230 93 91, Sytninskaya ul 10)* **Map 5** Entrees $2-6, main meals $3-7. Practically a St Petersburg institution, this place will not disappoint. It's a first-rate restaurant with mouth-watering dishes. Try the homemade cheese, and the lavash and khachipuri breads. A happier decor wouldn't hurt, though.

*Kafe Adzhika (☎ 310 26 27, Moskovsky pr 7)* **Map 7** Meals average $5. Open 24 hours. This cafe gives you the feeling of walking in on a well-decorated Georgian family's home. Service is friendly, the home cooking heavenly; a respite from the chaos of nearby Sennaya pl.

*Cheburechnaya (6-ya linia 19)* **Map 6** Just down from metro Vasileostrovskaya, this legendary place is a must, if only to try the delicious, thick Georgian soup *chanaxhi* for $1.50, and have a gander at the colourful locals. In late *perestroika* times, people from all ends of the city would come here for the meat soups (meat in the shops was a rarity for a while).

## Medieval

*Ivanhoe (☎ 230 72 12, Bolshoy pr 32A, Petrograd Side)* **Map 4** Entrees $4-6, main course from $7. Open 24 hours. A medieval-themed restaurant where meals are cooked in front of you in a stone oven. A large selection of food and a pleasant, unusual ambience makes this an appealing option. Food is served in plentiful portions, but it's usually so good you'll still want more.

*Valhall (☎ 311 00 24, Nevsky pr 22/24)* **Map 8** Main meals from $10. For a while, this restaurant, with its wild Viking decor and kitschy get-up on the waiters and waitresses cornered the exotic niche in town. It's still a hoot. Its Broadway musical-style cabaret ($15, 10pm, Wed-Sun) is unique in the city and ironic enough (especially considering the setting) to be amusing. The menu is European and Scandinavian.

## German

*Schvabsky Domik (☎ 528 22 11, Novocherkassky pr 28/19)* **Map 7** Buffet section – meals $3-8; restaurant No 1 – meals $5-12; restaurant No 2 – $7-20. Open 11am-1am daily. This food emporium, a combination of three restaurants in one, takes up an entire block. Something for everyone here amid a Bavarian decor which pushes the hokey barrier – from schnitzel, sauerkraut, potatoes galore (50 potato dishes in their Potato House section!), sausage and roast pork to more complicated recipes. The food is great (so is the German beer), the place fun. Visit each of the three dining halls before deciding where to eat – the menus vary quite a bit between them.

## French

*Bistrot Garçon (☎ 277 24 67, Nevsky pr 95)* **Map 8** Entrees from $3, main course $7-20. Open 9am-1am daily. This is an utter delight. Top-notch French cuisine in an atmosphere of rustic finesse. Small, cosy, friendly, with service that's just right, you can feast on classics like French onion soup ($3), escargot bourguignon ($12), stuffed eggplant ($7) and their large selection of French cheeses (Roquefort, Bouché

### They Deliver, Don't They?

Home delivery is a relatively new concept in Russia, but these places can turn a cosy night or day in into a culinary feast. **Laima** (☎ 232 44 28) will bring you some of their very fine 'fast food' (the word hardly applies to them) 24 hours a day, for about a 20% surcharge. **Orient** (☎ 327 74 44) will do the same at a 10% surcharge. **Swagat** (☎ 217 21 11) delivers their succulent Indian dishes for free. **Fujiyama** (☎ 234 49 22) will come to see you with sushi, but you'll probably want to run out to an ATM before they arrive. **Pizza Pronto** (☎ 315 89 48) will supply you with one of their finest, with a minimum order of $12, and only before 6pm (they're scared of pranks – if you convince them you're genuine, they may deliver later).

PLACES TO EAT

de chèvre etc). They also have a nice breakfast menu.

**Bistro Le Français** (☎ 315 24 65, Galernaya ul 20) **Map 6** Soups and entrees $4-10, main meals $8-18. Fine cuisine in a subtle, authentic decor, often frequented by nostalgic expats. Cap off a great meal with a Grand Marnier mousse ($7). They serve great breads and pastries.

## Pizza & American

**City Bar & Restaurant** (☎ 314 10 37, nab reki Moyki 20) **Map 8** Meals $4-9, some student discounts. For those nostalgic for burgers 'n fries and apple pie, this place's got em all, and them some. The fixins' are damn good! You can grab a game board and relax for awhile too, listening to music piped in directly from Internet radio stations. All in all, a pleasant place to hang loose.

**Montreal Canadiens** (☎ 310 95 26, Apraksin per 22, cnr Fontanka River) **Map 7** Entrees average $5, main courses average $10. A living shrine to the famous Canadian hockey team (whose all-star veterans visited in 2000 – proof is in their dozens of iconified photos on the wall!), with souvenirs, T-shirts and hockey sticks on display. A large screen plays sports events. It's a cosy but tavern-style place where the speciality is Montreal steak ($28), done with a special grill imported from Canada.

**La Strada** (☎ 312 47 00, Bol Konyushennaya ul 27) **Map 8** Salads from $4, pizzas average $12. This is a grand, spacious place with an enormous glass ceiling and an open kitchen area where you can watch the cooks prepare the pizzas. Portions are huge. Their baked potato dishes ($8) are super-filling.

**Pizza Hut** (☎ 315 77 05, nab reki Moyki 71/16; ☎ 327 26 42, Nevsky pr 96) **Map 8** Pizzas $6-16. Open noon-10pm Sun-Thurs, noon-11pm Fri-Sat. Both do countless varieties of pizza and have tiny salad bars ($5). The Nevsky location also does pizza by the slice (thank you!) for under $2.

**Pizza Pronto** (☎ 315 89 48, Zagorodny pr 8) **Map 7** Pizzas $4-15. Open 11am-11pm daily. A dependable Russian pizzeria with pasta dishes as well.

## Chinese

**Chopsticks** (☎ 325 60 60, Mikhailovskaya ul 1/7) **Map 8** Main courses $10-24. Open noon-11pm daily. This used to be the city's main contender, and while you can't call it overpriced, the food is no better than at more inexpensive venues in the city. Service is very precise, however.

**Golden Dragon** (☎ 114 84 41, ul Dekabristov 62, **Map 6;** ☎ 232 26 43, Kronversky pr 61, **Map 4**) Soups and egg rolls $2-5, main meals $5-13. The atmosphere at both the locations is a bit dull, but many of the 120 dishes are very good and reasonably priced.

**Jackie Chan** (☎ 315 34 51, Kazanskaya ul 33) **Map 6** Main meals $5-12, business lunch $3. Out of the way a bit, and it doesn't look like much from the outside, but there's a little bridge inside with real fish in the pond beneath, the staff go out of their way to please and the food is quite fine.

**Tinye** (☎ 323 22 29, 1-ya linia 18) **Map 6** Soups $2, main dishes $6-12. This is another good bet. Their huge soups are big enough for a meal, and the house speciality, eel on an iron plate, will cost you $10.

**Kharbin** (☎ 272 65 08, ul Zhukovskogo 34/2) **Map 7** Entrees $2-5, main meals $4-8. The staff is lovely here, and serve up dependably good Chinese food, including excellent fried eggplant in soy sauce with ginger ($4). You can cook up a storm at your table yourself for $12.

## Korean

**Korean House** (☎ 259 93 33, Izmailovsky pr 2) **Map 7** Main courses $6-11. Reputed to serve some of the best Korean dishes in Eastern Europe, their food is delicious, and all that garlic and spice is a treat after nonspicy Russian fare. Specialities are Korean-style beef and kim chi, with a good choice of vegetarian meals.

**Ariang** (☎ 274 04 66, 8-ya Sovietskaya 20) **Map 7** Main courses $10-25. A fancier venue with lots of free starters to keep clients happy.

## Indian

**Tandoor** (☎ 312 38 86, Voznesensky pr 2). **Map 6** Main meals $7-20, set meals $13-18, business lunch $10. This is the most central Indian place in town, but not the best. The menu – albeit Russianised – is varied, and their speciality is Vindaloo Palek, a tasty homemade cheese marinated in honey and spices.

*Swagat (☎ 322 21 11, Bolshoy pr 91, Vasilevsky Island)* **Map 6** Main meals $5-18. Open noon-11pm Tues-Sun. Diners leave here with dumb-looking expressions of total satisfaction on their faces after having partaken in a heavenly feast of northern Indian delicacies. Justice (a la tandoori, tikka, masala, curry) is done to chicken, prawns, beef and vegetables. The masala kulcha bread ($2) melts in your mouth. The sour lassi ($1.50) is a cut above the rest. There's sitar music and dancing nightly after 8pm, the service is darling (they do friendly things like bring you free nuts while you wait), the decor subdued. Convinced?

## Italian

*Da Vinci (☎ 311 01 73, W www.da Vinci.spb.ru, Mal Morskaya ul 15)* **Map 8** Main courses $10-15. Ostensibly Italian, this is one of those collage restaurants so popular in Russia – there's as much American and Mediterranean food on the menu as Italian, and the entertainment runs the gamut of jazz, Russian folk dancing and musclemen strip shows. Why yes, there's a children's menu too. And vegetarians haven't been forgotten about. The Web site is a hoot, and the place itself curiously fun.

*Mama Roma (☎ 314 03 47, Karavannaya ul 3/35)* **Map 8** Main meals $6-14, business lunch buffet $4. Great pizza and pasta in a generic setting.

## Vegetarian

*Gushe (☎ 113 24 05, Vladimirsky pr 5,* **Map 8**; ☎ 316 11 81, Moskovsky pr 74, **Map 7**). Meals $2-6. Open 9am-11pm daily. A vegetarian's delight (hard to believe, but there's not a shred of meat in the place). Soya and tofu casseroles (on display), vegetarian lasagna, salads, fresh juices and lots more in a pleasant space.

*Green Crest (113 13 80, Vladimirsky pr 7)* **Map 8** Meals under $3. Open 9am-11.30pm daily. Though the sign out front makes this look like a pharmacy, inside is a selection of cream-drenched salads (takeaways available) and a great vegetable stew ($1.50). This cafe also has salmon and meat dishes and Tinkoff beer on tap.

*Troitsky Most (☎ 326 82 21, Mal Posadskaya ul 2,* **Map 5**; ☎ 232 66 93, Kronversky pr 9/2, **Map 5**) Salads and soups $1-4. Open 24 hours. The original vegetarian place in town (it used to be the Hare Krishna cafe), there are vegie burgers, dry soya meals, potato cutlets and lots of salads.

*Café Idiot (☎ 315 16 75, nab reki Moyki 82)* **Map 6** Entrees $3-7, main meals $4-10. Open noon to 11pm daily. Despite it being always packed with expats, the atmosphere is excellent – funky lamps and tables, couches to lounge on, and several rooms with different ambiences (including one that's nonsmoking). Add live jazz on weekends, bookshelves packed with used books, magazines and board games and a good Sunday brunch. Check out their toilet, which is the definition of economical spacing.

## Seafood

*Bremen Morskoy Klub (☎ 318 91 39, Bol Morskaya ul 15)* **Map 8** Entrees $2-4, main course average $13. One of several boat-themed restaurants in the city, this one has a fancy feel to it in its two dining halls, one decked out like a, well, deck, and the other like a cosy captain's mess hall. Specialities include pike perch in white wine sauce ($10) and sturgeon in 'home' sauce ($14).

*Matrosskaya Tishina (☎ 164 44 13, ul Marata 54/34)* **Map 7** Main courses from $15. When you enter, you're not sure if you've stumbled upon a moored boat or a fish shop as portholes and fish nets blend with aquariums brimming with live lobsters and gigantic perch (those with a sadistic streak can pick which one they want for supper). Small but decidedly upscale. Food is great, but you won't leave here without paying $20 to $25 a person.

*Afrodite (☎ 275 76 20, Nevsky pr 86)* **Map 8** Main courses $7-15, business lunch $5.

Reputed to be the city's finest seafood restaurant, with a well-respected Portuguese chef, it boasts exotic dishes like barracuda and alligator.

**Khristofor** (☎ 312 97 61, Bol Morskaya ul 27) **Map 8** Entrees $6-8, main courses $10-15, business lunch $8. This one wins it for decor and atmosphere, with a wooden ship-shaped bar and subtle off-lighting. There's shark steak ($14), and delicious baked pike perch ($14), and meat dishes too.

## PLACES TO EAT – TOP END
### Russian
**Austeria** (☎ 238 42 62, Peter & Paul Fortress) **Peter & Paul Fortress Map** Meals $15-25. For location and service, nothing in this category comes close to touching this place. Dine outside and count on excellent Neva views, solid Russian food and live music nightly. They swear their recipes are from the time of Peter the Great.

**Nikolai** (☎ 311 14 02, Bol Morskaya ul 52) **Map 7** Meals $12-30. On St Isaac's Square in the House of Architects is this first-class, almost regal dining space – you'd think you were having lunch inside the Hermitage. Dress accordingly. The recipes are supposedly traditional Russian dishes from the era of Nicholas I.

**Kalinka** (☎ 323 37 18, Syezdovskaya linia 9) **Map 4** Meals $15-28. Some find this too touristy (it's a favourite stop for tour groups), but there's a reason for its popularity. The atmosphere is finely crafted 'traditional' Russian, there's live music on original old instruments and fine food (like bear in cognac pepper and rabbit with fruits for $21). Weekday visits are quieter.

### Japanese
**Fujiyama** (☎ 234 49 22, Kamennoostrovsky pr 54) **Map 4** Entrees $3-21, sushi $2.50-5.50 per piece, Sashimi about $16 for five pieces. This is top of the line and accordingly very expensive. There are 26 kinds of sushi, various succulent combo plates that cost up to $50 and a very nice miso soup ($3.50). The atmosphere is a bit sterile and rigid, but service is first-rate.

## Best Splurge

Money left over at the end of your trip? Feel like being pampered? Your best option (out of the many good ones) is **Taleon Club** (☎ 312 53 73, Ⓦ www.taleon.ru, nab reki Moyki 59) **Map 8** Soups $8-14, entrees $20-30, main courses $25-42, Sunday brunch $29. Open noon-3am daily. Men need a dinner jacket (ties not necessary but recommended) and proper footwear and women should be dressed neatly; the sumptuous surroundings make it easy to understand why. This building used to be famous businessman Yeliseev's mansion, and if you've already seen his store on Nevsky pr (see the Things to See & Do chapter), you know he had rarefied tastes. Every room here has its own style (the dining hall alone is half empire, half Ludwig XXVI). The in-house casino is a baroque fantasy with a socialist-realist painting on the ceiling by Izmailovich. The library room is in Russian baroque. The cigar room is out of a dream. You can lounge for a while in whatever room you like. Guided tours are available.

It was on this spot that the temporary Winter Palace was built for Empress Elizabeth. Later reconstructed, it still housed members of the court (from here, plotters left to strangle Paul I in his newly-built castle), then became a Literary Institute and in Soviet times the Institute of Marxism-Leninism. Much of the interior was, of course, left to go to pot, but you'd never know it now amid all the finely carved wood panels, stained glass windows and engravings.

Oh yes, the food. First-rate. In 1999 and 2000 it was voted best luxury restaurant in the city. There's a large choice of fish, meat and vegetarian dishes, and all things considered, quite reasonably priced. There are some grand specialities, though, like the Blancpain, a smorgasbord of six types of seafood for three people for $220. See their full menu on the Web site. There's a huge selection of wines (ranging from $15 to $3473 a bottle!). and two pages of cognacs. If you're modest, a full-course meal for two could be $150; if not, the sky's the limit.

*Sakura (☎ 315 94 74, nab kanala Griboedova 12)* **Map 8** Meals $20-50. Its reputation is more based on the fact that it's one of the city's most expensive restaurants than on its cuisine, but you can still expect the best here.

*Shogun (☎ 275 32 97, ul Vosstania 26,* **Map 7***; ☎ 314 74 17, Gorokhovaya ul 11/25,* **Map 8***).* Main courses $9-18. Everyone in town recommends Shogun for authentic Japanese cuisine, which has beautiful interiors, private shuttered rooms and absolutely lovely staff. The $15 business lunch is very popular. At the new ul Gorokhovaya location, they've opened the city's first real sushi bar where you get the same level of service and decor at less expensive prices (a light meal starts at $7). Treat yourself to their plum wine.

## Italian

*Rossi's (☎ 329 60 00, Mikhailovskuyu ul 1/7)* **Map 8** Entrees $7-15, main courses $18-35. A good Italian meal is an expensive proposition in this city, but at least you get what you pay for. Delicious freshly made pasta is served in very aesthetically presented portions in this casual but elegant hall.

*Milano (☎ 314 73 48, Karavannaya ul 8)* **Map 8** Main courses average $25. Put on your Sunday best, sit back and let yourself be pampered. There are sumptuous pasta dishes, but they specialise in seafood plates (their scampis are reputed to be the best in town). Leave the kids home – they aren't welcome here after 6pm, to ensure a relaxed atmosphere.

## European

*Landskrona (☎ 275 20 01, Nevsky pr 57)* **Map 8** Main courses from $15, Executive lunch $29. Named after a 16th- to 17th-century Swedish outpost near the centre of what is now St Petersburg, this restaurant has enjoyed a reputation as one of the city's best since the early 1990s. Its specialty is Mediterranean food, particularly Italian, but has a selection of delicious, exotic dishes. You're served a white wine sorbet between courses to cleanse the palette. In summer, an open-air terrace offers panoramic views of the city from within the Sheraton Nevskij Palace Hotel. The live jazz music is a welcome relief from the light classical and folk music in most other restaurants.

*Staraya Tamozhnaya (The Old Customs House; ☎ 327 89 80, Tamozhenny per 1)* **Map 6** Entrees $6-32, main courses $18-45. The atmosphere here is simply delightful, with vaulted brick ceilings, excellent live jazz, fantastic service and wonderful food. Nothing outrageous or particularly creative, just large portions of very well prepared Russian and European specialties, including steak, lamb, lobster and rabbit. Try the pumpkin cream soup ($6).

*Dvorianskoye Gnezdo (☎ 312 32 05, ul Dekabristov 21)* **Map 6** Meals $60-90. This is the city's most luxurious restaurant, inside the Yusupov Palace, a gourmet's fantasy come true. If you want to spend a packet – like Bill Clinton and Madeleine Albright did when they supped here – on good food, excellent wine and sensational service, this is the place to do it.

# Entertainment

St Petersburg is the arts and entertainment capital of Russia. The classical tradition in the city is among the best on the planet – ballet, opera, music and theatre – and there's a sizzling world of rock clubs, jazz joints and discos that has St Petersburg nightlife soaring to dizzying heights. Very heartening is the fact that nearly every one of the dozens of concert halls – large and small – and theatres are filled practically every night – a testament to this society's love of culture.

Be sure to check *Pulse* and the Friday edition of the *St Petersburg Times* for their comprehensive weekly club, pub, theatre and concert listings. Things change fast here. There are also posters plastered all over the city with events advertised.

## CLASSICAL MUSIC, BALLET & OPERA

September to June is the main performing season – in summer, though there's plenty to see and do, many companies are away on tour. An exception is the last 10 days of June, during the White Nights Dance Festival, with events ranging from folk to ballet.

### Tickets

Some of the city's largest venues charge a separate foreigner's price, many times the Russian price (see the boxed text 'Dual-Pricing System' in the Facts for the Visitor chapter). The Mariinsky, Mussorgsky, Hermitage and Maly Theatres all charge extra for your accent. It is still cheaper than what you'd pay for those tickets purchased through a top hotel's concierge or travel agency. If you can prove that you are working or studying in Russia, you'll pay the Russian price.

If you get a Russian ticket and are caught inside the theatre (a frustrating and embarrassing experience), you will be made to pay the difference by rabid babushkas. Scalpers usually sell last-minute tickets outside the theatre an hour before the show.

These will be Russian tickets, and if they're for a sold-out show, they can go for around $40 to $50 each. Make sure to check the ticket carefully and see that the date and seat position promised are correct; there are a number of fakes around. First floor is the *parter*; the mezzanine is the *beletazh*; and the balcony is the *balkon* or *yarus*.

The best booking office to buy tickets for classical and rock concerts, plays and ballet is the Teatralnaya kassa (Театральная касса; Map 8; ☎ 314 93 85, Nevsky pr 42), opposite Gostiny Dvor.

## Classical Music

See also the Things to See & Do chapter – many palaces, churches and museums host their own, more intimate musical evenings.

**Bolshoy Zal** (Big Hall; ☎ 110 42 57, Mikhailovskaya ul 2) **Map 8** Also known as the Shostakovich Academic Philharmonic Big Hall, this grand hall mainly hosts concerts by the renowned St Petersburg Philharmonic Symphony Orchestra, under different conductors.

**Glinka Capella** (Kapella imeni Glinki, ☎ 314 10 58, nab reki Moyki 20) **Map 8** Also known as the St Petersburg State Capella, this venue has high standards, featuring piano and violin concerts and the occasional vocal evening. The choir here was founded during Peter the Great's time. Its acoustics are heralded as among the best in the world.

**Maly Zal imeni Glinki** (Small Philharmonia; ☎ 311 83 33, Nevsky pr 30) **Map 8** This concert hall is the second venue at which the symphony orchestra plays. It was the city's main concert hall in the 19th century.

## Ballet & Opera

Aside from these classical venues, keep your eyes out for two troupes whose ballets have caused minor scandals and much delight wherever they perform: the Boris Eifman Ballet Theatre (they have taken more audacious chances in revolutionising ballet than any other troupe since it was formed in 1977) and Valery Mikhailovsky's St Petersburg All-Male Ballet (see Dance in the Facts about St Petersburg chapter). Both have travelled abroad widely, and have no permanent theatre.

**Mariinsky Theatre** (☎ 114 52 64, W www .kirovballet.com, Teatralnaya pl 1) **Map 6** The Kirov Ballet and the Kirov Opera both perform here. See the Facts about St Petersburg chapter under Dance for more information about this world-famous milieu which saw the premieres of Tchaikovsky's *Sleeping Beauty* and *The Nutcracker*.

The companies tend to go away on tour for about two months in the summer and unpredictably the rest of the year, but they usually stage five ballets and five operas per month. Some are standouts, but standards vary. The ballet's home shows are nearly always booked out; ticket sales from the theatre usually start 20 days in advance. Other visiting companies also perform here.

**Mussorgsky Opera and Ballet Theatre** (Teatr Opery i Baleta imeni Mussorgskogo; ☎ 318 19 78, pl Iskusstv 1) **Map 8** Cheaper and easier-to-get-into ballet and opera performances are staged here – they cover all the classics. The Small Theatre stages more contemporary works than the Kirov and standards are respectable.

**Rimsky-Korsakov Conservatory** (☎ 312 25 19, Teatralnaya pl 3) **Map 6** This theatre also stages a handful of popular operas each month.

**Hermitage Theatre** (☎ 311 90 25, Dvortsovaya nab 34) **Map 7** One of the most beautiful venues for performances since Catherine the Great's times, there are occasional concerts and operettas here.

## Modern Music

**Lensovieta Culture Palace** (☎ 346 39 02, Kamennoostrovsky pr 42) **Map 5** Pop and folk groups and other performances are mounted throughout the year at halls such as this.

**Oktyabrsky Concert Hall** (☎ 275 12 73, Ligovsky pr 6) **Map 8** On the site of a former church, this concrete concert hall hosts the biggest names in Russian pop and rock.

## THEATRE

Tickets for theatrical venues in town are available from the same sources as those for classical music.

**Maly Dramatic Theatre** (☎ 113 20 49, ul Rubinshteyna 18) **Map 8** Under the expert direction of Lev Dodin, there are unforgettable, often experimental pieces staged here. Don't miss *Gaudeamus*, *Claustrophobia*, or Dodin's 9½-hour version of Dostoevsky's *Besy (The Possessed)*.

**Lensoviet Theatre** (☎ 113 21 91, Vladimirsky pr 12) **Map 8** You can't go wrong here; seems like every performance is a winner, especially on their second, smaller stage where Bruchner's *Voychek*, Beckett's *V Ozhidaniy Godo* (Waiting for Godot) and Pinter's *Lyubovnik* (The Lover) will be formidable, even if your knowledge of Russian is mediocre.

**Pushkin** (☎ 110 41 03, pl Ostrovskogo 2) **Map 8** Also known as the Alexandrisky, this is the city's premier drama theatre. It stages (in Russian) the likes of Shakespeare, Maugham and many Russian works, usually on a grand scale.

**Tovstonogov Bolshoy Dramatic Theatre** (☎ 310 04 01, nab reki Fontanki 65) **Map 7** This is another leading mainstream drama theatre, considered the tops throughout the Soviet era.

**Teatr Satiry** (☎ 314 70 60, Sredny pr 48, Vasilevsky Island) **Map 6** Very clever, funny and off-beat plays are staged in this intimate space.

**Zazerkalye** (☎ 164 18 95, ul Rubinshteyna 13) **Map 8** This company specialises in children's theatre.

## CIRCUS & PUPPETS

**St Petersburg State Circus** (☎ 314 84 78, nab reki Fontanki 3) **Map 8** Tickets $10. Shows 7pm Tues, Wed & Fri, 3pm & 7pm Sat & Sun Sept-June. This is the address of the permanent venue of this circus, which sometimes seems very tired during rather typical comedy-acrobatic performances. To look at their current program, see W www .ticketsofrussia.ru/theatres/circus.

**Bolshoy Teatr Kukol** (☎ 272 82 15, Nekrasova ul 10) **Map 8** Tickets about $1.

ENTERTAINMENT

Shows 11.30am & 2pm Sat & Sun. Founded in 1931, this is the city's main venue for puppets, with 16 children's shows in their repertoire, and two for adults.

*Teatr Kukol-Marionetok* (☎ *311 19 00, Nevsky pr 52)* **Map 8** Tickets about $1. This venue has puppet and marionette shows on a varying schedule.

## PUBS, BARS & BEER GARDENS
Many of the clubs and discos double as bars and hang-outs as well.

### Inexpensive Bars
*Ot zakata do rasveta* (☎ *314 64 48, Bol Morskaya ul 31)* **Map 8** Open 24 hours. Its name means 'From Dusk to Dawn', and like the movie, this is a dark, fun place. Lots of wood, swinging doors, interesting toilets, decent chow, laid-back clientele, lively entertainment and overall good atmosphere.

*Zapravka* (☎ *235 28 16, Bolshoy pr 28, Petrograd Side* **Map 4** Open noon-midnight daily. This is a real find for those who like friendly, cosy, local hang-outs with great and inexpensive grub (if you can call dishes like salmon in cognac sauce grub!). It's so small (about 25 seats), you'd hardly think they could fit a band in there, but there's live music from Tuesday to Saturday after 7pm (worth checking out). The business lunch is a steal at $3.

*Bar O Meter* (☎ *315 53 71, Mal Morskaya ul 7)* **Map 8** Open 11am-6am daily. There are several things which make this place stand out: incredibly energetic and friendly staff (no sour-pusses here!); amazing pasta dishes ($6) expertly served (al dente and with a spoon!); and the metre-long 'glasses' of beer from which the bar takes its name (the whole place will cheer as you down the last drops!).

### Upmarket Bars
*James Cook Pub* (☎ *312 32 00, Shvedsky per 2)* **Map 8** This is geared to an upmarket clientele, but the ambience is anything but elitist. Divided into a cafe and tavern, this British pub has a wide selection of imported beers, including Japanese Asahi ($3), Hoegaarden ($4) and popular Cherry Beer ($4). The meals get pricey (up to $25) and the

speciality is sturgeon in 'home' sauce ($16). The cafe sells coffee beans and exotic loose tea, including the nearly narcotic silver tea ($35/50gr!).

*Tribunal* (☎ *311 1690, pl Dekabristov 1)* **Map 6** This spacious bar has always been at the forefront of the quest to coat sleaze in elegance, and succeeds with mixed results. Famous for the suggestive ads with scantily-clad women, the bar has greatly diversified and not only offer topless entertainment, but male striptease and transvestite shows. All this in a polished, high-class atmosphere. It's still quite popular with randy tourists.

*Chayka* (☎ *312 46 31, nab kanala Griboedova 14)* **Map 8** On any given night, this place near the corner of Nevsky pr is filled with foreign businesspeople and prostitutes who will sidle up to you while you're at the bar and say something coolly seductive like, 'I want peanuts. Buy me beer'. Worth avoiding if you're picking up the tab. Though, if you're a fan of German beer you will not be disappointed.

*Sadko's* (☎ *329 60 00, Mikhailovskaya ul 1/7)* **Map 8** Sometimes its happening here (within the Grand Hotel Europe), other times it's just stuffy and expensive.

### Irish Pubs
*Mollies Irish Bar* (☎ *319 97 68, ul Rubinshteyna 36)* **Map 7** This bar first brought the Black Stuff to the city on the Neva. It's still going strong – and it's not only foreigners filling the tills. The live bands can get ear-splittingly loud, but it's the kind of place where people will get up and dance spontaneously, so who cares! The pub food is also decent. Draught Guinness pints are $5 and lagers are $4.

*Shamrock* (☎ *219 46 25, ul Dekabristov 27)* **Map 6** Another energetic place, though it feels quite collegiate at times. This cool and cavernous place, opposite the Mariinsky Theatre, is another excellent Irish pub with a great atmosphere and similar prices to Mollies.

### Beer Gardens
There are several beer gardens right along Nevsky pr; most other bars in town offer a

fine assortment as well. Here are a few that specialise in making beer-lovers happy.

*Tinkoff (☎ 314 84 85, Kazanskaya ul 7)* **Map 8** Open noon-3am Sun-Thur, noon-5am Fri-Sat. This place will redefine beer drinking for you. Set inside a gigantic, gorgeous (now quite posh) brewery, it sells a large array of fresh microbrewed beers, like the delicious White Unfiltered, for $2 to $4 a half litre. There's also a full menu, but food prices are stellar (there's an ATM on the premises though). There's live music, but no dancing.

*Pivnoy Klub (☎ 279 18 52, ul Nekrasova 37)* **Map 8** Open noon-3am daily. The name means Beer Club, but it's way better than that simple moniker suggests. This is a totally relaxed place that has a pleasantly local feel to it. It manages to mix a subdued decor with a lively atmosphere. Bands perform most nights; best to reserve a table.

*The Bierstube (☎ 275 20 01, Nevsky pr 57)* **Map 8** Open noon-1am. This is pretty much what you'd expect: waitresses in *dirndl*, an Austrian setting, German/Austrian cooking and good but expensive beer (within the Sheraton Nevskij Palace Hotel complex). Draughts (0.5L) are about $5.

## ART & ALTERNATIVE BARS

*The Stray Dog (☎ 312 80 47, pl Isskustv 5)* **Map 8** Evening performances $3-5. Open 11am-midnight daily. From late 1912 to 1915, this bar was the focal point in futurist and avant-garde art culture in St Petersburg. Poetry recitals, lectures, spontaneous dance performances and ad hoc exhibitions were held here. Artists were admitted free, all others paid a heavy cover charge to see the likes of Mayakovsky, Akhmatova, Meyerhold and Diaghilev hanging out or expressing themselves. Reincarnated in early 2001, the new version hopes to unite the disjointed world of the city's young creators, as well as host concerts, screenings and exhibitions of all kinds. There's a great bar to hang out at and watch the proceedings. One of the city's more unique spaces.

*Manhattan Club/Katyol (☎ 113 19 45, nab reki Fontanki 90)* **Map 7** Cover $2-4. This bar used to be an artsy, 'Nouveaux Bohemian Wannabe' magnet, but has broadened its horizons with live music in a good, airy space and an interesting, mixed crowd. Thursday is Latino night.

*Fish Fabrique (☎ 164 48 57, Pushkinskaya ul 10)* **Map 8** Open 3pm-late daily. Set in the building that's the focus of the avant-garde art scene, this attracts some radical artsies and fun-lovers. The crowd gives this cramped space its edge, not its sparse, nonexistent decor. Art and experimental films are screened nightly at 6pm, and live bands kick up a storm at 10pm nightly.

*Psycho Pub (nab reki Fontanki 23)* **Map 8** Cover $1-4. A grunge dive to end all others, this dark place screeches 'authentic' at full volume. Located in a dingy courtyard of a building where street cleaners live, this tiny space thrives on its unwashed but friendly clientele and energetic bands playing rap-core, thrash or reggae. Its anything-goes ambience and inexpensive drinks make this pretty appealing.

## NIGHTCLUBS & DISCOS
While most young Russians are happy wandering the streets looking for adventure or playing guitar in parks with friends, there are crowded nightclubs for all tastes and expense accounts. No matter what you're into – tattoos and body art, strippers of all sexes and varieties, funk, techno, grunge or heavy rock, the city's hot spots are bursting with it, fuelled by a young and energetic crowd adamant about having a great time. This is a party city, and if you know where to go, you'll find the crowd that'll wind your crank.

## Small Clubs
*Griboedov (☎ 164 43 55, W www.mfiles .spb.ru/griboedov, ul Voronezhskaya 2A)* **Map 7** Cover free-$3. Open 5pm-6am daily. Located in an old bomb shelter, this has become the city's hottest club, with great bands and a no-pop-music policy that pleases its eager to shake crowd of alternative, early-20s fun-lovers. A good mix of attitude and grit gives this place a unique feel. Weekends get stiflingly crowded here – the best nights are Wednesday and Thursday.

ENTERTAINMENT

*Mama* (☎ 232 31 37, *Mal Monetnaya ul 3B)* **Map 5** Cover about $4. Open from 11pm Fri-Sat. Depending on the DJ, the energy in here can rise to fever pitch (DJ Kefir usually does the trick), but other times it's just packed with horny, drunk teens who like to go craaaazy, man! It's split level, with an Internet club and an outdoor courtyard for fresh air, and the music is usually house or disco. Get there early or late to avoid the huge crowds outside.

*Moloko* (☎ 274 94 67, **W** *www.moloko .piter.net, Perekupnoy per 12)* **Map 7** Cover $2-3. Open from 7pm Thur-Sun. Everything an underground club should be – dimly lit, modestly decorated and bubbling with the sense that something's about to happen. Great bands running the gamut of Latin, ska, metal-funk, reggae and blues. One of the city's most popular clubs.

*City Club & Money Honey* (☎ 310 05 49, **W** *www.moneyhoney.org/cityclub, Apraksin dvor 14).* **Map 7** Cover around $2. This double club is an excellent, lively place to go. Upstairs (City Club) there's a dance floor and pool tables and lots of space to mingle (the place attracts an over-20 crowd), and downstairs there's the Money Honey Saloon, which has great live rockabilly and country bands (you haven't heard *I Walk the Line* until you've heard the Russians do it!). Bands usually start at 8.30pm. The crowds' randiness sometimes spills over into rowdiness later on. Enter via the courtyard off Sadovaya ul.

*Studio 20* (☎ 355 31 67, *pr Korablestroyteley 20, korpus 2)* **Map 6** Cover from $2. Open 24 hrs. Out of the centre, and inside a student dorm building on Vasilevsky Island this is a funky student club. You'll probably be the only non-Russians there, so enjoy a sense of discovery and see how friendly and fun-loving students make a fuss in their own habitat. It's also a great space with an underground feel and occasionally kick-ass live bands.

## Major Clubs

*Plaza* (☎ 323 9080, *nab Makarova 2)* **Map 4** Cover $4-20. Open from 10pm Wed-Sun. This is *the* club at the moment in St Pete, voted best club in Russia in 2000. Spacious, European-style, lots of chrome and metal, and erotic dancers. On Wednesday, they play Russian music, Thursday has good, soulful disco, and weekends there are usually dance concerts (where cover prices can be exorbitant, depending on the act). The crowd is mixed.

*Akvatoria* (☎ 118 35 18, *Vyborgskaya nab 61)* **Map 5** Cover $4-20. A huge complex with something to please everyone – several dance floors, theme nights, modern, Euro decor, and if that doesn't do the trick, a bowling alley, casino and pool hall. The size of the place is a bit overbearing.

*Ostrov* (☎ 328 46 49, *nab Leytenanta Shmidta 37)* **Map 6** Cover from $6. Highlights include a snow and rainmaking machine that douses people dancing to Russian disco at unexpected moments.

*Metro* (☎ 166 02 04, **W** *www.metro club.ru, Ligovsky pr 174)* **Map 7** Cover $2-4. There are three dance floors in this emporium, with music on the pop-techno side, but there's an attempt to keep everyone happy. Every night there are different themes and shows, from amateur strip contests to lip-synching teeny pop bands. The crowd is young, the atmosphere lively, if sometimes pretentious.

*Havana* (☎ 259 11 55, *Moskovsky pr 21)* **Map 6** Cover $1-3. A real salsa and Latin club with a Cuban theme and imported dancers. The line-ups here are eye-opening – all these northern whiteys wanting to get down and let completely loose to Latino house! A fun place.

*Hollywood Nights* (☎ 311 60 77, *Nevsky pr 46)* **Map 8** Cover $6-35. Open 11pm-6am Wed-Sun. A bombastic tribute to Americana, this enormous disco has improved over the years as the Mafia set, which used to hang here, has gone elsewhere. Now this is a place for the young and wealthy and those who like to latch onto them. There are usually popular Russian bands lip-synching or shows. Music is Europop. There's an adjoining strip club too.

*Marstall* (☎ 311 06 84, *nab kanala Griboedova 5)* **Map 8** Free for foreigners. This bar/club will certainly make you feel special

– it's the one place where you pay less if you're a foreigner. If you're male (and this is a favourite among randy male tourists), you may be shown attention by the local females who hunt for sugar daddies here. Generally, the place has a lively, fun atmosphere, with good live bands.

## Sexy
*Xali Gali (☎ 246 3827, Lanskoe sho 15)* **Map 3** Cover $18. Open 9pm-4am daily. This infamous den of iniquity is renowned for giving its rapacious audience the unexpected in the midst of strip shows, naked magic acts, saucy comedy acts, sex shows and penis measuring contests (for each of your centimetres you get 1% discount off the price of drinks!). Wild and foul-mouthed MCs dictate the evening's excesses in the city's most audacious venue. Get there by 10pm – they may not let you in after the show has begun. From metro Chyornaya Rechka, head north along nab Chyornoy Rechki one block, turn right onto Landskoe sh, and try to lose your inhibitions along the way.

*Monro (☎ 312 13 31, nab kanala Griboedova 8)* **Map 8** Cover $2-4. Open 5pm-11pm daily. This was the first erotically-themed club to open in the city, with squeaky clean video booths and phallic, ancient Egyptian, Greek and Roman motifs. There is no sleaze here, though, just an open-minded atmosphere in which to dance to your favourite Russian pop tune or chill out in the lounge – but only until 11pm as they're located in a residential building.

*Golden Dolls (☎ 314 65 55, Nevsky pr 60)* **Map 8** Cover $12-22. The city's most famous and tacky strip venue faces Catherine the Great's approving nod on the other side of Nevsky pr. In the jamble of chrome and flesh, you'll be served a menu with items like Tequila Sex ($16) and Friction Dance ($30). You can do creative things like pay $40 to watch a girl eat a sausage or to eat ice cream off her tummy. You can guess what the crowd is like.

## GAY & LESBIAN VENUES
The city's gay nightlife has suffered many ups and downs over the years, with only one real success story to boast of. Still, the scene here is as focused on pretty boys, sex and (sadly) drugs as any other major Western city. Underfed rent boys haunt the bars for generous foreigners or rich sugar daddies, and the lesbian scene is very under-developed. The city in general has a gay-friendly clubland due to the adventurous nature of its club-goers, so don't feel you must restrict yourself to these card-carrying gay clubs.

*69 Club (☎ 259 51 63, 2-ya Krasnoarmeyskaya ul 6)* **Map 7** Cover $4-8 (men), $4-10 (women). This sleek, Euro-style bar-restaurant-nightclub turned the gay scene on its head in the city and became one of Russia's most popular clubs. It got co-opted by mafioso trying to seem hip and then military cadets trying to roll the clientele for cash, but has always been a good place to dance the night away. There are erotic dance shows and a dreary dark room. And it gets away with a face control policy and charging women more for entry!

*Jungle (☎ 327 07 70, ul Blokhina 8)* **Map 4** Cover $1-4. A true veteran, this club has somehow survived from the mid-1990s when it was very popular. It's still a hang-out for local gays and lesbians, but its atmosphere is often quite dour. Saturdays are best.

*Greshniki (☎ 318 42 91, nab kanala Griboedova 28/1)* **Map 8** Cover free-$3 (men), $5 (women). Ostensibly more into leather and chains (judging by the dungeon decor), this dark place boasts nude waiters and extravagant dancers. Drinks are reasonably priced, and the crowd, when there is one, is friendly. Overall, it's kind of creepy, however.

## JAZZ VENUES
*JFC Jazz Club (☎ 272 98 50, Shpalernaya ul 33)* **Map 5** Cover $2-4. Open from 7pm nightly. This excellent club is probably the best of its kind in the city, fulfilling all your expectations of what a jazz club should be. Small and New York-styled, it makes you feel like you are in the East Village. It's got a fun crowd, great beer and atmosphere, and really good jazz, blues, improv and folk bands from Russia and around the world.

ENTERTAINMENT

**812 Jazz Club** (☎ 346 16 31, Bolshoy pr 98, Petrograd Side) **Map 5** Cover $1-2. Opened in spring 2001, this little space is an alternative jazz club that hosts great jam sessions after its nightly concerts, which start at 8pm. Jazz, funk, reggae and Latin bands play to the last drop of sweat. Enter via the courtyard.

**Jimi Hendrix Blues Club** (☎ 279 88 13, Liteyny pr 33) **Map 7** Cover up to $4. Open 24hrs. Pretty good, depending on the band (jazz, rock and blues bands usually start at 7.30pm). Otherwise, Lenin and Brezhnev imitators are known to steal the stage, and while the atmosphere is congenial, there's often a sense that something is about to happen, then it doesn't.

**Jazz Philharmonic Hall** (☎ 164 85 65, Zagorodny pr 27) **Map 7** Cover from $2, student discounts. Concerts 7pm nightly. This famous venue represents the established, more traditional side of jazz. It has two bands – a straight jazz and a Dixieland – plus foreign guests doing mainstream and modern jazz, all hosted by co-founder David Goloshchyokin, who runs about being seen.

**Neo Jazz Club** (☎ 273 38 30, Solyanoy per 14) **Map 5** Cover $2. Open 9am-midnight daily. A pretty laid-back place with smoother, more mellow live jazz music. Most people go there for supper too (very good Armenian specialities for under $8) and to just chill.

## SPORTS BARS
**All Star Café** (279 90 17, ul Zhukovskogo 33) **Map 8** Open noon-5am daily. A real homey sports bar with big screen, dart games, good food (mostly meat meals for about $5) and genuinely friendly staff.

**Futbol Bar** (☎ 314 84 68, W www.football.ru, Karavannaya ul 28) **Map 8** Open noon-1am, Fri-Sat until 6am. A modern and sparkling clean, split-level sports bar with pool tables, monitors and large screens and enough rooms to find your favourite corner. Zenith rules here.

## CINEMA & VIDEO
Seeing foreign movies in Russian theatres is a cinema purist's nightmare, for everything is dubbed. The quality of dubbing has improved enormously over the years, though, and they now use more than just one voice for different characters! However, purchase video cassettes and you'll cringe as all your favourite actors are reduced to one nasal, monotone voice. Many cinemas (most along Nevsky pr) host film festivals or film weeks throughout the year.

**Crystal Palace** (☎ 272 23 82, Nevsky pr 72) **Map 8** $4-8. The city's first Western cinema, decked out with Dolby stereo, is on the site of the first commercial cinema to open in the USSR, in 1929. Mainly US-blockbuster fare.

**Mirage** (☎ 232 48 38, Bolshoy pr 35, Petrograd Side) **Map 4** The second Western-style cinema opened in summer 2001 and is an impressive entertainment emporium with billiards and a restaurant.

**Spartak** (☎ 272 78 97, Kirochnaya ul 8) **Map 5** Older, European or lesser-known Russian films are screened here.

**Westpost** (☎ 275 07 84, Nevsky pr 86) **Map 8** VCR/TV rental $25/45 weekend/week; membership $10; tape rentals $2-3 daily. Westpost rents combination VCR/TVs, and has a selection of nearly 2000 videos in English.

## SPECTATOR SPORTS
The pickings are rather slim here. There are occasional blood-thirsty kick-boxing and boxing matches advertised on posters along Nevsky pr, and for more specialised sport competitions, contact the Sports Complex (see Activities in the Things to See & Do chapter).

**Petrovsky Stadium** (☎ 119 57 00, Petrovsky ostrov 2) **Map 4** Zenith, St Petersburg's rather pitiful football team (yes that means soccer), which has a good season every few years, plays here, as do other clubs.

**Yubileyny Palace of Sport** (☎ 119 56 15, Dobrolyubova pr 18) **Map 4** The hockey season stretches from September to June, and here's where you can see St Pete's top team, SKA. At other times the space hosts expos on tattooing and the like.

Smolny Nunnery

Peter the Great's tree: visionary, yes, but not much of a town planner

Shemyakin's *Peter the Great*

A tram passes over Troitsky most towards the Peter & Paul Fortress.

A church through every archway

The Grand Cascade and Water Avenue, the uncontested centrepiece at Petrodvorets.

Statues adorn the Grand Cascade, Petrodvorets.

Musicians in period costume perform in the courtyard of the Grand Palace, Petrodvorets.

# Shopping

No-one comes here specifically for the shopping, but a lot of people leave with their wallets a lot lighter, now that St Petersburg has almost everything you'd want – often cheaper than at home. Nevsky pr is the obvious centre for your shopping needs with foreign and Russian stores of every variety and several of the city's biggest shopping centres on it. In addition to Gostiny Dvor and Passazh (see the Things to See & Do chapter), DLT, just up from Nevsky pr at Bol Konyushennaya ul 21/23, has fully-stocked departments of anything you'd want (but watch your wallet there – it's a pickpocket haven for some reason).

In addition, there are usually kiosk cities (a product of the perestroika era) around metro and train stations where you can find foodstuff and trinkets of variable quality. Again, except for beer, you should be wary about buying alcohol from these places.

## WHAT TO BUY
### Souvenirs
Souvenir stands set up shop around all major tourist attractions, especially at the Hermitage, in front of the Peter & Paul Fortress, and at the *souvenir market* (Map 7) which is diagonally across (north) from the Church on Spilled Blood and open year-round. Most shopping centres and hotel lobbies also sell a fair amount of folksy souvenirs. At each of these places, there are *matryoshka* dolls, wooden spoons, *palekh* painted boxes, military gear, Russian-language T-shirts and watches galore. A certain amount of bartering is perfectly acceptable.

*Khudozhestvennyye Promysly* (☎ 113 14 95, Nevsky pr 51) **Map 8** There's a large selection here, a bit pricey, but you're assured of decent quality.

### Soviet Memorabilia
If you want to bring some original Soviet souvenirs home, don't stop at the watches and pins available at tourist fairs. Many are manufactured especially for today's tourists.

Matryoshka dolls: favourite souvenir

LEE FOSTER

How about some truly beautiful Soviet-era commemorative stamps? They cost no more than $0.18 each and are available from the at the Main Post Office's *philately booth* (glavpochtamt; booth No 11; ☎ 312 83 02, Pochtamtskaya ul 9) **Map 6**. Or some colourful old children's games or wooden alphabet blocks (the box covers are a kitsch lover's delight)? They're under $1 each while they last, at the *Paper Supply Store* (Bolshoy pr 69, Petrograd Side) **Map 5**. You can always find cool items, though some are stolen, on the impromptu street junk markets sold by drunks. Try around the Our Lady of Vladimir Church, along the 6-ya and 7-ya linii down from metro Vasileostrovskaya and around the *Andreevsky Market* (Map 6) just down from that at the corner of Bolshoy pr.

*Voyentorg* (☎ 314 62 54, Nevsky pr 67) **Map 8** If army's your thing, you'd do no better than here. It sells original (as well as synthetic) articles of military clothing of all types and varieties (from soldiers' underwear – unused – to officers' caps and parade uniforms). Prices are very reasonable.

*Sekunda* (☎ *275 75 24, Liteyny pr 61)* **Map 8** Enter through the courtyard. This small place sometimes has great kitschy Soviet items.

## Arts & Antiques

There are dozens of art and antique shops throughout the city, but only some of them – generally the more expensive ones – will walk you through the customs clearing procedures.

*Free Arts Foundation* (☎ *164 53 71, Pushkinskaya ul 10)* **Map 8** Galleries have different opening times, but on Saturday afternoons, all of them are open. Often referred to simply by its address, this is gallery central as far as modern art is concerned. The guru here is Timur Novikov, and the numerous galleries have everything from paintings and sculpture to digital works. You might see people stoned out of their brains and philosophising against a backdrop of puzzling pieces of art in Victorian, frilly frames. Sometimes the space itself and its denizens are more intriguing than the actual art. Occasionally performance pieces take place, like poets firing live rounds of ammunition at bottles of Baltika beer.

*Sol-Art* (☎ *327 30 82,* W *www.solart gallery.com, Solyanoy per 15)* **Map 5** Open 10am-6pm daily. In the sumptuous surroundings of the Stieglitz Museum, this is a great place to buy local, contemporary art. There are thousands of paintings to rummage through, and there is a large selection of Russian souvenirs too.

*Palitra* (☎ *277 12 16, Nevsky pr 166)* **Map 7** Open 11am-7pm Tues-Sat. This a gallery with rotating exhibits of local artists and is well worth a visit.

*Art Gallery Borey* (☎ *273 36 93, Liteyny pr 58)* **Map 8** There's usually a good show on here, one of the cooler art galleries in town. The bookshop towards the back has very reasonably priced local art and some of the best art books in town.

*Artists' Union of Russia Exhibition Centre* (☎ *224 06 22, Bol Morskaya ul 38)* **Map 7** Open 1pm-7pm Tues-Sun. This place has galleries of art for sale and on exhibition on several floors. You really have to search hard for something impressive here, but it gives a good account of the more establishment side of St Petersburg's current art scene – all artists on display are members of the union. Check out the lovely wooden doors on the 3rd floor.

*St Petersburg Centre for Modern Art* (☎ *219 47 37, Nevsky pr 60)* **Map 8** This gallery has rotating exhibitions of Russian modern art paintings and sculptures.

*Association of Free Artists Gallery* (☎ *311 77 77, Nevsky pr 20)* **Map 8** Occasionally something quite unexpected crops up on display here. There's a sense that the artists on exhibition here are underdogs and I feel like rooting for them.

## China

*Lomonosova China Factory* (*Lomonosova Farforvy Zavod;* ☎ *560 85 44,* W *www.lom onosovporcelain.com, pr Obukhovskoy oborony 151)* **Map 3** Open 10am-7pm Mon-Sat, 11am-5pm Sun. There are great deals on fine china at this factory outlet shop, where you get anything from the company catalogue at prices lower than in the department stores. There are over 500 items on sale, including lovely teapots ($6) and serving dishes ($17). From Metro Lomonosovskaya, turn left (east), walk under the bridge to the embankment then left – the factory's ahead. The shop is inside the main door and to the right.

## Honey

*Pchelovodstvo* (☎ *279 72 62, Liteyny pr 42)* **Map 8** Open 10am-6pm Mon-Sat. 'I came all the way here to buy *honey*?' you ask? But step into this sweet shop and you won't be able to resist. You'll find many types of fresh honey from Russia's Rostov region, dozens of products, remedies and creams made from bee pollen, as well as unique teas, which make for nice gifts.

## Wine

*Intendant* (☎ *311 15 10, Karavannaya ul 18/37)* **Map 8** If you've saved a bunch of money buying cheap CDs, you may want to splurge on a $400 bottle of Chateauneuf du Pape at St Petersburg's finest wine shop. It stocks everything from fine table wines for $10 to a $2280 bottle of Chateau Petrus – and the proper glasses to drink them out of.

## Books

You'll finds books for sale everywhere – on street corners, pedestrian subways, even in grocery shops and suburban trains.

*Anglia (☎ 279 82 84, nab reki Fontanki 40)* **Map 8** The city's oasis of English language books is here, with a dizzying collection of art, history and literature books at dizzyingly Western prices (but ISIC card holders get a 5% discount). Get your Lonely Planet guidebooks here too (the HI St Petersburg Hostel also has a few, but here the selection is wide). There's also a large section of academic books for teachers of English. It's a great place to just hang out – they're used to people browsing – or coming in to check out their rotating art exhibitions. Allied with the British Council, it also hosts literary events regularly.

*Snark (☎ 164 93 66, Zagorodny pr 21).* **Map 7** This great store has several locations throughout the city (another is right on pl Vosstania) and was the first Russian bookstore in the city with a Western look and feel (where it's actually possible to browse!). This friendly, well-stocked place gives discounts to members, features monthly themes, and has lots for the kids.

*Dom Knigi (☎ 219 64 02, Nevsky pr 28)* **Map 8** The city's largest bookshop is always packed, and worth a trip in itself. Inside the pre-revolutionary headquarters of the Singer sewing machine company, it has two, newly renovated floors of mainly Russian books on every subject imaginable. Excellent souvenir and local history books are on the 2nd floor.

*Na Liteynom (☎ 275 38 73, Liteyny pr 61)* **Map 8** Open 11am-7pm Mon-Sat. This antiquarian bookshop in a courtyard has a good selection of old books, as well as a small antique collection.

*Isskustvo (☎ 312 85 35, Nevsky pr 16)* **Map 8** There are several shops near the corner of Bol Morskaya ul. In this one is a good selection of maps and art books.

*Abuk (☎ 312 20 81, Nevsky pr 18)* **Map 8** This shop has a selection of antique and rare books and prints.

*Staraya Kniga (☎ 232 17 65, Bolshoy pr 19, Petrograd Side)* **Map 4** A tiny, musty shop dealing in old and out of print books.

## Music, Videos & CD-ROMs

Copyright? Huh? Russia is the world's largest market for bootleg cassettes, CDs and CD-ROMs, which are available every few steps in kiosks, underground passageways, markets and all kinds of stores. Usually labelled in Russian or bad English, the tapes are of varying quality, but you shouldn't have any problems with CDs (for $2 to $3 a pop, it's not a huge risk). Here you'll find musical collections the likes of which the rest of the world has never seen. Also on sale are CD-ROMs loaded with MP3s, so you can get anyone from Madonna's to Brian Eno's entire artistic output on one disc for $2.50. There's a rumour that 75% of all computer program CD-ROMs sold in Russia have a defect or virus on them, but the $3 price tag tempts thousands every day to chance it.

*Saigon (☎ 315 58 73, Nevsky pr 7/9)* **Map 8** This is a safe bet for everything you'd want – cheap cassettes, legal and licensed CDs ($10 to $20) and a great selection of videos (some in original English or French) sold by knowledgeable staff.

*Titanik (☎ 310 49 29, Nevsky pr 52/54)* **Map 8** Open 24 hrs. It has several locations in the city, and have an overwhelming array of thousands of music CDs and videos.

*Melodia Records (☎ 232 11 39, Bolshoy pr 47, Petrograd Side)* **Map 4** This was *the* Soviet record label, and it's still around. It stocks CDs of mainly Russian musicians and composers.

## Sports Supplies

*Soldat Udachi (☎ 279 18 50, ul Nekrasova 37)* **Map 7**; *(☎ 232 20 03, Bolshoy pr 17, Petrograd Side)* **Map 4** There's more here than merely Spanish reproductions of antique weaponry (sabres, swords, guns, knives, martial arts equipment). They sell

Russian watches and a great selection of camping, hiking, hunting and fishing gear, including GPS devices, Swiss Army knives, MagLites and metal flasks for your fire water. Oh yeah, and a full-sized 'Knight in Shining Armour' for $2400, though you may have problems explaining it at the border.

***Techno Sport Centre*** (*☎/fax 322 60 60, Pl Morskoy Slavy 1*) **Map 6** Way out on Vasilevsky Island, inside the Hotel Morskaya complex is one of the city's best sports supply stores, mainly but not exclusively focusing on seafaring gear. It sells water jets, boats, rubber rafts, motors, water scooters, as well as telescopes, binoculars (Russian and foreign), fishing gear, and Nordic Line warm gloves.

***Sportivny Na Liteynom*** (*☎ 272 21 70, Liteyny pr 57*) **Map 8** Another great store with sports clothes, running shoes, camping and hunting supplies, skis, and the occasional mosquito-net hat (which could come in handy in the city, even if it looks a tad odd!).

## Markets

Most of the city's markets are for food, but the best one for trinkets, clothes, leather, technical appliances, and a huge music selection is ***Warehouse Market*** (*Map 3; ul Marshala Kazakova*), a fair way out from the centre. From metro Avtova, cross the street and hop express bus No 81 (a five- to seven-minute ride) straight there for $0.12. It's open 9am to 4pm Tuesday to Sunday, and on the weekends there are doll shows and street artists for the kids.

For cheap leather jackets and other clothes, people often head out to the stalls around and opposite metro Zvyozdnaya or around metro Ladozhskaya.

# Excursions

While Moscow's Golden Ring of ancient cities is famous world over for exciting side-trips away from the capital, St Petersburg is no poorer in its options for day trippers. Between 25km and 45km from central St Petersburg lie five splendid old tsarist palaces surrounded by lovely parks. Kronshtadt, a once-closed naval base 29km from the city, has one of the loveliest cathedrals in northern Russia. Further out towards the north-west is the old Finnish town of Vyborg, and eastward, near the banks of Lake Ladoga are the Nizhnezvirsky Nature Reserve, the beautiful village of Staraya Ladoga, the sand caves of Sablino and small, picturesque islands with monasteries – Valaam, Kizhi, and Konevetsky.

Though all of these are easily accessible by inexpensive public transport, you can easily book a tour of them (see also Organised Tours in the Getting Around chapter). All phone numbers in the chapter share the same area code as St Petersburg (☎ 812) unless otherwise stated.

## VYBORG
ВЫБОРГ

☎ 278 ● pop 81,000

Vyborg (**vih**-bork) is the main border town on the Helsinki–St Petersburg road, a lovely 13th-century city filled with old buildings, winding cobblestone streets, a romantic, if dishevelled, harbour, and a sprawling, magnificent park.

One of the oldest cities in Europe, Vyborg's central feature is the imposing medieval Vyborg Castle, built by the Swedes in 1293 when they first captured Karelia from Novgorod. Since then borders have jumped back and forth around Vyborg.

Peter the Great added it to Russia in 1710. A century later it fell within autonomous Finland, and after the revolution it remained part of independent Finland (the Finns call it Viipuri). Stalin took it in 1939, lost it to the Finns and Germans during WWII, and on getting it back deported all the Finns. Today

it's a laid-back, Finnish-looking city full of Russian fishers, timber-haulers, military men, and the usual border-town shady types. A good city history and nice photos are at W www.towns.ru/towns/viborg_e.

## Orientation & Information

Vyborg's compactness makes it easy to walk everywhere. The main street, Leningradsky pr, cuts south-west from the railway station at the north to the Pantserlax Bastion (1574).

The telephone office is on the corner of ul Mira and Moskovsky pr. Change money at Druzhba or Vyborg hotels or at Avtovazbank, ul Progonnaya 1. Maps are available at the book store, Knigi, at pr Lenina 6.

The Vyborg Travel Bureau (☎ 2 21 09, ul Pervomayskaya 6) can give you suggestions for tours and other practical information. Continent Club (☎ 2 47 60), a travel agency in the lobby of Hotel Druzhba, can also help you out.

## Things to See

**Vyborg Castle** (*Vyborgsky zamok;* ☎ 2 15 15; *adult/child $0.30/0.20, extra $0.20 to climb the tower; open 10am-7pm Tues-Sun*), built on a rock in Vyborg Bay, is the city's oldest building, though most of it now is 16th-century alterations. Inside is a small museum of local studies. Across the bridge is the **Anna Fortress** (Anninskaya Krepost), built in the 18th century as protection against the Swedes and named after Empress Anna Ivanovna. Behind this is the **Park Monrepo Reserve** (☎ 2 05 39), a massive expanse of wooded and lake-dotted parkland one could spend a whole day in. Laid out in a classical style, it also has a forest feel to it; as pretty as Pavlovsk's park, only wilder. Curved bridges, arbours and sculptures complete the picture. To read about the park's interesting history, see W www.oblmuseums.spb.ru/eng/museums/20/info.html.

There are lovely streets with centuries-old churches, bell towers and cathedrals, especially along and off ul Krepostnaya. A short walk from the 16th-century castle takes you to the **Kruglaya bashnya** (Round Tower), and the **Spaso-Preobrazhensky sobor** (Cathedral of the Transfiguration, 1787) which are all worth visiting.

On ul Storozevaya is a monument to 108 Finnish soldiers who died in the war of 1939–40. It was only erected in 2001 – a previous such monument was placed in 1996 but destroyed by vandals.

## Places to Stay & Eat

*Hotel Druzhba (☎ 2 57 44, Zheleznodorozhnaya ul 5)* Singles/doubles $32/40. Considered the city's best option, it also has two bars, an outdoor beer garden and a decent restaurant.

*Vyborg Hotel (☎/fax 2 23 83, Leningradsky pr 18)* Singles/doubles $28/37. Somewhat run down, but central and decent enough, with its own restaurant. Service is friendly.

*Korolenko Boat Hotel (☎ 3 44 78, anchored at the Salakka-Lahti Bay, 200m from Hotel Druzhba)* $12 per person. Clean but teensy-weensy cabins aboard a ship. It's a friendly place but the 24-hour bar can get noisy. The hotel also rents out row boats.

*Round Tower Restaurant (☎ 2 78 38)* Open noon-11pm daily. On the top floor of the tower itself, this is the nicest place in town, with excellent meals for about $3. The bar stays open 24 hours.

*Bar-Restaurant Nordwest (☎ 2 58 93)* Open 10am-midnight daily. Slick and just a bit tacky but with a great menu (try its salmon cream soup for $1.25), this is another good option.

The market just north of the Round Tower has fresh produce for the self caterer.

## Getting There & Away

Vyborg is about three hours by suburban train from St Petersburg's Finland Station. Trains go nearly every hour all day; on the big board at the Finland Station they're called Vyborgskoe. From St Petersburg, all buses to Helsinki stop at Vyborg. There are also at least eight buses a day to Vyborg, leaving the bus station and stopping in front of the western entrance/exit of the Ploshchad Lenina metro, on Botkinskaya ul. These make the trip about 20 minutes faster than the train, and cost $0.80.

## PETRODVORETS (MAP 9)
ПЕТРОДВОРЕЦ

Peter the Great had a cabin 29km west of St Petersburg on the Gulf of Finland, to oversee construction of his Kronshtadt naval base. He built a villa, Monplaisir, and then a whole series of palaces across an estate originally called Petergof, which is now called Petrodvorets *(Peter's Palace; ☎ 427 74 25; estate open 9am-9pm, Lower Park & Alexandria Park open daily)*. If you don't care about seeing the museums, you can wait until the ticket office closes at around 4pm, then enter the grounds for free.

All are set within a spectacular ensemble of gravity-powered fountains that are now the site's main attraction. This 'Russian Versailles' is probably the most impressive of St Petersburg's suburban palaces, certainly the most popular.

While Petrodvorets (pet-ra-dvar-**yets**) was trashed by the Germans in WWII (what you see is largely a reconstruction from photos, drawings and anecdotes), it suffered heaviest damage under Soviet bombing raids in December 1941 and January 1942 (according to more recent historians). Hitler, abandoning his hopes for a New Year's victory celebration inside St Petersburg's Hotel Astoria, planned to throw a party here, and drew up pompous invitations. Stalin ordered the place heavily attacked to thwart this.

## Things to See & Do

**Grand Cascade** The uncontested centrepiece is the Grand Cascade and Water Avenue *(fountains normally play 11am-7pm May-Sept)*, with over 140 fountains and canals partly engineered by Peter himself. The central statue of **Samson** tearing open a lion's jaws celebrates Peter's victory over the Swedes.

There are trick fountains – triggered by hidden switches (hidden, that is, by hordes of kids jumping on them) – designed to squirt unsuspecting passers-by.

**Grand Palace** Between the cascade and the formal Upper Garden is the Bolshoy dvorets (*Grand Palace;* ☎ *427 95 27; tour adult/student $8/4; open 10.30am-5pm Tues-Sun, closed last Tues of the month*). Peter's modest project, finished just before his death, was grossly enlarged by Rastrelli for Empress Elizabeth and later redecorated for Catherine the Great. It's now a vast museum of lavish rooms and galleries – a monument above all to the craft of reconstruction (which is still going on). Anything not nailed down was removed before the Germans arrived, so the paintings, furniture and chandeliers are original.

Highlights include the **Chesma Hall**, full of huge paintings of Russia's destruction of the Turkish fleet at Çesme in 1770. Of some 20 rooms, the last, without a trace of Catherine, is the finest – Peter's simple, beautiful study, apparently the only room to survive the Germans. It has 14 fantastic carved-wood panels, of which six reconstructions (in lighter wood) are no less impressive; each took 1½ years to do. Peter the Great still looks like the tsar with the best taste.

Tickets are sold inside, near the lobby where you pick up your *tapochki* (slippers).

**Monplaisir** Peter's outwardly more humble villa (☎ *427 91 29; admission $3.50; open 10.30am-4pm Thur-Tues summer only, closed last Thur of month*), with study and galleries facing the sea, remained his favourite and it's not hard to see why: wood-panelled, snug and elegant, peaceful even when there's a crowd – which there used to be all the time, what with Peter's mandatory partying ('misbehaving' guests were required to gulp down huge quantities of wine). The main hall has marble floors and a richly painted ceiling; the kitchen is Dutch style, a little study is Chinese.

To the left of Monplaisir is an annexe called the Catherine Building (☎ *427 91 29; admission $3.50; open 10.30am-5pm Fri-Wed summer, 10.30am-5pm Sat-Sun winter, closed last Fri of month*), built by Rastrelli between 1747–55, because Catherine the Great was living here – conveniently – when her husband Peter III was overthrown. On the right side is Quarenghi's 1800 Bath Building (☎ *427 91 29; admission $2; open 10.30am-4pm Wed-Mon summer, 10.30am-4pm Sat & Sun winter*). Tsarist families and their guests once purified body and mind here.

**Lower Park & Other Pavilions** Along the gulf is the Lower Park, with more fountains big and small, elegant and silly (watch out for more trick fountains), and more pavilions.

Near the shore, and finished soon after the Grand Palace, is a two-storey pink-and-white box called the **Hermitage** (☎ *427 53 25; admission $3; open 10.30am-6pm Sat & Sun*) which features the ultimate in private dining on the 2nd floor. Special elevators hoist a fully laid table into the imperial presence, thereby eliminating any hindrance by servants. The elevators are circular and directly in front of each diner, whose plate would be lowered, replenished and replaced.

Further west is **Marly** (☎ *427 77 29; admission $2.50; open 11am-4pm Sat & Sun*), another of Peter's mini-palaces and guest-houses. To the east an old **Orangery** contains a ho-hum exhibition of 49 figures of big-wigged Russians from the 18th and 19th centuries. Better is the **Triton fountain** outside, with its 8m jet of water.

**Alexandria Park** Even on summer weekends, the rambling, overgrown Alexandria Park is peaceful and empty. It was built for Tsar Nicholas I (and named for his tsarina) and it looks as though his heart just wasn't in it. Besides a mock-Gothic chapel, its diversions include the **Farmer's Palace** (1831), which vaguely resembles a stone farmstead and is now in ruins, and the 1829 **Cottage** (☎ *427 99 53; admission $3; open 10.30am-5pm Tues-Sun summer, 10.30am-5pm Sat & Sun winter, closed last Tues of the month*), which is modelled on an English country cottage and is now a museum.

**Petergof Palace Pharmacy** This unexpected tourist attraction is a renovated old-style apothecary (☎ *427 95 78, ul Pravlenskaya 6; open 8am-8pm Mon-Fri,*

**EXCURSIONS**

*11am-6pm Sat, 9am-8pm Sun)* with drawers full of medicinal plants – it looks (and smells) like the real thing. You can sip herbal teas, and if your Russian's good enough you can ask them about your medical peccadillo. It's just east of the Upper Garden.

**Petrodvorets Town** Don't miss the five-domed **SS Peter & Paul Cathedral** *(evening services 5pm, closes 6pm or 7pm except holidays, when night services are held)* across the road, built in neo-Byzantine style by V Kosyakov at the turn of the 20th century. One bus stop west of the main palace entrance is the **Raketa watch factory** *(☎ 420 50 41, Sankt Petersburgsky pr 60)*, which has a little boutique *(open 10am-6pm Mon-Fri, 10am-5pm Sat)*, selling *very* cool watches.

Six kilometres east of Petrodvorets is **Strelna**, another estate with parklands and two palaces built for Peter and later enlarged for Empress Elizabeth by Rastrelli. One of these, the Konstantinovsky Palace, was chosen by Putin as his summer residence, and repairs are underway.

### Places to Eat
There are a few cafes scattered around the Lower Park.

*Imperatorsky Stol (☎ 427 91 06, Razvodnaya ul 2)* Open 10.30am-6pm daily summer only. At the west side of the palace grounds is this restaurant serving traditional Russian meals.

*Vena (☎ 427 94 47, Sankt Peterburgsky pr 30)* Open 1pm-midnight daily. Another decent venue serving standard cafe fare.

### Getting There & Away
If you're not going there on a tour, the easiest way is to take comfy double-decker Bus No 849 or 851 from outside the Baltic Station ($0.30, 40 minutes), which leave regularly throughout the day and let you off at the main entrance on Sankt Peterburgsky pr. You can also take a suburban train from the Baltic Station to Novy Petrodvorets (not Stary Petrodvorets), departing every 30 to 60 minutes until early evening, but then you'll have to take any bus but No 357 to the fifth stop, another 10 minutes.

From May to September, a fine alternative is the *Meteor* hydrofoil from the jetty in front of St Petersburg's Hermitage, which goes every 20 to 30 minutes from 9.30am to at least 7pm. The trip takes half an hour and costs a whopping $15 each way.

## LOMONOSOV
## ЛОМОНОСОВ
While Peter was building Monplaisir, his right-hand man, Alexandr Menshikov, began his own palace, **Oranienbaum**, 12km east further down the coast. Menshikov never saw the finished product; following Peter's death and Menshikov's exile, the estate served briefly as a hospital and then passed to Tsar Peter III, who didn't much like ruling Russia and spent a lot of time at the Oranienbaum. After doing away with him, his wife Catherine (the Great) made it her private pleasure ground.

Oranienbaum was not occupied by the Nazis. After WWII it was for some reason renamed after the scientist-poet Mikhail Lomonosov and now doubles as a museum and **public park** *(open 9am-10pm year-round)*, with boat rentals and carnival rides alongside the remaining buildings.

### Things to See & Do
The complex of palaces and pavilions are all located at Dvortsovy pr 48, and all are open 11am to 5pm Wednesday to Monday, closed last Monday of the month. With semicircular galleries and a lower garden, Menshikov's **Grand Palace** *(☎ 423 16 27; adult/student $1.75/0.50)* impresses the most, though still under eternal renovations. Beyond the pond is **Peterstadt** *(☎ 422 37 56; admission $1.75)*, Peter III's boxy toy palace, with rich, uncomfortable-looking interiors and some Chinese-style lacquer-on-wood paintings. It's approached through the **Gate of Honour**, which is all that remains of a toy fortress where he amused himself drilling his beloved soldiers.

Most worth seeing is Catherine's over-the-top **Chinese Palace** *(☎ 422 37 53; admission $1.75)*, baroque outside and extravagantly rococo inside, with a private retreat designed by Antonio Rinaldi that

Lining up to see the Grand Palace, Petrodvorets

LEE FOSTER

JONATHAN SMITH

Peter & Paul Cathedral, Petrodvorets

JOHN KING

Hermitage Pavilion, Petrodvorets

JONATHAN SMITH

Another of Peter's mini-palaces and guesthouses, Marly, sits within the Lower Park, Petrodvorets.

JOHN KING

Modelled on an English design, the Cottage of Nicholas I sits among trees in Alexandria Park, Petrodvorets.

MARTIN MOOS

Royal seal of approval: Catherine Palace, Pushkin

CHRISTOPHER WOOD

Old stone bridge, Pavlovsk Park

GRAHAM BELL

Golden spires of Catherine Palace, Pushkin

includes painted ceilings, fine inlaid-wood floors and walls, and decoration probably unequalled in any of the other St Petersburg palaces. The most blindingly sumptuous is the **Large Chinese Room**, designed in the 'Oriental' style of the day.

The building that looks like a blue-and-white wedding cake is the **Coasting-Hill Pavilion** (☎ 423 16 39; admission $3), the launching pad for Catherine's private roller coaster, a multistoreyed wooden slide down which courtiers would fly on little carts or toboggans. The slide is gone but the pavilion's extravagant inner rooms are worth a look.

Perhaps Lomonosov's best feature is the several kilometres of quiet paths through pine woods and sombre gardens.

### Getting There & Away

The suburban train from St Petersburg's Baltic Station to Petrodvorets continues to Lomonosov. Get off at Oranienbaum-I (not II) Station, an hour from St Petersburg. From the station, walk north-east past a church and then cross pr Yunogo Lenintsa to the park entrance. There are also taxi-buses to both Petrodvorets and Lomonosov from outside metro Avtovo.

### PUSHKIN (MAP 10) & PAVLOVSK
### ПУШКИН И ПАВЛОВСК

The sumptuous palaces and big, beautiful parks at Pushkin and Pavlovsk, neighbours 25km and 29km south of St Petersburg, can be combined in a day's visit – but since they're both good places to relax, you might want to take them more slowly.

Pushkin's palaces and parks were created under Empresses Elizabeth and Catherine the Great between 1744 and 1796. The centrepiece is the vast 1752–56 baroque Catherine Palace (Yekaterininsky dvorets), designed by Rastrelli and named after Elizabeth's mother, Peter the Great's second wife. Pushkin used to be called Tsarskoe selo (Tsar's Village) but was renamed in 1937 after Russia's favourite poet, who studied here. The country's first railway opened in 1837 to carry the royal family between here and St Petersburg.

Pavlovsk's park of woodland, rivers, lakes, little valleys, avenues, classical statues and temples, is one of the most exquisite in Russia, while its Great Palace is a classical contrast to the Catherine Palace. Palace and park were originally designed by Charles Cameron between 1781 and 1786, on Catherine the Great's orders, for her son, the future Paul I.

### Catherine Palace

As at the Winter Palace, Catherine the Great had many of Rastrelli's original interiors remodelled in classical style. The palace (☎ 466 66 69, Sadovaya ul 7; adult/student $6/3; open 10am-4.30pm Wed-Mon, closed the last Monday of the month) was ruined by the Germans in WWII. Most of the wonderful exterior and 20-odd rooms have been beautifully restored – compare them to the photographs of the devastation left by the Germans.

All the rooms on show are upstairs. Visits normally start with the white State Staircase, an 1860 addition. South of here, only two rooms – both by Rastrelli – have been restored: the **Gentlemen-in-Waiting's Dining Room** and, beyond, the **Great Hall** (Bolshoy zal), the largest room in the palace, all light and glitter from its mirrors and gilded woodcarvings.

North of the State Staircase on the courtyard side are the **State Dining Room**, **Crimson** and **Green Pilaster Rooms**, **Portrait Room** and finally the **Amber Room** (Yantarnaya komnata). The latter was decorated by Rastrelli with gilded woodcarvings, mirrors, agate and jasper mosaics, and exquisitely engraved amber panels given to Peter the Great by the King of Prussia in 1716. But its treasures were plundered by the Nazis and went missing in Kaliningrad (then Königsberg) in 1945 (they're still looking!).

Most of the north end is Cameron's early classical work. The elegant proportions of the **Green Dining Room** (Zelyonaya stolovaya) on the courtyard side are typical. Also on the courtyard side are three rooms with fabulous, patterned silk wall-coverings: the **Blue Drawing Room** (Golubaya gostinaya), **Chinese Blue Drawing Room** (Kitayskaya golubaya gostinaya), and **Choir Anteroom** (Predkhornaya), whose gold silk, woven with swans and pheasants, is the original from the 18th century.

## Pushkin Parks

Around the south and east of the Catherine Palace extends the lovely **Catherine Park** (Yekaterininsky Park). The main entrance is just west of the palace, at the beginning of Pokaprizovaya doroga. The **Cameron Gallery** *(admission $1.50; open 11am-5pm Wed-Sun May-Oct, 11am-5pm Sat-Sun Nov-April)*, south of the main palace, has a display of 18th- and 19th-century costumes and carriages. Between the gallery and the palace, notice the south-pointing ramp which Cameron added for the ageing empress to walk down into the park.

The park's outer section focuses on the **Great Pond**, where you can rent a boat in summer. This section is dotted with an intriguing array of structures ranging from the **'Pyramid'**, where Catherine the Great buried her favourite dogs, to the **Chinese Pavilion** (or Creaking Summerhouse), **Marble Bridge** (copied from one at Wilton, England) and **Ruined Tower**, which was built 'ready-ruined' in keeping with a 1770s romantic fashion – an 18th-century empress's equivalent of prefaded denim!

A short distance north of the Catherine Palace along ul Dvortsovaya, the classical **Alexander Palace** *(☎ 466 60 71, Dvortsovaya ul 2; adult/student $3.50/1.75; open 10am-5pm Wed-Mon, closed last Wed of the month)* was built by Quarenghi in 1792–96 for the future Alexander I but Nicholas II was its main tenant. It's the least touristy palace, so in some ways the most pleasant. The overgrown and empty **Alexander Park** *(admission free)* extends on three sides of the palace and adjoins the Catherine Park in the south.

## Akhmatova Museum & Lycée

There's a small **Akhmatova Museum** in the Lycée *(☎ 470 77 92, Sadovaya ul 2; bus No 371 from train station; admission $1.75; open 10am-4.30pm Wed-Mon, closed last Fri of the month)*. There are special celebrations

on Akhmatova's birthday, 23 June. There is also a display here about Pushkin, who studied at this once-famous school, from 1811–17, as well as several other exhibitions. This was once an old wing of the Catherine Place, reconstructed by Stasov to accommodate the Lycée in 1811.

## Pavlovsk Great Palace & Park

Cameron's original palace *(☎ 470 21 55, ul Revolutsii; adult/student $6/4; open 10am-5pm Sat-Thur, closed first Fri of the month)* was a three-storey domed square with single-storey wings curving halfway round the existing courtyard. The palace was a royal residence until 1917, then burnt down two weeks after liberation in WWII when a careless Soviet soldier's cigarette set off German mines (the Soviets blamed the Germans), but was fully restored by 1970.

The finest rooms are on the middle floor of the central block. Cameron designed the round **Italian Hall** beneath the dome, and the **Grecian Hall** to its west, though the lovely green fluted columns were added by Brenna. Flanking these are two private suites mainly designed by Brenna – Paul's along the north side of the block and Maria Fyodorovna's on the south. The insane, military-obsessed Paul's **Hall of War** contrasts with Maria's **Hall of Peace**, which is decorated with musical instruments and flowers.

On the middle floor of the south block are Paul's **Throne Room** and the **Hall of the Maltese Knights of St John**, of whom he was the Grand Master.

If you skip the palace, it's a delight simply to wander round the sublime park grounds and see what you come across.

## Getting There & Away

Take one of the frequent suburban trains from the Vitebsk Station in St Petersburg. They go to Detskoe selo Station (zone 3 ticket) for Pushkin, and to Pavlovsk Station (zone 4) for Pavlovsk. It's about half an hour to either place. There are also many taxi-buses outside metro Moskovskaya which make the trip (cost about $0.50, about 20 minutes).

From the train station, a five-minute ride on bus No 370, 371, 378 or 381 takes you to within two minutes' walk of Pushkin's Catherine Palace. From Pavlovsk Station, you can reach the Great Palace either by bus No 370, 383, 383A or 493 (under 10 minutes); or by entering the park across the road from the station, and walking 1.5km across it to the palace. Walking at least one way across the park is a good idea.

## KRONSHTADT
## КРОНШТАДТ

Within a year of founding St Petersburg, Peter – desirous of protecting the city and his new Baltic toehold – started work on the fortress of Kronshtadt on Kotlin Island, 29km out in the Gulf of Finland. It's been a pivotal Soviet and Russian naval base ever since.

In 1921 the base was the scene of a short-lived mutiny against the Bolsheviks, one of the last overt signs of opposition to the revolution until perestroika. The Red sailors stationed there, ironically, were the most revolutionary, pro-Bolshevik element in 1917; Trotsky called them 'the pride and glory of the Russian Revolution'. Four years later, hungry and poor, they set up a Provisional Revolutionary Committee under Petrichenko and drafted a resolution demanding, among other things, an end to Lenin's harsh policy of War Communism.

The sailors repulsed a first attempt to stifle the mutiny by the Red Army, but on 16 March 1921 were overtaken when 50,000 troops crossed the ice from Petrograd and massacred nearly the entire naval force. Though bloodily suppressed, the event did cause Lenin to relax state pressure and scrap War Communism. It marked the end of the Russian revolutionary movement.

Kronshtadt was also the site of many scientific experiments (Russia boasts that the invention of radio, by A Popov in 1895, took place here), and where the chlorination of drinking water was first pioneered (1910). Today, the city of Kronshtadt, which was opened to foreigners in 1996, boasts one of the most beautiful cathedrals

in northern Russia. There are several cafes along its main north-south axis, pr Lenina.

## Things to Do

The city of 45,000 is pleasant to stroll around, and a walk along the southern end of the island, past the port where you can easily glimpse Russian warships, is a highlight. Yet the major sight here is the **Naval Cathedral** (Morskoy Sobor, 1903–13), designed by V Kosyakov, heavily influenced by the Istanbul cathedrals he visited. This neo-Byzantine wonder, built to honour Russian naval muscle, stands on Anchor Square, near an eternal flame for all of Kronshtadt's fallen sailors. It has an intricately detailed facade (anchors and all) and a haunting air of mystery. Sadly, the interior is off limits (since 1932 it has been used as a sailor's club and cinema), but a section of it is now the **Central Naval Museum** (☎ 236 47 13, Yakornaya pl 1; admission $1.20; open 11am-5pm Wed-Sun).

## Getting There & Away

There are numerous, daily tours leaving from in front of the Kazan Cathedral and Gostiny Dvor. By public transport, from metro Chyornaya Rechka, exit to your left, cross the street and veer right towards the bus stop where Bus No E510 and any number of taxi-buses or private cars will be waiting to make the half-hour trip. In Kronshtadt, the bus stop is on the corner of Grazhdanskaya ul and pr Lenina, and from there it's about a 400m walk south-west to the Naval Cathedral. City maps are available from the bookshop at pr Lenina 19.

## STARAYA LADOGA
## СТАРАЯ ЛАДОГА
☎ 263

This lovely, sleepy village, on the winding banks of the Volkhov River, is unknown to most tourists, though it's mentioned in every Russian schoolchild's history books. A three-hour trip by train and bus 125km outside St Petersburg, Staraya (Old) Ladoga acquaints visitors with one of the first points of settlement and trade in ancient Rus. Some say the first.

According to some ancient texts, when the Scandinavian Viking Rurik, along with his relatives Truvor and Sineus, swept into ancient Russia in 862, he first made his base and built a wooden fortress at present-day Staraya Ladoga (the town was known only as Ladoga until 1704 when Peter the Great founded Novaya (New) Ladoga to the north, as a transfer point for the materials arriving from afar to build St Petersburg). Scientists, historians, and archaeologists who work in Staraya Ladoga insist that it is at least one of the first capitals of ancient Rus. Indisputably, Ladoga was more than a simple village; it was a witness to and an active participant in the very birth of the Russian nation.

Archaeological expeditions continue to uncover a wealth of information about the town's past, and every summer, visitors can watch as 9th-century relics are unearthed in and around the town's fortress. At one point, six monasteries worked in this small region. Evidence of Byzantine cultural influences in the frescoes of the village's 12th-century churches point to the town as a cultural as well as historical and commercial cross-road.

Historians have given 753 as the village's birthdate, and so the town is gearing up to celebrate its own anniversary in tandem with St Petersburg's in 2003.

## Things to See

The **Giorgevskaya Church**, built in the second half of the 12th century, stands perched atop a hill by the banks of the Volkhov River, inside the fortress grounds. There are two permanent exhibitions here, one in the wooden **Church of Dimitri Solun** *(admission $1; open 9am-6pm Tues-Sun May-Sept, 9am-4pm Tues-Sun Oct-Apr)*. The church itself is open all year-round, but only during dry weather, to protect the delicate 12th-century frescoes still visible on the walls.

**Historic Architectural & Archaeological Museum** *(☎ 49 331, fax 13 524, admission $0.50, open 10am-5pm Tues-Sun)*. Located at the far end of the park on the northern edge of town, this houses a retrospective of

the area's history. Check out the unique works of local artist Tatiana Kozmina.

**Ioanna-Predtechi Church** (1695), located atop the highest hill in the area, behind the museum, is the only church with regular, weekend services in town. On this site was a 13th-century monastery. Nearby, by the river banks, is an ancient burial mount.

## Getting There and Away

*Elektrishkas* to Volkhov (the Volkhovstroy I station) leave the Moscow Station 11 times a day, cost $1 each way and take 2½ hours. From Volkhov, take bus or minibus No 23 headed towards Novaya Ladoga from the main bus stop outside the station, just across the square. It's a 20-minute trip to Staraya Ladoga and costs $0.30. The second of the three town bus stops lets you off just past the fortress.

In the town of Volkhov, the Volkhovskaya Zemlya travel agency (☎ 65 830) can organise visits to the Staraya Ladoga and Volkhov areas, arrange horse-riding along the banks of the Volkov River and transport from St Petersburg. There is also one mini hotel, the Staraya Ladoga (☎ 12 200, Sovetskaya ul 6), where you are set up from $7 a night.

## NIZHNEZVIRSKY NATURE RESERVE
## НИЖНЕЗВИРСКИЙ ГОСУДАРСТВЕННЫ ЗАПОВЕДНИК

On the south-eastern shore of Lake Ladoga, the 414-sq-km Nizhnezvirsky Nature Reserve *(☎ 81264-205 21, @ orlan@orlan .spb.su)* is an important stopover for migratory birds and home to a variety of animals, among them the Lake Ladoga ringed seal *(Phoca hispida ladogensis)*, a freshwater subspecies peculiar to the area. Arrangements to visit the reserve can be made directly, or through the American Association for the Support of Ecological Initiatives (AASEI). In St Petersburg, call Alexander Kaprenko of the AASEI's local branch Adonis (☎ 307 09 18, @ alexk@aasei .spb.su), or contact director Bill Wasch at its US headquarters (☎ 860-346 2967, fax 860-347 8459, @ wwasch@wesleyan.edu). There are several trains a day from the

Moscow Station to Lodeynoye pole (about four hours, $4), from where you'll have to met by a representative of the reserve and driven the final 50km.

## SABLINO CAVES

Along the delicate banks of the Tosna River, 40km south-east of St Petersburg, are a series of deep, sprawling sand caves, originally dug from the mid-19th-century for glass making. No imperial grandeur here, just gritty nature; this is a great day out. The catacombs are pitch black, moist, cool (a constant 4°C) and beautiful, filled with interesting formations. Nearby are two small waterfalls and lots of hilly, forested land ideal for picnics. You can only enter the caves on a tour (it's frighteningly easy to get lost in them). The city office of the Protection of Natural and Cultural Heritage (☎ 325 65 96, fax 232 09 42, Alexandrovsky park 4) organises excursions of groups and individuals. To get there yourself, take the suburban train from Moscow Station to Sablino (the second after Kolpino), cross the tracks and hop an hour-long bus ride on No 319, 334 or 439 and get off after it crosses the Tosna River. The caves begin to your left.

## LAKES LADOGA & ONEGA

For excursions even further afield, consider taking a boat excursion to the islands of Valaam (at the northern end of Lake Ladoga) and Kizhi (in Lake Onega). Boats of all shapes and sizes leave nearly every day in summer on one- to four-day excursions. See River Cruises in the Getting There & Away chapter for more details on how to book.

## Valaam
ВАЛААМ
The remote Valaam Archipelago, which consists of Valaam Island and about 50 smaller ones, sits in north-western Lake Ladoga (lah-da-ga). The main attractions here are the unique 14th-century Valaam Transfiguration Monastery (Spaso-Preobrazhenskii Valaamsky monastyr), its cathedral and buildings, and the pleasant village of 600 people that surrounds it.

## Kizhi Island
КИЖИ ОСТРОВ
An old pagan ritual site, Kizhi Island, 66km north-east of the Karelian city of Petrozavodsk (an eight-hour train ride north-east of St Petersburg) across Lake Onega, made a natural 'parish' for 12th-century Russian colonists, though none of the earliest churches remain.

Its centrepiece is the fairy-tale Cathedral of the Transfiguration (Preobrazhensky sobor, 1714), with a chorus of 22 domes, gables and ingenious decorations to keep water off the walls. Even so, it's now so rickety that the interior's closed, and in spite of Unesco protection nobody can agree on how to restore it. Next door is the nine-domed Church of the Intercession (Pokrovskaya tserkov, 1764).

There are more wooden churches outside the 'museum', and a hamlet with houses like the ones inside, but occupied. The whole place has a dreamy unreality to it.

## Getting There & Away
Valaam is such a popular destination that most travel agencies will have it on their itineraries. If you speak Russian, you can also deal directly with the monastery's centre in St Petersburg (☎ 271 22 64, ⓔ vmp@ mail.rcom.ru, Ⓦ www.valaam.karelia.ru, nab Sinopskaya 34/36). It organises a full range of year-round excursions (by boat or helicopter) and can set you up with a place to sleep inside the monastery. Prices start at $68 per person. It also has combined Vallam/ Kizhi tours.

River cruises regularly stop at Kizhi, and it's possible to go by yourself as well, by taking an overnight train to Petrozavodsk ($25, eight hours) and then a boat from the ferry terminal. It's a heavily touristed destination, and foreigners pay quite a bit more for the ferry there and entrance to the grounds than do Russians. Being part of a boat cruise will eliminate these extra costs.

## Konevetsky Island
Остров Коневец
A tiny dot in Lake Ladoga is the place where a male monastery was founded in

EXCURSIONS

1393 by Arseny Konevetsky. The monastery has re-opened since the early 1990s, and with Finnish funding, has undergone massive restoration. In Soviet times, it was an off-limits military base, and the destruction is still visible throughout the island. Some scientific experiments are still conducted on an off-limits corner of the island. School groups regularly visit the island, and several centres for drug rehabilitation use the grounds as part of their rest therapy. There are several chapels as well as the main Kremlin grounds, near which is a large guesthouse. On a huge boulder sits a lonely chapel; this was the site of pagan horse-slaughtering rituals. With peaceful, clean beaches and lots of forests to wander through, it makes a pleasant break for a day or so.

You'll need to contact the monastery's office in St Petersburg (☎ 311 71 94, Zagorodny pr 7) before heading out, to check the boat schedules and availability to stay overnight. It's about three hours by public transport (suburban train from Finland Station to Gromovo, direction Priozyorsk, then bus No 624 one hour to the last stop). One night including vegetarian meals should cost about $15. More information can be had via W www.orthodoxy.ru/konevitsa.

# Language

Just about everyone in Russia speaks Russian, though there are also dozens of other languages spoken by ethnic minorities. Russian and most of the other languages are written in variants of the Cyrillic alphabet. It's relatively easy to find English-speakers in St Petersburg and Moscow but not so easy in small cities and towns.

Russian grammar may be daunting, but your travels will be far more interesting if you at least take the time to learn the Cyrillic alphabet, so that you can read maps and street signs. For a more in-depth handling of Russian, see Lonely Planet's *Russian phrasebook*.

## Transliteration

There's no ideal system for going from Cyrillic to Roman letters; the more faithful a system is to pronunciation, the more complicated it becomes. The transliteration system used in this language guide differs from that used in the rest of this book (which follows the US Library of Congress System I – good for deciphering printed words and rendering proper names); it's intended to assist you in pronouncing Russian letters and sounds, with an emphasis on practicality. Most letters are transliterated in accordance with the sounds given in the alphabet table on page 176. In this system Cyrillic e (pronounced 'ye') is written as Roman *e* except at the start of words where it's *ye* (eg, Yeltsin). The combination кс becomes *x*.

Bold letters in the transliterations indicate where the stress falls in a word.

## Pronunciation

The 'voiced' (ie, when the vocal cords vibrate) consonants б, в, г, д, ж, and з are not voiced at the end of words (eg, хлеб, 'bread', is pronounced *khlyep*) or before voiceless consonants. The г in the common adjective endings -его and -ого is pronounced 'v'; 'Mayakovskogo', for example, is pronounced *Maya-kov-skovo*.

Two letters have no sound but are used to modify others. A consonant followed by the 'soft sign' ь is spoken with the tongue flat against the palate, as if followed by the faint beginnings of a 'y'. The rare 'hard sign' ъ after a consonant indicates a slight pause before the next vowel.

## Greetings & Civilities

Two words you're sure to use are the universal 'hello', здравствуйте *(zdrast-vuy-tye)*, and пожалуйста *(pa-zhal-sta)*, the word for 'please' (commonly included in all polite requests), 'you're welcome', 'pardon me', 'after you' and more.

Hi. (casual)
   *pri-vet*                Привет.
Good morning.
   *dob-ra-ye ut-ra*   Доброе утро.
Good afternoon.
   *dob-ryy den'*     Добрый день.
Good evening.
   *dob-ryy veh-cher* Добрый вечер.
Goodbye.
   *da svi-da-niya*   До свидания.
Goodbye. (casual)
   *pa-ka*               Пока.
Yes.
   *da*                 Да.
No.
   *net*                Нет.
Thank you (very much).
   *(bal'-sho-ye) spa-si-ba*
   (Большое) спасибо.
Pardon me.
   *pras-ti-te/pa-zha-lsta*
   Простите/Пожалуйста.
No problem/Never mind.
   *ni-che-vo* (literally 'nothing')
   Ничего.
Can you help me?
   *pa-ma-gi-te, pa-zhal-sta?*
   Помогите, пожалуйста?
May I take a photo?
   *mozh-na sfa-ta-gra-fi-ra-vat'?*
   Можно сфотографировать?

## The Russian Cyrillic Alphabet

| Cyrillic | Roman | Pronunciation |
|----------|-------|---------------|
| А, а | a | as the 'a' in 'path' (in stressed syllable) as the 'a' in 'about' (in unstressed syllable) |
| Б, б | b | as the 'b' in 'but' |
| В, в | v | as the 'v' in 'van' |
| Г, г | g | as the 'g' in 'god' |
| Д, д | d | as the 'd' in 'dog' |
| Е, е * | e | as the 'ye' in 'yet' (in stressed syllable) as the 'yi' in 'yin' (in unstressed syllable) |
| Ё, ё ** | yo | as the 'yo' in 'yonder' |
| Ж, ж | zh | as the 's' in 'measure' |
| З, з | z | as the 'z' in 'zoo' |
| И, и | i | as the 'i' in 'litre' |
| Й, й | y | as the 'y' in 'boy' |
| К, к | k | as the 'k' in 'kind' |
| Л, л | l | as the 'l' in 'lamp' |
| М, м | m | as the 'm' in 'mad' |
| Н, н | n | as the 'n' in 'not' |
| О, о | o | as the 'o' in 'more' (in stressed syllable) as the 'a' in 'hard' (in unstressed syllable) |
| П, п | p | as the 'p' in 'pig' |
| Р, р | r | as the 'r' in 'rub' (rolled) |
| С, с | s | as the 's' in 'sing' |
| Т, т | t | as the 't' in 'ten' |
| У, у | u | as the 'u' in 'put' |
| Ф, ф | f | as the 'f' in 'fan' |
| Х, х | kh | as the 'ch' in 'Bach' |
| Ц, ц | ts | as the 'ts' in 'bits' |
| Ч, ч | ch | as the 'ch' in 'chin' |
| Ш, ш | sh | as the 'sh' in 'shop' |
| Щ, щ | shch | as 'sh-ch' in 'fresh chips' |
| ъ | (no symbol) | 'hard sign' (see p.175) |
| Ы, ы | y | as the 'y' in 'busy' |
| ь | ' | 'soft sign'; (see p.175) |
| Э, э | e | as the 'e' in 'ten' |
| Ю, ю | yu | as the 'yu' in 'yule' |
| Я, я | ya | as the 'ya' in 'yard' (in stressed syllable) as the 'ye' in 'yearn' (in unstressed syllable) |

\* Е, е is transliterated Ye, ye when at the beginning of a word

\*\* Ё, ё is often printed without dots

## Meeting People

When introducing yourself use your first name, or first and last. Russians often address each other by first name plus patronymic, a middle name based on their father's first name – eg, Natalya Borisovna (Natalya, daughter of Boris), Pavel Nikolayevich (Pavel, son of Nikolay).

What's your name?
*kak vas za-vut?*   Как вас зовут?
My name is ...
*mi-nya za-vut ...*   Меня зовут ...
Pleased to meet you.
*o-chen' pri-ya-tna*   Очень приятно.
How are you?
*kak de-la?*   Как дела?
Where are you from?
*at-ku-da vy?*   Откуда вы?
I'm from ...
*ya iz ...*   Я из ...

## Language Difficulties

I don't speak Russian.
*ya ni ga-va-ryu pa rus-ki*
Я не говорю по-русски.
I don't understand.
*ya ni pa-ni-ma-yu*
Я не понимаю.
Do you speak English?
*vy ga-va-ri-te pa ang-liy-ski?*
Вы говорите по-английски?
Could you write it down, please?
*za-pi-shi-te pa-zhal-sta?*
Запишите, пожалуйста?

## Getting Around

How do we get to ...?
*kak da-brat'-sa k ...?*
Как добраться к ...?
Where is ...?
*gde ...?*
Где ...?
When does it leave?
*kag-da at-prav-lya-et-sya?*
Когда отправляется?
Are you getting off?
*vy vy-kho-di-ti?*
Вы выходите?

bus
   *af-**to**-bus*          автобус
taxi
   *tak-**si***            такси
train
   ***poy**-ezt*          поезд
tram
   *tram-**vay***        трамвай
trolleybus
   *tra-**ley**-bus*     троллейбус

map
   ***kar** ta*           карта
metro token, tokens
   *zhi-**ton**, zhi-**tony***  жетон, жетоны
railway station
   *zhi-lez-na-da-**rozh**-nyy vag-**zal***
   железнодорожный (ж. д.) вокзал
stop (bus, tram etc)
   *a-sta-**nof**-ka*   остановка
ticket, tickets
   *bi-**let**, bi-**le**-ty*  билет, билеты
transport map
   ***skhe**-ma*        схема транспорта
    ***trans**-par-ta*

## Accommodation

How much is a room?
   ***skol'**-ka **sto**-it **no**-mer?*
   Сколько стоит номер?
Do you have a cheaper room?
   *u vas est' di-**shev**-le **no**-mer?*
   У вас есть дешевле номер?

hotel
   *gas-**ti**-ni-tsa*    гостиница
room
   ***no**-mer*         номер
key
   *klyuch*           ключ
blanket
   *a-di-**ya**-la*       одеяло
toilet paper
   *tu-a-**let**-na-ya*  туалетная бумага
    *bu-**ma**-ga*

The ... isn't working.
   *... ni ra-**bo**-ta-it*  ... не работает.
electricity
   *e-lek-**tri**-chest-va*  электричество
heating
   *a-ta-**ple**-ni-ye*   отопление

| Signs | |
|---|---|
| Вход | **Entrance** |
| Выход | **Exit** |
| Мест Нет | **No Vacancy** |
| Справки | **Information** |
| Открыт | **Open** |
| Закрыт | **Closed** |
| Касса | **Cashier/Ticket Office** |
| Больница | **Hospital** |
| Милиция | **Police** |
| Туалет | **Toilet** |
|   Мужской (М) | **Men** |
|   Женский (Ж) | **Women** |

hot water
   *ga-**rya**-cha-ya*   горячая вода
    *vo-**da***
light
   *svet*            свет
tap/faucet
   *kran*           кран

## Around Town

House numbers are not always in step on opposite sides of the street. Russian addresses are written back-to-front, with Russia at the top of the address and the adressee at the bottom.

Where is ...?
   *gde ...?*        Где ...?
I'm lost.
   *ya za-blu-**dil**-sya* (m)
   Я заблудился
   *ya za-blu-**di**-las'* (f)
   Я заблудилась

avenue
   *pras-**pekt***      проспект (просп.)
boulevard
   *bul'-**var***        бульвар
church
   ***tser**-kof'*       церковь
highway
   *sha-**se***         шоссе
lane
   *pi-ri-**u**-lak*    переулок (пер.)

museum
  *mu-zey*        музей
square/plaza
  *plo-shchat'*   площадь (пл.)
street
  *u-lit-sa*      улица (ул.)
theatre
  *te-atr*        театр

## Directions
to/on the left
  *na-le-va*      налево
to/on the right
  *nap-ra-va*     направо
straight on
  *prya-ma*       прямо
here
  *tut*           тут
there
  *tam*           там
near
  *da-le-ko*      далеко
far
  *blis-ka*       близко
north
  *se-ver*        север
south
  *yuk*           юг
east
  *vas-tok*       восток
west
  *za-pad*        запад

## Bank, Post & Telecommunications
bank
  *bank*          банк
currency exchange
  *ab-men va-lyu-ty*  обмен валюты
money
  *den'-gi*       деньги
small change
  *raz-men*       размен
travellers cheques
  *da-rozh-nyye*  дорожные чеки
  *che-ki*

post office
  *poch-ta*       почтамт
postcard
  *at-kryt-ka*    открытка

stamp
  *mar-ka*        марка
telephone
  *ti-li-fon*     телефон
fax
  *fax/ti-li-fax* факс/телефакс
intercity telephone office
  *mizh-du-ga-rod-nyy ti-li-fo-nyy punkt*
  междугородный телефонный пункт
international telephone office
  *mizh-du-na-rod-nyy ti-li-fo-nyy punkt*
  международный телефонный пункт

## Shopping
I need ...
  *mne nuzh-na ...*  Мне нужно ...
Do you have ...?
  *u vas est'...?*   У вас есть ...?
How much is it?
  *skol'-ka sto-it?* Сколько стоит?

bookshop
  *knizh-nyy*      книжный магазин
  *ma-ga-zin*
department store
  *u-ni-vir-sal'-nyy*  универсальный
  *ma-ga-zin*          магазин
market
  *ry-nak*         рынок
newsstand
  *ga-ze-tnyy ki-osk*  газетный киоск
pharmacy
  *ap-te-ka*       аптека
good/OK
  *kha-ra-sho*     хорошо
bad
  *plo-kha*        плохо

## Time, Days & Dates
What time is it?
  *ka-to-ryy chas?*  Который час?
At what time?
  *f ka-to-ram*    В котором часу?
  *chi-su?*
hour
  *chas*           час
minute
  *mi-nu-ta*       минута
am/in the morning
  *ut-ra*          утра

pm/in the afternoon
  *dnya*              дня
in the evening
  **ve**-*chi-ra*     вечера
local time
  **mes**-*na-ye* **vre**-*mya*
  местное время
Moscow time
  *mas-***kov***-ska-ye*   московское время
  **vre**-*mya*

Dates are given day-month-year, with the month usually in Roman numerals. Days of the week are often represented by numbers in timetables (Monday is 1).

When?
  *kag-**da**?*       Когда?
today
  *si-***vod***-nya*  сегодня
tomorrow
  **zaft**-*ra*       завтра
yesterday
  *vchi-**ra***       вчера

Monday
  *pa-ni-***del'***-nik*   понедельник
Tuesday
  **ftor**-*nik*      вторник
Wednesday
  *sri-**da***        среда
Thursday
  *chit-***verk***    четверг
Friday
  **pyat**-*ni-tsa*   пятница
Saturday
  *su-***bo***-ta*    суббота
Sunday
  *vas-kri-***sen'***-e*   воскресенье

January
  *yan-***var'***     январь
February
  *fev-***ral'***     февраль
March
  *mart*              март
April
  *ap-***rel'***      апрель
May
  *may*               май
June
  *i-***yun'***       июнь

---

## Emergencies

I'm sick.
  *ya* **bo**-*lin* (m)    Я болен.
  *ya* *bal'-***na*** (f)   Я больна.
I need a doctor.
  *mne* **nu**-*zhin vrach*  Мне нужен врач.
Help!
  *na* **po**-*mashch!/*   На помощь!/
  *pa-ma-***gi***-ti!*     Помогите!
Thief!
  *vor!*              Вор!
Fire!
  *pa-***zhar***!*    Пожар!
hospital
  *bal'-***ni***-tsa*   больница
police
  *mi-li-***tsi***-ya*   милиция

---

July
  *i-***yul'***       июль
August
  **av**-*gust*       август
September
  *sen-***tyabr'***   сентябрь
October
  *ok-***tyabr'***    октябрь
November
  *na-***yabr'***     ноябрь
December
  *de-***kabr'***     декабрь

## Numbers

How many?
  **skol'**-*ka?*     Сколько?

| | | |
|---|---|---|
| 1 | *a-***din*** | один |
| 2 | *dva* | два |
| 3 | *tri* | три |
| 4 | *chi-***ty***-ri* | четыре |
| 5 | *pyat'* | пять |
| 6 | *shest'* | шесть |
| 7 | *sem* | семь |
| 8 | **vo**-*sim'* | восемь |
| 9 | **de**-*vit'* | девять |
| 10 | **de**-*sit'* | десять |
| 100 | *sto* | сто |
| 1000 | **ty**-*sya-cha* | тысяча |

one million
  *(a-***din***)* *mi-li-***on***   (один) миллион

## FOOD
Many restaurants have menus in English. If there's a service charge, it will be noted on the menu by за обслуживание (for service).

May we order?
   *mozh-na za-ka-zat'?*
   Можно заказать?
What is this?
   *shto e-ta?*
   Что это?
I'd like ...
   *ya by kha-tel* ... (m)
   Я бы хотел/
   *ya by kha-te-la* ... (f)
   Я бы хотела ...
I'm a vegetarian.
   *ya ve-ge-ta-ri-an-yets* (m)
   Я вегетарианец.
   *ya ve-ge-ta-ri-an-ka* (f)
   Я вегетарианка.
without meat
   *bis mya-sa*
   без мяса

breakfast
   *zaf-trak*          завтрак
lunch (afternoon meal)
   *a-bet*             обед
dinner/supper
   *u-zhin*            ужин
restaurant
   *ri-sta-ran*        ресторан
café
   *ka-fe*             кафе
canteen
   *sta-lo-va-ya*      столовая
snack bar
   *bu-fet*            буфет
waiter, waitress
   *a-fi-tsi-ant* (m)    официант
   *a-fi-tsi-ant-ka* (f) официантка
menu
   *men-yu*            меню
hot
   *gar-ya-chiy*       горячий
cold
   *kha-lod-niy*       холодный

## Menu Decoder
This glossary is a brief guide to some basics.

### Breakfast
блины            *bli-ny*
   leavened buckwheat pancakes; also eaten as an appetiser or dessert
блинчики         *blin-chi-ki*
   bliny rolled around meat or cheese and browned
каша             *ka-sha*
   Russian-style buckwheat porridge
кефир            *ki-feer*
   buttermilk, served as a drink
омлет            *ahm-lyet*
   omelette
творог           *tva-rok*
   cottage cheese
яйцо             *yai-tso*
   egg
яичница          *ya-ish-ni-tsa*
   fried egg

### Lunch & Dinner
Meals (and menus) are divided into courses:

закуски          *za-ku-ski*
   appetisers
первые блюда     *per-vi-ye blyu-da*
   first courses (usually soups)
вторые блюда     *fta-ryye blyu-da*
   second courses or 'main' dishes
горячие блюда    *gar-ya-chi-ye blyu-da*
   hot courses or 'main' dishes
сладкие блюда    *slat-ki-ye blyu-da*
   sweet courses or desserts

### Appetisers
The fancier appetisers rival main courses for price. The best caviar, икра *(i-kra)* is black (sturgeon) caviar, *i-kra chyor-na-ya*, also called *zer-ni-sta-ya*. Much cheaper and saltier is red (salmon) caviar, *i-kra kras-na-ya*, also called *ke-to-va-ya*.

грибы в сметане  *gri-by fsme-ta-ne*
   mushrooms baked in sour cream (also called жульен из грибов *zhul-yen iz gri-bov*)
салат            *sa-lat*
   salad

из помидоров     *iz pa-mi-**dor**-ov*
    tomato salad

салат столичный     *sa-**lat** sta-**lich**-nyy*
    salad of vegetable, beef, potato and egg
    in sour cream and mayonnaise

## Soup

борш     *borshch*
    beetroot soup with vegetables and some-
    times meat, usually served with sour
    cream and hard-boiled egg

лапша     *lap-**sha***
    chicken noodle soup

окрошка     *a-**krosh**-ka*
    cold or hot soup made from cucumbers,
    sour cream, potatoes, eggs, meat and *kvas*

рассольник     *ra-**ssol'**-nik*
    soup of marinated cucumbers and kidney

солянка     *sal-**yan**-ka*
    thick meat or fish soup with salted cu-
    cumbers and other vegetables

уха     *u-**kha***
    fish soup with potatoes and vegetables

харчо     *khar-**choh***
    traditional Georgian soup made of lamb
    and spices

ши     *shchi*
    cabbage or sauerkraut soup

## Poultry & Meat Dishes

антрекот     *an-tri-**kot***
    entrecote – boned sirloin steak

бефстроганов     *bef-**stro**-ga-nov*
    beef stroganoff – beef slices in a rich
    sauce

бифштекс     *bif-**shteks***
    'steak', usually a glorified hamburger
    filling

говядина     *gav-**ya**-di-na*
    beef

голубцы     *ga-lup-**tsy***
    cabbage rolls stuffed with meat

жаркое     *zhar-**koy**-e*
    meat or poultry stewed in a clay pot;
    most common seems to be:

жаркое по-     *zhar-**koy**-e*
домашнему     *pa-da-**mash**-ni-mu*
    'home-style', with mushrooms, potatoes
    and vegetables

из птицы     *iz **pti**-tsa*
    poultry

котлета     *kat-**le**-ta*
    usually a croquette of ground meat

котлета по-     *kat-**le**-ta pa-*
киевски     ***ki**-ev-ski*
    chicken Kiev – fried boneless chicken
    breast stuffed with garlic butter

котлета по-     *kat-**le**-ta pa-*
пожарски     *pa-**zhar**-ski*
    minced chicken

мясные     ***mya**-sni-ye*
    meat

пельмени     *pil'-**men**-i*
    meat dumplings

плов     *plov*
    pilaf, rice with mutton bits

свинина     *sfi-**ni**-na*
    pork

шашлык     *shashlyk*
    skewered and grilled mutton or other meat

## Fish

осетрина     *a-se-**tri**-na*
отварная     *at-**var**-na-yah*
    poached sturgeon

осетрина с     *a-se-**tri**-na zgri-**ba**-mi*
грибами
    sturgeon with mushrooms

рыба     ***ry**-ba*
    fish

судак     *su-**dak***
    pike perch

форель     *far-**yel'***
    trout

## Vegetables

гарниры     *gar-**ni**-ry*
    any vegetable garnish

горох     *ga-**rokh***
    peas

грибы     *gri-by*
    wild mushrooms

капуста     *ka-**pus**-ta*
    cabbage

картошка/     *kar-**tosh**-ka/*
картофель     *kar-**to**-fil'*
    potato

морковь     *mar-**kof'***
    carrots

зелень     ***zye**-lin'*
    greens

| овощи | *o*-va-shchi |
| vegetables | |
| огурец | a-gur-*yets* |
| cucumber | |
| помидор | pa-mi-*dor* |
| tomato | |

## Fruit

| абрикос | a-bri-*kos* |
| apricot | |
| апельсин | a-pel'-*sin* |
| orange | |
| вишня | *vish*-ni-ya |
| cherry | |
| банан | ba-*nan* |
| banana | |
| виноград | vi-na-*grad* |
| grapes | |
| груша | *gru*-sha |
| pear | |
| фрукты | *fruk*-ty |
| fruits | |
| яблоко | *ya*-bla-ko |
| apple | |

## Other Foods

| масло | *mas*-la |
| butter | |
| перец | *pyer*-its |
| pepper | |
| рис | ris |
| rice | |
| сахар | *sa*-khar |
| sugar | |
| соль | sol' |
| salt | |
| сыр | syr |
| cheese | |
| хлеб | khlep |
| bread | |

## Desserts

| мороженое | ma-ro-zhi-ne-ya |
| icecream | |
| кисель | ki-*sel'* |
| fruit jelly/jello | |
| компот | kam-*pot* |
| fruit in syrup | |
| пирожное | pi-*rozh*-na-ye |
| pastries | |

## DRINKS
### Nonalcoholic

water
| вода | va-*da* |

boiled water
| кипяток | ki-pya-*tok* |

mineral water
| минеральная | mi-ne-*ral*-na-ya va-*da* |
| вода | |

soda water
| газированная | ga-zi-*ro*-va-na-ya |
| вода | va-*da* |

coffee
| кофе | *ko*-fe |

tea
| чай | chai |

with sugar
| с сахаром | s *sakh*-ar-am |

with jam
| с вареньем | s far-*en'*-im |

milk
| молоко | ma-la-*ko* |

juice
| сок | sok |

lemonade
| лимонад | li-ma-*nad* |

soft drink
| безалкогольный напиток | |
| bez-al-ka-*gol'*-nyy na-*pi*-tuk | |

### Alcoholic

alcohol
| алкоголь | al-ka-*gol'* |

vodka
| водка | *vot*-ka |

Soviet champagne
| советское | sav-*yet*-ska-ya |
| шампанское | sham-*pan*-ska-ya |

red/white wine
| красное/белое | *kras*-na-ya/*bel*-a-ya |
| вино | vi-*no* |

brandy
| коньяк | ka-*n'ak* |

beer
| пиво | *pi*-va |

kvas (beer-like drink)
| квас | kvas |

To your health!
За ваше здоровье!
za *va*-she zda-*ro*-v'e!

# Glossary

**aeroport** – airport
**apteka** – pharmacy
**avtobus** – bus
**avtovokzal** – bus station

**babushka** – grandmother
**banya** – bathhouse
**benzin** petrol
**bilet** – ticket
**bufet** – snack bar, usually in a hotel, selling cheap cold meats, boiled eggs, salads, bread, pastries etc
**bulochnaya** – bakery
**buterbrod** – open sandwich

**dacha** – country cottage, summer house
**deklaratsia** – customs declaration
**dezhurnaya** – woman looking after a particular floor of a hotel
**dom** – house
**duma** – parliament

**elektrichka** – suburban train
**etazh** – floor (storey)

**gazeta** – newspaper
**glavpochtamt** – main post office
**gorod** – city, town
**gostinitsa** – hotel

**ikra** – caviar
**izba** – traditional single-storey wooden cottage
**izveshchenie** – notification

**kafe** – cafe
**kassa** – ticket office, cashier's desk
**khleb** – bread
**klyuch** – key
**kniga** – book
**krazha** – theft
**kvartira** – flat, apartment
**kvitantsia** – receipt

**magazin** – shop
**magizdat** – underground recording illegally distributed under communist rule

**manezh** – riding school
**marka** – postage stamp or brand, trademark
**marshrutnoe taxi** – minibus that runs along a fixed route
**mashina** – car
**matryoshka** – set of painted wooden dolls within dolls
**mesto** – place, seat
**militsia** – police
**mineralnaya voda** – mineral water
**morskoy vokzal** – sea terminal
**most** – bridge
**muzey** – museum
**muzhskoy** – men's (toilet)

**naberezhnaya** – embankment
**novy** – new

**obed** – lunch
**oblast** – area, region
**obmen valyuty** – currency exchange
**ostanovka** – bus stop
**ostrov** – island
**OVIR (Otdel Viz I Registratsii)** – Department of Visas & Registration

**palekh** – painted box
**Paskha** – Easter
**pereryv** – break, recess
**pereulok** – lane
**plan goroda** – city map
**ploshchad** – square
**pochtamt** – post office (*glavpochtamt* is the town's main post office)
**poezd** – train
**poliklinika** – medical centre
**posylka** – parcel
**prospekt** – avenue

**rechnoy vokzal** – river terminal
**reka** – river
**remont** – closed for repairs
**restoran** – restaurant
**Rozhdestvo** – Christmas
**rubl** – rouble
**rynok** – market

**samizdat** – underground literary manuscript
**samovar** – urn
**sanitarny den** – literally 'sanitary day'; the monthly day on which establishments shut down for cleaning (these days vary and often occur with little forewarning)
**schyot** – bill
**sever** – north
**sobor** – cathedral
**stary** – old
**stolovaya** – canteen, cafeteria

**tapochki** – slippers
**teatr** – theatre
**tserkov** – church
**tsirk** – circus
**tualet** – toilet
**tuda i obratno** – 'there and back', return ticket

**troyka** – horse-drawn sleigh

**ulitsa** – street
**uzhin** – dinner

**vkhod** – way in, entrance
**voda** – water
**vokzal** – station
**vostok** – east
**vorovstvo** – theft

**yug** – south

**zakaznoe** – registration of mail
**zal** – hall, room
**zaliv** – gulf, bay
**zapad** – west
**zavtrak** – breakfast
**zhensky** – women's (toilet)
**zheton** – token (for metro etc)

# Thanks

Many thanks to the travellers who used the last edition and wrote to us with helpful hints, useful advice and interesting anecdotes:

Glenn Ashenden, Kris Ayre, William Ballantine, Donald Bell, Richmod Bollinger, Jean & Guy Boney, Bob Cromwell, Joseph D Crowley, Joey Day, Ponor Doline, WF Dymond, P Ekerot, Vidar Frett, Jane Galvin, Eric Glerum, Daniel Granello, Ed Graystone, Yaniv Hamo, Dan Hedges, Katherine Hess, Kevin Jordan, Maureen Keogh, Kitty Lee, Andre Lehmann, Erik Lindqvist, Scott Lundell, Lachlan MacQuarrie, J Mak, Damian McCormack, Sonia Migliorini, David Montgomery, Martin Moore, Erin K O'Brian, Phil O'Brien, Lars Pardo, Irina Pavlova, Alex Phillips, Peter Relyveld, Jack Schwartz, Allan Sealy, Jonathon Smith, Walery Stukacz, Lesley Sumner, Soon Ju Tok, Whui Mei Yeo, Olga S Zamiatina

# Lonely Planet Guides by Region

Lonely Planet is known worldwide for publishing practical, reliable and no-nonsense travel information in our guides and on our Web site. The Lonely Planet list covers just about every accessible part of the world. Currently there are 16 series: Travel guides, Shoestring guides, Condensed guides, Phrasebooks, Read This First, Healthy Travel, Walking guides, Cycling guides, Watching Wildlife guides, Pisces Diving & Snorkeling guides, City Maps, Road Atlases, Out to Eat, World Food, Journeys travel literature and Pictorials.

**AFRICA** Africa on a shoestring • Botswana • Cairo • Cairo City Map • Cape Town • Cape Town City Map • East Africa • Egypt • Egyptian Arabic phrasebook • Ethiopia, Eritrea & Djibouti • Ethiopian Amharic phrasebook • The Gambia & Senegal • Healthy Travel Africa • Kenya • Malawi • Morocco • Moroccan Arabic phrasebook • Mozambique • Namibia • Read This First: Africa • South Africa, Lesotho & Swaziland • Southern Africa • Southern Africa Road Atlas • Swahili phrasebook • Tanzania, Zanzibar & Pemba • Trekking in East Africa • Tunisia • Watching Wildlife East Africa • Watching Wildlife Southern Africa • West Africa • World Food Morocco • Zambia • Zimbabwe, Botswana & Namibia
**Travel Literature:** Mali Blues: Traveling to an African Beat • The Rainbird: A Central African Journey • Songs to an African Sunset: A Zimbabwean Story

**AUSTRALIA & THE PACIFIC** Aboriginal Australia & the Torres Strait Islands •Auckland • Australia • Australian phrasebook • Australia Road Atlas • Cycling Australia • Cycling New Zealand • Fiji • Fijian phrasebook • Healthy Travel Australia, NZ & the Pacific • Islands of Australia's Great Barrier Reef • Melbourne • Melbourne City Map • Micronesia • New Caledonia • New South Wales • New Zealand • Northern Territory • Outback Australia • Out to Eat – Melbourne • Out to Eat – Sydney • Papua New Guinea • Pidgin phrasebook • Queensland • Rarotonga & the Cook Islands • Samoa • Solomon Islands • South Australia • South Pacific • South Pacific phrasebook • Sydney • Sydney City Map • Sydney Condensed • Tahiti & French Polynesia • Tasmania • Tonga • Tramping in New Zealand • Vanuatu • Victoria • Walking in Australia • Watching Wildlife Australia • Western Australia
**Travel Literature:** Islands in the Clouds: Travels in the Highlands of New Guinea • Kiwi Tracks: A New Zealand Journey • Sean & David's Long Drive

**CENTRAL AMERICA & THE CARIBBEAN** Bahamas, Turks & Caicos • Baja California • Belize, Guatemala & Yucatán • Bermuda • Central America on a shoestring • Costa Rica • Costa Rica Spanish phrasebook • Cuba • Cycling Cuba • Dominican Republic & Haiti • Eastern Caribbean • Guatemala • Havana • Healthy Travel Central & South America • Jamaica • Mexico • Mexico City • Panama • Puerto Rico • Read This First: Central & South America • Virgin Islands • World Food Caribbean • World Food Mexico • Yucatán
**Travel Literature:** Green Dreams: Travels in Central America

**EUROPE** Amsterdam • Amsterdam City Map • Amsterdam Condensed • Andalucía • Athens • Austria • Baltic States phrasebook • Barcelona • Barcelona City Map • Belgium & Luxembourg • Berlin • Berlin City Map • Britain • British phrasebook • Brussels, Bruges & Antwerp • Brussels City Map • Budapest • Budapest City Map • Canary Islands • Catalunya & the Costa Brava • Central Europe • Central Europe phrasebook • Copenhagen • Corfu & the Ionians • Corsica • Crete • Crete Condensed • Croatia • Cycling Britain • Cycling France • Cyprus • Czech & Slovak Republics • Czech phrasebook • Denmark • Dublin • Dublin City Map • Dublin Condensed • Eastern Europe • Eastern Europe phrasebook • Edinburgh • Edinburgh City Map • England • Estonia, Latvia & Lithuania • Europe on a shoestring • Europe phrasebook • Finland • Florence • Florence City Map • France • Frankfurt City Map • Frankfurt Condensed • French phrasebook • Georgia, Armenia & Azerbaijan • Germany • German phrasebook • Greece • Greek Islands • Greek phrasebook • Hungary • Iceland, Greenland & the Faroe Islands • Ireland • Italian phrasebook • Italy • Kraków • Lisbon • The Loire • London • London City Map • London Condensed • Madrid • Madrid City Map • Malta • Mediterranean Europe • Milan, Turin & Genoa • Moscow • Munich • Netherlands • Normandy • Norway • Out to Eat – London • Out to Eat – Paris • Paris • Paris City Map • Paris Condensed • Poland • Polish phrasebook • Portugal • Portuguese phrasebook • Prague • Prague City Map • Provence & the Côte d'Azur • Read This First: Europe • Rhodes & the Dodecanese • Romania & Moldova • Rome • Rome City Map • Rome Condensed • Russia, Ukraine & Belarus • Russian phrasebook • Scandinavian & Baltic Europe • Scandinavian phrasebook • Scotland • Sicily • Slovenia • South-West France • Spain • Spanish phrasebook • Stockholm • St Petersburg • St Petersburg City Map • Sweden • Switzerland • Tuscany • Ukrainian phrasebook • Venice • Vienna • Wales • Walking in Britain • Walking in France • Walking in Ireland • Walking in Italy • Walking in Scotland • Walking in Spain • Walking in Switzerland • Western Europe • World Food France • World Food Greece • World Food Ireland • World Food Italy • World Food Spain **Travel Literature:** After Yugoslavia • Love and War in the Apennines • The Olive Grove: Travels in Greece • On the Shores of the Mediterranean • Round Ireland in Low Gear • A Small Place in Italy

# Lonely Planet Mail Order

Lonely Planet products are distributed worldwide. They are also available by mail order from Lonely Planet, so if you have difficulty finding a title please write to us. North and South American residents should write to 150 Linden St, Oakland, CA 94607, USA; European and African residents should write to 10a Spring Place, London NW5 3BH, UK; and residents of other countries to Locked Bag 1, Footscray, Victoria 3011, Australia.

**INDIAN SUBCONTINENT & THE INDIAN OCEAN** Bangladesh • Bengali phrasebook • Bhutan • Delhi • Goa • Healthy Travel Asia & India • Hindi & Urdu phrasebook • India • India & Bangladesh City Map • Indian Himalaya • Karakoram Highway • Kathmandu City Map • Kerala • Madagascar • Maldives • Mauritius, Réunion & Seychelles • Mumbai (Bombay) • Nepal • Nepali phrasebook • North India • Pakistan • Rajasthan • Read This First: Asia & India • South India • Sri Lanka • Sri Lanka phrasebook • Tibet • Tibetan phrasebook • Trekking in the Indian Himalaya • Trekking in the Karakoram & Hindukush • Trekking in the Nepal Himalaya • World Food India **Travel Literature:** The Age of Kali: Indian Travels and Encounters • Hello Goodnight: A Life of Goa • In Rajasthan • Maverick in Madagascar • A Season in Heaven: True Tales from the Road to Kathmandu • Shopping for Buddhas • A Short Walk in the Hindu Kush • Slowly Down the Ganges

**MIDDLE EAST & CENTRAL ASIA** Bahrain, Kuwait & Qatar • Central Asia • Central Asia phrasebook • Dubai • Farsi (Persian) phrasebook • Hebrew phrasebook • Iran • Israel & the Palestinian Territories • Istanbul • Istanbul City Map • Istanbul to Cairo • Istanbul to Kathmandu • Jerusalem • Jerusalem City Map • Jordan • Lebanon • Middle East • Oman & the United Arab Emirates • Syria • Turkey • Turkish phrasebook • World Food Turkey • Yemen **Travel Literature:** Black on Black: Iran Revisited • Breaking Ranks: Turbulent Travels in the Promised Land • The Gates of Damascus • Kingdom of the Film Stars: Journey into Jordan

**NORTH AMERICA** Alaska • Boston • Boston City Map • Boston Condensed • British Columbia • California & Nevada • California Condensed • Canada • Chicago • Chicago City Map • Chicago Condensed • Florida • Georgia & the Carolinas • Great Lakes • Hawaii • Hiking in Alaska • Hiking in the USA • Honolulu & Oahu City Map • Las Vegas • Los Angeles • Los Angeles City Map • Louisiana & the Deep South • Miami • Miami City Map • Montreal • New England • New Orleans • New Orleans City Map • New York City • New York City City Map • New York City Condensed • New York, New Jersey & Pennsylvania • Oahu • Out to Eat – San Francisco • Pacific Northwest • Rocky Mountains • San Diego & Tijuana • San Francisco • San Francisco City Map • Seattle • Seattle City Map • Southwest • Texas • Toronto • USA • USA phrasebook • Vancouver • Vancouver City Map • Virginia & the Capital Region • Washington, DC • Washington, DC City Map • World Food New Orleans **Travel Literature:** Caught Inside: A Surfer's Year on the California Coast • Drive Thru America

**NORTH-EAST ASIA** Beijing • Beijing City Map • Cantonese phrasebook • China • Hiking in Japan • Hong Kong & Macau • Hong Kong City Map • Hong Kong Condensed • Japan • Japanese phrasebook • Korea • Korean phrasebook • Kyoto • Mandarin phrasebook • Mongolia • Mongolian phrasebook • Seoul • Shanghai • South-West China • Taiwan • Tokyo • Tokyo Condensed • World Food Hong Kong • World Food Japan **Travel Literature:** In Xanadu: A Quest • Lost Japan

**SOUTH AMERICA** Argentina, Uruguay & Paraguay • Bolivia • Brazil • Brazilian phrasebook • Buenos Aires • Buenos Aires City Map • Chile & Easter Island • Colombia • Ecuador & the Galapagos Islands • Healthy Travel Central & South America • Latin American Spanish phrasebook • Peru • Quechua phrasebook • Read This First: Central & South America • Rio de Janeiro • Rio de Janeiro City Map • Santiago de Chile • South America on a shoestring • Trekking in the Patagonian Andes • Venezuela **Travel Literature:** Full Circle: A South American Journey

**SOUTH-EAST ASIA** Bali & Lombok • Bangkok • Bangkok City Map • Burmese phrasebook • Cambodia • Cycling Vietnam, Laos & Cambodia • East Timor phrasebook • Hanoi • Healthy Travel Asia & India • Hill Tribes phrasebook • Ho Chi Minh City (Saigon) • Indonesia • Indonesian phrasebook • Indonesia's Eastern Islands • Java • Lao phrasebook • Laos • Malay phrasebook • Malaysia, Singapore & Brunei • Myanmar (Burma) • Philippines • Pilipino (Tagalog) phrasebook • Read This First: Asia & India • Singapore • Singapore City Map • South-East Asia on a shoestring • South-East Asia phrasebook • Thailand • Thailand's Islands & Beaches • Thailand, Vietnam, Laos & Cambodia Road Atlas • Thai phrasebook • Vietnam • Vietnamese phrasebook • World Food Indonesia • World Food Thailand • World Food Vietnam

**ALSO AVAILABLE:** Antarctica • The Arctic • The Blue Man: Tales of Travel, Love and Coffee • Brief Encounters: Stories of Love, Sex & Travel • Buddhist Stupas in Asia: The Shape of Perfection • Chasing Rickshaws • The Last Grain Race • Lonely Planet ... On the Edge: Adventurous Escapades from Around the World • Lonely Planet Unpacked • Lonely Planet Unpacked Again • Not the Only Planet: Science Fiction Travel Stories • Ports of Call: A Journey by Sea • Sacred India • Travel Photography: A Guide to Taking Better Pictures • Travel with Children • Tuvalu: Portrait of an Island Nation

# LONELY PLANET

You already know that Lonely Planet produces more than this one guidebook, but you might not be aware of the other products we have on this region. Here is a selection of titles that you may want to check out as well:

**Russia, Ukraine & Belarus**
ISBN 0 86442 713 1
US$27.95 • UK£16.99

**Russian phrasebook**
ISBN 1 86450 106 5
US$7.95 • UK£4.50

**Scandinavian & Baltic Europe**
ISBN 1 86450 156 1
US$21.99 • UK£13.99

**Eastern Europe**
ISBN 1 86450 149 9
US$24.99 • UK£14.99

**Europe on a shoestring**
ISBN 1 86450 150 2
US$24.99 • UK£14.99

**Read This First: Europe**
ISBN 1 86450 136 7
US$14.99 • UK£8.99

**St Petersburg City Map**
ISBN 1 86450 179 0
US$5.99 • UK£3.99

**Available wherever books are sold**

# Index

## Text

Bold indicates maps.

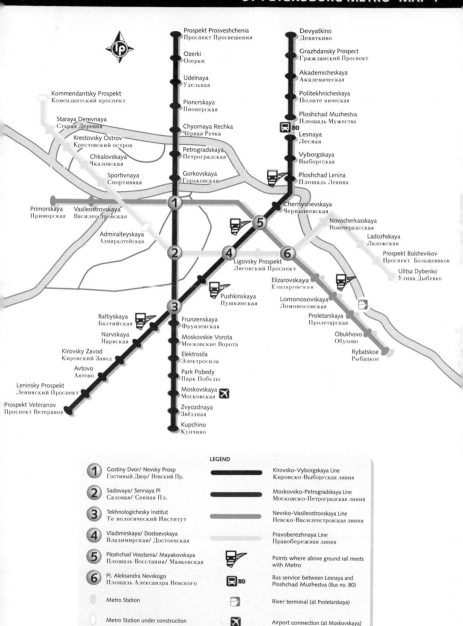

IP

Prospekt Prosveshchenia
Проспект Просвещения

Devyatkino
Девяткино

Ozerki
Озерки

Grazhdansky Prospect
Гражданский Проспект

Udelnaya
Удельная

Akademicheskaya
Академическая

Kommendantsky Prospekt
Комендантский проспект

Pionerskaya
Пионерская

Politekhnicheskaya
Полите ническая

Staraya Derevnaya
Старая Деревня

Chyornaya Rechka
Чёрная Речка

Ploshchad Muzhestva
Площадь Мужества

Krestovsky Ostrov
Крестовский остров

Petrogradskaya
Петроградская

80

Lesnaya
Лесная

Chkalovskaya
Чкаловская

Vyborgskaya
Выборгская

Sportivnaya
Спортивная

Gorkovskaya
Горьковская

Ploshchad Lenina
Площадь Ленина

Primorskaya
Приморская

Vasileostrovskaya
Василеостровская

(1)

Chernyshevskaya
Чернышевская

Admiralteyskaya
Адмиралтейская

(5)

Novocherkasskaya
Новочеркасская

Ladozhskaya
Ладожская

(2)

(4)

(6)

Prospekt Bolshevikov
Проспект Большевиков

Ligovsky Prospekt
Лиговский Проспект

Ulitsa Dybenko
Улица Дыбенко

Pushkinskaya
Пушкинская

Elizarovskaya
Елизаровская

(3)

Lomonosovskaya
Ломоносовская

Baltiyskaya
Балтийская

Frunzenskaya
Фрунзенская

Proletarskaya
Пролетарская

Narvskaya
Нарвская

Moskovskie Vorota
Московские Ворота

Obukhovo
Обухово

Kirovsky Zavod
Кировский Завод

Elektrosila
Электросила

Rybatskoe
Рыбацкое

Avtovo
Автово

Park Pobedy
Парк Победы

Leninsky Prospekt
Ленинский Проспект

Moskovskaya
Московская

Prospekt Veteranov
Проспект Ветеранов

Zvyozdnaya
Звёздная

Kupchino
Купчино

LEGEND

(1) Gostiny Dvor/ Nevsky Prosp
    Гостиный Двор/ Невский Пр.

Kirovsko-Vyborgskaya Line
Кировско-Выборгская линия

(2) Sadovaya/ Sennaya Pl
    Садовая/ Сенная Пл.

Moskovsko-Petrogradskaya Line
Московско-Петроградская линия

(3) Tekhnologichesky Institut
    Те нологический Институт

Nevsko-Vasileostrovskaya Line
Невско-Василеостровская линия

(4) Vladimirskaya/ Dostoevskaya
    Владимирская/ Достоевская

Pravoberezhnaya Line
Правобережная линия

(5) Ploshchad Vosstania/ Mayakovskaya
    Площадь Восстания/ Маяковская

Points where above ground rail meets
with Metro

(6) Pl. Aleksandra Nevskogo
    Площадь Александра Невского

80

Bus service between Lesnaya and
Ploshchad Muzhestva (Bus no. 80)

Metro Station

River terminal (at Proletarskaya)

Metro Station under construction

Airport connection (at Moskovskaya)

# MAP 2  AROUND ST PETERSBURG

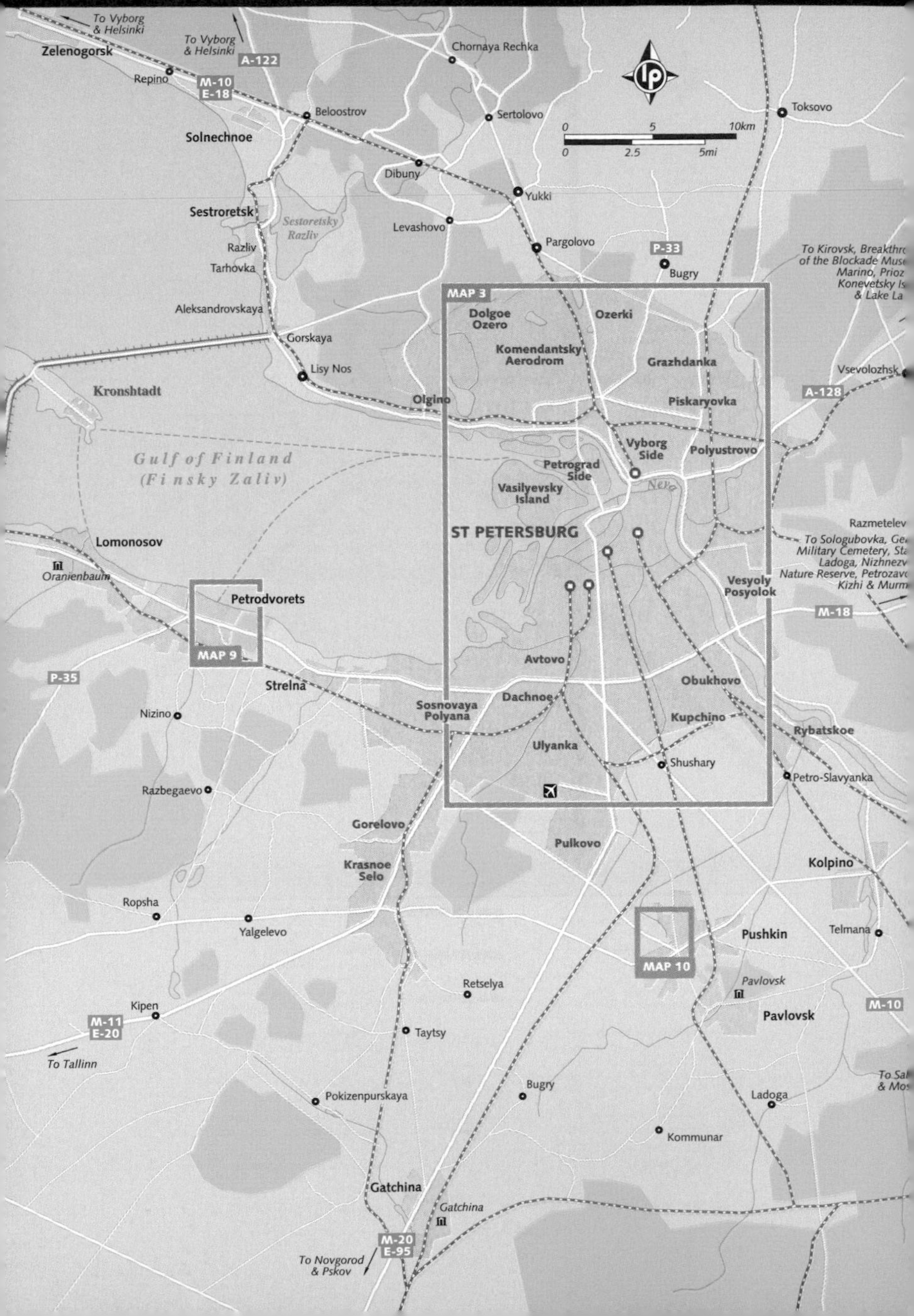

To Vyborg & Helsinki

Zelenogorsk

Repino

To Vyborg & Helsinki

A-122

M-10
E-18

Beloostrov

Chornaya Rechka

Solnechnoe

Sertolovo

Dibuny

Toksovo

Sestroretsk

Yukki

Razliv

Sestoretsky Razliv

Levashovo

Pargolovo

P-33

Tarhovka

Bugry

To Kirovsk, Breakthro
of the Blockade Muse
Marino, Prioz
Konevetsky Is
& Lake La

Aleksandrovskaya

Gorskaya

Lisy Nos

Olgino

MAP 3

Dolgoe
Ozero

Komendantsky
Aerodrom

Ozerki

Grazhdanka

Piskaryovka

Vsevolozhsk

A-128

Kronstadt

Gulf of Finland
(Finsky Zaliv)

Vyborg
Side

Polyustrovo

Petrograd
Side

Neva

Vasilyevsky
Island

ST PETERSBURG

Razmetelev
To Sologubovka, Ge
Military Cemetery, Sta
Ladoga, Nizhnevz
Nature Reserve, Petrozavi
Kizhi & Murm

Lomonosov

Oranienbaum

Petrodvorets

MAP 9

Vesyoly
Posyolok

M-18

P-35

Strelna

Avtovo

Dachnoe

Obukhovo

Nizino

Sosnovaya
Polyana

Kupchino

Rybatskoe

Razbegaevo

Ulyanka

Shushary

Petro-Slavyanka

Gorelovo

Pulkovo

Kolpino

Krasnoe
Selo

Ropsha

Pushkin

Telmana

Yalgelevo

MAP 10

Pavlovsk

M-10

Kipen

M-11
E-20

Retselya

Pavlovsk

To Tallinn

Taytsy

Bugry

To Sa
& Mo

Pokizenpurskaya

Ladoga

Kommunar

Gatchina

Gatchina

M-20
E-95

To Novgorod
& Pskov

0        5        10km
0    2.5        5mi

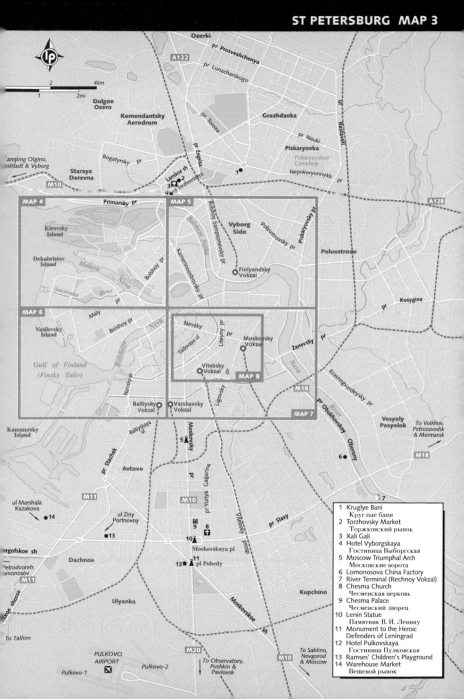

LP

2          4km
1          2mi

Ozerki
pr Prosveshchenya
A122
pr Lunacharskogo

Dolgoe
Ozero

Camping Olgino,
shtadt & Vyborg

Komendantsky
Aerodrom

Grazhdanka

pr Toreza

pr Nauki

Piskaryovka

Piskaryovskoe
Cemetery

Nepokoryonnykh

Staraya
Derevna

Bogatyrsky  pr

pr Engelsa

ul Rustaveli

M10
Landkoe sh                    2
3  ●● 1
Torzhovsk                      1

A128

**MAP 4**
Primorsky pr

**MAP 5**

Bolshoy Sampsonievsky pr

Vyborg
Side

Poluostrovsky pr

Piskaryovsky pr

Poluostrovo

Kirovsky
Island

Kantemirovtsky pr

Finlyandsky
Vokzal

Dekabristov
Island

Malaya

Bolshoy pr

Smolenka

River

Neva

pr Kosygina

Kosygina

**MAP 6**

Maly

Neva

**MAP 8**

Nevsky pr

Litevny pr

Moskovsky
Vokzal

Zanevsky

Vasilevsky
Island

Bolshoy pr

Sadovaya ul

Krasnogvardeysky pr

Gulf of Finland
(Finsky Zaliv)

Bolshoy pr

Vitebsky
Vokzal

Ligovsky pr

Neva

River

M18

**MAP 7**

pr Obukhovskoy Oborony

Kanonersky
Island

Baltiyskaya ul

Baltiysky
Vokzal

Varshavsky
Vokzal

Vesyoly
Posyolok

To Volkhov,
Petrozavodsk
& Murmansk

M18

Moskovsky pr

5

pr Gagarina

6

Avtovo

M11

7

ul Marshala
Kazakova

14

ul Ziny
Portnovoy

M10

9    8

13

10

Moskovskaya pl

pr Slavy

pr Yuriya Gagarina

Vitebsky prosp

Dachnoe

ergofskoe sh
etrodvorets
omonosov

M11

11  pl Pobedy
12

Kupchino

Ulyanka

Moskovskoe

To Tallinn

PULKOVO
AIRPORT

M20

M10

Pulkovo-2

Pulkovo-1

To Observatory,
Pushkin &
Pavlovsk

To Sablino,
Novgorod
& Moscow

1  Kruglye Bani
   Круглые бани
2  Torzhovsky Market
   Торжковский рынок
3  Xali Gali
4  Hotel Vyborgskaya
   Гостиница Выборгская
5  Moscow Triumphal Arch
   Московские ворота
6  Lomonosova China Factory
7  River Terminal (Rechnoy Vokzal)
8  Chesma Church
   Чесменская церковь
9  Chesma Palace
   Чесменский дворец
10 Lenin Statue
   Памятник В. И. Ленину
11 Monument to the Heroic
   Defenders of Leningrad
12 Hotel Pulkovskaya
   Гостиница Пулковская
13 Ramses' Children's Playground
14 Warehouse Market
   Вещевой рынок

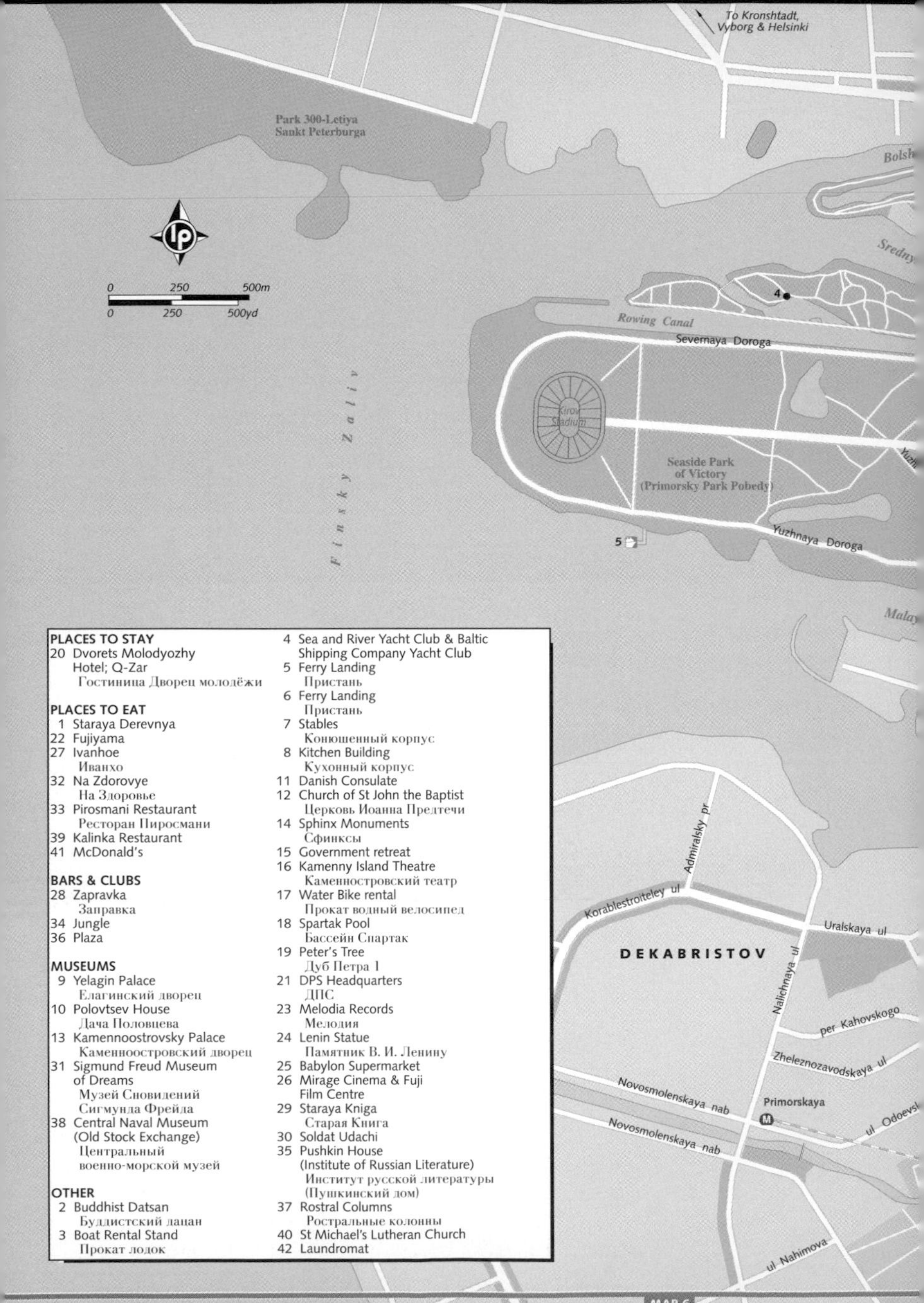

MAP 4

To Kronshtadt,
Vyborg & Helsinki

Bolsh

Park 300-Letiya
Sankt Peterburga

Sredny

0    250    500m
0    250    500yd

Rowing Canal

4

Severnaya Doroga

F i n s k y   Z a l i v

Kirov
Stadium

Seaside Park
of Victory
(Primorsky Park Pobedy)

Yuzhnaya Doroga

5

Malay

**PLACES TO STAY**
20 Dvorets Molodyozhy
   Hotel; Q-Zar
   Гостиница Дворец молодёжи

**PLACES TO EAT**
1 Staraya Derevnya
22 Fujiyama
27 Ivanhoe
   Иванхо
32 Na Zdorovye
   На Здоровье
33 Pirosmani Restaurant
   Ресторан Пиросмани
39 Kalinka Restaurant
41 McDonald's

**BARS & CLUBS**
28 Zapravka
   Заправка
34 Jungle
36 Plaza

**MUSEUMS**
9 Yelagin Palace
   Елагинский дворец
10 Polovtsev House
   Дача Половцева
13 Kamennoostrovsky Palace
   Каменноостровский дворец
31 Sigmund Freud Museum
   of Dreams
   Музей Сновидений
   Сигмунда Фрейда
38 Central Naval Museum
   (Old Stock Exchange)
   Центральный
   военно-морской музей

**OTHER**
2 Buddhist Datsan
   Буддистский дацан
3 Boat Rental Stand
   Прокат лодок

4 Sea and River Yacht Club & Baltic
   Shipping Company Yacht Club
5 Ferry Landing
   Пристань
6 Ferry Landing
   Пристань
7 Stables
   Конюшенный корпус
8 Kitchen Building
   Кухонный корпус
11 Danish Consulate
12 Church of St John the Baptist
   Церковь Иоанна Предтечи
14 Sphinx Monuments
   Сфинксы
15 Government retreat
16 Kamenny Island Theatre
   Каменностровский театр
17 Water Bike rental
   Прокат водный велосипед
18 Spartak Pool
   Бассейн Спартак
19 Peter's Tree
   Дуб Петра I
21 DPS Headquarters
   ДПС
23 Melodia Records
   Мелодия
24 Lenin Statue
   Памятник В. И. Ленину
25 Babylon Supermarket
26 Mirage Cinema & Fuji
   Film Centre
29 Staraya Kniga
   Старая Книга
30 Soldat Udachi
35 Pushkin House
   (Institute of Russian Literature)
   Институт русской литературы
   (Пушкинский дом)
37 Rostral Columns
   Ростральные колонны
40 St Michael's Lutheran Church
42 Laundromat

Admiraltsky pr

Korablestroiteley ul

Nalichnaya ul

Uralskaya ul

per Kahovskogo

Zheleznozavodskaya ul

**DEKABRISTOV**

Novosmolenskaya nab

Primorskaya

Novosmolenskaya nab

ul Odoevs

Primorskaya

ul Nahimova

MAP 6

MAP 4

MAP 5

Chyornaya
Rechka

Lipovaya al
Dibunovskaya ul
Serebryakov per
ul Oskalenko
ul Akademika
Shimanskogo
nab Adm Ushakova

ul Savushkina
Primorsky pr
Primorsky pr
Primorsky pr
Ushakovsky
most

3-y Elagin
most

nab r Bolshoy Nevki

12

3-y Cherny pr
Kirov
Park
nab r Sredney Nevki
KAMENNY
13

3
Nevka
8
Glavnaya al
7
nab r Maloy
Nevki
Kamennoostrovsky
most

YELAGIN
9
Teatralnaya ul
Bolshaya al
11
1-ya Beryozovaya al
14
Lopuhinsky
Gardens

3-y Yuzhny pr
17
1-y Elagin
most
Polevaya al
2-ya Beryozovaya al
15
Bokovaya
al
Levashova al
nab

6
16
Kamennoostrovsky pr

Nevka
2-y Elagin
most
nab r Krestovki
19
Maly Krestovsky
most
Vyazemsky
Gardens
Vyazemsky per

nab Martynova
Olgina ul
Malaya Nevka
ul Grota
Geslerovsky
most

Kemskaya ul
Deputatskaya ul
Esperova ul
Deputatskaya ul
Pesochnaya nab
Popova
Karpovsky
most
22
Ordina-naya ul

KRESTOVSKY
18
Vakulenchuka
Krestovsky
Ostrov
nab r Karpovki

ul Ryukhina
Krestovsky
Ostrov
Prohodnaya ul
Beloselskaya ul
Konstantinovsky pr
Grebnaya ul
Morskoy
20
ul Professora
Popova
Dahlya
21
nab r Karpovki

Krestovsky pr
pr Dinamo
Barochnaya
PETROGRAD
SIDE
Vsevoloda Vishnevskogo
Ordinarnaya ul

Krestovsky pr
Petrogradskaya ul
Krestovsky
most
Levashovsky
pr
Vishnevskogo

Nevka
Dinamo
Stadium
Sportivnaya ul
Spartak
Stadium
nab Admirala Lazareva
ul Bol Zelenina
Lenina
Lahtinskaya ul
Podrezova
Podkovyrova
Podrezova
Barmaleeva

Bol Petrovsky
most
Vyazovaya ul
Lazersky
most
Malaya Zelenina
Pionerskaya
Korpusnaya
ul Lodeynopolskaya ul
Chkalovsky pr
Gatchinskaya ul
Oranienbaumskaya ul
ul Shamsheva
24
23

ul Savnoy
Petrovskaya pl
PETROVSKY
Petrovsky pr
Zhdanovskaya ul
ul Krasnogo
Kursanta
Chkalovskaya
25
Kolpinskaya ul
26
Bol Pushkarskaya ul

SERNY
Balkika
Stadium
Pionerskaya
nab r Zhdanovki
Mal Razhnochinnaya ul
Mal Krasnoselskaya
Pionerskaya
Bol r
Mal
Rybatskaya ul
Monchegorskaya ul
27
28
Vvedenskaya ul

Uralskaya ul
Petrovsky
Park
pl Sports
Maly pr
31
29
30
Bolshoy pr
Sezzhinskaya
Zverinskaya
Tatarsky per

Zheleznovodskaya ul
ul Odoevskogo
Sportivnaya
33
32

Baltiysky
Yung
per
Petrovsky
Stadium
Sportivnaya
ul Blokhina
pr Dobrolyubova
34
ul Blokhina
Kronverksky pr

per Dekabristov
MALAYA NEVA
Bolshoy pr
Yubileyny
Sports
Palace
pr Dobrolyubova
KRONVERKSKY

Kumskaya ul
per Dekabristov
nab r Smolenki
nab Makarova
Tuchkov
most
Mytninskaya ul

2-ya i 3-ya linii
6-7 linii
8-9 linii
10-11 linii
12-13 linii
Sredny pr
Maly pr
4-ya i 5-ya linii
Syezdovskaya & 1-ya linii
ul Repina
nab Makarova
Volkhovsky per
Tuchkov per
MALAYA NEVA
Tiflissky per
Birzhevoy most
35
36
37
38

42
Vasileostrovskaya
41
40
39
Vasilevsky

MAP 6

MAP 5

MAP 4

pr Marshala Bly

Beloostrovskaya ul

Kanemirovskaya ul

M Lesnaya

nab Chyornoy Rechki

Vaz sky per

Krasnogvardeyskiy per

Bol

Sampsonevskiy pr

Harchenko

Gribalevoy

nab Adm Ushakova

Golovinsky most

Luch Stadium

1

Kantemirovskaya ul

Lesnoy pr

Diagonalnaya ul

Novolitovskaya ul

Polyustrovskiy pr

Kantemirovsky most

ul Aleksandra Matrosova

Novolitovskaya ul

Litovskaya ul

Aptekarskaya nab

ul Akademika Pavlova

2

Vyborgskaya nab

Gelsingforsskaya ul

Lesnoy pr

Chugunnaya ul

Mendeleyevskaya ul

VYBORG SIDE

ul Chapygina

Zenit Stadium

Belovodsky per

Tobolskaya

Chugunnaya u

ul Professora Popova

ul Prof Popova

Aptekarskiy pr

Smolyachkova

M Vyborgskaya

Silin most

Botanical Gardens

Aptekarskaya nab

Krapivny per

ul Literatov

Petropavlovsky most

nab r Karpovki

Grenaderskaya

7

8

Petropavlovskaya ul

Grenadersky most

Aptekarsky most

4

6 5

M Petrogradskaya

PETROGRAD SIDE

ul Fokina

Neyshlotsky per

Maly pr

9

pl Lva Tolstogo

ul Rentgena

ul Chapaeva

Evpatoriyskiy per

Vyborgskaya ul

Lesnoy pr

10

ul Ordinarnaya

ul Plutalova

Bobshoy pr

11

ul Lva Tolstogo

Pirogovskaya nab

Saharny per

Bol Sampsonevskiy pr

Botkinskaya

36 Pl Lenina

12

ul Rentgena

15

16 Monetnaya

ul Mira

Pinsky per

ul Chapaeva

Sampsonevsky most

37

ul Lenina

Bol Pushkarskaya ul

17

Divenskaya ul

Pecheny per

27 Posadskaya ul

34

35

Klinicheskaya ul

ul Akademika Lebedeva

Finsky per

Finland Station (Finlandsky Vokzal)

Pl Lenina M

13

Pushkarsky per

Kronverkskaya ul

Matveeva per

Syezzhinskaya ul

14

18

Avstriyskaya pl

26

Bol Posadskaya

Mal Posadskaya

Michurinskaya ul

Orenburgskaya ul

pl Lenina

Komsomol

Kresty Pri

19

ul Voskova

Sytninskaya ul

24

25

28

Mytninskaya ul

ul Kuybysheva

Penkovaya ul

33

nab Mikhailova

Arsenalnaya nab

38

20

Sytninskaya pl

29

30

22

23

M Gorkovskaya

Kamennoostrovsky pr

31

Liteyny most

39

21

Alexandrovsky Park

32

nab

nab Robespiera

Shpalernaya ul

Kronverksky pr

Petrovskaya

59

58

Shpalernaya ul

Kronverksky

Kronverksky

Kronverkskaya nab

Peter & Paul Fortress

Troitsky most

NEVA НЕВА

60

Zakharevskaya

57

56

Chernyshevskogo

54

Chaikovskogo

55

ZAYACHY

See Peter & Paul Fortress map

70

Prachechny most

Kutuzova

Gagarinskaya ul

Shpalernaya ul

69

ul Chaikovskogo

65

Furshtadtskaya ul

61

M Chernyshevskaya

53

50

Suvorovskaya pl

71

Verkhne-Lebyazhy most

Gangutskaya

Gagarinskaya

Mohovaya ul

67

Solyanoy per

64

63

Kirochnaya ul

52

51

72

Dvortsovaya nab

73

Mars Field

Summer Garten

nab Lebyazhyego canala

r Fontanki

66

68

Preobrazhenskaya pl

62

Manezhny per

Birzhevaya pl

Millionnaya ul

nab r Fontanki

ul Pestelya

4

Ermitazhny most

74

ul Ryleeva

MAP 7

# MAP 5

**LACES TO STAY**
5 Hotel St Petersburg
   Гостиница
   Санкт-Петербург
8 Holiday Hostel
5 Hotel Neva
   Гостиница Нева

**LACES TO EAT**
6 McDonald's
0 Laima
1 Café Marco
8 Bistro Samson
   Бистро Самсон
9 Kafe Tblisi
   Кафе Тбилиси
4 Troitsky Most
   Троицкий мост
26 Troitsky Most
   Троицкий мост
52 Idealnaya Chashka
   Идеальная Чашка
54 Sunduk
   Сундук
56 Kolobok
   Колобок
57 Sladkoezhka
   Сладкоежка

**BARS & CLUBS**
5 812 Jazz Club
9 Lensovieta Culture Palace
   Дом Культуры им. Ленсовета
27 Mama

58 JFC Jazz Club
66 Neo Jazz Club

**MUSEUMS**
15 Kirov Museum
   Музей С. М. Кирова
31 Museum of Political History
   Музей Русской
   политической истории
32 Peter's Cabin
   Домик Петра Великого
47 Tauride Palace
   Таврический дворец
69 Summer Palace
   Летний дворец
73 Marble Palace; American Center
   Мраморный дворец
67 Blockade Museum
   Мемориальный
   Музей обороны и
   блокады Ленинграда
60 Museum of Decorative
   and Applied Arts
   Музей прикладного
   искусства

**OTHER**
1 Akvatoria
   Водно-спортивный комплекс
2 Television Antenna
3 Polyuostrovsky Market
   Полуостровский рынок
4 St Sampson's Cathedral
   Сампсониевский собор

7 Telephone Office
8 Post Office
12 Paper Supply Store
13 Ipris
14 Playground
16 Estonian Consulate
17 Post Office
20 Sytny Market
   Сытный рынок
21 Amusement Park
   Аттракционы
22 Music Hall
   Мюзик Холл
23 Planetarium
   Планетарий
25 Lenfilm (Film Studios)
   Ленфильм
28 Gorky Statue
   Памятник А.М. Горькому
29 Sports Complex
30 Mosque of the Congress of Muslims
33 Cruiser Aurora
   Крейсер Аврора
34 Kalinka Stockmann's
36 Bus stop
37 Platform 1 Railway Ticket Office
39 Sphinx Monuments
   Сфинксы
40 Flower Shop
   Интерфлора
41 Flowers Exhibition Hall
   Выставка цветов
42 Dzerzhinsky Statue
   Памятник Ф. Дзержинскому

43 Smolny Cathedral
   Смольный собор
44 Smolny Institute
45 Lenin Statue
   Памятник В. И. Ленину
46 British Consulate
48 Lenin Statue
   Памятник В. И. Ленину
49 Bik Photo
50 German Consulate
   Консульство Германии
51 Sunny Sailing
53 Post Office
55 Finnish Embassy
59 SPIBA
60 GUVD Big House
   (former KGB Headquarters)
   ГУВД Большой дом
61 US Consulate
   Консульство США
62 Spaso-Preobrazhensky
   Cathedral
   Спасо-Преображенский собор
63 Spartak
   Кинотеатр Спартак
64 Central OVIR
   (Visa Registration) Office
   ОВИР
70 Summer Garden Landing
71 Statue of Suvorov
72 Eternal Flame
   Вечный огонь
74 Hermitage Theatre
   Театр Эрмитаж

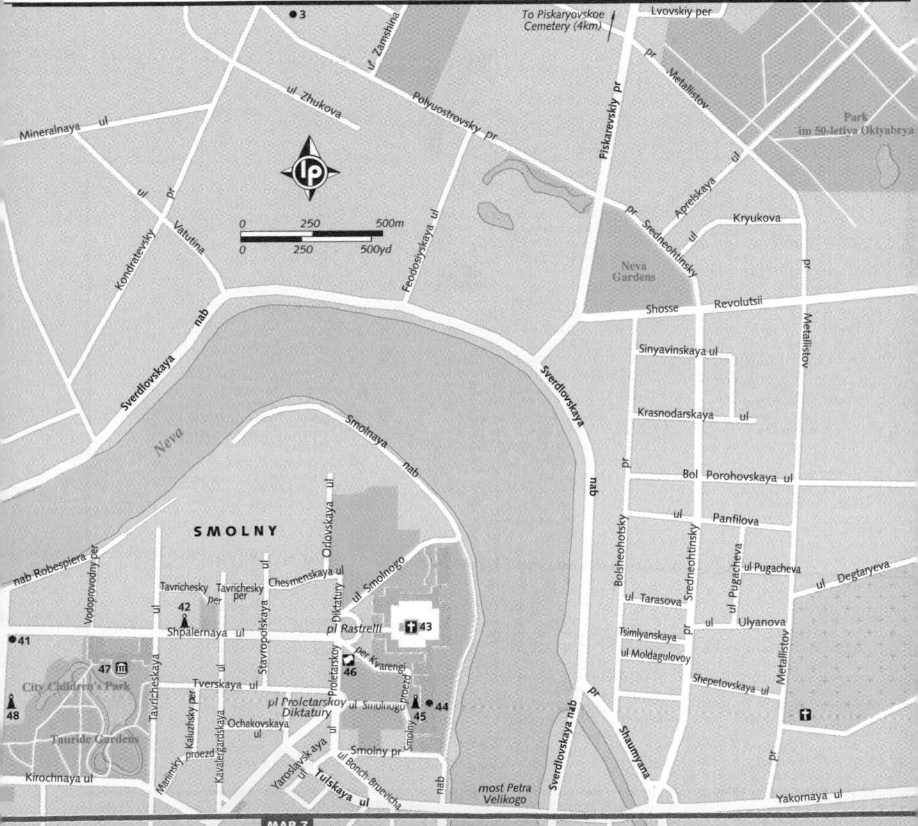

MAP 6

MAP 4

Michmanskaya

pl Baltiyskogo
Flota

Pribaltiyskaya
pl

ul Vorobstoricley

ul Nahimova

Nalichinty

Parusnaya ul

Shkipersky protok

Galerny proezd

Grebnoy Port

Shkipersky

protok

Kershdhima ul

Gavanskaya ul

Oporhin ul

Srednegavanskiy

Nalichnaya ul

Korzh Galernogo Farvatera

Opachlnsky
Gardens

pl Morskoi
Slavy

Finsky Zaliv

Gutnevsky kovs

Shonderskaya ul

Nevelskaya ul

0    250    500m
0    250    500yd

### PLACES TO STAY
2  Pribaltiyskaya Hotel
   Гостиница Прибалтийская
6  Hotel Morskaya
   Гостиница Морская
43 Matisov Domik
   Матисов Домик
58 Petrovskogo College
   Student Hostel

### PLACES TO EAT
8  Swagat
14 Cheburechnaya
   Чебуречная
16 Tinye
   Тинье
19 Staraya Tamozhnaya
   (Old Customs House)
   Старая таможня
32 Bistro Le Francais
37 Café Idiot
45 Golden Dragon
51 Dvorianskoye Gnezdo
   Дворянское Гнездо

### BARS & CLUBS
1  Studio 20
30 Ostrov
33 Tribunal Bar
49 Shamrock Bar

### MUSEUMS
3  People's Will D-2
   Submarine Museum
   Подводная лодка Д-2 Народоволец
10 Geological Museum
   Геологический Институт
17 Twelve Colleges &
   Mendeleev Museum
   Двенадцать коллегий и
   Музей Менделеева
18 Museum of Zoology
   Зоологический музей

20 Museum of Anthropology &
   Ehnography (Kunstkammer)
   Музей антропологии и
   этнографии (Кунтскамера)
24 Menshikov Palace
   Дворец Меньшикова
26 Academy of Arts Museum
   Музей Академии художеств
31 St Petersburg History Museum
   Музей истории
   Санкт-Петербурга
38 Museum of the History
   of Religion
   Музей Истории Религии
41 Bobrinsky Palace
   Бобринский Дворец
42 Palace of Grand Duke
   Alexey Alexandrovich
   Дворец Князя Алексея
   Александровича
44 Alexandr Blok
   House-Museum
   Музей-квартира Блока
50 Yusupov Palace
   Юсуповский дворец

### OTHER
4  LenExpo
   Ленэкспо
5  Sea Terminal
   (Morskoy Vokzal)
   Морской вокзал
7  Church of Mother of
   God the Merciful
   Церковь Милующй Боже Матери
9  Fire Department & Memorial
11 Lenin Statue
   Памятник В. И. Ленину
12 Latvian Consulate
13 Satiry Theatre
   Театр Сатиры
15 Church of St Catherine
   Церковь св. Екатерины

21 Lomonosov Memorial
   Памятник Ломоносову
22 Philological Faculty
   Филологический факультет
   Государственного Университета
23 Sindbad Travel
25 Sphinx Monuments
   Сфинксы
27 Andreevsky Market
   Андреевский рынок
28 Apteka #13
29 Temple of the Assumption
   Успенское подворье
   Оптина Пустынь
34 Dekabristov Landing
35 The Bronze Horseman
   Медный всадник
36 Manege Central Exhibition Hall
   Центральный выставочный
   зал Манеж
39 Central Post Office
   Главпочтамт
40 Main Post Office
46 Choral Synagogue
   Синагога
47 Leon
48 Mariinsky Theatre
   Мариинский театр оперы и балета
52 Rimsky-Korsakov Statue
   Памятник Н. А.
   Римскому-Корсакову
53 Rimsky-Korsakov Conservatory
   Консерватория Римского-Корсакова
54 St Nicholas Cathedral
   Никольский собор
55 Chinese Consulate
56 City Centre for Fighting AIDS
   Городской центр для
   борьбы со СПИДом
57 Euroline Office
59 Narva Triumphal Gates
   Нарвские ворота
60 Stalin Statue

MAP 6
MAP 4
MAP 7

Vasileostrovskaya

2-ya 3-ya linii
Sredny pr
Bolshoy pr
Maly pr
6-7 linii
8-9 linii
10-11 linii
12-13 linii
14-15 linii
16-17 linii
18-19 linii
20-21 linii
22-23 linii
24-25 linii
Klubny per
Detskaya pr ul
Kartaschevska ul
Shevchenko ul
Detskaya ul
prekt.
26-27 linii
nab Masterskoi
nab Makarova
Kosaya liniya
Kozhevennaya linya

VASILEVSKY

"Vasileostrovets" Gardens

Bolshoy pr
Shmidta
Leytenanta
nab Leytenanta
most Leytenanta Shmidta

University Botanical Gardens
St Petersburg State University
University
St Petersburg
State
University

Sredneokhtinsky pr
4-ya linii
Vladiky per
Bolshoy pr
ul Repina
Akademicheskiy per
Bugsky per
Akademicheskiy per

Birzhevoy
Universitetskaya nab

BOLSHAYA NEVA

Angliyskaya ul
Galernaya ul
pl Dekabristov
Admiralty Gardens

Angliyskaya nab
Galernaya ul
ul Truda
nab Admiralteyskogo kanala
Admiralteysky kanal
Konnogvardeysky bulvar
Konnogvardeyskiy per
ul Yakubovicha
Pochtamtskaya ul
Bol Morskaya

Galernaya ul
pl Truda
nab Kryukova kanala
nab r Moyki

Moyka

NOVOADMIRALTELSKY

Novaya Gollandiya

Kolomensky

pr Pisareva
ul Pisareva
pr Maklina

Bolshaya Neva

MATISOV

ul A Bloka
Drovyanoy per
Angliyskiy pr

pr Pryazhki
nab r Pryazhki
ul Vitebskaya
ul Perevoznaya
ul V Ermaka
Pskovskaya ul
Lotsmanskaya ul
Prsvect Rimskogo-Korsakova

Pryazhka

nab Pechatnika
Mesterskaya ul
ul Dekabristov
pr Soyuza Pechatnikov
Lermontovsky pr
pr Rimskogo-Korsakova

ul Dekabristov
Minsky per
Nikolsky per

ul Soyuza Pechatnikov

Teatralnaya ul

Nikolsky Gardens

Potseluev most
nab r Moyki
Pratchechny per
Fonarny per
ul Dekabristov
nab kanala Griboedova
Lviny most

Mogilyovsky most
Pikalov most
Staro-Nikolsky most

nab kanala Griboedova
Griboedov canal
kanala Griboedova

Pokrovsky

Alarchin most
nab Kanonerskaya ul
pl Turgeneva

Sadovaya ul
ul Labutina
Klimov per

Hikolskaya ul
Hikolsky per
Podyacheskaya per

nab r Fontanki
nab r Fontanki
Fontanka

Sadovaya ul

pr Moskvinoy

13 Krasnoarmeyskaya ul
8 Krasnoarmeyskaya ul
9 Krasnoarmeyskaya ul
10 Krasnoarmeyskaya ul
11 Krasnoarmeyskaya ul
12 Krasnoarmeyskaya ul

Staropeterhgofskiy pr
ul Tsiolkovskogo
Derptsky per
Revelsky per
ul Lodigina
Drovyannaya ul
ul Tsiolkovskogo

Rizhsky pr

Mezhevoy canal
Kurlyandskaya ul

Vindavskaya
Dvinskaya ul

GUTUEVSKY

nab Obvodnogo kanala

Bumazhnaya ul
Bumazhny canal

Ekateringofka
nab r Ekateringofki
Lifflyandskaya ul

Park Ekateringof

To School No348
& Kirov Statue

Turakanarka

Narvsky pr
Perekopskaya ul
Narvskaya
pl Stachek
ul Ivana Chyornykh

Baltiyskaya ul

ul Rozenshteyna
Shkapina ul
Metrostroevoy ul
Mozchajny per
Marshala Govorova
Mitrofanevskoe shosse

56

57
Baltic Station
(Baltiysky Vokzal)
Baltiyskaya

59

58

60

# MAP 7

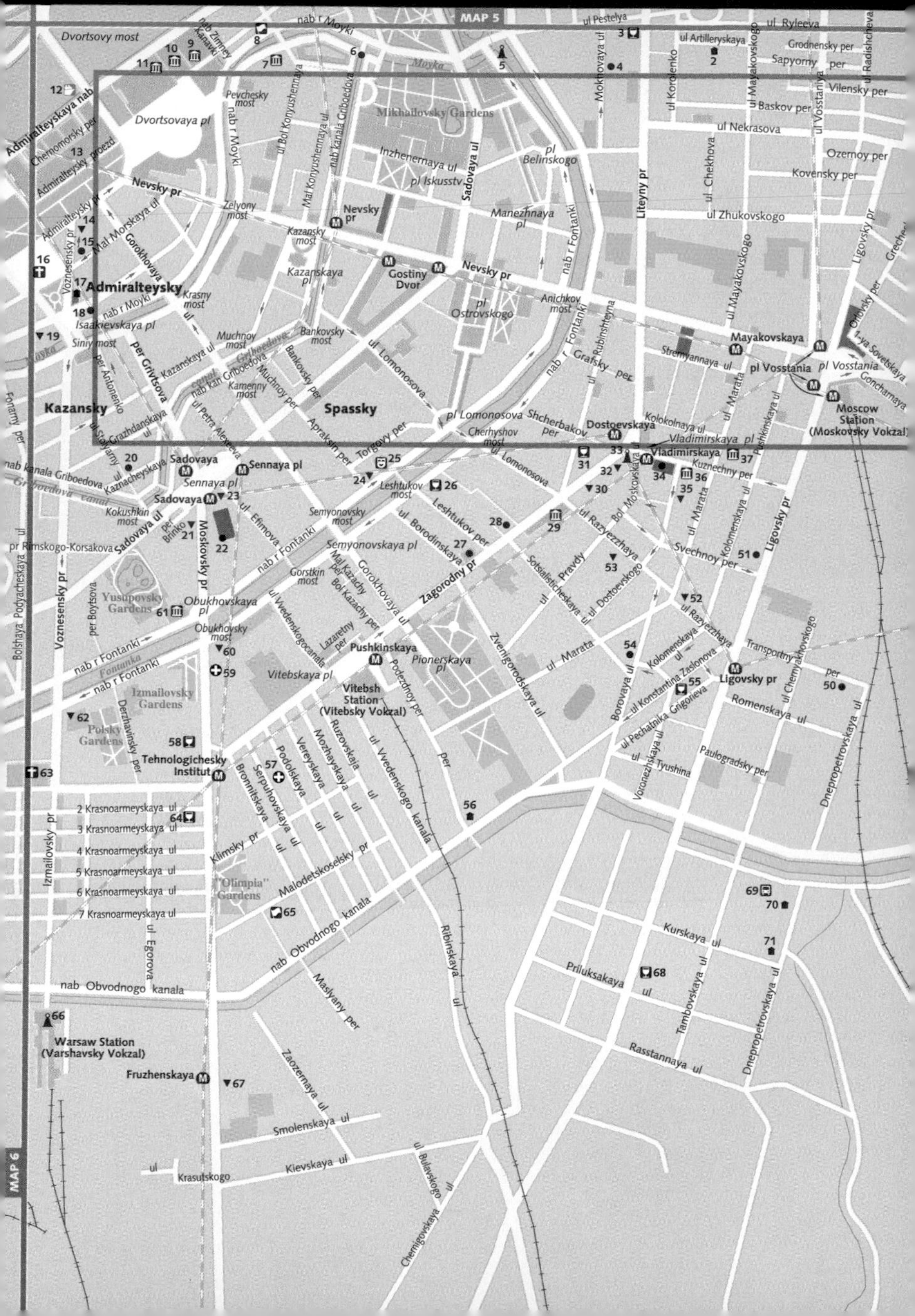

MAP 5

Dvortsovy most

nab r Moyki

ul Pestelya

ul Ryleeva

ul Artilleryskaya

Grodnensky per

Sapyorny per

Vilensky per

Baskov per

ul Nekrasova

Ozernoy per

Kovensky per

ul Chekhova

ul Zhukovskogo

Mokhovaya ul

Liteyny pr

Mikhailovsky Gardens

Dvortsovaya pl

Pevchesky most

Inzhenernaya ul

pl Iskusstv

pl Belinskogo

Manezhnaya pl

Nevsky pr

Zelyony most

Nevsky pr

Kazansky most

Gostiny Dvor

Nevsky pr

Kazanskaya pl

Anichkov most

pl Ostrovskogo

Admiralteyskaya nab

Chernomorsky per

Admiralteysky proezd

Admiralteysky pr

Mal Morskaya ul

Gorokhovaya ul

Admiralteysky

Krasny most

Isaakievskaya pl

Siniy most

nab r Moyki

nab r Fontanki

Grafsky per

Rubinshteyna ul

Stremyannaya ul

Mayakovskaya

pl Vosstania

pl Vosstania

Moscow Station (Moskovsky Vokzal)

Muchnoy most

Bankovsky most

ul Lomonosova

Kazansky

Spassky

Kamenny most

per Grivtsova

Kazanskaya ul

nab kan Griboedova

Ruchiyny most

Apraksin per

Torgovy per

pl Lomonosova

Shcherbakov per

Chernyshov most

Dostoevskaya

Vladimirskaya

Vladimirsky pr

Kuznechny per

ul Marata

Kolokolnaya ul

Vladimirskaya pl

pr Rimskogo-Korsakova

Sadovaya

Sennaya pl

Sennaya pl

Sadovaya

Kokushkin most

Leshtukov per

Leshtukov most

Semyonovsky most

ul Borodinska

Zvenigorodskaya ul

Bol Moskovskaya ul

ul Razyezzhaya

Kolomenskaya ul

Ligovsky pr

Svechnoy per

Voznesensky pr

Moskovsky pr

Semyonovskaya ul

Gorokhovoy ul

Zagorodny pr

Sotsialisticheskaya ul

Pravdy

ul Dostoevskogo

ul Marata

Kolomenskaya ul

ul Razyezzhaya

Ligovsky pr

Yusupovsky Gardens

Obukhovskaya pl

Obukhovsky most

Pushkinskaya

Pionerskaya pl

Borovaya ul

ul Konstantina Zaslonova

Ligovsky pr

nab r Fontanki

Fontanka

Vitebskaya ul

Vitebsh Station (Vitebsky Vokzal)

Podezdnogo kanala

Transportny per

per

Izmailovsky Gardens

Polsky Gardens

Dzerzhinskogo per

Tehnologichesky Institut

ul Pechatnika Grigorieva

Voronezhskaya ul

Tyushina ul

Paulogradsky per

Dnepropetrovskaya ul

Izmailovsky pr

2 Krasnoarmeyskaya ul

3 Krasnoarmeyskaya ul

4 Krasnoarmeyskaya ul

5 Krasnoarmeyskaya ul

6 Krasnoarmeyskaya ul

7 Krasnoarmeyskaya ul

ul Egorova

Klimov per

"Olimpia" Gardens

Malodetskoselsky pr

nab Obvodnogo kanala

Rybinskaya ul

Kurskaya ul

Pryazhka ul

Prilukskaya ul

Dnepropetrovskaya ul

Tambovskaya ul

nab Obvodnogo kanala

Maslyany per

Zaozernaya ul

Rasstannaya ul

Warsaw Station (Varshavsky Vokzal)

Fruzhenskaya

Smolenskaya ul

ul Krasutskogo

Kievskaya ul

ul Bakunina

Chernigovskaya

MAP 6

MAP 7

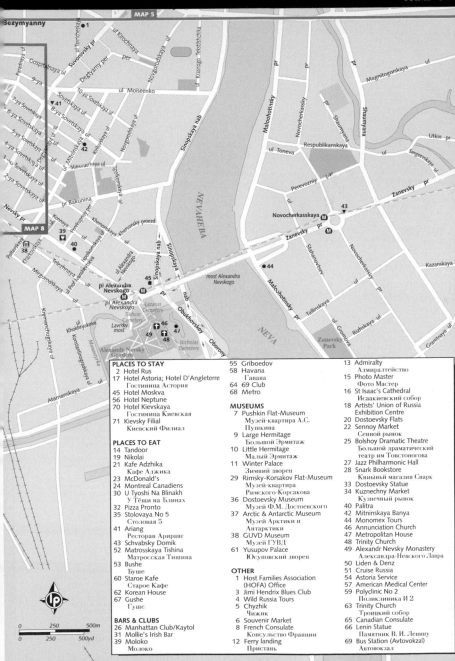

**PLACES TO STAY**
2 Hotel Rus
17 Hotel Astoria; Hotel D'Angleterre
    Гостиница Астория
45 Hotel Moskva
56 Hotel Neptune
70 Hotel Kievskaya
    Гостиница Киевская
71 Kievsky Filial
    Киевский Филиал

**PLACES TO EAT**
14 Tandoor
19 Nikolai
21 Kafe Adzhika
    Кафе Аджика
23 McDonald's
24 Montreal Canadiens
30 U Tyoshi Na Blinakh
    У Тёщи на Блинах
32 Pizza Pronto
35 Stolovaya No 5
    Столовая 5
41 Ariang
    Ресторан Ариранг
43 Schvabsky Domik
52 Matrosskaya Tishina
    Матросская Тишина
53 Bushe
    Буше
60 Staroe Kafe
    Старое Кафе
62 Korean House
67 Gushe
    Гуше

**BARS & CLUBS**
26 Manhattan Club/Kaytol
31 Mollie's Irish Bar
39 Moloko
    Молоко

55 Griboedov
58 Havana
    Гавана
64 69 Club
68 Metro

**MUSEUMS**
7 Pushkin Flat-Museum
    Музей-квартира А.С.
    Пушкина
9 Large Hermitage
    Большой Эрмитаж
10 Little Hermitage
    Малый Эрмитаж
11 Winter Palace
    Зимний дворец
29 Rimsky-Korsakov Flat-Museum
    Музей-квартира
    Римского-Корсакова
36 Dostoevsky Museum
    Музей Ф.М. Достоевского
37 Arctic & Antarctic Museum
    Музей Арктики и
    Антарктики
38 GUVD Museum
    Музей ГУВД
61 Yusupov Palace
    Юсуповский дворец

**OTHER**
1 Host Families Association
    (HOFA) Office
3 Jimi Hendrix Blues Club
4 Wild Russia Tours
5 Chyzhik
    Чижик
6 Souvenir Market
8 French Consulate
    Консульство Франции
12 Ferry landing
    Пристань

13 Admiralty
    Адмиралтейство
15 Photo Master
    Фото Мастер
16 St Isaac's Cathedral
    Исаакиевский собор
18 Artists' Union of Russia
    Exhibition Centre
20 Dostoevsky Flats
22 Sennoy Market
    Сенной рынок
25 Bolshoy Dramatic Theatre
    Большой драматический
    театр им Товстоногова
27 Jazz Philharmonic Hall
28 Snark Bookstore
    Книжный магазин Снарк
33 Dostoevsky Statue
34 Kuznechny Market
    Кузнечный рынок
40 Palitra
42 Mitninskaya Banya
44 Monomex Tours
46 Annunciation Church
47 Metropolitan House
48 Trinity Church
49 Alexandr Nevsky Monastery
    Александра-Невского Лавра
50 Liden & Denz
51 Cruise Russia
54 Astoria Service
57 American Medical Center
59 Polyclinic No 2
    Поликлиника И 2
63 Trinity Church
    Троицкий собор
65 Canadian Consulate
66 Lenin Statue
    Памятник В. И. Ленину
69 Bus Station (Avtovokzal)
    Автовокзал

# MAP 8 NEVSKY PROSPEKT НЕВСКИЙ ПРОСПЕКТ

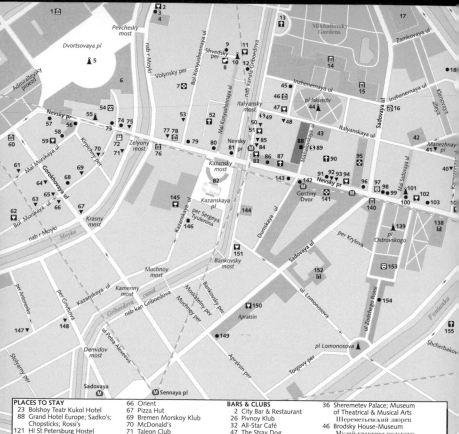

## PLACES TO STAY

23 Bolshoy Teatr Kukol Hotel
88 Grand Hotel Europe; Sadko's;
   Chopsticks; Rossi's
121 HI St Petersburg Hostel
   & Sindbad Travel
123 Hotel Oktyabrskaya
   Гостиница Октябрьская
124 Oktyabrsky Filial
130 Sheraton Nevskij Palace Hotel;
   The Bierstube; Landskrona
146 Herzen Institute Student
   Dormitory & State Pedagogical
   University
   Общежитие Института
   Герцена

## PLACES TO EAT

20 Arlekino
   Арлекино
24 Shogun
31 Kharbin
37 Milano
40 Mama Roma
41 Teremok
48 Kalinka Malinka
50 Sakura
53 La Strada
61 DaVinci
63 Khristofor
   Христофор
64 Shogun
65 Orient

66 Orient
67 Pizza Hut
69 Bremen Morskoy Klub
70 McDonald's
71 Taleon Club
75 Kafe Literaturnoe
   Кафе Литературное
77 Minutka
84 Gino Ginelli
85 Laima
92 Sever
93 Grillmaster
110 Propaganda; Café Stolovaya
115 Afrodite
117 Pizza Hut/KFC
118 Idealnaya Chaska
119 Carrols
120 Cheburechnaya
   Чебуречная
122 Orient
126 Baskin Robbins
127 Café Rico
133 Green Crest
134 Gushe
   Гуше
147 Jackie Chan
148 Kotletnaya
   Котлетная
160 Bliny Domik
   Блинный домик
165 Bistrot Garçon
166 Idealnaya Chaska
167 Depo

## BARS & CLUBS

2 City Bar & Restaurant
26 Pivnoy Klub
32 All-Star Café
47 The Stray Dog
51 Monro
59 Bar O Meter
62 Ot Zakata do Rasveta
   От заката до рассвета
83 Chayka
94 Hollywood Nights
102 Golden Dolls
104 Futbol Bar
106 Psycho Pub
145 Tinkoff
150 City Club; Money
   Honey Saloon
151 Greshniki
   Грешники

## MUSEUMS

1 Winter Palace
   Зимний дворец
14 Russian Museum
   Русский музей
15 Museum of Ethnography
   Музей этнографии
17 Engineer's Castle
   Инженерный замок
35 Akhmatova Memorial
   Museum
   Музей-квартира Анны
   Аматовой

36 Sheremetev Palace; Museum
   of Theatrical & Musical Arts
   Шереметьевский дворец
46 Brodsky House-Museum
   Музей-квартира родского
60 Museum of Political History
76 Stroganov Palace
   & Stroganov Yard Café
103 St Petersburg Centre
   Modern Art
135 Beloselsky-Belozersky Palace
   & Tourist Information Office
   & Museum of Wax Figures
   Дворец Белосельских-Белозерских
138 Anichkov Palace
   Аничков дворец
152 Vorontsov Palace
   Воронцовский дворец

## OTHER

3 Institut Français
4 Glinka Capella
   Хоровая капелла имени Глинки
5 Alexander Column
   Александровская колонна
6 General Staff Building
   Здание главного штаба
7 Petrofarm Pharmacy
   Аптека Петрофарм
8 Swedish Consulate
9 Ipris (copy centre)
   Иприс
10 Imperial Policeman Statue

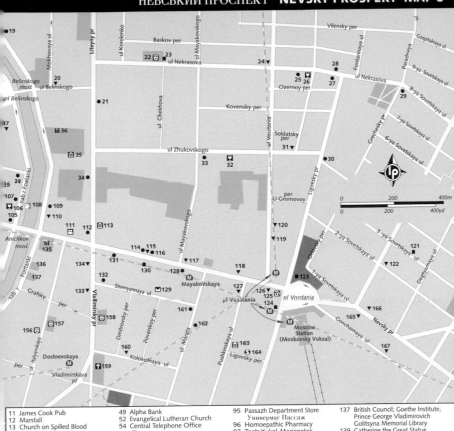

| | |
|---|---|
| 11 James Cook Pub | 49 Alpha Bank |
| 12 Marstall | 52 Evangelical Lutheran Church |
| 13 Church on Spilled Blood | 54 Central Telephone Office |
|    Храм Спаса на Крови |    Телефон |
| 16 Nordic | 55 Nevsky prospekt 14 |
| 18 St Petersburg State Circus |    (Siege Monument) |
|    Цирк | 56 Central Airline Ticket Office |
| 19 Anglican/Episcopalean Open | 57 Saigon |
|    Christianity Centre | 58 Ministry of Culture |
| 21 Pchelovodstvo | 68 ATS Telecom |
|    Пчеловодство |    Строгановский дворец |
| 22 Bolshoy Teatr Kukol | 72 Barrikada Cinema |
| 25 Soldat Udachi |    & Idealnaya Chashka |
| 27 Eclectica | 73 Isskustvo bookstore |
| 28 Maltsevsky Market |    Магазин Исскуство |
|    Мальцевский рынок | 74 Abuk Bookshop |
| 29 Wendy's Baltic Bread | 78 Association of Free |
| 30 Oktyabrsky Concert Hall |    Artists Gallery |
|    Концертный зал Октябрьский | 79 DLT Department Store |
| 33 Ost-West Kontaktservice |    Универмаг Д.Л.Т. |
| 34 Sportivny na Liteynom | 80 Valhall |
| 38 Finnord Office & | 81 Dom Knigi |
|    Bus station |    Дом книги |
| 41 Intendant | 83 Kazan Cathedral |
| 42 Zimny Stadion |    Казанский собор |
|    Зимний Стадион | 86 Maly Zal im. Glinki (Small Hall) |
| 43 Bolshoy Zal |    Малый зал им Глинки |
|    Большой зал филармонии | 87 St Catherine's Roman |
| 44 Pushkin Statue |    Catholic Church |
| 45 Mussorgsky Opera | 89 Promstroy Bank |
|    & Ballet Theatre | 90 Armenian Church of St Catherine |
|    Театр ореры и балета им | 91 Theatre Ticket Office |
|    Мусоргского |    Театральная касса |

| | |
|---|---|
| 95 Passazh Department Store | 137 British Council; Goethe Institute; |
|    Универмаг Пассаж |    Prince George Vladimirovich |
| 96 Homoeopathic Pharmacy |    Golitsyna Memorial Library |
| 97 Teatr Kukol-Marionetok | 139 Catherine the Great Statue |
| 98 Titanik | 140 National Library of Russia |
| 99 Photo kiosk at Nevsky pros 54 |    Российская Национальная |
| 100 Yeliseevsky Food Shop |    иблиотека |
|    Елисеевский Гастрономая | 141 Gostiny Dvor |
| 101 Small statues |    Гостиный Двор |
| 105 Apteka Baltik | 142 Excursions Ticket Booth |
|    Аптека алтика | 143 Town Duma |
| 107 Fuji Film Centre |    Дума |
| 108 Anichkov Bridge Landing | 144 Central Train Ticket Office |
| 109 Anglia bookstore |    Железнодорожные билетные |
| 111 Crystal Palace |    кассы |
| 112 Na Liteynom Bookshop | 149 City Excursions Bureau |
|    & Sekunda |    Городское кскурсионное бюро |
| 113 Art Gallery Borey | 153 Pushkin Theatre |
| 114 Westpost |    Театр имени А.С. Пушкина |
| 116 Cityline & City Telephone | 154 Vaganova School of Choreography |
|    Office |    Хореографическое училище |
| 125 Kro Magnon |    имени Вагановой |
| 128 Voyentorg | 155 Church of the Latter Day Saints |
|    Военторг | 156 Zazerkalye Theatre |
| 129 Post Office |    Театр Зазеркалье |
| 131 Khudozhestvennyye | 157 Maly Dramatic Theatre |
|    Promysly Souvenirs | 158 Lensoviet Theatre |
|    Художественные промыслы | 159 Our Lady of Vladimir Church |
| 132 Skin and Venereal Dispenser | 161 Nevskie Bani |
|    Кожно-венерологический | 162 Dzinn 24-hour store |
|    диспансер |    Джинн |
| 136 Mayakovskogo City | 163 Free Arts Foundation & Fish Fabrique |
|    Central Public Library | 164 Ligovsky |

# MAP 9 PETRODVORETS ПЕТРОДВОРЕЦ

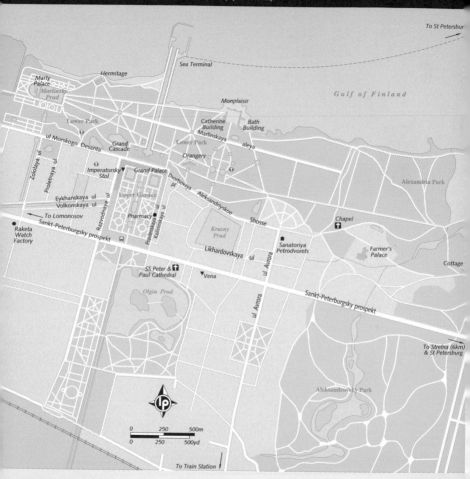

To St Petersbur

Sea Terminal

Gulf of Finland

Hermitage

Marly
Palace

Marlinsky
Prud

Monplaisir

Lower Park

Catherine
Building
Marlinskaya

Bath
Building

ul Morskogo Desanta

Grand
Cascade

Lower Park

aleya

Zolotaya ul

Proletnaya ul

Orangery

Alexandria Park

Imperatorsky
Stol

Grand Palace

Dvortsovaya
pl

Upper Garden

Aleksandriyskoe

Eykhanskaya ul
Volkonskaya ul

Razvodnaya ul

To Lomonosov

Sankt-Peterburgsky prospekt

Pharmacy

Praflenskaya ul
Kalinadskaya ul

Shosse

Chapel

Raketa
Watch
Factory

Krasny
Prud

Sanatoriya
Petrodvorets

Farmer's
Palace

Cottage

Likhardovskaya  ul

ul Avrora

Sankt-Peterburgsky prospekt

SS Peter &
Paul Cathedral

Vena

Olgin Prud

ul Avrora

To Strelna (6km)
& St Petersburg

Aleksandrovsky Park

| 0 | 250 | 500m |
| 0 | 250 | 500yd |

To Train Station

The fountains of the Grand Palace, Petrodvorets

To St Petersburg (24km)

Academichesky pr

Dvortsovaya ul

Oktyabrsky bul

Fermskaya doroga

Fyodorovsky Gorodok

Alexander Park

Pushkin Dacha

Arsenal

Pushkinskaya ul

P

Moskovskaya ul

Alexander Palace

Dvortsovaya

Tsetkovnaya ul

Malaya ul

Leontevskaya ul

Lenin

Mount Parnuss

Market Hall

Chinese Theatre

Znamenskaya Tserkov
Lycée

Carriage Museum

Srednaya ul

Orancheretnaya ul

To Detskoe Selo Railway Station & Kolpino

Chapel

Catherine Palace

Orangeries

Entrance

Volkhon skoe shosse

Park Entrance

Agate Rooms

Bus from Pavlovsk

Bus to Pavlovsk

Konyushennaya ul

Chinese Village

Kagul Obelisk

Cameron Gallery

Sadovaya ul

Podkaprizovaya doroga

Chinese Pavilion

Great Caprice

Naberezhnaya ul

Chinese Pavilion

Concert Hall

Granite Terrace

Grotto

Hermitage

Pavlovskoe sh

Catherine Park

Rampovaya alleya

Kybar kanal

Prudy

Boat Landing

Great Pond

Boat Landing

Kaskadnye

Marble Bridge

Ruined Tower

Pyramid

Turkish Bath

Chesma Column

Admiralty

Parkovaya ul

To Krasnoe Selo
Krasnoselskoe sh

Parkovaya ul

To Pavlovsk (4km)

Radishcheva ul

Gusarskaya ul

Ogorodnaya ul

Krasnoy Zvezdy ul

Zakharevskaya ul

0    200    400m
0    200    400yd

# MAP LEGEND

## CITY ROUTES

Freeway .................. Freeway
Highway ......... Primary Road
Road ..... Secondary Road
Street ........................ Street
Lane .......................... Lane
............................ On/Off Ramp

.............. Unsealed Road
................ One Way Street
.............. Pedestrian Street
.................. Stepped Street
........................ Tunnel
.................... Footbridge

## REGIONAL ROUTES

................ Tollway, Freeway
........................ Primary Road
.................. Secondary Road
........................ Minor Road

## BOUNDARIES

.................... International
........................ State
.................. Disputed
.......... Fortified Wall

## HYDROGRAPHY

................ River, Creek
........................ Canal
........................ Lake

.. Dry Lake; Salt Lake
........ Spring; Rapids
................ Waterfalls

## TRANSPORT ROUTES & STATIONS

........................ Train
............ Underground Train
........................ Metro
........................ Tramway
...... Cable Car, Chairlift

........................ Ferry
............ Walking Trail
.............. Walking Tour
........................ Path
.............. Pier or Jetty

## AREA FEATURES

............ Archaeological Site
........................ Building

........................ Campus
........................ Cemetery

........................ Market
........ Park, Gardens

........................ Plaza
........................ Swamp

## POPULATION SYMBOLS

○ CAPITAL ............ National Capital
◉ CAPITAL ............ State Capital

● CITY ........................ City
○ Town ........................ Town

◆ Village
........................ Village
........................ Urban Area

## MAP SYMBOLS

■ ........................ Place to Stay

▼ ........................ Place to Eat

● ........................ Point of Interest

⊠ .................... Airport
⊖ .................... Bank
.................... Bus Stop
.................... Bus Terminal
.................... Cathedral
⊞ .................... Church
⊟ .................... Cinema

⊡ .................... Embassy
⊡ .......... Ferry Terminal
⊕ .................... Hospital
⊡ .......... Internet Cafe
☼ .................... Lookout
⚑ .................... Monument
⊙ .................... Mosque

▥ .................... Museum
⊡ .................... Parking
⊡ .......... Police Station
⊡ .......... Post Office
⊡ .......... Pub or Bar
⊗ .......... Shopping Centre
⊡ ...... Swimming Pool

⊡ .................... Synagogue
⊡ .................... Telephone
⚑ .................... Temple
⊡ .................... Theatre
⊙ .................... Toilet
❶ .... Tourist Information
⊡ .................... Zoo

*Note: not all symbols displayed above appear in this book*

---

# LONELY PLANET OFFICES

## Australia
Locked Bag 1, Footscray, Victoria 3011
☎ 03 8379 8000  fax 03 8379 8111
email: talk2us@lonelyplanet.com.au

## USA
150 Linden St, Oakland, CA 94607
☎ 510 893 8555  TOLL FREE: 800 275 8555
fax 510 893 8572
email: info@lonelyplanet.com

## UK
10a Spring Place, London NW5 3BH
☎ 020 7428 4800  fax 020 7428 4828
email: go@lonelyplanet.co.uk

## France
1 rue du Dahomey, 75011 Paris
☎ 01 55 25 33 00  fax 01 55 25 33 01
email: bip@lonelyplanet.fr
www.lonelyplanet.fr

**World Wide Web: www.lonelyplanet.com *or* AOL keyword: lp**
**Lonely Planet Images: lpi@lonelyplanet.com.au**